# A NATION FORGED IN WAR

## ≫ How World War II Taught Americans to Get Along ≪

Thomas Bruscino

Legacies of War ★ G. Kurt Piehler, Series Editor

D1105507

The University of Tennessee Press / Knoxville

The Legacies of War series presents a variety of works—from scholarly monographs to memoirs—that examine the impact of war on society, both in the United States and globally. The wide scope of the series might include war's effects on civilian populations, its lingering consequences for veterans, and the role of individual nations and the international community in confronting genocide and other injustices born of war.

Copyright © 2010 by The University of Tennessee Press / Knoxville.
All Rights Reserved. Manufactured in the United States of America.
First Edition.

The paper in this book meets the requirements of American National Standards Institute / National Information Standards Organization specification Z39.48-1992 (Permanence of Paper). It contains 30 percent post-consumer waste and is certified by the Forest Stewardship Council.

LIBRARY OF CONGRESS CATALOGING-IN-PUBLICATION DATA

Bruscino, Thomas
A nation forged in war: how World War II taught Americans to get along / Thomas Bruscino. — 1st ed.
    p. cm. — (Legacies of war)
Includes bibliographical references and index.
ISBN-13: 978-1-57233-695-7 (hardcover)
ISBN-10: 1-57233-695-1 (hardcover)

  1. United States. Army—Military life—History—20th century.
  2. United States. Army—History—World War, 1939–1945.
  3. United States. Army—Mobilization—History—20th century.
  4. World War, 1939–1945—Social aspects—United States.
  5. World War, 1939–1945—Participation, European American.
  6. World War, 1939–1945—Participation, African American.
  7. African American soldiers—History—20th century.
  8. Race discrimination—United States—History—20th century.
  9. United States—Race relations—History—20th century.
  10. United States—Ethnic relations—History—20th century.
  I. Title.

D769.1.B78 2010
940.54'03—dc22
2009039637

*To Terrie, Dominic, Anthony, and Mariana*

# CONTENTS

# ILLUSTRATIONS

# FOREWORD

THE SECOND WORLD WAR TRANSFORMED AMERICA'S RELATIONSHIP WITH
the world, and the United States emerged as one of the preeminent superpowers. After victory over the forces of Nazi Germany and Imperial Japan,
Americans embraced internationalism and the newly created United Nations.
The Second World War reordered American society at home. The massive
Keynesian spending required to become the arsenal of democracy led to an
unprecedented wartime prosperity that endured after the cessation of hostili-
ties. The quest for victory fostered a range of new scientific and technological
breakthroughs that had profound implications for the postwar era: radar, the
modern computer, and, most ominously, the atomic bomb.

In sheer numbers, never before or since have so many Americans served
in the armed forces at one time—over 15 million men and women donned
uniforms in the period from 1941 to 1945. What was the legacy of this military service on their lives and the wider society? Thomas Bruscino makes
a convincing case that the experience of military service fundamentally
transformed American attitudes toward ethnicity and religion. In the opening decades of the twentieth century, Americans were profoundly divided
over who should be considered an American. Many native-born white Anglo
Saxon Protestants questioned whether the new immigrants from southern
and eastern Europe could be integrated into American society. In the 1920s
the Ku Klux Klan attracted a membership of millions, and this organization
deemed immigrants, Roman Catholics, and Jews as a threat to the Republic. When Roman Catholic Al Smith, governor of New York, ran for the
presidency in 1928, many mainstream politicians and intellectuals openly
questioned whether a member of the Catholic Church could ever hold the
presidency.

World War II fostered a far-reaching redefinition of the American identity. Part of this represented a deliberate policy of the federal government.
Official propaganda aimed at civilians and soldiers stressed the importance of
cooperating across ethnic, religious, and class lines to meet the threats posed
by Germany and Japan. But other policies were at work. As Tom Bruscino's
work shows, the U.S. Army in the area of religious policy stressed the need
for an ecumenical attitude not only on the part of chaplains but also within

the rank and file. Moreover, Bruscino makes a persuasive case that throwing together men from different regions, ethnicities, religions, and classes fostered a greater sense of tolerance and forged a new American identity among white Americans. His study is especially attentive to the dynamics of military life that encouraged a common cultural outlook. Those serving in the enlisted ranks endured basic training that sought to strip recruits of their individual identities and inculcate them in the ways of the military. For those who saw combat, the crucible of battle often forged a sense of cohesion that prompted more than a grudging tolerance but a real sense of brotherhood.

Of course, World War II should not be considered a halcyon era, and Tom Bruscino does not ignore the shortcomings of the era. Anti-Semitism may have been waning, but there remained plenty of bigots. With only a few exceptions, African Americans served in segregated units within the armed forces, and the war did little to chip away at either Jim Crow in the South or widespread discrimination in the rest of the country. Women served in armed services, but their numbers were few and they were not part of the "bands of brothers." In contrast to the Soviet Union, the United States by law and practice prohibited women from serving in any of the combat ranks. Moreover, many veterans returning home had a hard time readjusting to civilian life and often felt a profound sense of alienation. Some joined veterans' organization in part to maintain the camaraderie they had experienced in the service.

Despite these caveats, Bruscino shows that much changed as a result of the Second World War. Veterans were treated differently, for one thing. In the aftermath of the Armistice of 1918, political leaders on the right and left were for different reasons reluctant to grant veterans a bonus—even after they marched on Washington in 1932. The GI Bill of Rights enacted by Congress in 1944 provided those who served in the Second World War with an array of benefits designed to speed their reintegration into society. Not only did it provide millions of veterans access to vocational training or higher education, but it also offered low-cost loans to purchase a first home. Although an uneven process, anti-Semitism and anti-Catholic sentiment continued to wane; by the late 1950s it would be possible for the theologian Will Herberg to argue that there existed a distinctive American way of life that united Americans and an ecumenical sentiment that saw Protestantism, Roman Catholicism, and Judaism as "equal" religions. In the 1940s and 1950s, national leaders, while urging Americans to unite against the new common enemy—Communism—also insisted on a growing tolerance of ethnic, religious, regional, and, increasingly, racial differences. Although there are certainly parallels between the Red Scare that followed World War I and the

McCarthyism of the Cold War, America avoided a resurgence of nativism. In fact, Americans remained more willing to elect Jews, Roman Catholics, and those from diverse ethnic backgrounds to public office—a trend that culminated in the 1960 election of John F. Kennedy to the presidency.

Tom Bruscino's monograph inaugurates a new book series focusing on the legacies of war. In the works that follow, we aim to publish additional monographs, as well as memoirs, diaries, and autobiographies that examine these complex legacies and their effects not only on American society but also in other parts of the world. In the twentieth and twenty-first centuries, war has engulfed virtually all societies, and the lines between civilians and combatants are often elusive. We plan to include works that trace the lingering impact of war on veterans, civilians, and the wider society. How do societies reconstitute and reconfigure themselves after war? What are the ways society remembers as well as forgets about past wars? Future works will consider how societies and the international community grapple with rendering justice after genocide and other war crimes have been committed. In a small way, we hope a better understanding of the legacies of war will help scholars and the wider public forge a more peaceful world.

G. Kurt Piehler
The University of Tennessee

# INTRODUCTION

THEY ARE THERE, SMALL TRIBUTES SCATTERED ACROSS THE COUNTRY. TIME has worn them away, pushed them into the gray routine of everyday life. They can be found in chapels in Pennsylvania, Minnesota, Washington, Massachusetts, and New York, at the Pentagon and National Cathedral in Washington, D.C., at an elementary school in York, Pennsylvania, at a veterans' hospital in the Bronx, on a waterway in Ohio, and at a fountain in Virginia. They show up in the books of stamp collectors, on murals on buildings on unexpected corners, and in paintings on museum walls throughout the land. No less than two foundations carry on to honor their deeds, one housed in the *Queen Mary*, anchored in Long Beach, California. The Four Immortal Chaplains are there, faded reminders of a war and a time when America was a very different place.

Their names were Clark Poling, Alexander Goode, George Fox, and John Washington, and they died together in the winter of 1943, in the bitter cold waters of the North Atlantic. Poling came from Ohio originally; he was a Dutch Reformed minister from a long line of pastors in the church. Goode was a native of New York, the son of a Brooklyn rabbi who followed his father's vocation to minister to his people. Fox was a Methodist from Pennsylvania who had lied about his age to serve in World War I and rejoined the army when World War II broke out. Washington was an Irish Catholic priest from New Jersey. The war brought them together; the U.S. Army needed men to look after the spiritual lives of soldiers who came from all walks of life and represented every religious creed.

So it was that in January 1943 these four men found themselves in New York with nine hundred other Americans, boarding the transport ship *Dorchester*, bound for an army post in Greenland. They never made it. In the early morning of February 3, a German submarine spotted the ship and fired a torpedo into its hull. The explosion wrecked the *Dorchester*, and the ship immediately began to go under. In the melee that followed, the four chaplains made their way to the deck, helping the confused and wounded along the way. They passed out life jackets from a storage chest to troops who had forgotten to grab their own, and when the chest was empty, they took off their jackets and gave them to whoever was left. The chaplains never made it off the *Dorchester,* but they counseled courage to the end. As the doomed transport sank beneath the waves, the four men linked arms and prayed. They were never seen again.[1]

In the years to come, Americans showed surprisingly little inclination to commemorate the greatest of all wars. With few exceptions, the Iwo Jima memorial being the most prominent, the country did not construct great monoliths or grand sculptures in honor of the sacrifices made. Until years later, they did not even ask for a place on the Mall in Washington. They were content to let movies or television tell the tale, to name living memorials such as community parks and swimming pools after the fallen, and to have small local ceremonies to remember what had been done. The outcome of the war seemed to stand for itself.[2]

But within these small commemorations, within this relative quiet, the story of the four chaplains made more than its share of noise. It began in December 1944, in a very public and widely reported ceremony, when each of the chaplains was posthumously awarded the Distinguished Service Cross, the U.S. Army's second highest award. In the summer of 1947, the Bronx Veterans Administration Hospital dedicated a $250,000 therapeutic pool in their honor.[3] Later that year, a church in Philadelphia began work on the Chapel of the Four Chaplains, which was to minister to Protestants, Catholics, and Jews. The chapel opened in 1951 to an audience of twenty-five hundred, including President Harry Truman and Secretary of Defense George C. Marshall.[4] In 1948 Congress waived a time restriction to allow the special issue of a stamp to commemorate the chaplains. The stamp read, "These Immortal Chaplains . . . Interfaith in Action," and on the occasion of its release President Truman called the chaplains' actions "the greatest sermon that ever was preached."[5] On Armistice Day in 1949, the Four Chaplains Memorial Viaduct, a massive engineering project, opened in Massillon, Ohio. A stained-glass window depicting the men went into the chapel at West Point in 1952; windows at the National Cathedral, the Pentagon, and a number of other chapels around the country followed. Year after year in the 1950s and beyond, the American Legion used the February anniversary of the sinking of the *Dorchester* to kick off brotherhood and back-to-God celebrations.[6] President Dwight D. Eisenhower spoke at many of these functions, and in 1954 he gave a radio and television address to emphasize that "whatever our individual church, whatever our personal creed, our common faith in God is a common bond among us."[7] In 1954 a memorial to the chaplains went up in Ann Arbor, Michigan, and the next year a fifty-thousand-dollar fountain dedicated to the men went into a park in Falls Church, Virginia, just outside the capital.[8] Finally, in 1958, the U.S. Senate voted to award Poling, Goode, Fox, and Washington the Medal of Honor. Because of a bureaucratic snafu they could not get that award, so instead they received a special Congressional Medal of Valor, as close to the Medal of Honor as possible. The secretary of the army presented the medal to their surviving families in January 1961, in one of the Eisenhower administration's last acts in office.[9] The tributes slowed down after that—not to be renewed until the 1980s and 1990s, when popular interest in World War II picked up again—but the story of the four chaplains had a remarkable run in the postwar years.

Of the 902 men aboard the *Dorchester,* only 230 survived to be pulled from the water. Poling, Goode, Fox, and Washington were just 4 men among the 672 who died that night. And they were but 4 men of some 400,000 Americans who died in that war, in hundreds of thousands of stories of heroism and tragedy. Yet something about those four stood out. After the war Americans moved on. They packed up their mementos, swallowed their grief for those who never came home, and looked to the future. But on the rare occasions when they paused to reflect on the war, when they thought about what it all meant, the Four Immortal Chaplains were there. That war story, among so many, resonated in postwar America. It did so not because it provided meaning to the war, but because it reflected the meaning that was already there. World War II changed the United States in countless ways big and small, but most profoundly, most fundamentally, it taught Americans to get along. That was the symbolism, that was the lesson, that was the meaning drawn from the example of four men of four faiths who, on that cold February night, linked arms, prayed, and died together.

Nearly sixteen million Americans served in World War II. They sacrificed the best years of their lives to fight in faraway lands and change the world for the better. But the war changed them too. The experience of military service in World War II caused a dramatic shift from intolerance to tolerance in white ethnic and religious relations in America.

That shift was no mean thing—intolerance among Americans of different national and religious backgrounds had a history as old as the country itself. Anglo-Saxon Protestants founded the Republic, and they and their descendants tied the legacy of that achievement to their ethnic and religious character. But the nation they created and the opportunities it offered proved enticing to more than just Protestants from the British Isles. First Germans and Irish, then Scandinavians and, by the latter part of the nineteenth century, natives of southern and eastern Europe flocked to America's shores, upsetting the ethnic and religious balance of the country.[10] Traditional Americans all too often responded with nativism and religious bigotry, peddling in ste-reotypes and contempt.[11] They embraced the pseudo-sciences of so-called social Darwinism and eugenics to account for their supposed superiority, and by the mid-1910s they were joining organizations such as the second Ku Klux Klan to act on all their worst emotions.[12]

For all of this discrimination aimed at immigrants and ethnic and reli-gious minorities, it should be remembered that animosity cut both ways. Al-though a sizable number of immigrants believed that they could mix in Amer-ica's so-called melting pot, not everyone came to the United States with the intent to become American.[13] Economic considerations led many of them to choose to immigrate to the United States (rather than, for example, Argen-tina). Some figured they could make money and send it home. Others worked seasonally and returned to their native lands.[14] And although they faced ethnic prejudice, immigrants themselves were often not particularly open-minded to the diversity they found in the United States.[15] Many did not want any part of Anglo-Protestant, or any other, culture. The result was that the immigrants who did stay played their part in isolating themselves from other races, eth-nicities, and religions. They formed ethnic enclaves in big cities, where they maintained their own cultures, spoke their own languages, went to their own schools, and read their own newspapers.[16] In the days before the widespread transportation revolution made the country smaller, these geographic barri-ers were all the more insurmountable. People rarely traveled outside of their own region and rarely met the different folks who lived in different parts of the country. By the first part of the twentieth century, the ethnic and religious divides had become entrenched.[17]

World War I and the events of the 1920s made clear just how bad the situation had become. An atmosphere of cultural distrust and uncertainty grew during the war years, and it started at the very top. Before the United States entered the conflict, President Woodrow Wilson urged neutrality on the country while himself favoring the Allies, especially the British. Like the president, very few people chose to be neutral in their feelings about the war overseas. Everyone picked a side, and the decision often reflected ethnic or religious identity. Some immigrants driven by patriotic fervor returned to their homelands to fight. Irish, German, and Jewish Americans found them-selves in large numbers sympathizing with the Central Powers—the Irish because they were fighting against British, the German and Jewish Ameri-cans because many still felt an affinity for their native lands.[18]

Once the United States entered the war, the government adopted a broad policy of aggressive Americanization, primarily because of fear that its diverse citizens and residents might place their loyalties elsewhere. The government pushed English and citizenship classes, loyalty leagues, and crackdowns on speaking German, all with the intent of breaking its newest citizens from their Old World cultures. The most egregious excesses of the "100 percent Americanism" movement targeted Germans and German Americans. From the ridiculous—such as renaming hamburgers "liberty sandwiches," sauerkraut "liberty cabbage," dachshunds "liberty pups," and frankfurters "red hots"—to the severe, such as the lynching of a German immigrant in St. Louis, the war nearly destroyed German American culture in the United States. The government passed various espionage, sedition, and alien acts to punish suspected traitors. With beer seen as a German beverage, temperance and prohibition movements used anti-German feelings to get wartime anti-alcohol laws on the books and start the process toward a constitutional amendment prohibiting alcohol nationwide.[19] Even examples from popular culture that celebrated the diversity of the American military ended up parodying ethnic and racial minorities. Billy Murray, one of the nation's first popular recording artists, scored hits during the era with such tunes as "When Tony Goes Over the Top," "Indianola," "It Takes the Irish to Beat the Dutch," and "Oh You Coon." These songs included lyrics such as "When Tony goes over the top / keep your eye on that fighting wop." Though shocking now, the comedian-singer remained well within the mainstream of the time.[20]

Military service in World War I offered a counterexample, a chance to put aside all the regional, religious, and ethnic divisions that troubled the diverse nation. During the fighting, the newly created Selective Service drafted over 2.7 million men for the U.S. Army. Of those men, almost half a million, 18 percent, were foreign-born immigrants.[21] These immigrants represented a wide variety of ethnic and religious groups. Mixing these immigrants with native-born Americans—themselves from different backgrounds and regions of the country—made the U.S. Army in World War I a diverse armed service.[22] Military service created a bond among men, a bond greatly strengthened by serving together in combat.[23] Immigrant soldier Ludovicus Van Iersel from the Netherlands received the Medal of Honor for scouting out a German position by crossing a swift stream under heavy fire.[24] Van Iersel remembered the closeness of his unit and said of his military experience, "I learned to get along and respect all people."[25]

Lessons such as these were not easily forgotten, and the veterans of World War I remembered their experiences at war's end and tried to apply them to American society in general. The U.S. Army created a new unit of immigrant soldiers to display the efficacy of military programs for training future citizens.[26] A veteran chaplain named Chellis V. Smith wrote a book in 1925,

*Americans All: Nine Heroes Who in the World War Showed that Americanism Is above Race, Creed, or Condition,* in which he argued that despite doubts about the ability of new citizens to "turn against the Mother country. . . . We completely abolished the hyphen-American. Men from all classes came."[27]

Smith was not alone among veterans in seeking to apply these lessons of assimilation to postwar America. Drawing on their own experiences as servicemen, the two main veterans groups in the United States both supported some sort of universal military service or training. Among its reasons for such a stand, in 1928 a post of the Veterans of Foreign Wars (VFW) cited the "inculcation of patriotism and love for the flag and the nation it represents," the "Americanism of the different elements which compose American life," and the "democratization of our youth, making rich and poor alike learn, shoulder to shoulder, to perform our country's service when needed."[28] The American Legion had formed after the war because, as the organization's official history put it, the common wartime experiences of the men who served created "an immense fraternity" whose members had similar views and needs.[29] The legion initially stayed out of the political issue of universal military training (UMT) but eventually came to support it as long as there was no large standing army.[30] Despite this support, neither universal military service nor universal military training would become a reality in the antimilitary environment of the postwar years.

Having been through what they had been through, and seen the devotion to country of their foreign-born buddies under fire, neither veteran group could understand those in the United States who resisted what at the time was called Americanization. So with universal military service programs failing, they turned their attention to creating a better melting pot in civilian life. The VFW created its Americanization Program in 1921 to foster feelings of patriotism. The program established Americanization Day, supported the "Star-Spangled Banner" as a new national anthem, and "advocated that immigrants be naturalized, only English be spoken, and foreign language newspapers be ousted."[31] The American Legion also noted the contributions of immigrants to the war effort and Americanism but made clear its displeasure with those who had used their alien status to escape military service to enjoy the benefits of working in the wartime economy. One Polish immigrant veteran who had lost a leg in the war expressed the legion's view at an early meeting: To those "not wanting to fight for the greatest of all flags . . . I say, 'Damn him, kick him out of here!'"[32] Along the same lines, the legion conflated nonveteran foreign immigrants and what they saw as the anti-Americanism of labor radicalism. The legion came to support immigration restriction in the 1920s, but it always made the notable exception for veterans, no matter their background.[33]

The more aggressive aspects of the VFW and American Legion efforts at Americanization, while initially honest attempts at recreating the unity of the wartime military experience, had begun to reflect the larger trend toward increased intolerance in American society.[34] Whatever unity existed in the military, the war certainly did not engender a spirit of ethnic and religious cooperation on the home front. In the end, the veterans just did not speak with a strong enough voice to get their message across. Their war had been stripped of all its nobility and credibility by the postwar peace settlements. With the victors claiming their spoils, and the world clearly not more safe for democracy, Americans sought to cast blame for the sordid affair. The American role in World War I came to be associated with the perfidy of arms makers, industrialists, and bankers, not the brave efforts of the doughboys.[35] The veterans' credibility became so diminished that much of the country actually resented their demands for early payment of war bonuses at the beginning of the Great Depression.[36] Maybe most important, the U.S. Army had been just too small, and the American part of the war had been just too short, to inundate the World War I generation with the lessons of unity learned by servicemen, especially when they came home to a society so hostile to such ideas.[37]

The intolerance carried on and grew in the interwar period. For a brief time after the war, a sharp economic downturn helped foster Communist-assisted labor unrest and the subsequent first Red scare. This virulent anticommunism and antiradicalism merged with the ethnic and religious animosities of the era. Jews and Italians suffered the highest profile persecution. For example, Victor Berger, a German Jewish Socialist congressman, was convicted of violating the Espionage Act and imprisoned for opposing the war— in large part due to anti-German and anti-Semitic feelings. More famously, in 1920 two Italian immigrant anarchists, Nicola Sacco and Bartolomeo Vanzetti, found themselves charged with the robbery and murder of a man in Brockton, Massachusetts. The jury convicted them on evidence that is still in dispute and under a judge who was overheard to call the defendants "those anarchist bastards." Nevertheless, Sacco and Vanzetti were executed in 1927.[38] At the sentencing, Vanzetti famously declared, "I am suffering because I am a radical, and indeed I am a radical; I have suffered because I was an Italian, and indeed I am an Italian."[39]

Besides the economic downturn immediately after the war, the decade following the Armistice marked the most prosperous era in American history up to that point.[40] But even prosperity did not lead to greater tolerance; in fact, quite the opposite occurred. As Frederick Lewis Allen wrote at the decade's close, intolerance "took the form of an ugly flare-up of feeling against the Negro, the Jew, and the Roman Catholic."[41] President-elect Warren Harding wrote of the problem in 1920: "Here in America we have no racial identity. We are a blend or a mixture or an association of all the nations of the earth, but, unhappily, up to the time of the war we were very much a collocation of peoples; but from this time on we want to be a fraternity of Americans."[42] Harding wanted that fraternity to be based on service to America, an idea fostered by uniting the country. "I believe it is best served by wiping away distinctions of class, creed, race or occupation which separate Americans from Americans."[43]

In this postwar environment, the country ratified the final two progressive amendments to the Constitution, women's suffrage and Prohibition. Unfortunately, American women proved subject to many of the same prejudices as American men, and their gaining the right to vote did not stop the intolerant trends of the times.[44] And Prohibition fit those times perfectly. What historian Oscar Handlin wrote of New York could apply all over the country: "The saloon was evil because it was situated in the city and was frequented by the Irish. Prohibition thus gave expression to the anti-Catholicism widespread in the rural sections of [New York]."[45] For their part, the foreign born and their children, bunched into cities, by and large ignored the ban on alcohol.[46] What is more, the children of immigrants—Poles, Italians, and Jews especially but also the Irish—came to run the bootlegging and alcohol distribution businesses of the 1920s. The names Arnold Rothstein, Lucky Luciano, Dutch Schultz, John Torrio, Max Hoff, and, above all, Al Capone became synonymous with violence and lawlessness for their roles in the alcohol trade–induced gang violence of the era, thereby confirming all of the worst stereotypes of the ruin certain groups brought to American life.[47]

In part because of these violations of the Eighteenth Amendment, the Ku Klux Klan, a small but dedicated organization before the war, grew dramatically after the fighting.[48] Millions of individuals from regions all over the country joined the Klan's membership rolls in the 1920s. They elected senators and governors in states as diverse as Georgia, Oklahoma, Colorado, California, Tennessee, Ohio, Indiana, Oregon, Maine, and Wisconsin. The Klan had influence from the top to the bottom of white Protestant society and should not be dismissed as a movement of bored elites or overzealous poor folk. In the complex modern world, the Klan sold itself as a defender of traditional values, the values of white Protestant America. As such, one historian has written, "Anti-Catholicism, white supremacy, hatred of Jews, anti-radicalism, opposition to foreign immigration—these were the salients of Klan ideology."[49]

The widespread acceptance of bigoted views could also be seen in immigration restriction. The Quota Law of 1921, a temporary "emergency" act, restricted the number of European immigrants allowed per year to 355,000.

More important, the law was an attempt to restrict the numbers of the so-called new immigrants by limiting the immigration from any one country to 3 percent of the population of foreign-born individuals from that country living in the United States in 1910.[50] This first major act represented in part an attempt to help protect native American jobs from cheap foreign-born labor, but as one historian of immigration policy has noted, "biological factors" had replaced "economic considerations" by 1924.[51] When it became clear that the 1910 population provided too high a proportion of the inferior stock from southern and eastern Europe, Congress acted again. The permanent Immigration or National Origins Act of 1924 set the yearly quota on European immigrants at 150,000 and moved the proportion baseline back to 1890, when foreign-born immigrants from southern and eastern Europe were a much smaller percentage of the American population. The law had come to reflect the time's widespread social intolerance. The United States had rejected the idea that immigrants from inferior stock could be assimilated into the original American bloodlines.[52]

Yet within a few short years, the relationships among white ethnic and religious groups would change dramatically. In the broadest terms, at the beginning of the era Americans were starkly divided along ethnic and religious lines. Americans of all national backgrounds and religions by and large had very little tolerance for Americans of different national backgrounds and religions. After midcentury, at the end of the era, that active and aggressive intolerance was gone. The differences among white ethnic and religious groups just did not matter as much to Americans as they had before. Military service in World War II led to this shift.

Scholars have long noted that something important happened in these years to change ethnic and religious relations in American society.[53] Social scientists and historians influenced by the social sciences have tended to look at such issues in terms of patterns. These important and influential arguments make the general case that the development of tolerance was a process, usually broken down into generations. A vastly oversimplified version of such an argument reads that first-generation immigrants struggle and are rarely able to melt in to American society, those in the second generation have more mixed results, and the third generation begins to assimilate in earnest.[54] There are many variations on this model, taking into account a multitude of other factors, but as a general rule, such generational models divorce developing tolerance from the specific historical circumstances of the mid-twentieth century.

Historians and some historically minded social scientists have tried to put the changing relations into their time and place. For example, the immigration restriction of the interwar period meant that a greater proportion of ethnic minorities were fluent in English, and the common language accelerated second- and third-generation assimilation. Others have noted economic factors. Gary Gerstle and John Mollenkopf made the general case that the upward economic mobility of second-generation Americans in the middle part of the twentieth century "gradually blurred the formerly sharp distinctions between native white Protestants and young adult children of Catholic and Jewish immigrants."[55] Scholars such as Lizabeth Cohen and David Roediger have also emphasized the ways in which class identification began to supersede ethnicity through the vehicle of ethnically inclusive labor unions.[56] There is no doubt that generational differences, a common language, economic mobility, and mixing in labor unions helped set the conditions for the shift from intolerance to tolerance, but alone they do not account for when the shift occurred and the speed at which it happened. Military service, as will be shown here, does.

It should also be noted that measuring tolerance among white ethnic and religious groups is only one analytical tool with which to understand relationships during this era. There are other approaches. Some scholars have looked at the role ideology and growing mass media played in changing views. For example, cultural historian Lary May's study of Hollywood films in the middle part of the century argued that through movies "World War II and the Cold War . . . generated a major transformation in the national identity," creating "a homogenous American Way rooted in liberal capitalism and universal, classless values."[57] Philip Gleason also emphasized ideology in wartime. "Following upon a period in which ethnic factors had receded from prominence in [intellectual and academic] discussions of national identity," he wrote, "the war gave unprecedented salience to the ideological dimension" of the American identity. So after the war, being an American meant believing in American values, such as "democracy, freedom, equality, respect for individual dignity, and so on."[58]

Others have relied on the concept of assimilation to look at ethnic and religious relations. There has been a sizable and heated debate over the definition and existence of the American melting pot, and much discussion as to the nature and meaning of assimilation. In the first part of the twentieth century, many Americans looked at assimilation of immigrants only as a positive good. In the postwar years, especially in the later 1960s, that view began to shift. Students of the issue noted that in the process of melting or assimilating, individual groups either lost their special distinctiveness or subsumed their cultural traits to an overbearing majority. More recent scholarship has showed that ethnic and religious groups in America had long engaged in bargaining about what they would keep and what they would lose from their distinct backgrounds—keeping in mind that the bargaining was by no means uniform among or even within individual ethnic groups. Because the ideas of melting or assimilation are so complex, there is no consensus as to how to measure them, especially as they apply to groups.[59] That said, the overall processes of incorporation, acculturation, and assimilation of white ethnic and religious groups seemed to change collectively at midcentury.[60]

Race is yet another related tool for analyzing the era, and scholars of race and ethnicity have tended to focus on the concept of whiteness, especially for what are now considered white ethnic groups. Historians Noel Ignatiev, Matthew Frye Jacobson, David Roediger, and Matthew Guterl, among others, have been engaged in a vigorous discussion over these important issues. They generally agree that prior to the war, most people used the terms "race" and "ethnicity" interchangeably and used the former more often than the latter to describe everyone, including European immigrant groups. In the complex racial hierarchy of the times, European immigrants and their descendants clearly outranked African Americans, but that position did not make them pure white or Caucasian. After the mid-twentieth century, European immigrant groups and their descendants did become white or Caucasian, and ethnicity in the American context became distinct from race.[61]

These other analytical tools—ideology, assimilation, race—should not be seen as competitive with the idea of tolerance. In truth, all of these views are complementary; they provide focus for each other. The details of the mid-century ideological shift, the finer points about the relationships among ethnic groups, the particulars of if, when, and how individuals groups became assimilated, and the finer points of the changing meaning of race in America all make better sense in the context of the change in the overall relationships among all of these groups (except African Americans) from general animosity to general tolerance. Likewise, the transition to tolerance makes better sense when understood alongside ideological, assimilation, and race issues. Race is the best example, because the postwar ethnic and religious tolerance described here clearly excluded African Americans. The reason is as simple as it is tragic: The World War II military kept African American troops segregated from their white counterparts, and as a result white-black relations generally remained outside the story of developing tolerance. So the issue of race plays an important role in this story, as relations between whites and blacks provide an essential counterpoint to the main theme of the book.[62]

All that said, the argument about tolerance in this book is based on specific historical experiences rather than on the conceptual issues of degrees of assimilation or whiteness. The World War II military took millions of nonblack men from widely different backgrounds and mixed them together. Their experiences while in uniform profoundly and permanently changed the way they looked at one another, and they came home and took the lead in shaping an ethnically and religiously tolerant postwar American social, cultural, and political life. In theory, it is possible that ideological homogeneity, quickened assimilation, and a broadened definition of whiteness could have led to the clear improvement in relations among white ethnic and religious groups in the United States by 1945. But they did not. Nor was the tolerance that emerged in the United States after the end of World War II dependent on ethnic or religious groups assimilating or melting any more than they already had. Military service in World War II led to general tolerance among the groups as those groups had already developed in America.

Versions of this argument have been made in the past, usually in articles or as part of larger studies on American identity. Cornell sociologist Robin Williams first made the case in 1951: "As the war continued there was, at least for those in military services, a growth of common experiences—no matter how unpleasant at the time—which in the end left a new residue of shared values and traditions."[63] In the 1970s, historian John Morton Blum made some limited claims along the same lines for Italian and Jewish Americans.[64] By the 1990s, George E. Pozzetta had introduced the topic as an area of research and was working on a larger study of World War II and ethnic America when he passed away.[65] A more recent study by historian Gary Gerstle relied largely on the memoir *Goodbye Darkness,* written by retired marine William Manchester, to deal briefly with the subject and come to similar conclusions, although much of what Gerstle wrote was introductory and speculative.[66] In 2004, Deborah Dash Moore published an important and nuanced study of the effect of military service on Jewish Americans, but her work did not deal in detail with the broader issue of white ethnic and religious relations.[67]

To date there is nothing comprehensive on the subject of exactly how the World War II military experience related to the sea change in ethnic and religious relations in the twentieth-century United States. This study aims to fill that gap. To that end, it focuses on prewar and wartime ethnic and religious relations in America, the experiences of soldiers during the war, and how those experiences shaped the way they dealt with and shaped American life in peace.

In order to avoid confusion, certain terms require definition for the purposes of this study.[68] Unless otherwise indicated in the text, the term "white" refers broadly to those descended from Europeans. Even though it is a bit of an anachronism, "ethnic" refers to the most common understanding of the word

—specific national origin: Greek Americans, Irish Americans, Italian Americans, Polish Americans, and German Americans are all ethnic groups, despite the divisions within each of those groups. Other groupings present a few more problems. Even given their status today as a nonwhite racial group, Hispanic or Latino Americans are treated here as a white ethnic group for two interrelated reasons.[69] First, during World War II, Latinos made up a rather small percentage of the population—from the largest group, Mexican Americans, the first and second generations numbered roughly 700,000 people out of a total population of 132 million in 1940.[70] Second, although they experienced many unique issues as Latinos, other white ethnic groups in the military by and large treated Latinos the same as they treated one another. Likewise, Jewish Americans' status as both an ethnic and religious group made them unique, but they too are treated as a white ethnic group here. The main other religious groups in this study are Roman Catholics and the various denominations of Protestants (keeping in mind that groups such as the Mormons and Eastern Orthodox do not fit precisely into either category).[71]

In order to explain the role of World War II military service in the development of tolerance, this study traces a line through mid-twentieth-century U.S. history. It begins with a brief account of the presidential election of 1928 as the great example of widespread ethnic and religious intolerance in the interwar period. Chapter 2 then provides a description of the ongoing, and in some cases increased, ethnic and religious tensions in the country through the Great Depression and all the way until the end of the war. Contrary to some popular belief, neither the Great Depression nor the war years on the home front created unity among the nation's diverse white population.

Chapters 3 to 6 narrow the focus to deal specifically with the U.S. military. As the single largest branch of the American military in World War II, the ground and service forces of the army provide the best representative sample of military service in the war. Of course, there were differences among the experiences of the men who served in the U.S. Army, Navy, Marine Corps, and Army Air Forces. A mechanic in the engine room of an aircraft carrier, a marine landing on the beach at Tarawa, and a waist gunner in a B-17 on a bombing run over Europe all lived a different war from the men on the ground in the U.S. Army. Even within the ground army, there existed key disparities among armor, airborne, signal corps, engineers, headquarters, artillery, and infantry.

Despite these differences, and despite the very important pride men felt for their service branch and their role within that branch, there is little evidence to suggest that the general conclusions drawn by this study about ethnicity and religion and the World War II military experience vary from branch to branch or theater to theater. And in fact, the ground army best proved the point. As the largest single service branch, one that fought in large numbers against both the Germans and the Japanese and one that itself was divided into many distinct smaller parts, the army would probably have provided cases that deviated from the general experience. It did not. The differences therein were of degree, not kind.[72] As one army veteran who never left the United States during the war later wrote in his memoirs, for the army "noncombatants, too, the war was the most defining experience of their generation."[73]

For almost all of its history, the traditionalists who ran the U.S. military had denied its role as an institution of social experimentation. Their job was to win wars. But that does not tell the whole story. In World War II, the army ran a great social experiment by mixing white men from all different backgrounds. Chapter 3 is a description of World War II army personnel policy toward ethnic and religious groups and that policy's historical roots.

Chapters 4, 5, and 6 detail the experiences of the men who made up the rank and file in the army as those experiences related to ethnic and religious issues. For all the differences among the millions of individuals who served in thousands of different roles, they all shared a profoundly important and large common experience in the military. That commonality of experience is exactly what the military sought; it attempted through discipline, ideals, and experiences to make uniform millions of individuals in the pursuit of a common cause. Chapter 4 describes the shock of provincial Americans at the introduction to army life, the purposes and results of training, and how the men ultimately adjusted to this new world.

The majority of American soldiers never saw combat in World War II. Even those who did spent most of their time outside direct action. Most service in the army was pretty dull, so the men tried to occupy themselves with games, reading, food, drink, and women. As they did, they came in contact with people from all around the world. In their search for entertainment in foreign lands and with foreign people, they discovered many of the shared principles, assumptions, and biases that united them as Americans. The fifth chapter describes this process. Chapter 6 focuses on the time before, during, and after combat. Nothing made a mockery of ethnic and religious intolerance quite so much as the experience of being under fire. There the men relied on their buddies, regardless of background. What is more, the sacrifices made by men from all ethnic and religious backgrounds provided a powerful testament to the meaning of the war, a meaning the men would not easily forget.

These millions of veterans returned to civilian life profoundly changed by their experiences at war, and chapter 7 describes that transition. There is an inherent challenge in trying to describe the cumulative effect of veterans on American politics and society after World War II. They did not all join veterans organizations. They did not speak with one voice on most issues. They spoke out hardly at all on some issues. Yet their power in postwar America was undeniable. This chapter explains how and to what degree they came to dominate politics and society.[74]

There the story of their collective postwar lives often gets lost in a different narrative—tangled, jumbled, and scattered by an abstraction called the Cold War. The Cold War dominates the story of the postwar years, obscuring a deeper understanding of the effect of World War II on the American people. Beyond the obvious topics of diplomacy and military affairs, the historiography on the second half of the twentieth century overflows with studies of Cold War culture and politics. At the same time, the United States enjoyed an economic boom and the creation of a widespread suburbanized consumer culture.

Frustrated critics of the era, both at the time and later, saw it as a time of panic, oppression, and missed opportunities. The threat of the Cold War and nuclear weapons engendered a radical departure in foreign policy away from America's traditional isolationism. The fear of communism at home created an equally extreme reaction to the threat of radical ideological dissidents.[75] In everyday life, critics noted that white Americans had moved into uniform track housing in the suburbs, where they looked and acted the same as all of their neighbors. For the critics, postwar America became prosperous but empty, a conformist mass consumption society in which everyone lived with a latent fear of the atomic bomb.[76] These critics missed the fact that veterans were at the center of all these trends, and because of those veterans both the Cold War and conformist consumer culture, whatever else their problems, were remarkably ethnically and religiously tolerant. Chapter 8 describes how veterans used their positions of power to influence these postwar trends.

The study concludes with the presidential election of 1960 as the great test of postwar ethnic and religious tolerance. That election and that year is a natural stopping point, because the 1960s saw the emergence of a variety of forces that challenged the postwar consensus. Most important among these newly emergent forces was the black civil rights movement. The issue of the relations between white and black Americans is an important undercurrent throughout this study. When one discusses relations among ethnic and religious groups, race is bound to be a factor. But race quite consciously receives little systematic attention because segregation meant the exclusion of African Americans from the postwar tolerance. Yet by the 1960s, the failure to include African Americans in the World War II military was contributing to problems that would create new tensions in white ethnic and religious America.

The focus on failures should not obscure the successes. The prewar disputes among white ethnic and religious groups in America created real tensions and real intolerance. Americans who experienced those tensions and intolerance feared their power to fracture the country. It was no small thing that in postwar America the vast numbers of white ethnic and religious groups came to get along. And it was all because of the war.

For the mass of Americans who lived through it, World War II dominated their lives. It made the modern United States. The spirit of that truth inspired this book.

# 1

# THE AMERICA THEY LEFT BEHIND

When you were a youngster, what kind of people did your family dislike? Did you hear talk at home against the Jews or the Negroes or the Catholics or the Methodists or the Chinese? Did you hate city people or Bostonians or Southerners, or those who didn't speak English very well?

— "The Stab of Intolerance," *New York Times,* 1941

MOST OF THE TIME—IN EVERYDAY LIFE—AMERICA'S PREJUDICES STAY HIDden. Americans pass their lives working, spending time with family and friends, trying to get through the days within a comfortable and accepted order of things. But those prejudices lurk just below the surface, and they emerge when that comfortable and accepted order is challenged from time to time. One of those times came in 1928. That year, Alfred Emmanuel Smith ran for president.

The candidacy of Al Smith exposed nearly all of the hate and distrust of a people spread across a vast continent who came from all over the world, worshiped different gods in different ways, and were held together in their own estimation by lines on a map and not much more. Along came Al Smith, not only a New Yorker but from New York City. He was a child of Irish immigrants. He was a Roman Catholic. In support of one or more of these traits, millions of city folks, immigrants and their children, and Roman Catholics flocked to Smith's banner. In response to one or all of those same traits, millions of Americans temporarily left behind the relative calm of their everyday lives to stop this man, this symbol of all that could upset would it meant to them to be American.[1]

The assault began early, when in April 1927 Columbia Law School graduate and student of canon law Charles C. Marshall wrote an open letter to Smith in the *Atlantic Monthly.* Marshall relied on the *Catholic Encyclopedia* and papal encyclicals to make his case that "certain conceptions" held by "a loyal and conscientious Roman Catholic" such as Smith were "irreconcilable with that Constitution which as President you must support and defend, and with the principles of civil and religious liberty on which American institutions are based." In short, Marshall wanted to know how Smith could be loyal to the strict rules and hierarchy of Rome and the freedoms of the United States at the same time.[2]

In the next month's issue, Governor Smith replied in a long letter written by a team of advisors. He refuted Marshall's letter point by point, making the case that both by church law and his personal experience, none of Marshall's concerns were valid. Smith argued that American history proved that there was nothing incompatible between the Roman Catholic Church and American institutions, as two Catholic Supreme Court chief justices—Roger Brooke Taney and Edward Douglass White—and "the tens of thousands of young Catholics who have risked and sacrificed their lives in defense of our country" had shown. He concluded with a profession of his faith as an American Catholic:

> I believe in the worship of God according to the faith and practice of the Roman Catholic Church. I recognize no power in the institutions of my Church to interfere with the operations of the Constitution of the United States or the enforcement of the law of the land. I believe in absolute freedom of conscience for all men and in equality of all churches, all sects, and all beliefs before the law as a matter of right and not as a matter of favor. I believe in the absolute separation of Church and State and in the strict enforcement of the provisions of the Constitution that Congress shall make no law respecting an establishment of religion or prohibiting the free exercise thereof. I believe that no tribunal of any church has any power to make any decree of any force in the law of the land, other than to establish the status of its own communicants within its own church. I believe in the support of the public school as one of the cornerstones of American liberty. I believe in the right of every parent to choose whether his child shall be educated in the public school or in a religious school supported by those of his own faith. I believe in the principled noninterference by this country in the internal affairs of other nations and that we should stand steadfastly against any such interference by whomsoever it may be urged. And I believe in the common brotherhood of man under the common fatherhood of God.
>
> In this spirit I join with fellow Americans of all creeds in a fervent prayer that never again in this land will any public servant be challenged because of the faith in which he has tried to walk humbly with his God.[3]

Would that such a ringing declaration of his faith and beliefs have ended then and there the debate over the fitness of a Roman Catholic to be president. But it was not to be.

In the introduction to Smith's reply, the editor of the *Atlantic* wrote optimistically of the level of discussion: "Not in this campaign will whispering and innuendoes, shruggings and hunchings, usurp the place of reason and of argument. The thoughts rising almost unbidden in the minds of the least bigoted of us when we watch a Roman Catholic aspire to the Presidency of the United States have become matters of high, serious, and eloquent debate."[4] He could not have been more wrong. The "whispering and innuendoes, shruggings and hunchings" began almost immediately.

Not surprisingly, Smith's political opponents exploited the issue. Even Republican candidate Herbert Hoover was not completely innocent of taking advantage of the country's many divides. Hoover distanced himself from any explicit statements of prejudice in the campaign, but he could not actively work against such feelings without risking losing voters, so he did little to end the bigotry used on his behalf. A Presbyterian minister had it right that year when he credited Hoover for disavowing any anti-Catholic sentiments, but he nonetheless criticized the Republican candidate: "Unfortunately he can not, or at least he does not, restrain and check the pernicious activity of his supporters. . . . Hence, if their candidate should be elected, he would owe his election in part to the religious prejudice and anti-Catholic enmity which the cabalists have stirred up and marshalled to the polls." Such a result would be a "calamity" for religious freedom in America. "The spiritual call to arms goes out to every man and woman," he concluded. "Defend the religious liberty of America."[5] This Herbert Hoover would not, and if he wanted to win, could not, do. He looked away while many of his supporters did play on the religious issue.[6]

As indication of how deep the intolerance went, it expanded into Smith's own Democratic party. Democratic senator James Thomas Heflin of Alabama openly and repeatedly attacked Smith and the Roman Catholic church, speaking at Klan rallies and even letting loose his vitriol on the floor of the Senate. He warned of "a distinct program and deep-laid plan and purpose in the minds of many Roman Catholics to control this country and make it Catholic" and that "Governor Smith is the man selected by the Roman Catholic political machine to be the Roman candidate for President of the United States." Although repudiated in Congress by Arkansas senator (and Smith running mate) Joseph Robinson, and basically drummed out of the party for abandoning its candidate in 1928, Heflin's words and ideas reached across the country, where they found too many receptive listeners.[7]

Other Democrats had to face the issue. After he lost out on the bid for vice president on the Democratic ticket and offered his support to Smith, Kentucky Senator Alben Barkley received letters from Americans expressing doubt and anger about Smith's candidacy. The concerns stretched over the range of issues, from Smith's Tammany connections, to his stand on Prohibition, to his religion. Perhaps most striking were all the Democrats who explicitly refused to vote for Smith that year because of one or all of those issues. Everett McKeaege, a San Francisco attorney, wrote to Barkley, "I may be wrong in my estimate of the New York Governor but I have never yet been able to get any satisfactory evidence, which would in the slightest degree lead me to the conviction that this gentlemen is other than a 'dyed in the wool' protégé and cat's paw of Tammany Hall."[8] A letter from one R. W. Smith accused Barkley of selling out Kentucky and the Democratic party by supporting Al Smith, a man who clearly was not fit to be president based on "his stand with respect to . . . the Church, Heretics meriting death, The public school[,] the Government *Subserviant* [*sic*] to the *Hierarchy*."[9]

A widespread popular movement against Smith had begun. Circulars, pamphlets, road signs, editorials, and public statements from a variety of religious and secular groups openly and proudly condemned Smith as unfit for the presidency because of his stands on alcohol and immigration, and, most important, because of his religion. Early student of the election Michael Williams called it a "flood of calumny," and wrote:

> In attempting to deal with the main stream of the avowedly anti-Catholic outbreak of 1928, the difficulty in adequately sketching the subject within reasonable limits of space is well-nigh insuperable. The sheer mass of the literature distributed throughout the country was stupendous. Its character was so generally false and vile that reproduction even of the less offensive specimens, while necessary, is deplorable. That so large a part of the American people could believe, or consider credible, the sort of charges made against their Catholic fellow citizens . . . is in itself proof of how grave a menace to the unity and peace of the nation is contained in the anti-Catholic psychology when it is inflamed and organized.[10]

Another early study that generally downplayed the religion issue called it "the most insidious whispering campaign in history."[11]

Prominent religious leaders from a variety of Protestant denominations spoke out openly against the Catholic Smith, including Bishop James Cannon of the Methodist Episcopal Church, Southern Baptist Arthur Barton, and popular preacher Billy Sunday. Countless local churches picked up the theme.[12]

One observer reported that former governor of Michigan, Chase Osborne, told a Methodist conference that American Catholics should "secede from the rule of the Pope and . . . set up instead of that Allegiance a self-governed church."[13] The September 16 weekly bulletin for the Fountain Avenue Methodist Church in Paducah, Kentucky, declared that the hour had struck to stand up to the wet, Tammany, immigrant forces of Al Smith. The bulletin argued that Smith would repeal the highly restrictive immigration laws because it "is to the interest of Tammany and Political Rome to open up the flood gates and fill this country full of foreign-born." Prohibition would then be repealed. In response to this threat, the bulletin instructed, "Pray earnestly then answer your own prayer with your ballot" and concluded, "Let Us Vote To Keep Our Constitution Intact From the Attack of the Foreigner."[14]

Reports and editorials in religious and secular newspapers and magazines in Virginia, Kentucky, New York, Ohio, Florida, Georgia, Texas, Washington, D.C., and elsewhere around the nation sounded the same theme. The Lutheran editors of America, with a combined readership of some two million, held a convention and concluded publicly that the "claims, teachings and principles of the Roman Catholic Church are antagonistic to and irreconcilable with the fundamental principles set forth in the constitution of our country concerning the separation of church and state."[15] The editors of the *Christian Century* opposed Smith because they feared "the seating of a representative of an alien culture, of a medieval Latin mentality, of an undemocratic hierarchy and of a foreign potentate in the great office of President of the United States."[16] Several newspapers reproduced the fictional Knights of Columbus oath that had been circulating the country since the outset of the century. As this version had it, new members of the Knights swore, among other things, to "hang, waste, boil, flay, strangle and burn . . . heretics [Protestants]; rip up the stomachs and wombs of their women and crush infants' heads against the wall, in order to annihilate forever their execrable race."[17]

The rumors and attacks spread far beyond church meetings and reports in periodicals. Rumors spread that the pope planned to move to the United States to take control if Smith won. A photo showing the construction of the Holland Tunnel with the claim that it was a passage directly to the Vatican even made the rounds.[18] A group calling itself the Knights of Luther released a small pamphlet from Toledo, Ohio, listing facts meant "to open the eyes and conscience of every true American citizen." The pamphlet warned of the disproportionate representation of Roman Catholics in all forms of American life, from politics to schools to police forces—all working at the behest of the church in Rome to take over the United States. Such a takeover would have dire consequences on American vice and virtue because the Catholic church denied all of the country's fundamental freedoms, even forbidding "its own people to read the Bible." The presidential election represented "Two Mighty World Theories of Government in Deadly Conflict."[19]

A handbill passed around in Mississippi insisted that Smith would use the American military to put Catholic priests back into Mexico. Another handbill that saw circulation in the South and Midwest showed a cartoon of Governor Smith kneeling before an enthroned Italian Cardinal. The caption read, "—and he asks the American people to elect him President."[20] From Aurora, Missouri, came a pamphlet titled *30 Reasons Why Protestants Should Be Sure to Vote for Alcohol Smith*. The author included among his reasons:

> To contribute a boy to fill a drunkard's grave,
>
> To furnish a daughter to add to the Red Light District by the gin-fizz route,
>
> To have your wife and daughter when they join the President's Church for social prestige, to be asked questions in the confessional by a bachelor priest that you would not dare ask them yourself. . . .
>
> To see the Bible, your mother loved, now already driven by Roman Catholics from the public schools, spit upon and burned as in Roman Catholic Brazil, but not noted by our loud-mouthed Irish-American aposles [*sic*] of TOLERANCE. . . .
>
> To see the pope . . . move his political household to American shores and occupy the heavy stone fortresses Roman Catholicism has built commanding the heights of Washington, D.C., the better to direct his campaign to rule the world. . . .
>
> . . . to barter your Protestant birthright for a mess of political pottage and preferment by an unholy alliance with those who would destroy the Constitution, the schools, the church, the homes of free-born Americans, freedom of speech and press and all the blood-bought heritage handed down by your American forefathers, to get your share of the spoils while swelling the retinue of an Italian pope, May the God of your fathers have pity on your poor recanting Protestant soul, and in mercy mete out to you your just deserts [*sic*] here and hereafter, while you VOTE FOR AL SMITH.[21]

The rhetoric could hardly get more heated, yet such was the norm in the campaign of 1928.

Al Smith and his supporters tried to rise to the challenge. They put out campaign literature of their own, including a pamphlet drawn from several newspaper editorials rhetorically asking, *What was the Religion of the*

*Unknown Soldier?* The pamphlet pointed out that no one visited the tomb of the soldier and asked his religion "because love leads them there—and love is kind." Nor did his fellow soldiers or even God ask, "Are you Jew or Gentile, Protestant or Catholic?" Yet, the pamphlet continued, "to our shame—today a man's fitness for higher office is being questioned . . . because he is a Catholic." Even worse "are the ceaseless and senseless accusations made against this man Smith by women, wives and mothers, from whose lips little children must get the foundation of their knowledge of right and wrong, and all because Smith is a Catholic."[22]

Smith tried speaking out about tolerance in places such as North Carolina and Oklahoma but did not find receptive audiences.[23] When that did not work, his campaign sent old stock Protestant Democrats to campaign for him in the South and Midwest, centers of the most acute anti-Catholic prejudice. The future secretary of labor, Frances Perkins, stumped for Smith, stressing to these devout people that they should want a man in the White House who said his prayers and followed God's laws. According to Perkins, many agreed, "but they were bothered by the sign of the Cross and the Rosary. The Democrats in many of those areas voted against him, but for the most part they never quite forgave themselves."[24] Those who did vote for Smith risked alienation in their communities. In rural Indiana, reporter Ernie Pyle's parents voted for Al Smith in 1928 "because they thought he was a better man than Hoover," even though they were Protestant and prohibitionists. Afterward, Pyle recalled, "some of the neighbors wouldn't speak to them for months because they had voted for a Catholic and a wet."[25]

The efforts of Smith and his supporters to control the religious and ethnic issues were no use. In part the problem came from Smith himself. He believed vehemently that individual accomplishment, regardless of background, demonstrated Americanism.[26] He thought he answered the questions about his religion in the *Atlantic.* So afterward he treated the ongoing religious assaults with contempt, refusing even to acknowledge that he had some responsibility to convince the people that his religion should not be an issue. Smith's bluntness went on display shortly after the election. "It is amazing in this day and age that such countless thousands of people are so stupid as to believe the absolutely false and senseless propaganda that was whispered around during the last campaign," he wrote.[27] This attitude led one historian to write of the candidate, "He seemed determined to flaunt what was most controversial about his candidacy."[28] But even if he had made the effort, that kind of convincing was beyond the power of one man.

What was clear, but what Al Smith did not quite understand and could never really avoid, was that the issue was the issue. As long as his Irish immigrant city background and his Catholicism were part of the debate in 1928, he was in trouble. The intolerance and bigotry of the United States in the 1920s was visceral, emotional. The people were set in their ways. Logic and reason, fairness and understanding, had nothing to do with their actions when it came to issues of religion and ethnicity. The 1928 election exposed the ugly intolerance behind all the key religious and ethnic divides in the United States. Even as he tried to face down the issue, for most of the country Al Smith represented the cities, he represented the new immigrants, Catholics, and Jews who lived in the cities, and he represented the repeal of Prohibition those groups wanted. Though progressive and tolerant personally, Herbert Hoover represented traditional Anglo-Saxon Protestant Americanism.

Hoover won in a landslide. Some of the Solid South voted for the Republican candidate. Smith even lost his home state of New York. That is not to say that tolerance would have tipped the election in Smith's favor. Hoover enjoyed advantages as a candidate that had nothing to do with religion or ethnicity, but the results still went far beyond a prosperous economy and Hoover's charming personal success story. Certainly not every voter cared about the religious issue, but millions obviously did. The proof came from the campaign more than the election results themselves. Those who opposed Smith clearly believed that the most compelling arguments against the New Yorker involved issues of religion and ethnicity. If the voters rejected those arguments, that rejection did not show up at the polls. In that sense, the 1928 election represented a nationwide referendum on tolerance. The measure failed.[29]

It has long been the impression that the 1920s, and especially the 1928 election, marked a high point in animosity and intolerance. There is a simple reason for this impression: In the years after World War II, almost everyone recognized that ethnic and religious intolerance had decreased dramatically, but almost everyone also misidentified the origins of that change, which led them to misdiagnose the primary causes. In truth, the ethnic and religious animosity of 1930s and early 1940s was more quiet than in the 1920s. It was hard to be as loud as the Klan, immigration restriction, and the 1928 election. But the quiet of the 1930s was only relative to the noise of the 1920s and not an indicator of increased tolerance. In reality, the level of intolerance stayed at a steadily high state throughout the decade. Even the war itself did not lead to tolerance on the home front. In fact, the prejudices exposed in the 1928 election continued unabated, lurking under the surface and emerging throughout the 1930s and 1940s. The men and women who served in the military in World War II spent their youths in a divided country, and almost none of the political and social trends in the 1930s and 1940s indicated that all that was headed toward a change.

Ironically, the national politics of the era, as dynamic as they were, and Franklin Roosevelt, as dynamic as he was, had more than a little to do with sustaining the status quo. The explanation for that paradox can be found in the rapidly changing demographics of national politics. One of the reasons 1928 was so spectacular in its nastiness was because ethnic and religious relations had begun to be crucially important in state and federal politics.[30] Nowhere was this more evident than in the Democratic party. After Reconstruction, the Democrats became the only real party in the South, but they needed more than that region if they were to return to national prominence. They recruited from the most unlikely of places: urban machines. Machine politics had played a key role in the political life of immigrants in the cities in the last half of the nineteenth century.[31] Urban new stock Democrats appealed to their constituencies through a variety of policies, and they increasingly became tied up with the national Democratic party through prominent leaders, including Al Smith.[32] In this way, the Democratic party became the party of the immigrant in the North. But the Democrats were still the party of Jefferson, the party of agrarians, and the party of the South. For the Democrats to take power nationwide, the two wings needed to be brought together. Woodrow Wilson temporarily did the job in the 1910s, but by the 1920s the coalition had fractured regionally, culturally, and ideologically between their traditional southern and western rural base and the newly assertive urban immigrants.[33] The problem for the Democrats was that the two branches were opposites on a variety of issues, including the party's stand on Prohibition, which the urban branch decidedly opposed and the rural branch decidedly supported. Thus split, the Democrats could not offer much of a challenge to the Republicans during the decade.[34]

The Great Depression afforded an opportunity for the rise of an ambitious politician whose career had been put off for the better part of a decade by a debilitating disease. When Franklin Delano Roosevelt surveyed the national political scene from his home in Hyde Park, New York, in the late 1920s, at least one thing was clear. Immigrant and ethnic groups had become a force in American electoral politics, a new and powerful constituency that could no longer be ignored. But it would take an extraordinary effort to harness that power without alienating the large segment of the American population that had so vehemently rejected Catholics and other new immigrants in 1928.[35]

President Hoover's inability to manage what was probably an unmanageable economic crisis meant that the Democratic nominee in 1932 was virtually a lock to become president. Roosevelt had learned the lessons of 1928 and was not about to waste the hidden blessing of his polio, which had kept him out of the divisive party battles of the 1920s. "Aware that Smith would continue to be powerful in the cities," one historian has written, "Roosevelt acutely perceived the necessity of emphasizing traditional policies to attract traditional votes—to play down Prohibition and the religious issue, to avoid antagonizing either the Tammany or the anti-Tammany forces, to emphasize aid to agriculture and tariff reform."[36] When the 1932 Democratic convention rolled around, he had positioned himself perfectly. Though a New Yorker like Smith who could attract the urban vote, Roosevelt was also the classic upper-class Anglo-Saxon Protestant who did not carry the stigma of being a big city Catholic child of immigrants. In 1932, Franklin Roosevelt could appeal to both sides of the big urban-rural divide enough to get the nomination. Once he had the nomination, there was little chance of losing to Hoover in the general election. As expected, Roosevelt won big that year.[37]

From there, though, things would no longer be so politically straightforward for the new president. Roosevelt recognized that he would have to work much harder to win reelection in 1936. He needed to rebuild the coalition, a large part of which would be made up of the new immigrants. So as president, Roosevelt began to make some efforts on behalf of individual ethnic and religious groups. In speeches and policies aimed at these various crowds, the president encouraged nondiscrimination on the basis of religion or national origin. Most important, he appointed unprecedented numbers of Catholics and Jews to federal positions. As a result, American political life was more open to the participation of immigrants and their children during the Roosevelt years, and the president's policies and appointments were popular with the individuals involved and the people within those specific ethnic and religious groups.[38]

But those policies and appointments were not harbingers of a new more tolerant age because they did not exist in a political vacuum. While Roosevelt was a tremendously popular president, he was not without his critics. Conservatives in and out of the Republican party, not to mention Al Smith and the other disaffected Democrats who formed the Liberty League, challenged the president from a traditional ideological standpoint and within the mainstream political system.[39] In addition, new political faces in the 1930s, such as Huey Long with his Share the Wealth program, Francis Townsend and his old age pension plan, and Father Charles Coughlin, reviving the old silver-coining inflationary panacea, gained widespread support with their populist platforms.[40] Roosevelt rightly saw these groups as a threat to his reelection campaign; he had to avoid aiding them, or even worse uniting them, by alienating old stock Americans.

The result was a masterpiece of politicking that goes a long way toward explaining the scattershot and sometimes contradictory nature of the New Deal. What looked like pragmatic experimentation to find a way to end the Depression also included a healthy dose of political maneuvering. The New Deal included something for everyone—from farmers and bankers to labor and business. With so much going on, it became more and more difficult to keep track of it all. Rexford Tugwell, one of the original members of Roosevelt's Brains Trust, later wrote that President Roosevelt's seemingly helter-skelter policies and stands really represented "political necessity" as he worked toward some larger general objectives:

> He had to find a broad base of support, and he had to have the specific
> consent of the powerful groups he must work with. . . . Further than this,
> he must not alienate dangerous non-governmental groups—businessmen,
> the newspapers, the lobbyists, the immigrant conglomeration, the Catho-
> lic Church. Or, rather, he must not alienate enough of them at once to
> give real trouble. He must have the balance of consent necessary to allow
> him the tolerance he needed. But at the same time he must maintain
> enemies—convenient enemies such as he had always cultivated.[41]

Roosevelt's convenient enemies included the super rich, financiers, and the money changers he promised to drive from the temple. The Depression afforded Roosevelt the opportunity to focus the country's attention on an amorphous rich—all while he quietly but effectively catered to the individual interest groups that made up his coalition. Among those individual interest groups were the various ethnic and religious minorities who benefited in the Roosevelt years.

The repeal of the Eighteenth Amendment served as the perfect example of Roosevelt's skill in these matters. By the end of the 1920s, broader public opinion had turned against Prohibition. However, the 1928 election made clear that when the debate over Prohibition became coupled with ethnic and religious issues it could split the Democratic party. So as governor of New York, Roosevelt waffled on the issue while he searched for a compromise position that would achieve repeal without it appearing that he was catering to the urban ethnic vote. Many people were unhappy that both he and his wife defended the repeal of Prohibition in 1932, as it had been written into the Democratic platform. During and after the election, Franklin and Eleanor Roosevelt received stacks of letters both for and against repeal. The letter writers, especially those opposed to repeal, could be adamant in their views. A concerned citizen of Wray, Colorado, wrote to the president:

Dear Sir:—

    I first thot [*sic*] you were headed right by the power of God to help bring things aright, but alas thou art deceived by beer and wine and art weighed in the balance and found wanting.

    "Wine is a mocker, strong drink is raging and whosoever is deceived thereby is not wise."

        Yours truly

        Moses[42]

Mrs. Roosevelt came under even more severe reprobation after giving a radio address in late 1932 during which she hinted that because of Prohibition the average girl of the day did not know how to stick to the proper quantity of whiskey and gin when she drank. Letters flooded in to the soon-to-be first lady from churches, women's groups, temperance societies, and individual citizens all over the country.[43] One of the most biting letters came from one W. E. Graves of Toledo, Ohio:

Dear Mrs. Roosevelt,

    Permit me to add a word of appreciation for your sincere and helpful elevetation [*sic*] of that great American Institution, The Medicine Show. . . . Now we have a blue-blood society lady, born, bred, and reared in the purple, in a patronizing voice, giving us all kinds of advice. What a wonderful uplift this has been.

    The effect has been magical.

    Our girls are useing [*sic*] Ponds Face Balm and trying hard to see much synitheic [*sic*] gin they can carry. . . . Me, I have tried to drink Ponds Extract, but it did not have much kick, so I gave it up.[44]

Such heated words indicated that Prohibition still had the potential to be a divisive issue. But Roosevelt the politician sold the issue in different ways to different crowds. The wets in the cities, many immigrants and their children, loved that he embraced their position. The drys in the country were less comfortable, so Roosevelt turned repeal into a states' rights and economic issue. In one campaign speech he said, "The experience of nearly one hundred and fifty years under the Constitution has shown us that the proper means of regulation is through the States." To others he repeated the economic and class themes: "I favor the modification of the Volstead Act to permit States to authorize the manufacture and sale of beer just as fast as the law will let us. This is a way to divert three hundred million dollars or more by way of taxes from the pockets of racketeers to the Treasury of the United

States."[45] That the voters bought it, or at least bought it to the extent that they did not split the Democratic camp in large enough numbers to swing either the 1932 or 1936 elections, was testament to Roosevelt's skill as a salesman. Yet it was also true that they were much more inclined to buy from a salesman who was an old line Protestant upstate New Yorker rather than an Irish Catholic second-generation New York City native.[46]

Repeal of Prohibition was just one issue among many that required Roosevelt's deft touch. Despite the hiring of Catholics and Jews, despite the limited calls for tolerance, Roosevelt knew it was not politically expedient to appeal too much or too loudly to ethnic and religious minorities as a whole. He already had their votes; he would only erode his traditional rural base by talking too much of tolerance. So he subtly avoided the issue. For example, although the president repeatedly told local Works Progress Administrators "to follow the principle of nondiscrimination in religion, race, and political affiliation," the huge administration was by necessity decentralized, so local administrators could effectively follow any policy they wished.[47] President Roosevelt also dodged the tricky issue of immigration restriction by making no public pronouncements on the topic during the 1932 campaign, all while he quietly supported maintaining restrictions as long as the Depression continued.[48] At times it appeared that the administration thought about letting in more immigrants, especially political refugees, but the political reality stopped the president. At a March 1938 cabinet meeting, a discussion arose over refugees from countries that had been affected by Nazi and Fascist victories. The president was amenable to allowing in political refugees, and maybe even amending the immigration restrictions, but Vice President John Nance Garner noted that they could never get any amendment into law. In fact, Garner argued, "if the matter were left to a secret vote of Congress, all immigration would be stopped."[49] So President Roosevelt made public statements extolling the United States as a safe haven for political refugees—and made some quiet efforts for Jewish refugees especially—then made clear that he expected no overall change in immigration policy.[50] The delicate balancing act performed by Roosevelt could be seen in 1936, when the president began to face accusations that the New Deal really just catered to Catholics and Jews. As a response, the president brought in the former editor of a Protestant publication to join his campaign and act "as its emissary to the Protestants; his assignment was to bring 'Feminism, Piety and Pacifism' back to the Democratic camp."[51]

It worked. By 1936 Roosevelt had created his coalition, what would become the base of the national Democratic party for years to come. The coalition included Protestants from the South; farmers from the Midwest; Jews,

Catholics, and African Americans from the cities; members of labor unions; liberals; and even some radicals.[52] Politicians from both parties who saw Roosevelt's success at appealing to ethnic minorities tried to follow suit.[53] The general condition of ethnic and religious minorities improved even more. But the reason that the improvement of general condition did not lead to a decline in intolerance is because none of these policies focused on unification. The politicians appealed to the individual groups as individual groups. Yes, Roosevelt got the ethnic vote, but it would be more precise to say that he got the Jewish vote, the Catholic vote, the Irish vote, the Polish vote, the Italian vote, and so on. Of course there was some overlap, but Roosevelt had an uncanny ability to regiment these various interest groups so that they all voted for him for similar reasons, but not together.[54] The truth was that ethnicity and religion were still divisive enough issues that had the various interest groups who voted for Roosevelt known whom they were agreeing with, they might not have gone along. Conditions improved, or appeared to improve, for many ethnic and religious minorities in the 1930s because of the policies of the Roosevelt administration, and for that the president deserves much credit. But Franklin D. Roosevelt did little—politically could do little—to create a more tolerant pluralistic society before the war.

Although the Roosevelt administration and national politics did not lead to tolerance, there were some other trends during the 1930s that might have improved the situation. Many have argued that restrictions on immigration allowed a natural progression toward assimilation among second- and third-generation Americans.[55] Others have maintained that Depression-impoverished Americans from every ethnicity and religion were often too busy trying to survive to worry about their differences, especially considering new immigrants were restricted from entering and thus competing for jobs.[56] One of the ways some working-class ethnics survived was through identifying themselves as a common interest group by class. And indeed there was some movement during the decade for the working class away from ethnic and religious identification to a new more ethnically (but not racially) tolerant class consciousness rooted in mass culture, the Democratic party, and the CIO.[57]

Also important were the new efforts of some elite groups to push for increased tolerance.[58] For example, the years after the 1928 election saw the creation of the National Conference of Jews and Christians,[59] an organization dedicated to creating greater unity and understanding among the major religious groups in America.[60] Along the same lines, some progressive educators in the 1930s sought to find ways to alleviate some of the ethnic and religious tensions by recognizing the contributions of immigrants and their cultures to American society. They organized events like folk festivals in New York City to celebrate the artistic skill of America's various peoples. At one such festival they intoned the words of Franklin K. Lane, the former secretary of the interior: "Whatever the lure that brought us, each has his gift. Irish lad and Scot, Englishman and Dutch, Italian, Greek and French, Spaniard, Slav, Teuton, Norse, Negro—all have come bearing gifts and have laid them on the altar of America."[61]

A more popular example achieved national acclaim in 1939. That year the famous African American singer Paul Robeson gave a stunning rendition on CBS radio of a song called "Ballad for Americans." The ballad was an eleven-minute celebration of American history, starting with the Revolution and carrying through the Civil War and on to the present. Most telling was the song's long definition of who was American. The answer included all manner of professions, from factory workers and engineers to musicians and farmers. But it also included a lengthy, and unwieldy, section on race, ethnicity, and religion, beginning with the question, "Am I an American?"

> I'm just an Irish, Negro, Jewish, Italian, French and English, Spanish, Russian, Chinese, Polish, Scotch, Hungarian, Litvak, Swedish, Finnish, Canadian, Greek and Turk and Czech and Double Czech [American].
>
> And that ain't all, I was baptized Baptist, Methodist, Congregationalist, Lutheran, Atheist, Roman Catholic, Orthodox Jewish, Presbyterian, Seventh Day Adventist, Mormon, Quaker, Christian Scientist and lots more.[62]

Such efforts to push tolerance, along with the relative quiet of the 1930s, can give the impression that the country itself was becoming more united. But that was decidedly not the case. The view that immigration restriction led to more tolerance can only go so far. After all, restriction was basically government-mandated discrimination based on nationality. Furthermore, immigration restriction did not mean expulsion of immigrants who were already in the country. In 1940, 34.6 million of the 131.6 million people in the United States were still first- or second-generation Americans, 26 percent of the total.[63] During the 1930s, fewer than half of those immigrants living in the United States were naturalized as citizens—except Jews, who naturalized at much higher rates.[64] And even as these immigrants and their children began to participate more in American political life, they maintained strong ethnic identities. They kept up contact with their countries of origin and shopped at stores owned by individuals within their ethnic and religious groups.[65] They tended to vote along ethnic lines.[66] And individual groups had their own concerns that further separated them from other groups. For example, Italian immigrants and Italian Americans often sympathized with—or in some fairly rare cases, outright supported—Benito Mussolini's Fascist regime in Italy.[67] And American Catholics were set apart in their particularly strong anticommunism in both foreign and domestic affairs.[68]

In many cases, and despite population mobility during the Depression, the ethnic communities also remained isolated from one another and the rest of American society. To be sure, unlike African Americans, most European nationalities were not subject to written restrictive covenants excluding them from neighborhoods, but intolerant attitudes toward ethnic minorities helped contribute to "informal mechanisms of exclusion."[69] As one contemporary report noted, "The presence of 1,000 or more aliens or colored people in a county usually creates such a problem of racial relationships because these groups are not scattered evenly through the population but segregated into unified communities, set apart from the life of the majority group by the differences in physical appearance and in culture."[70] A first-generation American wrote in 1940 of most of the newer immigrants that "when they say 'we,' [they] don't mean 'we Americans' or 'we the people of this town.' But 'we who live in this section and are of Polish or Armenian, etc., origin or background.' When they say 'Americans,' they don't mean themselves."[71] One student of religion in America told a story, possibly apocryphal, of a Norwegian Lutheran visiting a friend in Minnesota in the late 1930s. The two were driving through town when they came to an intersection with a church on each corner. The visitor noted that they seemed to be in a very religious city and asked about the churches. The friend replied, "Yes, that is a German Lutheran church, that is a Swedish Lutheran Church, that is a Finnish Lutheran church, and that is a Danish Lutheran church." The author downplayed the differences as superficial, but the story illustrated the divisions in American society based on nationality, even within one denomination of Protestantism.[72] Michael Patrone, the son of Italian immigrants, described a similar phenomenon in his Ohio hometown with the two Catholic churches: "The Irish, most of them, all went to St. Stephen's. The Italians all went to Mount Carmel."[73]

One group that tried to move out of their traditional neighborhoods, second-generation Jews, faced serious discrimination in their attempts to buy new homes. In fact, many of them did not want to abandon the close relationships of the old immigrant neighborhoods, even as they sought out the middle-class American life. The result was that they ended up living together in middle-class neighborhoods and the suburbs of places such as

New York. This migration actually led to more segregation than before. The numbers were stark. As historian Deborah Dash Moore has written, "In 1920 only 54 percent of New York's Jews lived in neighborhoods at least 40 percent Jewish in population. By 1925 the percentage jumped to 64 percent, and at the end of the decade 72 percent of Jewish New Yorkers resided in sections with a critical mass of Jews." As the Depression slowed down mobility, Jews would stay by and large in their own neighborhoods right up until the war.[74] The Jewish case was but one example. New Deal housing policies began the process of encouraging ethnically mixed white suburbs, but ethnic and non-ethnic enclaves stayed largely undiluted right up to the end of the war.[75] Even at the points where they did mix, such as schools, the second generation of the new immigrants had a difficult time getting along with their peers in the years before the war.[76] Intermarriage rates, although very difficult to track across the whole population, also indicated a general resistance to ethnic mixing throughout the period.[77]

Nor is there any evidence that economic hardship created real unity. Such a long and intense tradition of intolerance would not be shed lightly, least of all in hard times. In fact, the Depression probably played a role in exacerbating those divisions, as various religious denominations tried to survive in part by focusing on what made them unique and important.[78] One observer believed that the Depression actually had "been effective in increasing prejudice and intolerance," in part because when jobs were cut, ethnic and religious minorities were the first to go. The result was that "the tendency became for various groups to stay together and hold onto their 'foreign' sections, which in better times had begun to show signs of disintegration."[79] Working-class solidarity crossing ethnic and religious bounds can also only go so far. For some, white working-class unity, in part built on the exclusion of blacks, superseded or replaced ethnic or religious identity, but as will be discussed below, it certainly did not create a new era of tolerance across the nation.[80]

Finally, whatever their intentions, the efforts of elite groups to encourage tolerance did not bring about a new era of happy pluralism. In truth, their programs were a reaction by the relatively few against how entrenched the divisions in the country had become. Their actions represented a great fear that the bad could become even worse, because they understood that in many ways, the intolerant had won. The relative quiet of the 1930s came in large part from the fact that the intolerant did not need to agitate as much; they had everything they wanted. They could sit back and enjoy; even the laws, for example, immigration restriction, agreed that their views were correct. Although speaking more about class divisions in American society, one scholar's description of the Ku Klux Klan's decline also applies to racial, ethnic, and religious divisions: "On most fronts, Klansmen could feel, if not triumphant, at least relieved by mid-decade."[81] Relative silence, although better than open hostility, did not equal tolerance or anything like it. The United States in the age of Roosevelt remained strongly divided along religious and ethnic lines.

The same elite groups that tried to encourage tolerance noted the severity of ethnic and religious divisions. A 1937 edited collection of writings from students of immigration, race, and culture called *Our Racial and National Minorities* began, "No problem in American life is more acute or of greater concern than that of our racial and cultural minorities and their initiation into our democratic life."[82] The goal of the book, according to the editors, was to "supplant irrational attitudes with reasoned judgment, and prejudice with understanding."[83] So entrenched were the views of foreigners as lawbreakers that one chapter of the book was devoted to the question "Are Our Criminals Foreigners?"—to which the author offered an "unqualified and emphatic" answer: "No!"[84] In 1935, the National Conference of Jews and Christians held the Williamstown Institute of Human Relations at Williams College to look at the problems of relations among Protestants, Catholics, and Jews. They found that non-Protestants distrusted Protestants for their militant nationalism, discrimination against non-Protestants in schools and jobs, and their confused mixing of religious devotion with bigotry. Many non-Catholics believed that Catholics had divided political allegiances because of their relation to the pope, that parochial schools were divisive and un-American, and that Catholic leaders would not work with Protestants, in part because non-Catholics thought that Catholics believed Protestants could not be saved. Finally, common stereotypes of Jews included being overaggressive, unethical in business, having undue economic power, tending to be more politically and socially radical, and sacrificing patriotism to internationalism.[85]

As American Jews gained various government jobs in the 1930s, they also became more publicly prominent. As they did, discrimination against Jews increased during the decade. Universities and private schools stopped hiring Jewish faculty, and jobs in the private sector explicitly advertised for Christians only.[86] Things got so bad that by 1938 some Jewish Americans were afraid of the potential backlash over the appointment or election of prominent Jews to high offices.[87] They had reason to worry. One study found that nearly all of the 119 active anti-Semitic organizations in the country in 1941 had formed since 1933. These organizations were spread around the country, and their members were predominantly urban middle-class people with average education.[88] Prominent among them were the so-called Silver Shirts, the

American Fascists, led by William Dudley Pelley, a man who was primarily anti-Semitic but had no great love for Catholics either.[89] At least one of these anti-Semitic groups, the Defenders of the Christian Faith, also took on an explicitly anti-Catholic position. The founder and leader of the Defenders was an untrained evangelical minister named Gerald B. Winrod. By the Reverend Winrod's accounting, the "rapidly developing cooperation of Catholics and Jews in gaining control of the American government was illustrated when Al Smith and Jim Farley (Catholics) united their efforts recently in supporting Governor Lehman (Jew) for reelection in New York." Such a relationship was a surprise because Winrod assumed that Catholics should have been strongly against the "filthy Jewish motion picture industry." However, Winrod found reasons to be optimistic, as the "final destruction of the Greek Orthodox and Roman Catholic Churches in the end-time of this age is anticipated in Revelation 17:16."[90] The issue was confused when Catholic radio priest Father Coughlin joined the anti-Semitic cause and began serializing the hoax tract *Protocols of the Elders of Zion* in 1938.[91] Illustrating the irony of Coughlin's participation in the anti-Semitic movement, one contemporary student of the issue described the sentiment of Protestant anti-Semites: "We don't want a damn Catholic leading our movement against the damn Jews."[92]

Even the outbreak of war in Europe in 1939 did not improve the situation, despite the nearly frantic efforts of some American elites in the government and in private organizations to promote acceptance and tolerance in the American people. The seriousness of the state of affairs could be seen in the sheer volume of their efforts. In 1940, the Common Council for American Unity, formerly the Foreign Language Information Service, began to publish a periodical called *Common Ground* with the explicit purpose of creating unity and understanding among the American people and overcoming "intolerance and discrimination because of foreign birth or descent, race or nationality."[93] At the same time, the U.S. Office of Education aired a series of twenty-four radio programs called *Americans All . . . Immigrants All* to foster "human understanding and tolerance." The program included episodes on just about every ethnic and racial group in America.[94] Each episode focused on the contribution of its race or nationality to American history and culture as an attempt to break "down the barriers that frequently exist between racial and national groups."[95]

Likewise, in 1941 the Immigration and Naturalization Service of the Department of Justice prepared a series of broadcasts by naturalized Americans under the title *I Am an American*. Among the most famous names were

Albert Einstein, Thomas Mann, and Claudette Colbert, but there were representatives from all over Europe and even a few from Latin America. Archibald MacLeish wrote that the intent of the broadcasts was "in part to remind Americans of all bloods and origins that America was once, and must still remain, the land to which the lovers of freedom, the refugees from intolerance, the fighters for liberty of man and mind, can always turn."[96] Afterward, the Justice Department convinced President Roosevelt to designate an I Am an American Day.[97] Even the newsreels got into the act; the *March of Time* for February 1941 was called "Americans All" and was "a salute to loyal foreign-born American citizens and a plea for unity and harmony among America's diverse racial and religious groups."[98]

After Pearl Harbor, the United States entered the war and the need to improve relations and foster unity grew more pressing.[99] The president himself noted the problem in January 1942, stating, "Remember the Nazi technique: 'Pit race against race, religion against religion, prejudice against prejudice. Divide and conquer!' We must not let that happen here."[100] With and without such prodding, social scientists tried to do their part to promote tolerance.[101] In September 1942, the *Annals of the American Academy of Political and Social Science* dedicated an entire issue to *Minority Peoples in a Nation at War*.[102] Like the *Americans All . . . Immigrants All* radio program, the authors of the various articles in *Minority Peoples* focused on the contributions of various racial, ethnic, and religious groups to American society. But the wartime publication certainly had a different tone from prewar efforts for unity. Several of the articles acknowledged the presence of "subversive individuals of minority status" and the efforts of foreign governments and organizations to foster disloyalty among American immigrants and their children.[103] The majority of the articles stressed the loyalty of immigrants and their descendants, but as one contributor wrote, "the war emergency has shown that distinctions of color and nationality are still a major problem confronting statesmanship in this country."[104]

Hollywood also did its part in encouraging ideas of racial, ethnic, and religious tolerance. Filmmakers' efforts began even before the United States entered the war. For example, in the 1940 film *Knute Rockne, All American*—most famous for costar Ronald Reagan and for the Notre Dame coach's "Win One for the Gipper" speech—made a point of celebrating the American immigrant heritage, with Rockne, an immigrant from Norway, a great exemplar.[105] Perhaps most famously, wartime movies consistently depicted small units in the military as a hodgepodge of nationalities, religions, and, sometimes, race. The so-called ethnic platoon became a fixture in World War II

"No loyal citizen of the United States should be denied the democratic right to exercise the responsibilities of his citizenship, regardless of his ancestry.

"The principle on which this country was founded and by which it has always been governed is that Americanism is a matter of the mind and heart.

"Americanism is not, and never was, a matter of race or ancestry.

"Every loyal American citizen should be given the opportunity to serve this country wherever his skills will make the greatest contribution—whether it be in the ranks of our armed forces, war production, agriculture, government service, or other work essential to the war effort."

THE PRESIDENT OF THE UNITED STATES, FEBRUARY 3, 1943

The U.S. government went to great lengths during the war to emphasize tolerance and unity. This 1943 Office of War Information poster quoted one of President Franklin Roosevelt's many statements on the shared responsibilities and inclusive definition of citizenship. Courtesy of Northwestern University Library World War II Poster Collection, http://www.library.northwestern.edu/govinfo/collections/wwii-posters/.

movies, from wartime films such as *Bataan* and *A Walk in the Sun* to later efforts such as *The Young Lions* and *Saving Private Ryan.*[106]

These wartime programs for tolerance extended to food. Though not necessarily the most high profile aspect of prejudice, unique eating habits set apart individual ethnic and religious groups.[107] According to one scholar, "This explains why food has traditionally been a prominent feature of ethnic slurs"—thus "beaners" for Mexicans, "krauts" for Germans, and "mackerel snappers" for Catholics.[108] Aware of this type of prejudice based on ignorance, the Office of Civilian Defense created the Food Fights for Freedom national campaign during the war and asked the Common Council for American Unity for help. They began a series of "What's Cooking in Your Neighbor's Pot?" parties, tasting and sharing recipes of Greek, Scandinavian, western Mediterranean, Asian, Slav, and American regional foods. Clearly the gender roles of the day played out in these parties, as in the words of one of the organizers, the gatherings served in part to explain "some of the concrete contributions the foreign-born housewife can make to the solution of the problems of the general American housewife in wartime."[109] More important, though, the meetings represented an attempt to unite a diverse and divided population.

Many of the most direct discussions of these issues targeted children. In March 1944 the National Education Association, an organization representing two hundred thousand American teachers, initiated a plan to urge every school and college to teach tolerance. "All of our people must be taught the tragic error of generalizing about groups of people," said a statement released by the organization.[110] The next year saw the publication of *This Way to Unity,* an edited collection designed to be used as a textbook of tolerance for young people. The book chronicled contributions made by all the various groups to American history and culture but also dedicated a large section to examples of the threats presented by prejudice and intolerance in American life. Using excerpts from the writings and speeches of prominent Americans, the book made the case that, in the words of one of the samples,

> it is to the advantage of all groups to unite militantly in stamping out every manifestation of intolerance. Once the beast is let out of the cage, there is no telling where it will run wild, when it will stop. Today it is the Jew who is attacked; tomorrow it is the Christian. Today it is the Negro; tomorrow it is the "poor white" or the Irish American or the New Englander or the labor unionist or the capitalist. Some night, even, the persecutor himself, the very instigator of intolerance, will be awakened and see the face of the creature in his own window, will cringe helpless and terrified before the monster he had created.[111]

Even Frank Sinatra participated in the efforts. In a speech to the World Youth Rally in March 1945, the twenty-nine-year-old singer told his audience that they had a chance to move away from the intolerance of the years when he was growing up in New Jersey and kids would throw rocks at him and call him a "little dago" or when kids heard their fathers "running down a 'big dumb mick' or a 'greasy wop' or a 'stingy Jew.'"[112] Sinatra repeated the theme in a short film made that same year, *The House I Live In*. In the movie, the young crooner stops some boys from picking on another boy because of his religion. He explains to them the folly of intolerance and concludes with the song "The House I Live In," which includes the lyrics "The children in the playground / The faces that I see / All races and religions / That's America to me."[113]

*This Way to Unity* and *The House I Live In* were far from the only examples from the end of the war years concerned with the ongoing threat of disunity and intolerance. As the editor of *Look* magazine wrote in the foreword to a 1945 work titled *One Nation*, "Some eighteen months ago . . . the Editors of Look became increasingly aware of what seemed a growing wave of intolerance and prejudice." As a result, they commissioned writer Wallace Stegner and the photographers of *Look* to put together a study that explained the plight of various minorities, including Catholic and Jewish Americans. Stegner explained that though the nun might wear an "unusual costume," and the rabbinical beards, special holidays, and "unfamiliar customs" marked off Jews from the rest of America, that was no justification for the desecration of Catholic and Jewish cemeteries and other acts of discrimination. They were decent people, he argued, who needed to be treated as individuals in the interest of national unity.[114]

For the first and only time, the *March of Time* newsreels reused a title for a different film. They resurrected "Americans All" (first used in February 1941) in July 1944, once again to press for "harmony and cooperation between citizens of diverse racial and national origins."[115] The editors of the 1937 publication *Our Racial and National Minorities* revised and updated their collection to republish it under the new title *One America* in 1945. They chose to focus on the good signs, specifically the way first- and second-generation Americans had remained loyal to the United States. They saw this as an important first step toward a more tolerant future. "The war has telescoped the gains and losses of decades of social change into a few years," they wrote. "It is necessary to describe these changes and to appraise them *in the light of their potential continuance in the postwar period*."[116] The fact that the editors were so enthusiastic that newer Americans did not turn against their adopted country in a time of war suggests something about the low level of expectations the divisions in American society had engendered well into the 1940s.[117]

The effects of all of this work toward improving ethnic and religious relations are hard to gauge, but they certainly did not lead to any clear improvement. A 1948 work summarizing the various studies of efforts in the 1930s to reduce prejudice found decidedly mixed results. School and college courses on tolerance, specific propaganda, and even limited contact with members of other ethnic and religious groups far from guaranteed friendlier attitudes among participants.[118] What historian Charles Alexander wrote of anti-Catholic feelings in America easily applied to all of the prejudices of the American people: "Anti-Catholicism had always been a fact of religious, social, and political life in America, and not even the surging national unity inspired by the war could wipe out three centuries and more of distrust."[119]

Indeed, for all of these efforts to build goodwill, the war effort exposed countless examples of ongoing intolerance. The most clear-cut cases of distrust affected Americans who had origins in Japan, Italy, and Germany. The Japanese American story has been well told, but less well known is the fact that shortly after the war started the government required that all German and Italian noncitizen residents, no matter how long they had lived in the United States, register at local post offices.[120] Numbering over 1.1 million (more than 600,000 Italians), these people took on the status of "enemy aliens" and had to carry photo identification "alien registration certificates." These enemy aliens faced government-imposed curfews, restrictions on travel, and tight rules concerning possession of potential weapons or long-range signaling devices.[121] The government even evacuated and interned a few thousand Italians and Germans. It was not until the autumn of 1942 that the government lifted the enemy alien status from these people.[122] Certainly these fear-driven efforts against the Italian American and German American communities pale in comparison to the much larger internment of Japanese Americans during the war, but they show a serious level of distrust for those two ethnic groups, especially the Italians.

As the wartime economy led the country out of the Depression, discrimination extended into both private and public employment. The Fair Employment Practices Committee (FEPC), created by executive order by President Roosevelt under pressure from the African American community to ensure fair and equal employment in the federal war industries, found that discrimination extended beyond race. Nearly 10 percent of the 4,081 complaints lodged to the FEPC between July 1943 and June 1944 claimed discrimination based on religion—mostly from Jews but also from some Catholics and other groups—and usually involving "the restriction of employment opportunities as a result of questions about religious beliefs on application forms."[123] Throughout the war, companies from Eastern Airlines to Western Union to Prentice-Hall asked about religion or national descent on their employment applications. The Coca-Cola Bottling Company of New York, operating nearly thirty plants and with both U.S. Army and U.S. Navy contracts, had race and religion codes on its application forms: "*W* for white, *X* for Christian, *P* for Protestant, and *PR* for Puerto Rican."[124] The New York state Committee on Discrimination investigated a job agency that kept track of both religion and "Parents' Descent" on its applications.[125]

The FEPC was not alone in its findings. The less well-known House Select Committee Investigating National Defense Migration under the chairmanship of California representative John Tolan, found similar issues in its public hearings. At the San Diego hearings in the summer of 1941, the Tolan committee received testimony alleging discrimination on the part of Consolidated Aircraft against Mexican American boys who had "been turned down [for employment] because they are too dark."[126] In the eastern part of the country, the committee found discrimination focused on both national origin and religion. The director of the Connecticut State Employment Service testified in Hartford in June 1941 that the problem of discrimination with German Americans was "not very acute," but, though improving, Italian Americans faced much greater problems.[127] In New Jersey, a representative of the mayor of Newark testified that there was "a tremendous amount of discrimination" against blacks, Jews, and Italians.[128] In New York, the state Committee on Discrimination in Employment reported a particular concern with two types of discrimination: one against nationality, barring German and Italians Americans from jobs, the other against race and religion, making it difficult for blacks and Jews to find work.[129]

The obvious conclusion to draw from the findings of discrimination against German and Italian Americans was that it stemmed from distrust of those related to America's soon-to-be enemies on the battlefield. But something more was going on than just distrust of the enemy.[130] Witnesses' testimonies suggest that Fascist Italy and Nazi Germany had little to do with hiring discrimination. In fact, when asked directly whether discrimination came from "the activities of Mussolini and Hitler," the witness replied, "I don't believe discrimination is due to that" because an employer had told him that "they had a number of Italians in their plant and they were very good workers, but he said the trouble was that they were 'excitable,' and that they were 'temperamental.'"[131] Another witness believed that what little discrimination there was against German Americans came from "fear of disloyalty and sabotage":

> But our Italian population in the State is substantial, and I do not
> think the discrimination against them has been so much the effect of fear

of sabotage, or the fact that Italy is in the war, as it is—well, I don't know how to express it—a feeling that Italians were originally brought into the country to take the lower-paid jobs, and that they are made for cheap labor.

There are also some contentions by manufacturers that their work habits are not too good. Invariably when we try to pin a firm down which is not taking its proper proportion of Italians, that is the answer—that their work habits were "not too good." It is alleged that they are "inclined to complain," and they are "not as satisfactory workers" as people of other racial extraction.

[Tolan committee member Rep. John Sparkman of Alabama:] In other words, that discrimination would be one of normal times, and not necessarily attached to the defense program?

[Witness:] You notice it more now, as you get further down into your labor pool, and a higher percentage of them remain.[132]

Since the Tolan committee focused its attention on citizens who were either immigrants or descended from immigrants from Axis power countries, and since the testimonies were limited to a few states with higher proportions of groups such as Italian Americans, it is hard to gauge if discriminatory hiring practices extended to other nationalities.[133] Still, it was clear that wartime discrimination in hiring practices came at least in part from long-held stereotypes and prejudices toward Jews, Catholics, Italians, and various other ethnic groups.

Ethnic and religious intolerance extended beyond just discrimination in hiring in the war years. New York City park commissioner Robert Moses wrote in 1943 that "Jews are still frozen out of certain business concerns as well as clubs, and there are quarters in which Italians and even Irish are not entirely welcome."[134] The former dean of Harvard Divinity School, Willard Sperry, said of religious relations during the war, "We have already had ugly incidents: inflammatory journals, defacing of churches and synagogues, clashes of street gangs."[135] Wartime polls backed such conclusions. In a 1944 poll, almost 25 percent of the respondents believed Jews to be a threat to the United States.[136] An American Institute of Public Opinion poll taken in 1942 asked respondents to rank seventeen different nationalities in comparison with the people of the United States. Canadians, the English, the Dutch, Scandinavians, and the Irish took the first five spots, followed, in order, by the French, Germans, Greeks, South Americans, and Jewish refugees. At the bottom of the list were Poles, Russians, the Chinese, Spaniards, Italians, Mexicans, and the Japanese. Obviously, such a poll is given to problems, but the fact that the nationalities of the new immigrants polled so low among

Americans in 1942 was testament to the lasting power of ethnic and religious animosity even into the war years.[137] As a pollster wrote in 1944, "Although democratic in his social outlook, the average American is snobbish about other races. . . . He discriminates against other nationalities in an undemocratic and unfair manner."[138]

The boys and men who would serve in the World War II military grew up in the middle of all this rancor. The earlier generations passed on their prejudices to their children, and then those beliefs were reinforced by peers. A variety of studies ranging from 1929 into the war years found ethnic and religious prejudice among children as young as four or five years old. This prejudice was taught by older playmates, adults, and especially parents, as young children learned from observation that "their parents or other adults despise members of the ethnic group."[139] One student of second-generation ethnics in schools noted how their memories of education up until the war were not dominated by tolerant or intolerant teachers, but by the intolerance of their fellow students: "Over and over again the life stories of newcomers use the word 'ridicule' to describe how other children treated them when they were 'greenhorns' new to this country. Peers and playmates made fun of their accents, their clothes, their food, their ignorance of American children's ways and games."[140]

These children saw many of their sports heroes subjected to open discrimination. In the 1930s, major league baseball players increasingly reflected the diversity in the United States (with the notable exception of African Americans). It was particularly tough for the few Jewish players. No player took more abuse than Detroit Tigers star Hank Greenberg. Greenberg remembered stepping to the plate everyday and having to listen "to some son of a bitch call you a Jew bastard and a kike and a sheenie and get on your ass. . . . If the ballplayers weren't doing it, the fans were." The slurs and prejudice extended to other groups. In 1936, Tigers player-manager Mickey Cochrane called Al Simmons (born Aloys Szymanski), his new addition to the team, "the big Polack." As more and more Italian Americans entered the game, players and fans taunted them as "wops" and "dagos," and managers and journalists wondered why they were suddenly so successful in the sport. One manager said, "The Tonies take to baseball quicker than they take to spaghetti."[141]

The younger generations picked up on this intolerance. Phyllis Lorimer grew up well off in Connecticut. She recalled, "My only knowledge of what people do about anything was to keep Polacks from moving in. I truly believed, as a child, the bridge across the canal from Southampton was to keep

Jews out of the country club."[142] The men who would serve provided the greatest evidence of such feelings. At a general level, even years later, the men who grew up in that generation often defined who they were by their ethnicity and religion. John E. Bistrica was "an American born . . . of Croatian ancestry in Youngstown, Ohio."[143] Dean Joy of Colorado had great pride in his Presbyterian, Scots-Irish parents.[144] Joseph Barrett talked about geographic divisions when he entered the service and met a group of Jewish men: "They came from Strawberry Mansion, a Jewish enclave, some ten blocks west of 22nd St. and Lehigh Ave., where I lived in Swampoodle, an Irish neighborhood in North Philadelphia."[145] Some of the young avoided the bigotry all around them. Robert Easton remembered that growing up in Santa Maria, California, his "friends included Japanese, Portuguese, Mexican, Italian and Jewish kids. . . . There were feelings of prejudice among some of our elders, true, but little of this rubbed off onto us."[146] Robert Thobaben lived on the East Side of Cleveland in an upper-middle-class community made up mostly of Anglo-Saxon Protestants but where his friends from school included Jewish and Italian kids.[147] But these few were exceptions to the rule.

Samuel Hynes described growing up in Minnesota with a father who "despised the Irish: there were only two kinds, he said, lace-curtain Irish and pig-in-the-parlor Irish, and both kinds were awful." In addition "he hated Catholics. He was a Mason and a Protestant Republican; he had voted against Al Smith in 1928 because he believed that if Smith won he'd dig a tunnel from the White House to the Vatican." Hynes's widower father then went and married an Irish Catholic widow—a sin for which he never forgave himself—and the family said two graces, one Protestant and one Catholic, before meals on Sunday.[148] Hynes's stepmother was not much better on such matters, mocking Bohemians and telling the boy when he asked if his older brother was going to marry a girl he was dating, "No, he's not. She's *Lutheran*."[149] A descendent of Czech immigrants, Michael Warish recalled, "I was raised Catholic in an Irish neighborhood, and there the Catholics didn't talk to any Protestants, and none of us Protestants and Catholics spoke to the few Jews who were there, and there were no Baptists around." He continued, "I don't think I'd be very far from the truth if I said that the pastor of our church wouldn't be caught dead talking to a Protestant minister."[150] Frank Mathias witnessed both anti-German and anti-Catholic prejudice growing up in Kentucky.[151] Mario Puzo, growing up in New York's Hell's Kitchen, found the reality of Italian immigrants and their children far different from movies and stories that portrayed "clichés of lovable Italians, singing Italians, happy-go-lucky Italians."[152] Robert Peters recalled that his home region in Wisconsin "was thoroughly anti-Semitic."[153] Carl Becker, from southwest Ohio, described it best:

> I brought to the [artillery] battery the baggage of vague and stereotypic notions about the character of non-Anglo-Americans. Nurtured by a community where an ethnic coherence had created a narrow parochialism, I was held hostage to biases that I now regret and reject. . . . As a Protestant from a small town, I saw the many Catholics as somehow alien to American life. . . . Though no one ethnic group was numerous, of course I had no hesitancy in identifying several sons of Italy as distinct character types: emotional and temperamental, talkative with their hands, short and swarthy.[154]

So prevalent were such ideas that when the young men of the 1930s began to enter the U.S. Army as it mobilized for the coming war, a council against intolerance distributed a booklet that urged the new soldiers to look at their upbringing: "When you were a youngster, what kind of people did your family dislike? Did you hear talk at home against the Jews or the Negroes or the Catholics or the Methodists or the Chinese? Did you hate city people or Bostonians or Southerners, or those who didn't speak English very well?"[155]

Intolerance defined ethnic and religious relations at home in the United States all the way through the war. This was the environment the World War II soldiers grew up in; this was the America they would leave behind.

Amid all of the ethnic and religious strife in the United States, and in the face of those who claimed that men in the armed services would soon join the causes of intolerance, emerged a powerful example that put shame to the prejudiced and intolerant. A fictionalized story of a Jewish boy trying to go to a beach in South Boston recounted in a 1945 book illustrates the point. The boy was stopped by a gang of other youths who tell him that they did not "allow kikes around Southie." One of the boys continued, "Wait'll the guys in the army get home. Just stick around and see what happens to all you Jew bastards that have been coining dough out of the war while Christians fight it. Wait till all the guys from around here get back from the army; you'll see what the war was about." The Jewish boy replied that his brother was killed on Guadalcanal. A fight ensued. Though dramatized, there were those who believed that the returning soldiers would take revenge on the groups, especially Jews, who sat out the war.[156]

But something very different was happening to Americans fighting the war in the armed forces, hinted at by the story of the Jewish boy whose brother died in the service. In the *New York Sun*, in February 1944, journalist George Sokolsky told a story from the fighting in the South Pacific. A young

Irish American sailor asked a lieutenant to check on the graves of his brothers on an unnamed island. The lieutenant honored the request and found the brothers lying next to each other, with graves marked by the Star of David on either side. When told of the gravesite, the young Irish American sailor began to cry. He quietly said, "Gee, [Lieutenant], my brothers always did keep swell company." Though he had changed the names, Sokolsky swore the story was true. But more important than whether it was true or not was the meaning Sokolsky gave to his tale, a moral that portended a great change in America:

> I hope this story is read by those who desecrate graves, who paint swastikas on synagogues and hammers and sickles on Catholic churches. I hope it will be read by those who believed that there are deep, sinister movements of hate that influence and affect our people. I hope that it will be read by those who are thriving on the cultivation of hate—hate of the Jew, hate of the Catholic, hate of the Protestant, hate for hate's sake.
>
> This is a living example of the rejection of hate. . . .
>
> The boys who are fighting on many fronts, when they return, will laugh at the songs of hate which the home bodies sing so lustily in these days of distress. In the foxholes they know that they are brothers because their blood and sweat mingle with the earth of the battlefield in defense of their country. In the tanks and planes and ships that fight on the seas, they cannot hate the comrade who stands beneath the same fire and the same danger for the same cause.
>
> Some day . . . you will glory in pride that Americans called Ross, Canelli, Clinton, Skvoznik, Vincent, Greenbaum, Bayforth, and Stoner—that every kind of an American—can take the ordeal of torture and certainty of death with equal and fervent daring. There is no hate for each other among such Americans.[157]

Such Americans left behind an American long divided by anger and intolerance. They went to war and discovered a whole new world.

# 2

# THE ETHNIC ARMY

All of us Holy Joes are switch hitters.
—*Battleground,* directed by William Wellman (MGM, 1949)

THE U.S. ARMY CAME FROM AMERICAN SOCIETY. ITS INDIVIDUAL MEMBERS harbored the same prejudices as any other Americans. In fact, many prominent military men were worse than the average American when it came to ethnic and religious tolerance. On the surface, there was no real reason to expect that the army would be the great engine of change. Yet during World War II, it was the army that brought together Americans and taught them to get along. How such a seemingly hidebound institution made such a notable achievement needs explaining.

The army had long experience dealing with diversity. From the beginning of the Republic, Americans distrusted and disliked standing armies. As a result, the country maintained during times of peace a tiny army, relegated to uncomfortable and mostly boring coastal defense and frontier service. America's best and brightest avoided soldiering as a career, and the enlisted men came from the lowest ranks of society, ranks in the United States that traditionally included many immigrants. As early as the 1840s and 1850s, Irish (mostly Catholic) and German immigrants made up somewhere between one-half and two-thirds of the army's ranks.[1] Such immigrants played a major part in the drastic expansion of the Civil War army in the North. At its peak in 1865, the Union army numbered more than 1 million men. All told, nearly 2.7 million men served in the Union army during the course of the war. Of these, hundreds of thousands were immigrants or their children—again primarily Irish and German but also various Scandinavian groups. Many of these men served in their own ethnic regiments, but the majority of Germans and Irish and other groups served in regiments with no ties to ethnicity, and they enlisted and fought for all the same diverse reasons as any other American soldiers.[2]

Once again the army saw its numbers drastically reduced for peace-time—by 1871 the total strength of the regular army dropped below thirty thousand, where it stayed until 1898. Even before Reconstruction came to its conclusion, the old American distrust for standing armies returned. Though the country consistently elected veterans of the war to high political offices, soldiering once again became a career to be avoided.[3] Despite efforts to improve recruiting, the army remained undermanned, and again men from the lower levels of American society filled the ranks, including immigrants.[4] By the mid-1870s, half of all of the enlisted men in the army came from outside the United States, and as before the war, these men mostly hailed from Ireland, Germany, and Great Britain.[5] Then the so-called new immigration brought new names and faces to American shores, and they began to join the army in search of a stable career. Among foreign-born soldiers, the Irish, Germans, English, and Canadians dominated, but they began to be joined in increasing numbers by Russians, Swedes, Danes, Poles, Austrians, and Hungarians.[6] The enthusiastic response to war with Spain in 1898 greatly accelerated the army's recruitment of more native-born, English-speaking Americans, but foreign-born men still made up 14 or 15 percent of the new recruits after the war.[7] That basic ratio would continue until World War I, only with decreasing proportions of Irish and English recruits relative to Germans, Russians, Austrians, Hungarians, and Italians.[8] Overall, some 12 percent of the army in this era were foreign born, mostly German, Irish, and, increasingly, Russians.[9] The expansion of World War I meant that immigrants—not counting their children or grandchildren—made up approximately one-fifth of the U.S. Army.[10] Through all of these years, the army was the most diverse institution in American life.

The question for the army was how to handle that diversity. The army's leaders were men of American society, subject to the same prejudices and biases as everyone else. White Anglo-Saxon Protestants—many of them New Englanders and almost all of them native born—made up almost the entirety of the officer corps.[11] In 1890, one such officer weighed the pros and cons of Irish, English, German, and native troops and concluded that the "pluck, intelligence, and self-reliance inherent in the Anglo-Saxon are the qualities which, properly handled, must make the best soldier for the modern army."[12] By the end of the nineteenth century, many in the officer corps came under the influence of the biological explanations of race of the era and looked with a skeptical eye on the new immigrants. One lieutenant wrote in the *Infantry Journal* that the country was accepting the "hide, hoof, and horn of European offerings."[13] A major worried about strong American bloodlines mixing with "the swarthy, low-browed and stunted peoples now swarming our shores."[14]

Restrictions on recruiting developed in the 1890s reflected these concerns. The army looked for single men in their twenties or early thirties who were "citizens . . . or have declared their intention to become citizens, and must be able to speak, read, and write the English language."[15]

During this time, a variety of officers displayed serious anti-Semitism in their words and actions. They repeated all of the worst charges against Jews, calling them at various points hard-headed, calculating, weak, selfish, dishonorable, cowardly, malingerers, criminals, cunning, physically defective, and so on.[16] Some individual officers took it upon themselves to oppose promotions for some of the Jewish men, who by best estimate made up some 6 percent of the army before World War I. An officer at the School of the Line at Fort Leavenworth even wrote a paper arguing that Jews despised physical labor and lacked any patriotism and thus had no real business in the military.[17] There can be no denying that many men in the army's officer corps accepted and perpetuated the prevalent bigotry of the day.

Despite these intolerant officers—and the intolerant society that spawned them—immigrant soldiers did well in the army. After the Civil War they received language and vocational training on their frontier posts when necessary. More important, they enjoyed a measure of respect from their fellow soldiers and the citizens who lived near their posts. A small 1904 report on the life of the enlisted man in the army from the Office of the Inspector General did not distinguish by nativity or religion in assuring its readers that new, more stringent recruiting standards meant that "a large proportion of the soldiers of the Army are self-respecting, well-conducted men and faithful and efficient soldiers" and "the young man intending to enlist can feel assured that he will not be thrown in with undesirable companions."[18] The report also noted that the new recruits faced joking from the old hands, and that sometimes old soldiers took advantage of the new guys, but overall "soldiers are very good at helping one another"—again, apparently regardless of nativity or religion.[19] For their part, foreign-born soldiers reenlisted in the army at high rates.[20]

By the turn of the century, a striking contradiction had developed between the ethnic and religious intolerance of American society, including army officers, and the relative tolerance of everyday army life.[21] No doubt a sizable part of the army's tolerance came from pure pragmatism. It was too inefficient to keep the wide variety of Irish, German, Russian, or any other European immigrants in segregated units, as they did African Americans. It did not make any sense for the army to fixate on differences when it needed trained soldiers for the ranks. But pragmatism was only part of the answer; other multiethnic societies had kept their militaries segregated along racial, ethnic, and religious lines and functioned just fine.[22] There was another foundation to the tolerance in the U.S. Army that had less to do with efficiency and more to do with idealistic notions of what America was.

From the very beginning of the Republic, many recognized that the army was one area in American national life where different people from different backgrounds could come together as enlisted men on relatively equal terms. Harkening back to the Continental army, no less than George Washington declared,

> In the general Juvenal period of life, when friendships are formed, & habits established that will stick by one, the Youth, or young men from different parts of the United States would be assembled together, & would by degrees discover that there was not just cause for those jealousies & prejudices which one part of the Union had imbibed against another part. . . . What, but the mixing of people from different parts of the United States during the War rubbed off these impressions? A Century in the ordinary intercourse, would not have accomplished what Seven years association in Arms did.[23]

President Washington was making the case for some sort of national university, but his point was clear: Mass military service had tremendous unifying power. Similar arguments emerged during the Civil War. After the Battle of Chancellorsville, when the German Americans of the Army of the Potomac's Eleventh Corps came under severe criticism, the *New York Times* defended the beleaguered men and added that

> their active service under the flag of the Union, their fighting side by side with the descendants of those who laid the foundations of the Republic, will do more to Americanize them and their children than could be effected in a whole generation of peaceful living. . . . Our people hereafter will be far more homogenized and fraternal. The blood that mixes in the battlefield, in one common sacrifice, will be a cement of American nationality nothing else could supply.[24]

Concern about cementing American nationality became a more pressing issue with the influx of the new immigrants at the turn of the century, only this time it accompanied the progressive impulse to reform. That impulse extended to the army, where individuals such as Secretary of War Elihu Root and Gen. Leonard Wood worked to bring the army into the twentieth century.[25] They looked to the future and predicted with great concern that any major war would require huge numbers of soldiers. The army's personnel policies had to try to balance the realities of American society with the need to prepare to rapidly mobilize hundreds of thousands or even millions of troops.

A serious debate ensued between advocates of universal military training, such as Theodore Roosevelt and Leonard Wood, and those who wanted to maintain a reliance on the traditional idea of the American citizen-soldier—the National Guard and wartime volunteers.[26] In the course of that debate, many supporters of universal military training came to see their cause as a cure-all for America's ills—a way toward preparedness in an unstable world (especially after the war broke out in Europe), a way to curb radicalism, and a way to assimilate the new immigrants.[27] The Americanization of those whom many believed to be unable to assimilate became a major selling point for military service. "I would have the son of the multimillionaire and the son of the immigrant who came in steerage, sleep under the same dog tent and eat the same grub," Theodore Roosevelt argued. "It would help mightily to a mutual comprehension of life."[28] For all the different groups in America, Roosevelt maintained that the "military tent where they all sleep side by side will rank next to the public school among the great agents of democratization."[29] In 1915, Leonard Wood wrote an article, "Heat Up the Melting Pot," that more explicitly made the case:

> Great masses of new peoples are coming into our land. We are doing far too little in the way of making them real Americans. Naturally they come in racial groups. Under the conditions which surround their early years in this country they go largely to race schools and only too often remain in racial areas and are fed upon a dialect press. They do not come into contact sufficiently with the older residents, with the native American, and as a result they do not have imprest upon them the fact that thru their reception and naturalization they have become an integral part of the American people. . . .
>
> What is needed is some kind of training which will put all classes which go to make up the mass which is bubbling in the American melting pot, shoulder to shoulder, living under exactly the same conditions, wearing the same uniform and animated by a common purpose. This "something" will be found in a system of universal training . . . , where all classes of men, Jew and Gentile, rich and poor, Protestant and Catholic, upper and lower social classes, work shoulder to shoulder, animated by a common purpose, that purpose being to better prepare themselves to discharge their military duties in case of trouble.

One of the most important results these efforts, Wood concluded, would be that "men will learn to think more in terms of the nation and less in those of the individual or the small community."[30]

These military progressives harbored an interesting mix of values. They understood and accepted much of the prevailing wisdom concerning nationality as race, and they embraced a fierce nationalism and jingoism. Such a combination might have led to an ideology of isolation and exclusion, but Roosevelt, Wood, and their ilk were jingoists and nationalists of the proselytizing sort. That is, they wanted to convert people at home and abroad to what they truly and honestly believed to be superior American values. Their ideas were heavy-handed, but they were also idealistic at a time when most Americans wanted to exclude, or worse, minority nationalities and religions. The army gave Roosevelt and company the perfect opportunity to convert immigrants.

Their great chance came in World War I, when the new Selective Service System drafted men from across the demographic spectrum. All adult male citizens or immigrant aliens who declared an intent to become citizens—by filling out the first citizenship forms—had an obligation to serve.[31] In the end, immigrants made up about one-fifth of the World War I army. Pragmatism and efficiency played a key role in how the military used these men. Some of the immigrants and the children of immigrants served in heavily ethnic and religious regional regiments and divisions, but Selective Service was first and foremost a program to get soldiers into the army, trained, overseas, and into the war as soon as possible. The army faced a modern war, and America's allies in the fight needed assistance soon against a determined German foe. Efficiency dictated as much uniformity as possible—in raising, training, equipping, and distributing the troops. As a result, plenty of immigrants and second-generation men served in units alongside men from diverse backgrounds.[32]

But progressive idealism also affected the wartime efforts. The inability of large numbers of eligible recruits to speak or read English led to more active army policies concerning these men.[33] The problem was obvious; soldiers who could not understand English could not very well take orders from officers and noncommissioned officers speaking English. The linguistic difficulties led to a waste of manpower, with non-English-speaking men sent to depot brigades in the South where they performed simple labor duties.[34] Recognizing the waste, the War Department created within its bureaucracy the Foreign-speaking Soldier Subsection (FSS) in January 1918. Under the leadership of the FSS the army developed a training system for the non-English-speaking troops at several camps, most prominently, Camp Gordon

In World War I, the U.S. Army gained extensive experience dealing with ethnic and religious diversity. The gold star honor roll on this propaganda poster emphasized the sacrifice of the diverse military population. Courtesy of University of North Texas Libraries Digital Collections, http://digital.library.unt.edu/permalink/meta-dc-386/.

in Georgia. There the army divided the men by ethnicity into companies led by foreign-language-speaking immigrants or second-generation officers. The men underwent intensive training in soldiering, English, and Americanization in the form of civics and citizenship classes.[35] The army kept up these Americanization efforts for the duration of the fighting. And indeed the army became the primary vehicle for over 150,000 alien soldiers to become citizens of the United States during the war.[36] The service used its men more efficiently, and the idealists had made good Americans.

The Americanization policy continued after the war. One again, the army progressives pushed for some kind of universal military training or service. The Americanization programs were a crucial aspect of this effort. As Gen. John J. Pershing testified before the House of Representatives about military training,

> Experience shows conclusively that it encourages initiative and gives young men confidence in themselves. Through the preparation for service to the country it increases their patriotism. It broadens their views through association with men of all classes and is thoroughly democratic. It prepares young men for the duties of citizenship. Such training is especially needed among our alien population, a large proportion of whom are illiterate. If these men were taught our language and were made familiar with the spirit of our institutions we should have less lawlessness and fewer I.W.W.'s [International Workers of the World].[37]

Beginning in 1919, the army sent illiterate and non-English-speaking recruits who had declared their intent to become citizens to Camp Upton, New York, where they were to learn English and citizenship. In fact, the War Department put so much stock in these efforts that they continued to recruit aliens and non-English-speaking citizens in peacetime, even before the legislation to do so had passed Congress.[38]

At Camp Upton, English language lessons overlapped with the instruction in civics and soldiering. Beyond basic language and writing skills, the intent of the lessons were obvious. From the earliest, the men learned to write sentences such as "Every good American wants to write good English," "A good soldier loves his home and his country," and "I will fight for my country for I am a good American soldier."[39] Later lessons emphasized the contributions of famous Americans and immigrants to the United States. In the lesson titled "Americanism," the men read that "millions of other new Americans came here from all the countries of the world and did their part to make the land of freedom a land of prosperity also. After all, the real Americans are those who believe in the principles of justice and freedom that America stands for."[40] The army offered the best place to learn those American principles, especially how to get along with each other, no matter the ethnic or religious background. One language lesson described a fight breaking out between "José" and "Rudolf":

> And as José seized a knife from the mess table, Rudolf picked up a chair and swung it at the wrathful José's head.

With a leap, Sergeant Hart sprang between the two men. "Stop that!" he ordered. "Drop that knife and put down that chair. If you fellows want to fight you will fight the American way. We will not stand for any European methods of settling arguments around here. Come with me."[41]

The sergeant arranged for a boxing match, and at the end of the match he told the men, "Each of you has shown the other fellow that he is a good man. Forget your argument and be friends. In that way you will be playing the game like American soldiers."[42]

The army progressives did not win outright or for long.[43] Whatever the best intentions of some in the army, their funding came from the civilian Congress, and by the early 1920s civilian America was caught up in a wave of antiradical, anti-immigrant, anti-Semitic, and anti-Catholic feelings. In a near-hysterical national environment that led to the passage of the emergency legislation to curb immigration, it is no surprise that Congress would not support the army's inclusive programs. In fact, Congress stopped supporting almost all army programs, including recruitment and educational and vocational training. The old American distrust for large standing armies reappeared, and as the successive Republican administrations of the 1920s encouraged budget cuts, the army was a ready target. The National Defense Act of 1920 stripped down the regular army in favor of a fairly large but entirely voluntary National Guard and Organized Reserve. The budget trimming reduced the regular army even more, so that by 1922, the total strength of the regular army had dipped from a wartime high of nearly 2.4 million to less than 150,000. By the end of the 1920s and into the 1930s the new popular disillusionment with the munitions-making "merchants of death" who had supposedly dragged the country into war bolstered the antimilitary trend. As a result, the active strength of the regular army would not grow to more than 190,000 until 1940.[44] Gen. Peyton March, former chief of staff, wrote in his memoirs of World War I that some American political leaders wanted on their own to reduce the army down to "the same number that the Allies had imposed on Germany after the war to make her impotent."[45] At the same time, the general wealth of the country made it difficult to recruit troops.

If the prosperity of the 1920s kept away recruits, the Depression of the 1930s drove away funding. During the early part of the Great Depression, recruiting was no longer a problem. Plenty of men wanted the stability of a job in the army, but Congress saw the service as a target for spending cuts.[46] The situation grew so dire that Chief of Staff Douglas MacArthur had to choose to cut spending on materiel so he could keep men.[47] When those cuts were not enough, he said he would rather cut all of the enlisted men to keep a core of knowledgeable officers than deal with any more across the board personnel trimming.[48] MacArthur's desperation illustrated the depth of the army's budget woes in the 1930s.

Through all of these ideological and funding disputes, the military moved away from more active policies for dealing with diversity. Most officers came to believe that the wisest course of action in dealing with the fickle American populace was generally to avoid partisanship and other contentious biases—to take on the veneer of "a disinterested servant."[49] Those who had once advocated using the army as the vehicle of assimilation now retreated into a more passive policy of ignoring ethnic and religious differences. And given the tensions in the larger society, ethnic and religious relations in the army stayed remarkably congenial. As quoted by historian Edward Coffman, Alphonso Zawadski, serving at Fort Meade, Maryland, in the 1930s, remembered that "'there was very, very, little prejudice' in that 'melting pot' of men of Polish, German, and Italian descent."[50] The army used as a recruiting tool the story of John Hunter, an Irish immigrant who learned to be a plumber in the army and eventually returned to civilian life and found a well-paying job as a plumber in Chicago.[51] A representative from the National Jewish Welfare Board sent to investigate the influence of Nazi propaganda in the U.S. Army in 1936 noted, "While, of course, occasional instances of anti-Semitism have been brought to my attention, I do not believe that it is widespread in the service, and certainly is less evident than in civil life."[52] It is telling that Maurice Rose, an up and coming officer in the interwar period, seemed to have little or no trouble with the other men, even officers, for being Jewish.[53]

At the same time, the more idealistic and proactive policies toward diversity remained embedded in army tradition, and revealed themselves from time to time in the interwar years. For example, throughout the 1920s and 1930s, the army quietly ran Citizens' Military Training Camps (CMTCs) during the summers to carry on the cause of preparedness. The entirely voluntary program offered a modicum of military drill and custom to as many as forty thousand young men a year in the late 1920s. These men literally came from all over the country; the adjutant general reported in 1924 that CMTC program received applications "from all but 247 of the 3,089 counties in the United States, and actual enrollments were secured from all but 420 counties."[54] The army did not segregate these white enrollees in any manner, whether by region, ethnicity, or religion (there were a few separate camps for African Americans). Not surprisingly for the era, some of the trainees faced prejudice from the other young men—one Jewish New Yorker had some serious confrontations with two anti-Semitic tentmates—but by and large the army's policy allowed them to work out their differences.[55] And in fact one contemporary defense of the CMTC invoked Gen. Leonard Wood's words in arguing that the camps were an outgrowth of his Plattsburg idea and thus "a real melting pot, in which the various, and often discordant elements which are now swarming to our shores will be fused into one common mass of Americanism."[56]

Franklin Roosevelt's New Deal gave the army a chance to work with a larger diverse population with the work programs of the Civilian Conservation Corps (CCC). The idea was to help alleviate the pressure on families by giving young men public works jobs such as clearing national forest lands and building roads. All told, the CCC would enroll more than 2.5 million Americans between 1933 and 1942. Several federal agencies played a part in the corps, but the army ran the camps that served as bases of operation for the men.[57] The CCC worked all over the country with brigades of young men from every region.[58] The only restriction related to ethnicity or religion was that aliens could not enroll; otherwise the law stated that "in employing citizens for the purposes of this act no discrimination shall be made on account of race, color, or creed."[59] The result was a group that reflected the country's diversity: 22 percent of the men had foreign-born parents at a time when roughly 20 percent of all Americans had foreign or mixed parents.[60]

As the organization that actually ran the camps and controlled the educational program, the army had its policy toward diverse ethnic and religious groups put to the test.[61] The only active acknowledgment of the enrollees' diversity came in the educational program, which in part strived to teach the men the values and responsibility of citizenship. The lessons certainly favored a vision of American citizenship built around the country's values toward patriotism, work, and gender roles in those times, but the message stayed positive toward the contributions of those of all backgrounds.[62] Of course, there were cases of discrimination among the young men, but by and large the men later remembered the CCC as a real positive in their lives, and enrollee after enrollee noted that they learned to get along better with new and strange people.[63] James Allen said that the kids from different states got along well and they "all buddied up."[64] According to Raymond Shuster, "The fellows learned to get along with each other."[65] Frank Delgenio recalled that the CCC "taught me discipline, how to take orders, how to be a good friend with your buddy in the bunk next to you. We were all good friends. I don't think there was an enemy in the camp."[66] To the extent that the CCC made good Americans out of these young men, the idealists would have been pleased.

By the outbreak of World War II the pattern had been set; only the specific issues changed.[67] Two problems of diversity were by and large gone and could be by and large ignored. First, because of immigration restriction during World War I and after, by 1940 the army really did not have to deal with a lot of aliens, enemy or otherwise, in the age cohort from which they would draw their troops.[68] Altogether no more than 112,000 aliens were inducted into the army during the whole war, making up almost 1 percent of the total force.[69] Second, immigration restriction and improved education across the country led to an almost imperceptible problem with the inability to speak English among recruits. The army set up small special training units to teach English and reading to those who were functionally illiterate in the English language, including non-English-speaking recruits. The non-English speakers numbered so few that the army did not deal with them as a special problem among illiterates, nor did the service have to group men based on their national background or language skills.[70]

Despite low numbers of alien soldiers, the World War II army, drawn mostly from Selective Service, remained an ethnically diverse force.[71] The specific numbers of different ethnic groups in the World War II army are difficult, if not impossible, to ascertain. The army did not keep track of national background, and the religious records are unclear as to specifics. None of this was for lack of effort from various groups in the country to try to figure out the extent of their role in fighting the war. Newspapers in heavily ethnic areas, politicians concerned with their ethnic constituents, and ethnic and religious organizations all tried to come up with estimates of the numbers of their various groups serving in the military. What numbers there are usually come as estimates from such groups. For example, the Jewish Welfare Board used reports from over two hundred volunteer boards around the country to estimate that 550,000 Jewish Americans fought in the war.[72] A history of Armenian Americans in World War II put their number at 18,500 (out of a total of 220,000 Armenian Americans in the entire country).[73] A newspaper in Chicago claimed that Italians Americans made up 10 percent of the servicemen from Chicago.[74] One private government memorandum from the Office of Facts and Figures in 1942 got more specific. The author stated that "the largest group of foreign descent in the U.S. Army is that of Italian descent—18½ of all foreign-born soldiers or soldiers with one or more foreign-born parents."[75] The sources of all of these numbers are unclear—they were often educated estimates based in part on contemporary newspaper accounts—but they indicate to an extent the diversity in the army.[76]

That diversity was the most important point. For all of the debates about the details of Selective Service, and with the ongoing exception of African

Americans in particular, the army deliberately made every effort to create a force that reflected the economic, occupational, and regional diversity of the male population of the country. Lewis Hershey, the longtime director of Selective Service, was an heir to the idealist tradition. He had seen the opportunity for unity presented by World War I, and he wanted to repeat the experiment. To him the draft was "an excellent force for the solidification and unification of America."[77] The demographic numbers did not match up perfectly with the general population—deferments, exemptions, and rejections built into the system meant that soldiers had slightly more education, were physically and mentally more sound, and were more likely to be single than the total civilian male cohort. Still, the numbers stayed close. The Selective Service state-by-state quota system based on the population demographics of the state meant that each state contributed almost its exact proportion of males of service age.[78] These proportions quickly extended to regionally specific National Guard units because those units were undermanned when mobilization began in earnest. As early as June 1941, Selective Service inductees made up between 33 and 58 percent of the enlisted personnel of the eighteen National Guard divisions.[79] Those proportions would only increase as the war progressed.

Because the World War II army represented the full spread of the economic, occupational, and regional diversity of the male population, it stands to reason that it also represented the full spread of the United States' ethnic population. In 1940, first- and second-generation Americans—immigrants and their children—numbered nearly thirty-five million, more than 25 percent of the total population of the country. Of these, Germans numbered nearly five million, Italians over four million, Poles nearly three million, Irish two and a half million, and Czechs, Hungarians, Swedes, Norwegians, and Mexicans all about one million.[80] Many of these folks were obviously too old to serve in the war, and many had other deferments. Of course, none of these figures take into account third- or fourth-generation Americans, many of whom at the time still maintained strong ethnic identities. The point stands that the pool was diverse. And since Selective Service drew fairly and equally from the pool, the army had the same diversity.[81]

As evidence of this diversity, a World War II manual for officers repeated the advice of Maj. Gen. David C. Shanks from his 1918 guide, *Management of the American Soldier:* "America is a composite nation embracing many distinct elements. The great national melting pot has not yet made us one homogenous people with easily distinguished national characteristics." He continued, "Take the average white American company. It will be composed of men of many nationalities. The Irish, the Swede, the Pole, the Jew, the Italian, and many others will be represented. These men possess widely different characteristics."[82] The people who ran the draft also noted the ethnic variation in their job—and in the process gave a glimpse into some of the popular regional understandings of race and ethnicity during the war—in the Selective Service periodical from March 1944. Under the headline "A Polyethnic Panel," it read:

Local Board No. 1, Faribault, Minn., claims to have one of the most poly-ethnic personnels in the Selective Service System. The names and races of the members of the board and its clerks are: Chairman Fred A. Wolf, German; Secretary Joseph W. Douda, Bohemian; Dr. F. U. Davis, Yankee; Clerk Osmond A. Felland, Norwegian; and Assistant Clerk Mera G. Ballis, Greek. And all, obviously, are good Americans.[83]

Many in the army might have been happy to keep up the interwar policy of ignoring ethnic and religious issues, but the reality of a diverse mass citizen army made such a policy impossible. The men came from a starkly divided society, and the army had to deal with that fact. To do so, army leaders turned to their institution's long history of pragmatism and idealism to handle their diverse population. As a result, the army consciously and purposely enacted policies that sought to unite men of all different backgrounds in the pursuit of a common cause.

Most simply, official army rules and regulations did not distinguish among ethnic groups. The army followed the same standard as Selective Service when it came to personnel policy concerning white ethnic groups: no discrimination based on creed or national background. That policy began in basic training. The officers and noncommissioned officers charged with training the men by and large followed those rules and regulations, and all of the men were held to uniform standards in training and discipline. Yet there was more to the training then just fairness of treatment. The World War II army was seeking in its soldiers to strike a balance among individual initiative, discipline, and teamwork. The private citizens who made up the army came about individual initiative easily enough, and the army had long experience with teaching discipline. Fostering teamwork fell within the traditional bounds of army training, too, but it also meant that the army had to deal more directly with the divisions among the men.[84]

Army leaders did not think that just having the men train together did enough to overcome intolerance, so they adopted some of the larger country's efforts at propaganda to create unity. The army and the government worked with Hollywood to make movies that stressed themes of ethnic and religious cooperation. The result of their efforts has been represented in what countless observers have called a cliché, the so-called multiethnic platoon. Film critics and cultural historians derisively point out that Hollywood willingly went along with the government's wartime propaganda program, including presenting the American soldier, sailor, and marine fighting in small units made up of Jews, Italians from New York, Irish Americans, Texans, and country boys. This hodgepodge of Americans always worked together despite their differences to defeat the enemy. War film after war film told the same story—what one critic described as the "ceaseless Hollywood roll calls of Spinellis, O'Haras, Dombrowskis, and Steins [to] highlight the *e pluribus unum* of it all: an ethnically diverse nation unified by democratic ideals"—and the tale that had a basis in reality became a cliché, prevalent in World War II movies down to the present day.[85]

The U.S. Army and government worked in other media and with a number of stars who wanted to do their part for the war effort. Author Stephen Vincent Benét penned a series of radio scripts that sounded the themes of tolerance and teamwork, especially in the army. In 1942 Benét wrote *Dear Adolf,* a series of six scripts based on actual letters written by Americans. William Holden read the "Letter from an American Soldier"—a note that included a long roll call of soldiers with names from all over the world. "Chinese, Italian, Greek, Bohemian, British, Mexican—the sons of the men who fought six wars and won them—the sons of the men who came here to get away from wars," the narrator intoned. "But they're all Americans now Adolf—and all against you."

> Against you and the Nipponese pals you sicked on us at Pearl Harbor—
> against you and all your ideas and ways. We don't like being ordered
> around, though we'll take it and like it in wartime. We think one man's as
> good as the next and maybe better. If we feel like going to church, we'll
> go to the church we pick out and the next guy can go to his. If we want to
> get married, we'll marry the girl we like—and the guy who makes a crack
> about her ancestry had better look out for his teeth.[86]

"Your Army," written in 1942 and broadcast as part of a radio series in 1944 with Tyrone Power as the lead voice, sounded a similar theme: "We know this is the army. Our army. A people's army, raised and equipped and run by free people, made up of Bill Jones and Bennie Cohen and Stan Woczinski, Burt Anderson and Charlie Pappas."[87]

The most direct way by which the army brought propaganda into training came through the use of various training films and filmstrips. Some of the men later in the war watched an animated short produced by the military called *Weapon of War.* The weapon in question belonged to the Nazis: race and religion hatred. In the movie, a liquid tonic sold by a nasty Nazi salesman represented that type of hatred, and that tonic was for sale to the United States, with its sixty-one different nationalities and 259 different religions. The Nazi salesman appealed to bigotry and claimed to have the cure for Armenians, Peruvians, Scandinavians, Greeks, Poles, Mexicans, Negroes, Chinese, Catholics, Presbyterians, Jews, Baptists, and just about any other group the soldiers may have grown up hating.[88]

The army also showed many of the men at least part of the *Why We Fight* movie series. Produced under the direction of Frank Capra, the seven movies sought to educate the men as to the nature of the free world and its enemies. In part because Capra was Catholic and a very religious individual, religion played a key role in the films. The Allies, including the Soviets, came across as the defenders of all things religious, the defenders of the great traditions passed down from Moses, Mohammed, Confucius, and Jesus. Each religious leader taught, according to the film, that "in the sight of God all men are created equal." Conversely, the filmmakers portrayed the Axis powers, particularly the Germans, as intensely antireligious. In *Prelude to War,* the first and most widely seen of the films, the Nazis were shown to be trying to replace God with the state and its greatest symbol, Hitler himself. At one point, a voiceover quoted Alfred Rosenberg, a Nazi ideologist, saying, "Catholic and Protestant churches must vanish from the life of the people."[89] As one scholar has written, "Capra showed Americans of diverse religious, class, ethnic, and regional backgrounds putting aside differences and disagreements in their embrace of the nation."[90]

The focus on religion in the *Why We Fight* movies, and the issue of Jews in the army in general, illustrated a fact the army could not ignore. The men in the army continued to have faith in their various religions. The army had no choice but to deal openly with at least that level of diversity. The president recognized that fact and sought from even before the war to make clear that the American effort would be divided fairly among its many religious denominations. At the first draft lottery in the fall of 1940 he read letters from Protestant, Catholic, and Jewish leaders.[91] Such an effort at incorporating various religions and denominations did not stop with the president. The army played its part, and the task fell primarily to the Chaplain Corps.

Chaplains had served in all of America's wars. Early on, they tended to serve in a less official capacity. Religious men often would not wait for government recognition before going off to minister to the men in times of war. In peace, post chaplains did not even have to be ministers at all. The mass mobilization of the Civil War led to the induction of regimental, post, and hospital chaplains, often at the rank of captain and including for the first time in any numbers Catholic, Jewish, black, and Indian chaplains. After the war, the handful of chaplains who remained in the army reported to the adjutant general, who almost always treated them as an afterthought. It took the modernizing and organizational impulses of the progressive era to affect reform, including the creation of the Board of Chaplains in 1909. Still, confusion over roles and numbers in World War I led the army to finally organize the chaplains into a more coherent unit. Most important, the National Defense Act of 1920 created a chief of chaplains to head up the Chaplain Corps.[92]

World War I had created new conditions, but even after that conflict, the army did not spend a great deal of time managing its Chaplain Corps. The result could be seen in both the CCC and CMTCs. In both cases the chaplains who saw to the spiritual needs of the young men generally got high marks, but it was also clear the army had not put much thought yet into setting official policy for dealing with a religiously diverse population. Several young men complained of being encouraged or even forced to attend services that were not their religion.[93] Also, no rabbis served in the regular army in the interwar period, although a few were in the reserves. Jewish cadets at West Point found that they had to go to Protestant chapel on Sundays, but eventually reserve rabbi chaplains began to hold services at the academy, and the army apparently put up little or no resistance to Jewish soldiers celebrating their holiest days. Yet throughout all of the time up until World War II, Protestants, particularly Episcopalians, dominated the chaplaincy, even though Roman Catholics had become the largest single denomination in the country (followed by Methodists and Southern Baptists).[94]

The professionalization of the World War II army and the issues created by mass mobilization made a diverse and capable corps of chaplains particularly important. The army put more emphasis on troop morale than ever before, including the role religion played in that morale.[95] Some in the army anticipated these issues, and by the outbreak of the war the army had official regulations governing chaplains and their training program. The chief of chaplains—for the duration of the war William R. Arnold, a Roman Catholic, served in the post—held broad powers to coordinate and supervise all of religious work of the army. Army regulations mandated that the chaplains perform duties "closely analogous to those performed by clergymen in civilian life," with one notable exception: The "peculiar conditions attaching to military life," meant that each chaplain had to "serve the moral and religious needs of the entire personnel of the command to which he is assigned." In that capacity, the regulations stipulated that "chaplains will serve as friends, counselors, and guides, without discrimination, to all members of the command . . . regardless of creed or sect."[96] The technical manual for the chaplain expanded on this definition of duties, calling for open-minded men who believed in the spirit of cooperation. "The chaplain is the servant of God for all," the manual instructed, "and no narrow sectarian spirit should color his utterances, nor should his personal work assist only a special group."[97] That said, army policy also stated, "No man shall be ordered, or forced wither by direct or indirect means, to attend any religious service or formation contrary to his conscience."[98]

The spirit of tolerance pervaded chaplain training. The chaplains were in the front lines of the army's efforts to overcome the potentially divisive religious and ethnic diversity of the troops. They had to overcome their own parochialism first. In training, the men marched, trained, and prayed together. After February 1943, the army deliberately assigned men of diverse denominations to the same dorm rooms.[99] Over and over again, the army impressed upon chaplains in training that they were to minister to all the men, if need be, and never discriminate based on religious differences.[100] Chaplain Roy Honeywell later wrote that the "indiscriminate mingling" of chaplains from various faiths became more striking in light of "the background of misunderstanding, distrust, and rivalry which has stimulated and perpetuated the divisions among religious groups." That mingling led to a much greater level of understanding among the men.[101] Rabbi Isaac Klein, who later wrote about his training experience, agreed:

> All differences, ethnic, cultural, theological and social, were forgotten.
> We were all possessed by an awareness of a common task ahead of us. This
> awareness accompanied us through the war years, and was responsible for
> the splendid spirit of cooperation that was the hallmark of the Chaplains'
> Corps throughout the war years. During the postwar years I often looked
> with nostalgia to those days of genuine brotherhood when I compared
> it with the artificial efforts of cooperation of the interfaith activities that
> became popular in the later years. Our minds gave compelling reasons for
> those interfaith projects, but our hearts were not in them. During the war
> years our hearts and souls were in the common effort to serve the soldiers,
> all soldiers.[102]

That spirit of unity usually continued long after training. The Four Immortal Chaplains were the most famous example, but there were plenty of others.

For example, when a civilian Catholic bishop complained in January 1945 that the army did not care for Catholic issues, a chaplain based in Virginia felt compelled to write to the chief of chaplains and say, "From my experience in the Army I have not seen where the Protestant and Jewish Chaplains have seriously interfered with the Catholic Chaplains in their services. In most cases there has been splendid cooperation among the Chaplains of all faiths."[103] And a Jewish chaplain stationed in Rhode Island wrote the chief of chaplains to describe the tremendous success he and his fellow chaplains had achieved with a series of "Brotherhood Services" for the men of Catholic, Protestant, and Jewish faiths.[104]

Also important to defining army policy toward religious diversity were the actions of the offices of the adjutant general and the chief of chaplains during the war. By regulation, the adjutant general dealt with most personnel correspondence and the chief of chaplains handled most of the correspondence concerning religious matters. Both offices thus dealt with a wide variety of issues relating to the religious makeup of the army. In case after case, on issue after issue relating to religion, they made every effort to treat the army's

*Left to right:* Chaplain Fred W. Thissen (Catholic), Chaplain Ernest Pine (Protestant), and Chaplain Jacob Rothschild (Jewish) were students together in 1942 at the U.S. Army Chaplain School at Fort Benjamin Harrison, Indiana. Such scenes were common in World War II chaplain training. Library of Congress.

diverse religious population fairly and equally. For example, some religious groups, most prominently Jews and Seventh Day Adventists, celebrated the Sabbath on days other than Sunday (usually Saturday), and some members of those groups would not work on their Sabbath. The army responded by looking at each case to try to determine the true strength of the religious convictions held by the individuals in question. A general rule emerged from this process, dictating that in nonemergencies, those who sincerely celebrated the Sabbath on Saturday could take the day off and do the equivalent work on Sunday.[105] A similar decision came from the chief of chaplains in response to a request from some Catholics that their men be allowed some time for worship on holy days specific to the Catholic Church.[106] Chaplain Arnold advised the army that the request should be granted as long as it did not interfere with important military work because attendance at such services would boost morale. He also pointed out that "any directive issued should have a general application to avoid the possibility of any member of any religious group feeling that his group has been omitted from consideration and thereby is the object of discrimination."[107]

The most potentially divisive issue came from religious groups at home using troop personnel numbers to make the case that one religion or another fought and died disproportionate to their overall population numbers. It would make sense that the various religions and denominations of the Chaplain Corps would reflect the religious background of the men who made up the army. Nevertheless, the precise numbers of Jews, Catholics, Baptists, Orthodox, Methodists, Lutherans, Presbyterians, Mormons, and so on are impossible to find. The army did not track the religion of its soldiers as a matter of policy.

General Arnold, the chief of chaplains, best described the reasoning behind this policy in a 1942 letter to a church leader who had made some suggestions for distributing chaplains: "Because I have been close to this problem of denominational allotments in the Army for thirty years and am familiar with every attempt to solve the difficulty I am not . . . sanguine of a satisfactory solution." According to Arnold, no simple way existed to break down denominations into broad categories, because, "for instance, Greek Catholics, Old Catholics, and National Polish Catholics do not wish to be classified with Roman Catholics; three distinctive groups of Jews demand separate consideration; some groups claim that the word 'Protestant' is not an exact term for them." The policy for distributing chaplains by denomination had to remain fluid: "Since the average regiment has men from twelve to fifteen denominations and there can be only one chaplain to a regiment or similar unit you can see the difficulty we are up against."[108]

Instead of taking a religious census of the troops as they entered the service, the Chaplain Corps acted under "the assumption that the religious basis in the Army is a cross section of the population of the United States."[109] For most of the war that meant chaplain distribution came from quotas set up early in the interwar period based in part on a pre–World War I census of religion in the United States. That system led to chaplain ratios that were disproportionate with the overall population, so in 1945 the War Department set up quotas for the various denominations based on the data for the overall population gathered by the 1936 census of religious bodies in the United States.[110] At the outset of the mobilization, the chief of chaplains wanted to have one chaplain for every one thousand to twelve hundred soldiers in the army. Troop mobilization planning for the war called for an army of over eight million men, so the chief of chaplains based the chaplain quotas on that figure.[111] The corps very nearly achieved that objective. In the summer of 1945, with roughly 8.2 million men serving in the army, 8,171 chaplains were also in the service, almost exactly 1 for every 1,000 soldiers.

In the final wartime quota system, Roman Catholics by far represented the single largest denomination, with a quota number of 2,589, more than 30 percent of the total. Next came Methodists (935, 11 percent), followed by Southern Baptists (756, 8.9 percent), Colored Baptists (612, 7.2 percent), Jewish (315, 3.7 percent), Presbyterian Church (USA) (310, 3.65 percent), Protestant Episcopal (248, 2.92 percent), and Disciples of Christ (199, 2.34 percent). The Missouri Synod Lutherans, United Lutherans, and American Lutherans together had a quota number of 547, roughly 6.5 percent of the total. Another sixty religions and denominations also had quota numbers or had chaplains serve from their groups. Because Selective Service and U.S. Army distribution centers generally did such a fair job of distributing the men for assignment, the denominations spread out among all of the branches and units of the wartime army. The chief of chaplains faced the daunting task of distributing chaplains as equally as possible (and occasionally as need dictated).[112] He could only do so much.

The relatively small numbers of chaplains, the size and distribution of the army, and the conditions in the various war zones dictated that sometimes Protestant, Catholic, or Jewish chaplains had to run services for men of all faiths. Chaplains of various faiths filled in for each other wherever the army went. For example, Rabbi Isaac Klein, who served in Europe, recalled having to arrange for Protestant and Catholic services from time to time. A Jewish soldier recalled an Episcopalian chaplain doing a wonderful job filling in and presiding over a Passover seder in 1945. The wartime correspondence between a rabbi and a priest told the story of a Jewish chaplain hearing a confession from an Irish Catholic soldier.[113] Such efforts explained why the chaplain in the 1949 movie *Battleground* told the men fighting in the Battle of the Bulge, "All of us Holy Joes are switch hitters."[114]

At the same time, the army could be of little help to those outside the military who wanted to make an issue of the contributions of various religious groups to the war effort. The army developed a standard response to such queries. Over and over the adjutant general or the chief of chaplains wrote to correspondents that although the country should be proud of the efforts of all of its diverse people, "it is the policy of the War Department to refrain from making a complete religious census of army personnel. Such information that has been and is now being received is obtained on a purely voluntary basis, and, although not complete, will be for official use only. The Department, therefore, is not in position to comply with your request."[115]

The army dealt with a number of other sensitive religious issues. Some religious groups and individuals wrote to complain about religious identification on dog tags. When the men enlisted and received identification tags, their religion was represented on those tags by a single letter. Thus they faced the option of C for Catholic, P for Protestant, or H for Jewish. But some Orthodox Christians, for example, thought it unfair that they did not have the option of O for Orthodox.[116] As a practical matter the army could not use a different single letter stamp for every denomination in the United States, and they told correspondents that, but they did try to work with groups that did not like their choices. The adjutant general suggested that the army would have no problem with individuals wearing an additional self-furnished identification tag.[117]

The distribution of antagonistic religious literature offered another challenge to army policy. The chief of chaplains encouraged discretion, cordiality, and cooperation among chaplains concerning the distribution of literature and the display of religious symbols on bases where the various denominations shared a chapel.[118] In the summer of 1944, the chief distributed to the Chaplain Corps a strong statement on the issue of offensive and antagonistic literature: "A gratuitous attack on the good will or good faith of another person never promotes the cause of truth or charity. In the army where men must live shoulder to shoulder and where a fraternal spirit is so vitally important, anything which even approaches the violations of freedom of conscience will be disastrous."[119]

The army, especially through the Chaplain Corps, was most clear and consistent with its policy when responding to overt cases of discrimination within the ranks. Not surprisingly, not all chaplains worked well with other religions and denominations. A Baptist chaplain based in San Francisco wrote to the chief of chaplains in June 1944 to announce that he resented the fact that Catholic chaplains could hold their own services while Protestants had to give more general services that ministered to all Protestants. "Frankly," he concluded, "I am very tired of being pushed around by a bunch of rum soaked, dissolute, idol worshiping men who so sanctimoniously call themselves 'father,' and who seem to have all the privileges in the army."[120] Chaplain Roy Honeywell wrote a diplomatic reply on the behalf of the chief of chaplains, ignoring the attack on Catholics and explaining that for practical reasons Protestants could more easily worship together than with Catholics or Jewish groups, but that the army encouraged additional denominational services if chaplains could find sufficient numbers to attend.[121] The answer did not satisfy the San Francisco chaplain, who wrote back to argue that he was not a Protestant because a "protestant church is one which protested against the evils, false teachings and abominable [sic] practices of the catholic church. . . . Now, my church was never in the catholic church to protest. The Lord Jesus Christ established my church when He was on earth, and it has existed since that time."[122]

Honeywell, who in addition to being a chaplain was also a professional academic historian, began his reply with "No doubt your definition of the word 'protestant' was substantially correct four centuries ago, though some insist that the true meaning as derived from *protestari* must be one who advocates or affirms something." He continued, "There are a number of religious bodies which make claims about their origins or relationships which seem to many students of the subject to have no trustworthy basis in fact and no significance if their truth were to be demonstrated, but they deserve respectful treatment from other Christians as long as these claims are held sincerely." However, cooperation and tolerance was "much more important to the success of any chaplain than group distinctions and terminology":

> The reputation of being narrowly sectarian or of claiming a superiority
> among Christians will impair the usefulness of any chaplain and repel
> earnest men. It is quite proper for a Baptist, Lutheran, or other chaplain
> to conduct communion or other service for his denominational group in
> addition to his general program of religious services for all Protestants.
> If he is unable thus to adapt himself to the general Protestant usages and
> viewpoint, he has missed his best opportunity for a greater usefulness.[123]

In other words, the office of the chief of chaplains declared that chaplains who did not embrace the more tolerant policies of the army were essentially useless.

By World War II, the army as an institution had a long history of dealing with ethnic and religious diversity in the ranks. That history led to army personnel policies during the war that integrated almost all of the various white ethnic and religious groups of the United States on an equal basis, and a religious policy that consciously sought to encourage tolerance. These policies were in large part pragmatic—the most fair and thus least controversial way to mobilize a diverse population for war. But the army's history had also produced a legacy of idealism among some officers responsible for personnel decisions. Even in the face of intolerance, these army men put great hope in the experiment of mixing the soldiers. When a Jewish officer wrote to complain about anti-Semitism among some of his men, an assistant to the chief of chaplains replied,

> This office regrets deeply the prejudice and injustice which frequently
> spring from differences in race, nationality, or creed and is eager to exert
> and proper influence which may tend to prevent or remedy such attitudes.
> One of the benefits resulting from the close associations of military ser-
> vice is that men come to know better the men of other groups with whom
> they serve, and from this better acquaintance grow mutual respect and a
> spirit of comradeship.[124]

Whatever the combination of pragmatism and idealism, the World War II army put white men together without barriers based on ethnicity or religion. If anything were to come of this great experiment, the soldiers themselves would have to do the rest.

# 3

# INTRODUCTION TO THE ARMY

Rich or poor, light or dark, the educated and the ignorant—
all were thrown together to accomplish the same objective,
mainly that of learning military skills; and we all were subjected
to the same rude Army discipline. Our inert qualities were discovered and the superficial appearances soon wore off.

—Raul Morin, *Among the Valiant,* 1963

THEY CAME BY THE MILLIONS—MEN AND BOYS, MARRIED AND UNMARRIED, fathers and the childless; those who had worked long on professional careers, those who labored in fields and factories, and many who had just finished school. They believed in God, went to church or synagogue, or had little use for religion. The tall and the short came, the skinny and stocky, the strong and the weak, with blond, brown, and red hair, or no hair at all. They were the average American soldier in World War II.

Such a diverse group of people defied generalizations. They could not even agree on whether or how much they wanted to be there. Millions volunteered, but most came by way of the draft. Some resented the call to military service, which had disrupted their family lives or career paths.[1] Others questioned the cause itself. One such man wondered, "Is this really my war? For whose benefit do I suffer? . . . For whom or what are we wasting our lives and bodies?"[2] Then there were those who, for a variety of reasons, could not be more happy to join. The army gave such men the chance to escape their prewar lives. A child of immigrants in the inner city recalled, "When World War II broke out, I was delighted. There was no other word, terrible as it may sound. My country called. I was delivered from my mother, my family, the girl I was loving passionately but did not love. And delivered WITHOUT GUILT. Heroically."[3] Others looked to military service as a way to put food on the table. A transient during the Depression said, "When the war came, I was so glad when I got into the army. I knew I was safe. I put a uniform on. . . . I had money comin', I had food comin'."[4] For most of the men, though, there was a feeling that they had some sort of duty to serve, yet very few could or would put words to that feeling. Leonard Herb explained that "at twenty one you're not very up on those things." Yet something pulled at them. "Everybody had to go," Herb continued, "and so you could see that it was a necessity, so everybody did it more or less willingly."[5]

More or less willingly, twelve million of these Americans served in the U.S. Army in World War II, and the diversity of their reactions to the call to service was an indication of just how different they all were. They came from all over the country and from all different economic backgrounds. They represented the full range of the country's ethnicities and religions, and they harbored the full range of the country's prejudices and misunderstandings. Yet common threads ran through their experiences in the army because that was what the army did. The army needed, the war required, that soldiers find at some level what united them. So when it came to getting the men to basic training, the army did not care whether they wanted to be there or what sense of duty had delivered them to the service. When it came to making soldiers out of the recruits, the army did not particularly care about the men's economic, ethnic, or religious backgrounds. And when it came to making an army out of those soldiers, the army certainly did not care about all of the men's personal anxieties or stories. In World War II, men from a freewheeling diverse society met a rigidly uniform institution. It was a great shock, and it had a profound effect.

It began with the physical examinations. Before they even officially joined, the army began tearing down the individuals with degrading and embarrassing tests. Doctors examined the eyes, ears, noses, teeth, and throats of the men. They listened to hearts, checked feet, examined buttocks, and took urine specimens.[6] A sergeant explained the goal of the exam when the older men at one center struggled to improve their appearances by sucking in their stomachs. A recruit at the examination recalled, "Some of the men were getting purple in the face when a sergeant said: 'Okay. Relax. Slide your bellies back where you usually carry them. This is no Mr. America contest. . . . We'd just like to know how many of you should be able to walk a mile without a repair job.'"[7] That modest objective did not make the exam any less of a shock for the inductees. One soldier recalled, "We were all herded into a cool room and stripped of all of our clothes and I might add, our dignity as well."[8] Another described the frantic confusion: "There was that line. Orders! Orders! Take your clothes off. Get that Bottle. Put your hands behind your back and stand close. What did you hear? What do you see? Stand on your toes. Oh, my feet! How they hurt and ache. Nude and perspiring, hot and stinking. Would this never end? Finally the signing on the dotted line and I knew I had made it."[9]

That first physical examination also introduced the men to what they came to call the "short arm inspection," wherein army medical personnel would inspect the genitalia of each man for signs of venereal diseases. In order to expedite the process, the men would line up naked or wearing just an overcoat. Either way, army doctors did not care about the individual pride or privacy of the men in this particular, very personal, and all-too-frequent roll call. As an indication of the regularity of the short arm inspections, one doctor said that by the time he embarked to go overseas, he "knew the corporal features of my men better than their faces."[10] The inspections continued throughout the war in theaters all over the world, and the men remembered them well.[11] The troops became so familiar with the exams that they could be pretty crass and familiar about the process. As the men in one unit lined up for a medical inspection that would not include a check for venereal diseases, one called out, "Don't the docs want us to squeeze our cocks for them, corporal?"[12]

The army had literally stripped down the recruits to their essentials, and it was a harrowing experience. The men learned early on that personal pride or modesty had no real place in the army. Physical inspections were not the only place where the army violated personal privacy. The tents and barracks buildings at the camps and forts where the men did their training did not divide the troops into cozy individual rooms. The men slept and dressed in full view of each other. John Jenkins wrote of army accommodations, "It is quite different, this being thrown in with 59 strangers with no opportunity for privacy."[13] Likewise, the showers were open. As one man wrote home, "The shower is another hullabaloo. About 600 guys all crowd into one place."[14] Even men who had plenty of experience with nudity from the swimming hole or the locker room and were not bothered by the barracks or showers were shocked by another army facility: the latrines. There, in most cases, the men had to urinate and defecate in full view of dozens of other people. One man recalled that "none had partitions: imagine sitting with a dozen defecating men, knees almost touching, with shorts or trousers bunched around your ankles."[15] A revelry came to surround this lack of privacy: "Answering nature's call meant subjecting yourself to loud and detailed criticism—perceptive and merciless descriptions of your sex organs, ranging from glowing admiration; brilliant critiques of your style of defecation, with learned footnotes on gas-passing."[16] Even generals were exposed to some of this behavior. Later on in the war, as his 82nd Airborne Division flew over the English Channel for their drop on D-Day, Gen. Matthew Ridgway described the efforts of the men in

The close and open quarters of military facilities led to open familiarity among the soldiers, regardless of ethnic or religious background. Courtesy of Robert T. Davis II.

his plane to relieve themselves in a bucket: "A man strapped and buckled into full combat gear finds it extremely difficult to reach certain essential parts of his anatomy, and his efforts are not made easier by the fact that his comrades are watching him, jeering derisively and offering gratuitous advice."[17]

The men also had to deal with the fact that they no longer controlled their physical appearance. One guide for new troops informed them that "the army clothes you from the skin out," and indeed the army provided everything a soldier should or could wear, including shirts, trousers, socks, and underwear.[18] All soldiers had and wore the same clothing, and not all of them liked the uniforms. "It embarrasses [the American soldier] to wear one," wrote one veteran. "He resents the fact that he must. . . . Your American likes variety and he likes to wear what he pleases, when he pleases."[19] By design the uniforms were, for lack of a better word, uniform. So too were haircuts—as much as they could be. The army made sure that every man had similarly short haircuts, haircuts that were not of the style of the day. As one captain announced to his new troops, "The Company Barber will standardize you to look like the rest of us."[20] Like the uniforms, it was not a standard all of the men appreciated. After induction, Warren Lloyd said, "I was too embarrassed about having my hair cut so short and didn't go home that weekend."[21] Wrote

Kenneth Connelly of the strict controls of military life, "The Army . . . practices the most thorough communism—the same clothes, . . . the same diet, the same tooth-brushes—absolute division of 'wealth.' However ideal it may be from an ethical standpoint, temperamentally I can't stand it."[22]

Removal of physical pride proved to be just one of several steps in separating the inductees from their civilian lives. The men also came to realize that their familiar social structures, whether with family or friends or work, did not exist in the army. Some friends joined at the same time and place and they made it into the same units, but by and large the new recruits entered the company of strangers. To deal with the shock, men embraced anything familiar, such as the recruit who considered it a stroke of luck to be in the same company with five or six strangers from his same home city.[23] Not only were the majority among strangers, but more often then not they found themselves traveling by train to distant and unfamiliar areas of the country for training, far from any homes they knew. The recruits tried to distract themselves from the anxiety brought on by this dislocation. Some read, but many other participated in what would become a common experience for the men in the military: gambling. On the train to boot camp, one volunteer remembered card games and craps breaking out in the aisles and between the seats. He joined in and quickly got cleaned out.[24] His was a common experience.

When not distracting themselves from the anxiety of traveling far from home, they examined the new lands through which they traveled. An older man who served as a chaplain in the Pacific wrote home while riding cross country, "It would be very 'right' if every group going overseas could cross the continent as we have done—could see America, even fleeting glimpses from a flying train. They would leave America with a more definite and reasonable pride in the nation which they serve and of which they are a part."[25] That may have been true, and probably was in retrospect, but at the time the trip just overwhelmed many of the younger men. John Hinton of Tennessee trained in Alabama: "What an experience this was! I was all of 18 years old at the time and had never been away from home over a week at a time."[26] Texan Audie Murphy recalled that when he got on the bus for the induction center, he had never been more than a hundred miles from home.[27] Ohioan Maynard Marquis said, "We pulled into Camp Wheeler, near Macon, Georgia. It was hot and sticky. I had never been this far from home before. I got pretty homesick for a couple of days."[28] George Wilson of Michigan also went to Camp Wheeler: "Everything was very strange and new to me. I had never been away from home for more than a week and was totally ignorant of the Army."[29]

Many of the army's training camps were located in the South, a new environment to the millions of northerners in the service. Their observations of the alien land ranged from climate to geography to social issues. One recalled, "I'd thought the South would be hot all year round, but it wasn't, it was chilly down here."[30] Another wrote, "I'd never been farther south than Washington, so the landscape—the woods, mountains, deserted streams, poverty-stricken villages along the tracks, occasional small cities with factories bordering the rivers—all this was novel. So, as we inched southward, was the heat in the cars, airless even with all windows opened."[31] The culture, especially racial relations, also made the South a foreign land. Wayne Colwell from New York wrote that he never saw any discrimination in the service, but he "quickly saw [discrimination] in Mississippi and other Southern states."[32] Richard O'Brien of California "trained in the South and observed Jim Crow signs, etc.," and, he added, he "didn't like it."[33]

After the physical exams and as the men struggled to adapt to new clothes and new physical environments, the disorienting process of getting the men in the army continued. In the days and weeks to come, army medical personnel administered painful shots to the men to inoculate them from diseases like typhoid and smallpox.[34] If that was not enough, the new recruits found themselves taking an exam, the army's General Classification Test. The test divided the men into five classes based on their scores. Only those with higher scores could get into the more coveted roles in the army, such as Officer Candidate School, the Army Specialized Training Program, and the U.S. Army Air Forces. Lower scores usually led to the infantry, where the men would have a much greater chance of getting into combat. In the midst of all the other new and disorienting experiences, the men found themselves taking an exam that went a long way to determining where they would serve in the army and whether or not they would serve under fire.[35]

This process of being stripped of their dignity, separated from the friends and family, placed in a strange land, poked, prodded, and tested represented nothing less than a personal upheaval. That upheaval made the early part of army service extremely trying. Missouri native Lawrence Dowler trained in California and recalled that "basic training was hard on some of us. First time away from home at 19 years of age and seeing a different way of life. Instead of being asked to do something, we are told what to do and do it now."[36] Andrew Nelson agreed. "I think the toughest time for young soldiers is the first weeks in the service," he stated. "All parts of your former life are missing and you think of combat in war. You feel unable to cope with what is ahead."[37] Of course, some men adjusted easier and carried themselves with more confidence, but in almost all cases the experience so shocked the men that they became at least partially unmoored from the pride born of prior experiences and expectations.[38]

The army deliberately used the short haircuts, uniforms, and cramped communal traveling and living conditions to upset the men, to level their appearances, to make them look and feel the same. But appearances could be deceiving. The army may have knocked down some of the pride of these individual Americans, but that was just the first step, and it still left a long way to go in developing the type of camaraderie the army needed to make an effective fighting force. "I confess that a large number of Americans I met in the army amazed me by their differentness," Glenn Gray later recalled. "Nothing else could have made me realize how narrow the circle in which we move in peacetime is."[39] Soldiers in World War II came from a stratified and regimented society where ethnic and religious differences went a long way in determining all of the important aspects of their lives, from where they lived and what they ate, to whom they knew and whom they distrusted or disliked. Men from such a society quickly noticed the differences among their fellow soldiers.

Even the least discerning soldier could fairly easily spot disparities in economic and regional backgrounds. Housed in barracks at training, Daniel Hoffman remembered that "Barracks B was for me an experiment in group living, among men mostly quite different from the college boys I'd known. They were a mixed lot, some few highly qualified and educated technical specialists, plus a lot of men from blue-collar backgrounds doing blue-collar jobs. . . ."[40] Robert Healey recalled a discussion during which "some city kids got into an argument about whether or not a hen could have eggs if there was no rooster around. . . . Finally, one country kid who knew all about it said, 'Oh, you dummies. Of course a hen can have eggs. The only thing is they won't be fertilized if there's no rooster, and there won't be any little chickies coming out of them!'"[41] Another man told his parents, "You would die laughing at some of the northern city fellows who haven't had chiggers before. They call the little creatures 'jiggers.'"[42]

Specific regional differences led to some interesting interactions and observations from the men. A man from Pittsburgh noted the tendency of the Texans in his unit to brag up their state. So he and the other non-Texans teased the Texans about the Lone Star State, and in response the Texans called them "Jersey Jerks, Brooklyn Bums and Smoky-City Rats."[43] One class of officer candidates in training received the privilege of going to a dance in San Antonio, where the local girls' mothers "ordinarily wouldn't let these young ladies within ten yards of a Yankee, but since we, as officer candidates, were certified as gentlemen, the girls were permitted to dance with us."[44] One vet from Massachusetts said, "No one, but no one, can tell a story like an Oklahoman."[45] A New England soldier who received specialized training at Ohio

University wrote home, "The OU girls . . . are uniformly good-looking and built sort of stocky and husky (the latter attribute must come from the corn). Our New England guys who don't appreciate these local farmers call 'em 'Just Plain Corn-Fed Hicks.' The OU girls think all the New Englanders are ane-mic."[46] These regional differences could be incorporated into the relationships among the men. A soldier serving in an armored unit recalled, "The men came from Brooklyn, Louisiana, Illinois and Pennsylvania, so we called our vehicle the 'BLIP.'"[47]

Not surprisingly, the men invariably noticed the ethnic variety among their new compatriots. The multiethnic World War II squad, platoon, or company became a cliché in American popular culture even during the war. But any other portrayal of small units in the army would be inaccurate. The ethnic variety shocked the soldiers. That shock led them to describe, both during and after the war, finding themselves a part of a multiethnic unit. The story stayed the same across theaters, divisions, and branches of service. For example, Robert Easton wrote home from basic training in the United States, "Among us are three whose parents were born in Germany, who could speak almost no English when they began school. There is Chapeno the gentle Mexican bred in Texas. . . . There is Brun the freckled sunburned Norwegian. . . . There is Erickson from Minnesota who plays the drums in a jazz band and Adolf, the Bohemian, whose father is a well-to-do dairyman."[48] In his diary, Nap Glass wrote of the men he met on the train ride to basic training, "There were a couple of Jewish boys I knew. One of the boys I talked to was Italian and as dumb as they make them. . . . The other was Polish and seemed to have a little more brains."[49] At one point in his training, Dean Joy described the various foods he and his roommates received in packages from home: "Lueck's mother sent Thuringer sausages [a German sausage], Eddington's sent cakes and pies, and Longo's sent jars of Italian antipasto."[50] Angus Nott, who would fight in the Pacific theater, said, "Our company had Italians, Jews, Irish, French and WASPs."[51] A veteran paratrooper later remembered from training his "two best buddies. Joe and Eddie. . . . Joe was of German descent, tall hard, and lean. Eddie was a Jewish boy, medium in height and weight, and master at knowing foreign languages. (They are both dead now, Joe and Eddie, killed in action behind German lines in Belgium. My friends.)"[52]

The men did more than write home about the diversity of their units. From when they first met each other, they pointed out their differences, usu-ally through crude humor. Over and over, soldiers made fun of their new companions, often by ethnic group. That fun could come out in pretty rough terms, and it no doubt offended some of the troops. But most understood that the joking did not come from bad intentions as much as insecurity born of young men trying to cope with a whole new way of life. There was "good-natured give-and-take among all the men with different backgrounds, religions, etc.," as paratrooper Carwood Lipton remembered.[53] Likewise, Gordon Carson did not notice any ethnic or religious animosity in his outfit, though they did "tease about ethnic[ity] and the various states you were from."[54] Jerry Davis in the Eleventh Airborne remembered, "We had a lot of Poles who we called ski and a few Jewish Abe's, but it was all in fun and never any hard feelings."[55] The men in Italian American paratrooper Bill Guarnere's unit called him "Gonorrhea," but he did not take too much offense at the nickname.[56] According to historian Deborah Dash Moore, Jewish GI Howard Sachs told a similar story: "Occasionally someone might have said to him, 'hey jewboy' And so he responded in kind, 'hey dago, or wop,' he recalled. These slurs did not 'make anyone angry.'"[57] Frank Armstrong later wrote that "the names they called each other were a good-natured carryover from the past and not taken seriously . . . viewed in retrospect, it reinforced our overall unity."[58] Hollis Stabler, an Oklahoman, recalled, "I ran into Rednecks [and] every now and then being a full blood Indian they called me chief." But, he continued, "I did not mind that [unless] they used the term in a derogatory way."[59]

As Stabler made clear, the kidding among the men was not always good-natured. Tone and context mattered. The soldiers gave names to "people they liked and those they hated," according to Charles Henne.[60] As a result of the latter, sometimes the noting of differences became outright bigotry. Not surprisingly, members or descendants of the newer immigrant groups and those groups that exhibited certain clear physical traits faced the problem more often. Bailey Tyre believed that in his unit "language reflected prejudice, ie Kike, Dagos, Niggers, Krauts, Japs."[61] James Sammons remembered that "Italian[s], Filipino[s]—Any dark skin person" occasionally confronted discrimination.[62] Junior officer Alexander Davit noticed "a bit of discrimination against Mexican/Indian types on one occasion."[63] Another man claimed that while still stateside, "Mexicans were not liked for their behavior relating to eating. They would empty the whole bowl of food onto their plates."[64]

As direct as they were about ethnicity, the men tended to be more reserved in discussions of religion, especially early on in training. Merritt Bragdon recalled, "People simply kept their views (and/or prayers) to themselves."[65] When the men did share religious beliefs, the process was casual and quiet. One veteran remembered that "most men let you know in conversations what denomination they belonged to and their own convictions."[66] Albert Schantz agreed that the troops handled religious issues with a sense of discretion. Schantz said that religion often came up in discussion, "but no one got upset."[67] Jack Foley made the point more explicitly: "I had no discrimination as a Roman Catholic nor was I ever aware of such among friends who were Jewish, Latter Day Saint, Protestant."[68] That is not to say soldiers never took offense over religious issues, far from it. Richard O'Brien remembered one such incident: "While waiting in a movie line in the States a group of officers were discussing the bombing of Rome, one suggested that they should bomb the Vatican too. I was offended by the remark but being a new recruit on my first pass I did not say anything to him."[69] But by and large, the men focused more on regional background and ethnicity when discussing the differences within their units.[70]

Jewish soldiers made up a special case.[71] When the men spoke of their Jewish comrades, they usually meant Jewish in an ethnic, not religious, sense. However, as both religious and ethnic minorities, Jews dealt with a complex situation. Of all the fully integrated groups within the army, Jewish Americans faced the most incidences of discrimination. Many of the men, both Jewish and Gentile, remembered cases of anti-Semitism. For example, James R. Jones saw one instance of anti-Semitism by one man in his unit, and William U'Ren recalled that "a couple of non-coms made life miserable for one Jewish soldier in a company I was in in the states."[72] Donald Dehn of the 44th Infantry Division remembered a fist fight between a Jewish soldier and an Irish soldier.[73] Italian American soldier Nicholas Scotto transferred to a new unit and met a sergeant from the South who would not speak with him because the sergeant mistook Scotto for Jewish. The sergeant apologized when he realized his mistake, but not for his animosity toward Jews.[74] A rabbi chaplain confirmed these accounts, recalling that in his experience, anti-Semitism "cropped up sometimes, though rarely, I am glad to say."[75]

Most of this discrimination toward Jewish soldiers came from outright ignorance. An extreme example came from a soldier from New York who remembered that "southern boys thought Jews must have horns."[76] More commonplace was the mistaken belief that somehow American Jews were not doing their part in the fight. While serving in the 11th Airborne Division, Andrew Nelson heard one soldier express an oft-repeated view of anti-Semites before the war: "Jews always get the breaks in America."[77] During the war, that view turned into the nasty rumor that Jews somehow always managed to avoid service, especially combat service. While that idea was far more pervasive out of the service than in, it did make its way into some army units. A man in the 35th Infantry Division said that some of the men he knew were prejudiced against Jews because Jewish soldiers "were in non-combat units."[78] At times, such ignorance meant that a relatively small dispute could bring out the worst in the men. One man recalled just such a time in the winter of 1943 at a headquarters in the United States: "Every G.I. wanted to go home for Christmas, when suddenly it was discovered that some of our Jewish comrades had put in for a pass." He continued, "A near riot ensued. . . . 'You guys killed Christ,' some hollered loudly. 'Now you want to celebrate His birthday.'" As a result of the furor, the Jewish soldiers agreed to go home for New Year's instead.[79] These types of individual incidents of anti-Semitism in the ranks continued throughout the war.[80]

The cases of anti-Semitism often triggered telling responses in regard to army policy toward ethnic and religious minorities. Even the men noticed that the army tried to ameliorate ethnic and religious tensions. Sometimes that meant separating the men who were having difficulties. Junior officer Edwin Mann recalled that in his unit stateside "a Jew that said he was being picked on for being a Jew—Someone was checking this out and I was surprised as I did not know he was Jewish and most of the men did not know or care—anyway they transferred him out of the Div. before leaving USA."[81] Other times, the threat of retribution from the army could solve the problem. Franklin Gurley had to deal with a situation while in his specialized training program. When a Jewish man who had immigrated from Palestine earned a promotion to cadet company commander, a couple of men in the unit became angry and demanded that all the Jewish cadets had to move out of the dormitory floor that they shared. "We've had enough of being so closely associated with those people," one of them said. The rest of the non-Jewish men on the floor unanimously opposed the two inflamed cadets, and told them so. Gurley himself became angry and said, "We're in this war to fight some nasty bastards, and we've got to avoid becoming like them in the process." When Gurley and the majority threatened that the army would punish the two anti-Semites, they backed down.[82]

That such a threat would work indicated that some of the men recognized that the army could and would act to oppose open bigotry among ethnic and religious groups in the ranks. As a result, cases of open discrimination remained limited. Generally, the men experienced problems on an individual basis, if at all. Later, when asked about ethnic or religious discrimination, a junior officer in the 11th Airborne Division responded, "Being Jewish I experienced minor anti-Semitic slurs by one individual but [I] can't point to any specific action."[83] Many veterans, regardless of unit or theater of war, gave similar answers to the same question.[84] "Sure, there were some bigots," Kensinger Jones said, "but they were ridiculed."[85] Paratrooper Kenneth Lytton wrote, "I was in a white unit with some Latinos but we had no discrimination within the unit."[86] Paul Miller, another man from the airborne, said, "No—We had almost all religious groups—ethnics were called as one seen them but with respect."[87] Outside of jokes, William McLaughlin could remember little religious or ethnic discrimination.[88] Junior officer Fred Martin from the 1st Cavalry Division said, "No. When the Div. first went overseas it had a high Mexican descent but a mix of a lot of backgrounds. I was Baptist and one of my best friends was the Catholic chaplain as were many of my friends."[89] William A. Bonds answered, "None—my unit was all white and had only one Jew, and a few Spanish and all other nationalities were represented (Irish, German)."[90] West Point graduate and infantryman Joel Thomason from Virginia recalled, "No ethnic or religious discrimination was seen or noted."[91] Missourian Eugene McConachie replied, "None—in my company we had 3 Jews—quite a few Catholics—some Hispanics, no Blacks. I'm a Methodist—we had a number of other denominations. The man in the bunk next to me was a Hispanic, we were good friends."[92] Charles Henne also could not remember any ethnic or religious bigotry.[93]

Even some men from the most besieged groups avoided cases of open bigotry. One example was William Lessemann, who remembered, "As a Jew, I did not feel any discrimination."[94] The issue of holiday leave, which had nearly caused a riot at one base, did not always lead to strife. Caesar Abate of California served in the Pacific theater. His unit had a lot of Jewish soldiers from New York and New Jersey: "They did K.P. [kitchen patrol] on our holidays—we did K.P. on [theirs]."[95] Lloyd Magee had a similar experience: "Jewish soldiers had their holidays off as well as Christian ones. Later, they volunteered for the duties on Christian holidays—never was a major problem, however."[96]

As can be seen from these examples, it was not that the differences in the men necessarily led to hostility. Indeed, some saw this mixing of Americans as a chance to expand horizons, such as Kentuckian D. C. Perguson, who enjoyed meeting "every kind of person."[97] For others, the wide variety of people was just another surprise of army life. As Boston native Christopher Mauriello put it in a letter home, "What an assortment of characters we have collected here."[98] However, the primacy the men put on noting their differences indicated the breadth of the divides between them. Their focus on differences said something about the society from which they came and the way they saw themselves and their fellow countrymen. They looked around in the army and saw southerners and westerners, city boys and country bumpkins, Catholics, Jews, Baptists, Methodists, Lutherans, Germans, Irish, Mexicans, Poles, Italians, and so on. The did not see each other as just soldiers or, more important, just Americans.

For the army, stopping or limiting open ethnic or religious discrimination among the troops was one thing, getting the men to actually get along was something else entirely. Randomly mixing men from all over the country and stripping them down so they were without their familiar clothes, haircuts, friends, or homes was just the beginning of this process, but it was an important beginning. These stripped-down, friendless, out of place individuals could look around and see that for all their ethnic and religious differences, the strangers around them were just as stripped-down, friendless, and out of place. The men had that, at least, in common. The rest of their lives in the army would build on that common ground. Once the army had thrown these various men together and literally stripped them down to their basics, it began the process of building them up as equals.

The haircuts and uniforms were just the start. Once training began, the army laid down specific rules for nearly every aspect of the men's lives. A great deal of time early in training consisted of learning military culture and regulations. As any veteran could testify, adjusting to military life involved absorbing a dizzying array of specialized details. New recruits had to become conversant in army jargon, including terms and abbreviations such as "tattoo," "latrine," "mess," "KP," "PX," and "PT." They had to learn the army ranking system; the differences between enlisted men, noncommissioned officers, and commissioned officers; and the uniform insignias that went with each rank. They had to learn when to salute, who to call "sir," and when to take off their caps. Different uniforms had different names, and the men had to know the appropriate uniform for any given situation. In addition, the army insisted on a clear arrangement for everything, from making beds to placing shoes in a specific spot, to stowing bags or trunks in a specific way. The focus on details could be seen in the diary entry of one man: "Again we were marched back to the barracks and were shown how to make up a bunk by placing one sheet over the mattress and making square corners and then placing the second sheet with a blanket over it, then folding down one end of this second sheet and blanket in eight inch folds. The two other blankets were placed folded at the head of the bed on which you placed the pillow."[99] The army had a reason for this attention to detail, this focus on the little things. As one written guide assured the new recruits, the purpose of army privileges and regulations were "to give all men, within the respective ranks and grades, the same rights and the same obligations, regardless of financial status, social prestige, race, color, or religion."[100] Everyone had to make the bed the same way.

Once they understood the basic regulations, the men spent the bulk of their time at close and extended order drill, marching and physical training, and weapons and tactical training.[101] A typical training day consisted of the men waking sometime between 5:00 and 5:55, a march and reveille, a wash-up and shave before breakfast by 6:30, drill and training from breakfast to lunch at noon, drill and training again all afternoon with a short break before supper, free time after supper until tattoo, the call to quarters, and taps. The army also spent some time every week educating the men on the causes and goals of the war, something about which the men generally did not like talking.[102] Part of the process involved watching the *Why We Fight* series, including the episodes that focused on equality and tolerance in the United States. It is unclear whether the movies truly convinced the men of the greatness and justness of the Allied cause, but the men did remember the images portrayed in the films long after viewing them.[103] The movies clearly affected at least one soldier, who later recalled, "I loved every one of those Frank Capra films, which to my eighteen-year-old mind perfectly summed up why we were doing what we were doing."[104]

The other areas of training, especially the physical activities, more clearly helped to engender camaraderie among the men. Close-order drill was one such area. The army had its reasons for lining the men up in tight formations and teaching them how to stand, turn, hold their rifles, and march in unison. As one guide for new soldiers explained, close-order drill helped "to get a group of men from one place to another in the shortest time and without confusion, and to train soldiers quickly to co-ordinate mind and body" to prepare them for advanced training. "A secondary function of close-order drill is that it develops a smart-looking company or regiment," the guide continued. "That, in turn, builds morale."[105] At least one soldier actually enjoyed close-order drill, mostly because of an excellent instructor. He recalled, "Close-order drill, intended to make men instantly responsive to commands, also works to weld them together through their being parts of maneuvers in unison, a physical bonding at the same time partaking of the primitive elements of rhythm and something akin to dance."[106] He may have been correct, but nevertheless almost all of the men found close-order drill insufferable. As one veteran said, "Too much time is spent on close order drill, which is pretty but doesn't make fighters. You won't stop a tank by doing present arms in front of it!" Surveys of the troops during the war found an overwhelming dislike for drilling both during and after training.[107] Close-order drill helped create camaraderie not so much by getting the men to act in unison as by creating among the men a mutual dislike for drill itself.

Along the same lines, it was not too long in training before the army introduced the men to KP, kitchen patrol. All of the mouths to feed meant a lot of food to prepare and pots, pans, dishes, and facilities to clean. Men on kitchen patrol prepared that food and cleaned those dishes. Bruce Carson described his KP assignments in a letter home: "The first time, I worked in the butcher shop quartering big slabs of bacon, scraping the floor, sanding, mopping, and finally loading and unloading big quarters of beef. My second visit with the K.P. was spent in the dining room. Here I mopped, scrubbed, mopped, scrubbed till well past eight. As a little reward for services well rendered, I received two nice red apples from the Sergeant as I left."[108] So reviled was the duty that enlisted men often drew KP as punishment for various transgressions. In the regular course of army life, everyone had to take their turn at the KP, and everyone hated it—so much so that it was one thing they could all agree on. As one man wrote of his experience in the kitchen, "There is nothing like K.P. to draw the men together and make them forget little misunderstandings that might cause friction." With no small amount of irony he concluded, "K.P. is wonderful."[109]

The same went for forced marches with heavy packs. The army sought to build stamina in the troops so they could handle the extensive marching ahead of them in the war, but the men saw the marches as torture. One veteran told a story shortly after the war that illustrated how much the men came to despise forced marches. O. A. Kennerly recalled waking at five o'clock in the morning dreading the thirty mile hike to come. He contemplated feigning illness or insulting the sergeant to get in trouble so he could do anything but the march. When he noticed the other men sleeping past the five o'clock whistle, he yelled, "Hit the deck, you goldbricks. If I can't sleep, then you sure as hell can't." Kennerly concluded, "A shower of G.I. shoes rained down on me and I heard glorious words and wonderful news: 'Go back to sleep, you fool. This is Sunday.'"[110] The men's mutual dislike for the marches, like their dislike for close-order drill and KP, united them. One man from what would become the 10th Mountain Division even wrote a song called "Ninety Pounds of Rucksack" about the camaraderie his unit developed in training from lugging huge packs around their training camp.[111] More and more the men found things in the army to dislike and distrust other than one another. Like it or not, they were in it together.

If the men resented together close-order drill, kitchen patrol, and forced marches, they at least saw some utility in combat training and larger maneuvers. In one survey, 70 percent of officers who had not yet gone overseas said they needed more training in how to train their men in weapons, equipment, and tactics.[112] Upon looking back from combat, the majority of men in another survey thought long forced marches helped soldiers out in the war, but not nearly as much as "going through tough, realistic battle conditions on maneuvers."[113] Since most of the men liked, or at least understood, maneuvers, a different sort of camaraderie developed out of the physical training in the field.

For one thing, the men developed a casual acceptance of the physical familiarity that had so shocked them at first. The troops shared certain physical ailments that became prevalent because of physical training. The running, forced marches, and extended maneuvers wore at the feet of the soldiers. Blisters became a common problem, and as a result the men got to know each other's feet pretty intimately. Some of the men training in the South met chiggers, small insects that dug in under the skin and had to be removed one by one. These pests led to gatherings of soldiers in various stages of undress as either their buddies or aid men helped to remove the vermin from hard to reach places.[114] If checking feet for blisters and removing chiggers from delicate areas were not enough, the troops in training became even more familiar with the bodily functions of their comrades. Of course, all the while the men continued to sleep in open barracks or tents and bathe, urinate, and defecate in full sight of each other, but training added some new twists. For example, paratroopers in training who embarked on their first training jumps could share a fear that manifested itself in a very physical way. Of his second jump, George Veach remembered, "I wanted to heave up my guts. I looked around and saw my green-faced buddy, who was vomiting into the bucket. By the time he had made way for me, it was too late. Up it came, all over my legs and the floor."[115] Men in field exercises also had to relieve themselves, and one soldier with a penchant for drawing penned a cartoon for a letter home from field training called "Mutual Support Latrine." It depicted two men holding themselves up by squatting back to back with their pants pulled down.[116] All of the physical familiarity brought out ribald humor from the men. A running joke in Carl Becker's training unit involved goosing—"poking between the buttocks"—during morning roll call. The goose would illicit a shout from the victim and muffled laughter from the rest of the men.[117]

At times the physical familiarity led to sexual confusion among some of the troops. Boys who had little or no experience with close physical contact with anyone, male or female, before entering the army all of a sudden found themselves faced with a variety of young men with a variety of sexual interests.[118] These men had to grapple with physical attraction toward some fellow soldiers in an army that treated homosexuality as a serious crime.[119] Whether or not sexual feelings toward their comrades entered the minds of most soldiers, the point was that army training brought the men closer together physically. They learned the lesson that vomiting, diarrhea, blisters, chiggers, thirst, hunger, and exhaustion affected everyone, no matter their ethnic or religious backgrounds.

Another camaraderie developed out of the loneliness, frustration, and exhaustion created by training: The men began to find friends among the strangers. The soldiers became buddies. Individual soldiers paired up and became fiercely loyal to each other. The choice of buddies tended to be pretty arbitrary in the beginning. The men made friends with those who happened to be nearest them in the barracks. As two veterans wrote, "The unfamiliar situation and the need felt for someone to share the discomforts and perplexities of the new life were sufficient basis for the buddy relationship."[120] Andrew Nelson, who thought the first few weeks in the service were the toughest, wrote, "Gradually this wears off and you get your confidence from training and those around you. Particular attention should be paid to the morale of the new recruit. The Buddy system is a real important factor in keeping morale up."[121]

Some men only had one close friend, but the buddy system did not always limit itself to pairs. The troops often belonged to a circle of close friends. The buddy system and expanded circle of friends helped the men adjust to army life. One soldier wrote home to his mother, "Now that I'm here I'm satisfied. Already I have made friends and have a feeling of companionship. I've never had it before. They call me 'Minnesota' because most of us can remember the state rather than the name."[122] Because the soldiers did not pick who bunked near them, these friendships necessarily crossed ethnic and religious lines. Even later on in training and service, when many of the men began to make friends based on their interests or occupations as civilians, those friendships continued to ignore ethnic and religious differences.[123]

In the later months of training and as the soldiers moved out of training camps and on to their stateside posts, they began to have more free time to relax and spend the money they had earned for their service. Since the army took care of food and board, the men tended to be frivolous with their spending, and they did so as buddies. Gambling became pretty standard early on in training, especially once the men drew their first pay. They played all sorts of card games, and craps continued at camp. "On pay day you could hear the dice hit against the latrine wall," one soldier remembered.[124] Sometimes individual ethnic groups among the troops helped the men enjoy their time off more. Kensinger Jones said, "We had a large Hispanic contingent and they brightened our lives with music."[125] Raul Morin, a Mexican American soldier, agreed that Mexican American soldiers brought a culture of music to the army, and songs such as "Soldado Razo" (Common Soldier) were popular among those troops.[126]

Later in training or in stateside posts, relaxation could involve visiting the towns near the training camp or base. More often than not, the off-duty soldiers looked to alcohol to help blow off steam on these excursions. "Up to that time, I'd drunk a beer or two but had never gotten plastered or even well organized," Charles Kelly wrote, "but now I began to discover that a few beers could be a lot of fun."[127] A paratrooper training in Panama had a similar experience, only with an added twist, courtesy of the treatment for malaria:

"It seems strange that beer and quinine can make men so drunk and crazy in such a short time."[128] So prevalent was this drinking on and around military camps that civilians took notice. As a result, some civilian groups mobilized to try to get the government to try to restrict the sale of alcohol to soldiers. One such appeal to President Roosevelt implored him to "take action to stop the sale of beer in commissaries, to prevent the sale or gift of intoxicating liquors including beer to soldiers and sailors in uniform anywhere and to do all that is within your power to erase vice from around our military establishments."[129] Despite such protests and limited efforts on the part of the army to curtail drinking, soldiers found plenty of alcohol throughout their service. And not all of the alcohol went to benders. One man recalled spending a furlough with one of his buddies. He went to the hospital for the birth of his friend's little boy. Afterward, they celebrated over some beers. The friend died in the Philippines when an artillery shell blew off his leg.[130]

Some soldiers took longer to make friends and adjust to army life. Raymond Gantter, who was older and had more education than the average, found that he had quite a bit of trouble relating to the other men. "And that was the hardest thing to bear," he later wrote, "the sense of being shut out from some warm and mysterious camaraderie that . . . was the only thing that could make army life tolerable." Despite his background, Gantter eventually made his way into that camaraderie. "The astonishing thing," he later commented, "is that in spite of regional differences, social differences, religious, political, and economic differences, men learn to work together and live together."[131]

A few individuals never quite fit in with the rest of the men. Maynard Marquis of Ohio was one such man. He recalled, "I was assigned to H Company, 2nd Battalion. . . . This was originally the Maryland National Guard. Most of the men were from Maryland, Virginia and Pennsylvania. I had nothing in common with anyone. They were all friendly and we got along fine, but I did not form a close friendship with anyone. I became a loner. I depended on myself only."[132] Nor did every man like what he learned about his comrades. Ray Mitchell told his wife that "the men I served with were some of the meanest individuals I've ever known."[133] Likewise, Roscoe Blunt "felt segregated from the rest of L Company." He wrote fifty-five years after the war's end, "My squad was not a closely-bonded unit. In fact, I would be hard pressed to name them."[134] A man who eventually served in the 4th Infantry Division explained the position of most of the men: "There was a lot of the guys that I liked that were good soldiers. You're always going to find rotten apples in any outfit, no matter where you are."[135]

Although a few of the men remained loners, most buddied up and formed circles of friends. But friendship was not the only form of camaraderie in the military that crossed ethnic and religious lines. The army also managed to foster feelings of unit and branch pride. As the men progressed through training and settled into their specific squads, platoons, companies, troops, batteries, battalions, regiments, and divisions, they increasingly began to identify themselves with those units. The feeling began with the squads and platoons and then expanded. In a letter to his wife from basic training, Robert Easton wrote, "I wish you could know the comradeship our platoon—particularly my 6th section—has developed."[136] Robert Thobaben considered his training platoon the "psychic home" of his military experience.[137] Morris Pockler saw his war from the perspective of "a company and squad."[138] For a variety of reasons, companies in the army had special importance for many men. At a prescribed strength of 200 to 250 men (but in practice usually somewhat smaller), the company was the largest unit that still felt small enough for the men to know one another. The company was the lowest level in the army command system to have an administrative structure and staff. Companies often felt like a family to the men, with the company commander and first sergeant acting as sort of surrogate parent figures, especially overseas.[139]

Unit pride extended beyond companies, troops, and batteries, but in a different way. Important as they were to the soldiers, the smaller units did not usually show up on maps or in newspapers. One of the most common complaints of the fighting men in World War II was that from their positions on the ground they had no understanding of the big picture of the war.[140] The big picture would help them to understand what they were doing, and just as important, they wanted the people at home to recognize their role in the fight.[141] To grasp the big picture, to explain their role in the war, the men had to look higher than companies, troops, and batteries. Regiments and divisions, and eventually corps and armies, gave the men a broader perspective and made it possible for friends and families at home to follow their war. As a result, all men made sure their loved ones knew their regiment and division, and most veterans identified with those units. One of many examples came from two veterans who wrote their unit's history. They served in "K Company, of the 333rd Infantry Regiment, 84th Infantry Division."[142] When the men on the front in that K Company read periodicals on the war, they would most likely not find their company in stories or on maps. But the 333rd Infantry Regiment and 84th Infantry Division covered larger swaths of territory and fit more easily into larger descriptions of the fighting. Similarly, people outside the military could not follow K Company in newspapers or newsreels but maybe could follow the 333rd Infantry Regiment and certainly could follow the 84th Infantry Division. This process of identifying with regiments and divisions began in training, and it led many of the men to feel some pride for their larger units. Some even found that their regiment or division had a long and proud history. Jack Gray explained the feeling when he spoke of the mystique of the 1st Infantry Division: "Somehow or other, you take a new man, a recruit, and when he put that number one on his shoulder, he becomes a different man. Pride in any outfit makes any outfit. Regardless if it's army, business, home or whatever it is, if you've got pride, you got it all."[143] Franklin Gurley found that he had an intense pride in his 100th Infantry Division and the infantry generally by the end of his training.[144]

The army even did a fairly good job of engendering pride in the men for the various branches in which they served. In some cases this process was easier. The more technical fields like the signal corps, the quartermasters, ordnance, and engineers offered soldiers an opportunity to practice more specialized skills. As a result, the men tended to have pretty high opinions of their branches.[145] Elite units, like the Rangers, mountain troops, or especially the airborne forces, enjoyed the advantage of being specialized. The men in those areas took great pride in their expert status or the difficulty of their work.[146] A Jewish paratrooper explained of the arduous life in an airborne division, "In the parachute troops we were all usually 'in the same boat.'"[147] At first glance, the infantry might seem to be an exception to the rule, but it was not. With the public, and new recruits, the infantry did suffer from the worst reputation of all the branches. Infantry was the place where the army sent all of the least qualified recruits to be grunts. Of the respondents to one wartime survey of three divisions in training, 25 percent of infantrymen liked their own branch the least in the army, while only 28 percent liked it the most.[148] But over time, and especially after they went overseas, infantrymen began to feel a kind of underdog pride in their branch—a feeling that only the toughest could survive the dirty assignments and scant respect given the infantry.[149] The army encouraged this pride by awarding the Expert Infantryman Badge for excellence in training and the famous blue Combat Infantryman Badge for infantrymen who saw battle.[150] The wartime squad, platoon, company, troops, battery, regiment, division, and branch became a lifelong fraternity that transcended ethnicity or religion. The men who served in those units in World War II would always have that bond, at least.

Throughout the war, one of the other ways the men built camaraderie was by defining who was outside of it. Enlisted men made up the bulk of the army, and their list of outsiders almost always included officers. As the buddy system and unit and branch pride developed, these smaller social groups of enlisted men reacted against the hierarchical army system. Nothing symbolized the army hierarchy like saluting. One book for new soldiers insisted that there was no caste system in the U.S. military, that officers earned their status due to merit, not background. In any case, the guide insisted, "You are not saluting the officer as a person. You are paying your respects to the position he holds and the responsibilities he bears."[151] But the men saluted because they had no choice. It was not that they necessarily resented the act of saluting, just that saluting was part of a rigidly hierarchical social structure that went counter to their individualistic instincts. As two veterans noted, the army was a place where two friends from before the war, an officer and enlisted man, "walked around an Army camp for three hours, as there was no place on the post where they could go together."[152] The men resented such a system and the pettiness of officers abusing their status and power.[153]

A good example was Company E of the 506th Regiment of the 101st Airborne Division, which in training had a company commander who was nearly universally reviled by the men under his command. As the unit prepared for combat, one man recalled, "Addressing his platoon sergeant, and to all within speaking range, he said, 'Sergeant, I want you to understand that you have my permission to shoot any man who does not obey any order given from here on out.' I thought this was a hell of a pompous statement to make. We are soldiers, and soldiers are conditioned to obedience. Why make such a remark?"[154] This particular officer happened to be Jewish, which led to some verbal barbs. As Walter Scott Gordon said, he saw no discrimination in the service, "except we disliked a Jewish company commander and we salted our language with references of him being Jewish and of doubtful parentage."[155] In this case, the ethnic and religious slurs were a side effect of a different disdain. The men of that unit, of all backgrounds, credited that officer with uniting them against him because of his behavior and actions.[156] One officer in the unit recalled that the company commander's "disciplinarian actions, which went too far in many cases, became the catalyst that made E company into one unit. The men seemed to hate him so much that they were bound together."[157] His was an especially acute and personal case, but it was just as true that the enlisted men united against officers for perceived or real slights.

The men gave this type of behavior a name: "chickenshit" (sometimes abbreviated to "chicken"). Chicken, wrote two veterans, "refers to the emphasis on petty regulations, such as polishing shoes, keeping the area clean, and saluting . . . [or] any order which is given for the sake of military regulation rather than for the performance of some particular purpose."[158] As one veteran said, "Chickenshit can be recognized instantly because it never has anything to do with winning the war."[159] One survey found that 70 percent of the enlisted men who participated thought they had to put up with too much chicken in the army.[160]

The system did not necessarily convince the men that they were inferior or superior because of rank. Most of the men looked forward to the day when they would be out of the hierarchical military and thus be able to prove they were better than their officers, especially the ones they considered chickenshit. And plenty of officers at various ranks got along quite well with enlisted men. Once the men entered combat, company commanders in particular seemed to be well respected by the men.[161] But at some point the large mass of men saw themselves as united in opposition to officers at one level or another who did not understand the experiences of the men or exploited their positions at the expense of the men.

At the Second Army Tennessee Maneuvers in May 1943, the soldiers of Company F, 347th Infantry Regiment, Eighty-seventh Infantry Division stand by for inspection. Army training had the dual effect of making the men look uniform while building camaraderie among the new soldiers. Courtesy of U.S. Army Center of Military History.

The men knew that their training and stateside service had begun to change the way they looked at themselves and their fellow soldiers. Everything about life in the army helped them realize that they could work and live together despite the differences that had seemed so important before the war. Bruce Carson wrote to his family about the men in his advanced training, "One meets the usual percentage of natural comedians, sneak thieves, office boys, country boy 'slickers' . . . , ex-bank clerks, preacher's sons, truck drivers, school teachers, and just plain tramps that one might find in any cross section of the country." But, he continued, "the fact that we're all in the 'same boat,' and all have the same worries, the same jobs, the same pleasures helps a lot to make living together easier."[162] In Warren Fitch's unit, "there was an even mix of rural, city, and religions, so everybody had to work at the main goal."[163] One veteran who served in the Chaplain Corps wrote of the training experience, "The change from civilian to military life came very fast and went smoothly. . . . The donning of a uniform, being quartered with other men of varying backgrounds, the meticulous following of an imposed routine to which you submit without question, had the effect of shock treatment. You were transformed, as it were, in one operation from a civilian into a member of the armed forces, or into a G.I., as the army lingo termed it."[164]

The new connections touched many of the men. Louis Banks remembered that as a soldier he "felt proud to salute and look around and see all the good soldiers of the United States."[165] Timid before joining, Robert Lekachman discovered in the army that he "could cheerfully get along with various kinds of people."[166] Robert Thobaben said of his training platoon, "We started our training isolated and estranged from one another. But three and one-half months later we were a genuine unit. We were bound by a hundred common experiences. We had become friends."[167] For Robert Easton, the bonds created by military service elicited even deeper emotions. He wrote to his wife, "I never knew what it meant to love a fellow human until I came into the army—not man-woman love, of course, but that abiding recognition of a link, a bond, a common source and destiny."[168]

Perhaps no one summed up the experience of induction and training quite as well as Mexican American soldier Raul Morin:

> Basic training life was a very interesting experience. Finding ourselves in a new setting away from the old surroundings, with new faces, new friends, and everyone in the same boat, put us on an equal status. Most impressive was the smooth way that Americans of all nationalities were assimilated in their new life. . . .
>
> We were so engrossed in our new chores of soldier life, and so aware of an uncertain future, that no room was left for anyone to be choosy about

his neighbor. No one went about demanding special treatment, or complaining about unequal opportunities.

Here we learned all there was to know about each other. In the course of our continuous association, all characteristics, personal traits and individualisms were openly revealed so that no one could hide anything from the other.

Rich or poor, light or dark, the educated and the ignorant—all were thrown together to accomplish the same objective, mainly that of learn-ing military skills; and we all were subjected to the same rude Army discipline. Our inert qualities were discovered and the superficial appearances soon wore off.[169]

Induction, training, and service in the United States turned millions of men and boys from all over the country and of all different backgrounds into American soldiers. Their relationships as soldiers transcended ethnicity and religion, but it was just the beginning. The military experience in World War II still had plenty to teach them about what it meant to be an American.

# 4

# HOURS OF BOREDOM

By contrasting their memories of home with their observations abroad, our soldiers learn overseas what makes America a good place to live in.

— "What We Have Learned Overseas
About America," *Army Talk,* 1945

LIFE CONTINUED AMID THE MAELSTROM. FOR ALL THAT HAPPENED IN THOSE
epochal years, service in the army in World War II actually proved to be pretty
boring most of the time. The boredom was especially acute after the shock
and excitement of induction and training. Often the men did not train with
a unit slated for regular service, so it was not until after basic that they would
join their outfits for deployment overseas. The process of mixing with the
other men began again, but by then the soldiers had experience with making
new comrades. The transition to the more permanent units did not equal the
shock of induction into army life, and the daily responsibilities did not grind
on the men the same way the busy basic training schedule had. Except for the
occasional maneuver, a rather dull routine dominated their lives.[1]

Even when the men did get overseas, they spent a lot of time looking
for something to do. They did not disembark in North Africa, Europe, or the
Pacific and immediately go into combat. In fact, most of the men spent little
or no time under fire. The U.S. Army in World War II only placed a fraction
of its troops in the front lines. When the army was at its greatest strength
in the spring of 1945, only slightly more than a third of the troops in the
ground and service forces actually served in ground combat units.[2] Most of
the soldiers in the service forces never heard a shot fired in anger; many of
the men in combat divisions served in noncombat roles. And even those who
did spend significant time at the front and in battle also spent much of the
war out of the line of fire. All the men, no matter their branch, had a lot of
down time. The old aphorism goes that war is hours of boredom punctuated

by instants of excitement or terror. American soldiers had to fill those hours somehow. Much of what they did to alleviate boredom involved activities that in a variety of ways subtly reminded them that what they had in common far outweighed their ethnic and religious differences.

When the men came together in opposition to their officers and the army's hierarchical system in basic training and later, they revealed the other side of camaraderie. Comradeship was inevitably exclusionary. The military experience was like that—groups of men coming together based in part on real or perceived differences between their group and all kinds of other groups. In most cases, this grouping and exclusion proved to be relatively harmless. But there were notable exceptions.

Most prominent among these was the segregation of African Americans in the army. For a variety of reasons—economic benefits, patriotism, the chance to prove themselves and dispel stereotypes—African Americans wanted to serve in their country's military in World War II. By the end of the war nearly one million black soldiers had filled army ranks. These men faced a hidebound army system that reflected the prejudices and bigotry of larger American society. The army maintained its unfortunate traditions of segregating black soldiers from their white counterparts and assigning large numbers of black troops to physical labor duties. The army also insisted that the best officers for what they called "Negro troops" were white southern men who supposedly knew how to handle African Americans.[3] Of course, all of these hurdles were in addition to the already very difficult transition to army life that all soldiers faced.[4] Black soldiers who wanted only to prove themselves to their country dealt with frustrations at every turn. The positive record of their service was a testament to their constancy.

Yet by and large their white counterparts did not know it. Segregation actually succeeded in keeping many of the white men from engaging in active discrimination against African Americans. One example was paratrooper Herbert Garris, who did not remember much racial discrimination "since the 101st was first-off White." The rest of the troops, he wrote, "blended with a fine workable mix of religious, ethnic, and national components."[5] As Garris's comments indicated, a key effect of segregation was that all the lessons white ethnic and religious soldiers learned about each other did not extend to African Americans. All of the prejudices the white men carried into the war against African Americans went mostly unchallenged.[6] When the white soldiers gathered themselves together as buddies, units, branches, or any other groups, black troops were excluded. That exclusion of black troops all too often took on nasty terms, reflecting all the worst prejudices and discrimination of the day. The white troops remembered it well.

An unusually sensitive soldier described the situation in his Officer Candidate School in 1942: "The white officers are civil but there's no real mixing. What a national disgrace the whole matter is! I discovered last night that Daniels, our one Negro candidate, lives in a room alone where all other 'private' rooms . . . contain at least 3 candidates. He was out so I left a package of cigarettes I'd bought for him on his bed and went away downstairs ashamed of my countrymen—and myself."[7] In April 1944, that same man overheard a fellow officer say, "You can't make soldiers out of jigaboos. Modern war's too complicated. . . . It's too much for a college graduate, let alone a jig!"[8] Edward Tipper said that in his unit, "anti-black feelings were common."[9] Gail Thomas saw several "conflicts between soldiers from southern states and blacks."[10] And officer Richard Winters remembered of his service in the 101st Airborne Division, "In WWII the army was segregated. Most [regiment] and [battalion] C.O.'s were Southern, West Point Officers. We had a lot to learn after the war was over."[11] The unfortunate reality was that the white ethnic and religious soldiers did not get to see their black counterparts in the same light as they saw each other.

Among those white troops, the boredom of army service and the new experiences found overseas strengthened the bonds created in training, while at the same time they gave the men whole new groups to exclude from their circle of camaraderie. Among the most prominent of these groups were the other arms of the military, especially the U.S. Navy. In some cases, the rivalry could reflect a resigned acceptance that the other services, especially the Marine Corps, represented something of an elite force. Because of early personnel policies that sent many of the better educated and more enthusiastic recruits to the navy and marines, even an official army history said those arms "had the character of hand-picked organizations."[12] And the soldiers knew about their reputation. An extreme example came when marine Eugene Sledge met some army men in the Pacific and one of the GIs called him "soldier." Sledge later wrote that the GI's "buddy grabbed him by the shoulder and yelled, 'Stop calling that guy soldier. He's a Marine. Can't you see his emblem? He's not in the army. Don't insult him.'"[13]

For the most part, however, soldiers did not surrender any superiority to other arms. Their pride could be based on friendly competition. For example, most of the men felt like they had a personal stake in the great annual college football rivalry between the army and navy service academies. That loyalty defied individual backgrounds. William Jones came from landlocked southwestern Pennsylvania and never actually got overseas during his service in the navy. When asked which team he backed in the big game he replied, "Who the hell do you think I cheered for?"[14] Army surgeon and German immigrant Klaus Huebner described the scene in 1944 Italy: "December 3 is a big day. The Army-Navy game will be rebroadcast to us tonight. We wait all day for this event."[15] That particular game had special meaning for the soldiers. After losing to Navy for five straight years, Army completed a perfect season in 1944 behind legendary players Glenn Davis and Doc Blanchard. They repeated the feat the next year in front of more than one hundred thousand fans.[16] This interservice competition could be friendly but serious. In the summer of 1944, before embarking for the Continent, Gen. George S. Patton sought to inspire the men of his Third Army by insisting, "We want to get the hell over there. We want to get over there and clean the goddam thing up. And then we'll have to take a little jaunt against the purple-pissing Japanese and clean their nest too, before the Marines get in and claim all the goddam credit!"[17] Sometimes the rivalry became violent. The experience of Carl Becker, who saw several fights break out between soldiers and marines at one port, was all too common.[18]

The trips overseas gave the men plenty of time and reasons to build camaraderie with each other and rivalries with outsiders. Traveling aboard ship across vast oceans proved to be a harrowing ordeal for the men. That is not to say they all hated the voyage, the sailors, or the ships that gave them the ride. In fact, of the respondents in one wartime survey, 54 percent said that their treatment on board ship was very good or pretty good, while 35 percent said it was not so good or very poor.[19] Some men obviously did not mind the trip, and no doubt they could be forgiving later in official surveys because they understood in retrospect the difficult circumstances of their travels.[20] Most likely, those surveyed meant that the treatment was good or pretty good given those circumstances. This retrospective understanding and moderation did not mean that the men did not have plenty of complaints about life at sea. Indeed the voyages overseas and later trips aboard ships actually became something of a microcosm of their entire service—conflating physical familiarity, boredom punctuated by moments of intense excitement or fear, and new or renewed rivalries.

No matter their final destination—and of ground and service soldiers, approximately three million were in Europe in April 1945, with a little over one million in the various Pacific theaters—the men universally complained of cramped and nasty conditions aboard ship.[21] The American military was doing everything it could to get as many men as possible to distant ports. That meant packing the soldiers in tight. As an indication of the crowded conditions, one man in the 10th Mountain Division won a bet by standing in the middle of the men's bunks and touching forty-two individual bunks with his rifle, all without moving his feet.[22] If the cramped conditions were not bad enough, most of these men had never been on an oceangoing vessel, and they found themselves susceptible to severe cases of seasickness in choppy waters. One veteran recalled that on ship the men "were too crowded to turn around or do anything except be sick to our stomachs, but we did that constantly."[23] There were many variations on this story of misery. For Roscoe Blunt it was "that 6,500 men were being crammed aboard into smelly, temporary living quarters" where they had to deal with "the nauseating stench of diesel fuel."[24]

For Joseph Barrett and the thousands of men aboard his Liberty Ship, a particular problem came from the insufficient and overwhelmed toilet facilities:

> It was a long metal trough with a five inch board on either side which ran along the inside of the hull. The type used on farms to feed pigs. I had to climb in an open doorway at one end and eventually exited at another doorway some 20 feet away. To get there I had to straddle the trough by placing a foot on either board and hobbled along until I found a space big enough to squat. If several soldiers were ahead of me having a not too peaceful crap, I literally stepped over their heads. This was not all that easy. The weather was cool. We were wearing heavy sweaters and field jackets and our ever present steel helmet. Sometimes, if it was at a busy hour, we had to squeeze between the two other men. The view from behind, and I really mean from behind some who is squatting, is not exactly like the view of Mount Everest in early morning covered with mist. The damn ship was rolling and pitching in the heavy sea, while a strong stream of sea water was roaring along the narrow, shallow trough like a tidal wave barely beneath naked rumps.[25]

Sidney Bowen's transport had individual toilet bowls, but there "wasn't an individual flushing system; a master tank overhead periodically flushed the toilets. Certain of the tricky bowls gave a cold sea-water douche to whatever anatomy hung into them." Of course, once the ship got to sea and the passengers encountered their first wave of seasickness, "the latrine was a scene to upset the strongest of stomachs. Vomit covered the floors and fixtures. No one was apparently assigned to clean the place."[26] Dean Joy said it smelled like a locker room in the cramped quarters, and even the saltwater showers they took every other day "left us feeling sticky with salt and the residue of caustic GI soap lather."[27]

Ben Hurwitz, a twenty-year-old soldier, drew this picture during his trip across the Atlantic and later commented, "This is what the hold of the ship looked like: bunks going all the way up and one ladder. Once you got down there, of course, all of you weren't going to be able to go up the ladder in an emergency. I think there were probably several companies of men down there. It was very noisy and every night was a crap shooter's paradise in the center of the floor." Courtesy of Joshua Brown.

In addition to all the physical travails, the soldiers found little with which to occupy themselves. James McAtamney said, "Life on the ship was boring. We could play cards, tell lies, joke a lot with each other, learn a little bit about each other's background. . . . [But] for most of the army personnel, it was a totally new experience. We came from different parts of the country—first exposure to the ocean, first exposure to a ship."[28] To fill the time the men picked up the gambling they had started back on the trains to basic training. One man even recalled the bizarre spectacle of a card game and religious services held in the same general area. He commented that the soldiers in those rooms had the chance to hear two very different types of prayers at the same time.[29]

In their boredom many of the men read, both on board and later when they spread around Europe and the Pacific. Many of the men who had less education and had never really read preferred to stick with the comic books of their youth. Once they made landfall in the Mediterranean theater, one man described his friends hiding in bushes to get out of KP duty until the sergeant came down, "got a big stick and whacked the big bushes and leaves until he hit a G.I. all snuggled down with *Flash Gordon* and *Little Orphan Annie.*"[30] D. C. Perguson lamented the fact that his fellow soldiers read and passed around comic books instead of reading better literature.[31]

In fact, many of the men who had never before had much of an interest in books turned to reading them, beginning on ship. As demand increased, the government worked with the publishing industry in the United States to print a staggering number and variety of books, all provided free for American servicemen. These books were small paper-bound editions, printed on cheap paper with two columns per page, and bound on the short side of the pages. From 1943 to 1947 almost 123 million copies of some 1,322 different titles of these strange Armed Services Edition books made their way into the hands of soldiers and sailors all over the world.[32] The best example of the widespread distribution of the books came in May 1944, when the men preparing to board their ships for the invasion of Normandy each received an Armed Service Edition along with candy and cigarettes.[33]

The men were profoundly grateful for the diversion. Thanks to the Armed Services Edition books, on the boring trip overseas Joseph Barrett read "great authors from Herman Melville and Walt Whitman to Dorothy Parker and Robert Benchley."[34] Robert Kotlowitz said that because of the editions, every time his transport crossed the Atlantic, "it unloaded another well-read division in the ETO."[35] A chaplain in the Pacific recalled from distributing the books to the troops that "a big item in their morale was having something to read in these long days and long nights that they had in the Pacific."[36] Accompanying the invasion fleet, war correspondent A. J. Liebling reported that the men sprawled all over the decks of their various crafts reading the books. "These little books are a great thing," one private from Brooklyn told him. "They take you away."[37] A tank commander recalled reading Betty Smith's novel *A Tree Grows in Brooklyn* as he waited to embark.[38] Later a veteran would write that he carried a copy of Carl Sandburg's short history of the Civil War, *Storm Over the Land,* in his helmet throughout the Battle of Saipan. "During the lulls in the battle I would read what he wrote about another war and found a great deal of comfort and reassurance," he recalled.[39] A man who drove trucks in New Guinea wrote an illustrative letter to the Council on Books in Wartime after the war:

> In looking back over my short Army career, I find I could have made it much easier for myself if I had done more reading.... The days when no mail is received are not so lonesome when there is an unfinished story around. Then, too, reading takes the mind away from the experiences we have that are so different from the environment we left and keeps you from

concentrating on all the discomforts we have, always looking for things to annoy you, and becoming a slave to self-pity.

You have many readers. I have traded many books with truck drivers. They are worth their weight in gold on those long waits we have at the docks, many times arriving there before the boat is even docked. You will find them in the pockets of the boys who operate the bulldozers. On the Army's new weapon, the landing boats, I have seen a small book with three or four in it fastened to the wall of their engine compartment so they will be dry and easy to find. There are many others who, like myself, find that having so many books available helps us to fill in that time when there are no shows and no letters to answer. They also keep me away from the gambling tables.[40]

The wide distribution of Armed Services Edition books acted as a springboard for the booming paperback book industry that emerged after the war.[41] And clearly all of the reading had an effect on the men themselves. Some college professors noted after the war how their new veteran students were well read in some books. And the authors of the various books in the editions received thousands upon thousands of grateful letters from servicemen who had read their work while in the military.[42] Most important, despite some limited attempts at censorship—for example, from congressional conservatives led by Senator Robert Taft on the eve of the 1944 presidential election—the Armed Services Edition books incorporated a wide selection of titles, many of them exploring controversial issues. The men probably did not consciously notice the egalitarian nature of this variety. "Yet," as one student of the editions has written, "the complete library of ASE volumes—from George Lowther's pulpy *Adventures of Superman* to Lillian Smith's complex study of interracial love, *Strange Fruit*—suggests that the members of the Council and army's ASE selection committee were sensitive to, and in many ways anticipated, the pluralist conception of democracy and culture that was to become an important animating principle of liberalism in the immediate postwar period."[43] And in fact, the reasoning behind censoring the one book that the government chose not to print during the war supports this conclusion. Zane Grey's adventurous western *The Riders of the Purple Sage* originally made the cut but was later dropped because of its negative portrayal of Mormons.[44]

For all of the dull hours to be filled with gambling and reading, the voyages were not all boring—there was, after all, a war on, and the Atlantic Ocean was especially dangerous to crossing ships. German submarines prowled the Atlantic Ocean, looking for Allied vessels to sink, including troop transports. Almost all troop ships came through unscathed, but that did not mean that there were not moments of helpless fear for the soldiers on board or that some ships did not sink. When rumors of German subs in the area spread through the hold, and they invariably did, the soldiers knew they could do nothing to help. They had to trust in hope—hope that the convoys would protect them, hope that the Germans would miss them, hope that they would survive attacks and the cold North Atlantic and be rescued.[45] Although the anxiety was real, actual attacks came up pretty rarely for the soldiers going to Europe. Indeed, less than one-quarter of 1 percent of all the troops shipped to Europe died during the passage.[46] And with the navy in control of vast swaths of the Pacific Ocean, men traveling to destinations in that theater worried less about the threat of submarines than their counterparts on the Atlantic. In fact, quite a few men took advantage of the warmer climes to sun bathe on deck.[47] But they found themselves just as packed in and just as bored as the soldiers on the Atlantic.[48]

When the men were not gambling or reading or dealing with the real and imagined fear of attack, they were antagonizing or being antagonized by the U.S. Navy crews that ran many of the ships. The trips overseas and the jaunts around the war zones only heightened the rivalry between the U.S. Army and U.S. Navy. These men found that each service branch had serious differences of perception. One soldier remembered that he and his fellow soldiers on his transport ship just "couldn't identify with these coast guard men or navy crewmen."[49] Combat engineer Sam Daugherty recalled that the commanding officer of his ship for the Normandy invasion "was so prissy about his ship that he had it roped off so that the troops that were to be passengers could only walk in a very limited number of places." Daugherty continued, "Here we were, the cocky veterans of quite a number of combat landings. So we subjected him to the usual variety of non-Navy terms like 'Where's the toilet?' 'Oh, it's at the front of the boat,' and 'Which side is it on?' 'The right side or the left side?'" The soldiers, Daugherty remembered, took advantage of "every chance we got to put down the Navy a little bit."[50]

The U.S. Navy did not always run the ships that carried the men overseas. For some, the voyage abroad introduced them for the first time to their British allies. The meeting made an impression, though not always a positive one. A major part of the problem came from culinary issues. "It was my first experience with British cuisine," noted one American of the foreign food. "We were served porridge, herring and corned beef."[51] John Bistrica said of the meals on his voyage, "The food was terrible. It was English. If it wasn't for the Oreo cookies, Coca Cola, and the jelly rolls that we had bought from the cooks I think we would have gone hungry."[52] Felix Branham agreed: "Aboard the Queen Mary while we were coming across, we were fed two meals a day, which consisted of corned beef, some powdered eggs occasionally. We would have pickles and mustard and mackerel, and golly, we were so hungry, because the food was just terrible."[53] John Hooper lamented that English sailors "appeared to do their worst" with food. "Some very thick and bitter coffee, and an oatmeal-like gruel with bread and marmalade provided breakfast."[54] Several of the men grew tired of one particular British staple: mutton. "Mutton is served endlessly," wrote an army doctor. "The British must have saved their mutton for years, just for us. . . . I would give a month's salary for a steak."[55] The differences extended beyond food. An enlisted medical technician working on a hospital ship based in England talked about the differences onboard between the Americans and British: "Being a British ship, they had separate messes for privates, for non-coms, officers, British officers, Welsh sailors had their own mess, Scottish engineers and also Irish stewards. . . . The British wanted us to have separate mess and quarters, as per British army, but we changed all that, and all the enlisted men ate and roomed together."[56]

The proximity and conditions shipboard led the men to feel as though, in one doctor's words, "they had lost their identity, and seem to be only numbers."[57] Fortunately, as in training, they were in it together. At times the trips gave them a chance to continue to make new acquaintances. One soldier of Irish descent thought it important to note that two of his new friends met on ship had Italian blood.[58] Through it all—the nasty conditions shipboard, the boredom and fear of the trip, the rivalries with the American and British sailors—they shared their fears and misfortunes onboard as soldiers and as Americans, not as ethnic groups and rarely as religious groups.

Conditions once the men disembarked overseas, whether in Europe, the Mediterranean, or the Pacific, drew the men even closer. The army continued to crowd the troops together, most famously in the railroad cars known as "forty and eights" because they could hold forty men or eight horses.[59] They also packed into the backs of trucks that offered little protection from adverse weather conditions.[60] So even when the men had a little room to move, they sometimes had "to huddle together as the cold in the back of the trucks worsened."[61] At one point late in the war, Dean Joy's unit rode in cattle trailers. "They had no benches, so we sat on our packs and duffle bags," he recalled. "About forty miserable infantrymen were packed like sardines in each vehicle."[62]

These conditions overseas meant that the men got to know each others' bodies, habits, and ailments even more intimately than they had in training.

Men who had not seen a bar of soap in weeks showered or bathed next to each other, all happy just to have some hot water.[63] Describing traveling to a nearby stream in New Guinea, one soldier said, "We no longer regarded it as curious or improper to walk entirely nude along a highway, or to bathe in full view of traffic, since the traffic was invariably military and thus presumably shockproof."[64] In many Asian and south Pacific locales the weather and water were warm enough, and the environment foreign enough, that the men abandoned self-consciousness and embraced naturalism.[65] For men from the quartermaster corps on New Guinea that meant unloading cargoes from arriving trawlers "stark naked, with waves pounding over their heads."[66]

The men in Europe faced a different problem. In the warmer summer months, many of the soldiers made the mistake of trying to lighten their load by jettisoning heavy and bulky extra clothing. When the weather turned cold, these men missed the extra layers. The issue became more severe when the army struggled to keep the troops supplied with winter gear like overshoes. These men had to turn to each other for warmth. George Wilson remembered what he called "refinements in the art of survival" for the cold of the winter of 1944–45. "Our foxholes were just wide enough for two men to sit up facing each other with each one's feet shoved under the other guy's butt," he wrote. "In this way we escaped the surface wind and also trapped enough warm breath and body heat for continued survival."[67] Mortar observer Preston Price described life at the front in Europe that same winter:

> As the temperature continues to drop each day and high winds begin to make the temperature seem even colder, we are forced into "bundling," an expedient for warmth at night. Each night my radio operator and I huddle as close to each other as possible and draw what blankets we have around our bodies to keep out the cold. Higgins tells me on several occasions that I am as warm as a hot-water bottle. I cannot say the same for Higgins, who seems to be a cold-blooded person. . . . Nevertheless, I am grateful for what little added warmth this brings, and we continue to sleep together in our sleeping holes until the bad weather abates.[68]

When the weather chilled them to the bone, the men could care less about the ethnicity or religion of the warm body of the other soldier in the foxhole.

That kind of proximity also meant that the men had a pretty intimate knowledge of the bodily functions of their comrades. For example, if one of the men in a unit had a painful condition like hemorrhoids, the rest of the men knew about it.[69] Just before D-Day, Leo Lick had a buddy who "thought that he had better have his hemorrhoids taken care of. They took him to the aids station, gave him a local anesthetic, removed the hemorrhoids, and returned him to the barracks. Needless to say he was in misery for the next couple of days, but when we hit the cold salt water on the Normandy beach the U.S. Army, the doctors, the Germans, and the war had some choice names assigned to them that weren't fit to print."[70]

For troops serving in more tropical settings, the cause and frequency of some ailments were different but the familiarity the same. The men there dealt with a foreign environment where it could rain all the time but they would be short of potable water. They encountered strange new flora like the tall sharp kunai grass of islands like New Guinea and Guadalcanal that could slice open a man's exposed skin if he did not pay attention.[71] They worried about odd and frightening creatures like crocodiles, poisonous snakes, centipedes, and all manner of biting insects. They contracted malaria, dengue fever, and scrub typhus, and a host of other maladies.[72] The men, regardless of background, shared the knowledge and fear of all of these threats.

Diarrhea was one malady that followed the army no matter where it went. It was so common, in fact, that the men developed a new term to describe its universality among soldiers: "the GIs." The Pacific and Asia theaters especially saw large numbers of cases of diarrhea as a result of dysentery. One veteran of the China-Burma-India theater recalled the common fact that he could not help but know that almost all of the men in his unit had diarrhea.[73] The same went for the European theaters. Hebert Campbell recalled, "I had a friend by the name of James Boyle, and they had issued us long underwear. . . . Well, anyway, he had on his long underwear, and one night he had to go to the latrine, so he went tearing out, it was probably 50, 75 feet from our tent, so he went tearing out, and he came back with no underwear. He said, 'I just couldn't make it.'"[74] Raymond Gantter had diarrhea while on the front line. He described the problem: "It's not modesty that bothers us . . . it's snipers. . . . We wipe on the run—our naked and chilled buttocks quivering in anticipation of a bullet—and button up again when we're once more safe in the dugout."[75]

The close proximity of the men and the circumstances of the war meant that they also shared knowledge of normal bodily functions. When trapped in foxholes by enemy action or inclement weather, either alone or in pairs, men had to improvise to answer nature's call. According to an officer in Europe, the "choice . . . would be a form of constipation or, in cases of extreme emergency, measures too indelicate to mention."[76] Another veteran explained that "when a man had to defecate, he did it in his K-ration box and threw it over the side; when he had to urinate he did it in a C-ration can or his helmet or in the bottom of his hole. Conditions were primitive and you learned quickly to improvise."[77] The personal habits and lack of sanitation among the men became common knowledge. One man recalled of a fellow soldier, "You know, steel helmets we used for everything. He used them to dig a foxhole, he used them to cook in, he used them to do your laundry in, and when you're on a ten mile hike, when you're on a break, you used them as a pillow. Well . . . one night, he invited me over for some hot chocolate. He had taken a D-bar, you shave 'em up, put water in 'em, heat it, you've got hot chocolate. So I turned down the invitation, because the night before, he had been there washing his socks and underwear out in his helmet, so I didn't feel like I wanted any part of it."[78]

Adventures in illness and bodily functions neither filled the time nor alleviated boredom. John Barnes had a common experience behind the lines: "For weeks we did nothing but lay around in our tents writing letters and talking and going to movies and talking and playing cards. It was boring to begin with, but it was also beginning to get tense. We began to talk too much and play football too hard."[79] In a few cases, the boredom itself sufficed to unite the troops. Not everyone went to the more famous zones of the war. The Allies maintained bases in isolated locations like Greenland. The cold emptiness on that huge island offered little to distract the men, so they grew even closer as they sought "to ease the bleakness of almost total isolation."[80] In all cases, the soldiers tried myriad activities to fill the hours of boredom. They wrote letters, played games, gambled, and listened to music.[81] They hunted for souvenirs of the war, even to the point of looting from battlefields, civilian homes, and churches. Barnett Hoffner of New York had to stop two men from taking money from a box on a church in Normandy. The men, he noted, "were from Alabama and they knew nothing of the Catholic religion. They wanted the coins as souvenirs."[82]

They joked with one another, looking for a cheap laugh to kill time. "In the military . . . tension and frustration were kept in check by laughing at others and their misfortunes," wrote one veteran. "It was accepted behavior. You either laughed or were laughed at, and to take offense was not allowed."[83] Joseph Barrett remembered a bad day at war as part of a long convoy: "Everyone was tired and hungry and someone would call out in a perfect imitation of President Roosevelt: 'I hate waahr. My wife Eleanor hates waahr. My dog Fala hates waahr.' And everyone would laugh. The tension was broken."[84] Artilleryman Jerry Kimball remembered, "There were lots of times when everything was quiet and most men had nothing to do. On one of these occasions several men were sitting around, lots of conversation was going on. One boy said, 'The first thing I am going to do when I get home is go to bed with my Old Lady,' others agreed. One guy that had been real quiet said, 'You know the second thing I am going to do . . .' After several others inquired what, his answer was 'Set down my suitcase.'"[85]

In addition to being bored, the relatively well fed U.S. Army seemed always to be hungry. To alleviate both boredom and hunger, American soldiers went on what seemed like a worldwide scavenger hunt for food to supplement and spice up their regular diet of army rations. Sometimes the food came from the troops themselves, in the form of care packages or homemade dishes. Robert Easton wrote to his wife and described a sergeant cooking an Italian dish called pasta fagioli (pasta with beans) at a camp in the United States. "The result," he wrote, "is beyond description."[86] One Italian American soldier wrote home and announced that he had received a package containing "cheese sticks, pepperoni, lots of gum, a can of ravioli, and lots of bicourti [sic]. The boys here are crazy over biscourti [sic]."[87] The same soldier complained about the lack of pepperoni in a later package, claiming, "Pepperoni is the favorite food here." In any case, he added later, "It's the Italian touch that we missed."[88] This diverse fare only whetted their appetites for more food and more variety.

Unfortunately for them, they often struggled to find good food in foreign lands. Millions of the men who traveled to Europe and the Mediterranean spent some time in England, and hundreds of thousands who went to the Pacific theaters went through Australia.[89] They found much of the local diet as unpalatable as the food aboard British ships. August Bruno said, "The thing is they used to give us a pass—I forget how many days—to go to London for two or three days. . . . The food was a little different for us there. We had Brussel sprouts, no end, and mutton, which I don't want to look at again."[90] Robert Peters, who also did not take to British cuisine, recalled "sausages made of animal fat mixed with farina [a type of cereal], greasy eggs, and horrid kidney and pork pies that were often rancid and moldy. We despised tea. . . . We also hated their 'sandwiches,' small triangles cut from saw-dust bread, smeared with too much butter, on top of which they plunked a shaving of peculiar cucumbers resembling no cucumber of any kind we knew at home."[91] Ray Aebischer recalled his time in England before D-Day: "Aldbourne, the name of our village, was a two-pound taxi jump from Swindon, so we visited there quite often, hoping to see some bright lights, but found only blackout, most of the pubs closed, and long queues in front of fish and chip shops that were open. For weekend and 3 day passes, London was the favorite place, with numerous Red Cross Clubs that had meals, and various forms of recreation."[92] In Australia, American money went far, and the men spent it on goods such as ginger beer and meat pies. Generally, though, the men ate American food on American bases and did not find the main staples of Australian food any more appetizing than their compatriots found British fare (with the exception of the much-loved Australian steaks). One soldier recalled the men joking that "the mutton might not have been so bad if only they'd sheared the sheep more closely before cooking it."[93]

Many of the men who went to the Pacific never stopped in Australia, and they found their local food choices even more limited in the islands. E. J. Kahn said of New Guinea, "That the natives and the Americans basically had little in common is perhaps best proved by the fact that the former regarded bully beef as a treat. . . . They had other bizarre tastes; after one American rifleman had shot a crocodile, the body didn't come up to the surface for three days, and then some natives leaped upon the mellowing corpse, cooked it, and urged the Yanks to join the feast. The invitation was declined with polite shudders."[94] The soldiers in Europe had more luck, but the pickings could still be pretty slim. On the way to Italy, the men in one unit asked a couple of Italian American comrades "if they had decent spaghetti where we were going."[95] They did occasionally find a cheap or free meal in Italy, France, or elsewhere on the Continent, but most of the time they would happily settle for the rare fresh egg, a staple of their diets at home. All of the trouble finding good food overseas was a reminder of what they all expected at home in the United States, regardless of their supposed differences.

When the American troops were not looking for food, they had drinking in mind. In Italy and France soldiers found new ways to inebriate themselves. A soldier in the 10th Mountain Division visited an Italian village and enjoyed hot soup and grappa with an Italian family. "The grappa," he wrote, "burned a ring down my throat."[96] In the campaigning through northern France, the men pretty much universally experienced a local liquor called calvados, apple brandy. It was strong stuff and not to everyone's liking. One man said that after one sip he "vowed once again to remain a teetotaler."[97] Sometimes the local drinks did not prove strong enough for American tastes. "Some of the guys had gotten a hold of some of French wine, or apple cider," a man in the artillery recalled. "They put it in these five gallon water cans, so they set these five gallon water cans on an old stove in a house somewhere, and they had taken some old copper gas lines . . . and made a little five gallon still out of it, and . . . it'd be trickling or running pure cognac. And they had quite a time. The battery commanders didn't care, because they'd give them a little and give a first sergeant a little, and he was happy."[98] Some men, such as Preston Price, procured liquor in more traditional ways. As a replacement on his way to the front in fall 1944, Price recalled his "chief occupation [was] drinking a rather watery Cognac bottled locally and sold for exorbitant prices," yet he found "the Belgian Cognac strangely to my liking."[99]

Robert Crousore remembered an incident in Germany when he and his unit found a wine cellar full of champagne: "And we'd often heard of this champagne, you know, all 22–23 year olds, so we thought, 'Man, try that.' So, we got a bottle of this, and it just tasted just like Ginger Ale. So everybody was sitting around, we had a bottle apiece, we were just sitting around having a good time and about chow time it had started to work. And the guys were going through the chow line, and a few there waiting in line to get up there and one guy just sort of staggered and over he'd go."[100] Charles Kelly also tried champagne for the first time while in Europe. "To me it tasted like soda pop or 7-Up," he recalled.[101] In Germany many of the Americans also discovered schnapps, with predictable results.[102]

In the Pacific, the methods of procuring and the varieties of alcohol were slightly different, but the results the same. The locals provided only a few drinks that the Americans could stomach—arrack in India and Ceylon, tuba in the Philippines and Guam, and the deadly mao-tai in China.[103] At one point, the enlisted men in the Eleventh Airborne got hold of some Japanese sake wine and had a good time, but that kind of good fortune proved to be an exception.[104] The troops had to fend for themselves—so they traded, stole, or made their own liquor.[105] In places such as New Caledonia and India, American soldiers paid as much as twenty dollars for a bottle of spirits.[106] A great deal of effort and ingenuity went into the homemade manufacture of alcohol. In what was a common story from Americans in all branches and all theaters, the men in Eli Bernheim's unit in New Guinea built a still to manufacture "jungle juice."[107]

The drinking could become ridiculous or even tragic. After being wounded in the Battle of the Bulge and going to Bastogne, paratrooper Gordon Carson recalled the medics giving him a bottle of crème de menthe. When the Germans bombed the city, he remembered, "I got sick and thank God for that helmet. I had already had about half of that crème de menthe. . . . All green in my helmet."[108] One man remembered reading a story in *Stars & Stripes* describing how eighteen Americans died because they drank German rocket fuel. "I had seen men squeeze Sterno heating jelly through a woman's silk stockings to get a few drops to drink," he wrote, "but 'buzz bomb juice' was just too much."[109] Scores of American soldiers suffered serious harm from drinking aftershave soaked through bread, medical alcohol mixed with fruit juice or water, wood alcohol, and anything else that might get them drunk.

In a letter home, a soldier blamed the army for making drinkers out of the men: "An informal frank poll in the room tonight revealed that most of the boys did not swear, or drink before leaving home. Now the boys confess they swear all the time and get drunk every time they get a large quantity of liquor."[110] Even a self-professed teetotaler admitted that he became a drinker when introduced to German beer.[111] The drinking began in training and while in service stateside and only accelerated overseas. The boredom or army life, the escape from home, peer pressure, the fear of combat, and wanting to forget the horrors of war all contributed to one degree or another to the heavy drinking, and many of the veterans would bring that unfortunate habit home with them after the fight. But during the war, drinking was a nearly universal vice, and one that certainly crossed all lines of ethnicity or religion. When troops went on a bender, they did it together.

The young men shared other needs. American troops sought female companionship, often in the form of sex, and for many of the same reasons they sought food and drink—boredom, fear, peer pressure, escape, and just plain desire. Women in any form were much lusted after in that predominantly male world. Military life created a heightened awareness of sexuality and sexual desires, and the men sought to outdo each other in their masculinity. When they saw movies, the men preferred either comedies or romances starring beautiful women. They painted pictures of women on planes and tanks. Pin-up girls, led by Betty Grable, adorned American barracks, huts, and tents no matter where the U.S. Army went. And soldiers did not have to

In a typical wartime scene, soldiers gamble on a bunk. The wall behind them is adorned with pin-ups and pictures of naked women. Courtesy of Robert T. Davis II.

go to any special lengths to procure such pictures. Periodicals for the men, such as *Yank*, almost always included a pin-up of the month. The pin-up girls represented the ideal—the perfect American woman against whom the men would judge all others. As one historian has written of Grable's popularity, "She best exemplified the sex appeal of the all-American girl-next-door. Women liked her too, which suggests that Grable's real appeal was less erotic than as a wholesome symbol of American womanhood."[112]

The ideal was nice, but the men craved the real thing. As one man wrote to his wife about seeing some Women's Army Corps members in his camp, "Don't worry. They aren't pin-up girls—though, to be frank, any woman looks good to our deprived eyes."[113] USO shows helped some, and the greatest female star of those shows also said something about the desires of those men. If Betty Grable was the all-American girl, Marlene Dietrich brought something more foreign, more sensual, more blatantly sexual to the troops. Dietrich became the huge draw of the USO shows. As her appeal indicates, the men did not just crave companionship, they lusted for something more.

Sexual flings and visits to prostitutes began at home, but they greatly accelerated overseas. The men knew that they were stretching moral conventions, but they had a whole new perspective. "By most people's standards we were immoral, but we were young and could die tomorrow," one soldier recalled.[114] Armed with such a justification, and as they drew farther from the constraining influence of home, the soldiers sought to fulfill their sexual desires with the women they found abroad. In Europe especially, sexual liaisons with local women happened all the time.[115] One chaplain lamented, "The havoc that military service played with the sex-morality of the soldiers was a great shock to me."[116] So pervasive were such activities, and the subsequent cases of venereal disease, that some higher-ups in the army briefly contemplated officially sanctioned and monitored army brothels. Such a move would have triggered an enormous backlash at home and among some of the more abstemious troops, so the army quickly cashiered the idea.[117] Still, the men managed.

In fact, the American soldier was infamous in England for being "overpaid, over-sexed, and over here." Some of these liaisons represented wartime flings, some were outright sexual assaults, and others led to real and lasting romances. Between 1941 and 1950, nearly thirty-eight thousand women from the United Kingdom went to the United States as wives of American citizens. The situation in England also triggered another example of the white troops setting themselves apart from their black counterparts. The white Americans resented the fact that English women seemed to have no compunction about romantic and sexual relationships with black troops.[118] Writing from

England, M. D. Elevitch said, "Over here there is no race problem—Negroes are accepted as readily as whites—They even go to dances with white girls—Somehow—the average man in our outfit can't bring himself to understand or tolerate this."[119] A Wisconsin soldier in the 87th Infantry Division wrote of the issue, "There were negros [sic] here a few months ago and they told us that some of the English girls went with them the same as with any other soldiers. Some of them are even going to have babies from them. That sure lowered my opinion of the English people."[120] At the time, even racially progressive white troops could not understand or tolerate even a legitimate and lasting romance between a black man and a white woman.

In the war zones of the Continent the sexual liaisons rarely had anything to do with romance. The army encountered prostitution wherever it went, and the soldiers proved to be enthusiastic customers, despite the best efforts of military medical personnel and chaplains.[121] From North Africa to Germany, prostitutes enticed the soldiers. Jack Gray remembered a sign on a bar in North Africa that advertised one woman for fifty cents.[122] One veteran recalled that upon arrival in Italy, "little boys would come up to you with their filthy faces and say, 'Fichi, fichi. Wanna fuck my sister?'" Still, he continued, "a lot of guys had no compunctions."[123] In a letter home from Germany, M. D. Elevitch described visiting a "whore house district" with some friends who solicited prostitutes while he sat in a waiting room reading a paper, "barbershop style."[124]

Even in combat situations some men sought companionship from local women. Shortly after D-Day, one Ranger sought to proposition a French farm girl he saw taking care of one of the few cows that survived the combat in the area. On his way over, a German soldier jumped out of hiding and the American shot and killed him. According to the soldier, "I looked around . . . and that French gal was gone. . . . I looked back at that old SS trooper and I thought to myself, 'You son of a bitch, I ought to shoot you again. You probably knocked me out of a piece of ass.'"[125] Victor Fast said, "I also remember one of our H.Q. Rangers who boasted that he was going to have sex with a French woman within eight hours after he hit the beaches. Sure as hell, Herb Epstein cracked a door when we were clearing Vierville and he saw the knucklehead in the act."[126]

Although one veteran from the Pacific recalled that "there were none of the European diversions," this type of behavior went on in those theaters also.[127] Men sometimes got leave to Australia, where they did plenty of drinking and carousing.[128] The men were quite pleased to find the women of Australia very friendly to Americans.[129] Sex with the local female population did not happen as frequently on the other islands in the Pacific. A man on New Guinea noted that the Americans took notice of some of the half-naked native women, but they also noticed that these ladies did not resemble what they saw as the "lovely, passionate flowers" depicted in movies set in the south seas.[130] If appearances of women in the Pacific theater did not please the men, that was nothing compared to the cultural shock. A returning veteran told reporters that a native leader on Guadalcanal offered the American marriage to either of his daughters, but the veteran declined, as "one of them was 14 years old and the other only 12."[131] Yet it was far from unheard of for the soldiers to have sexual liaisons with island women. One of the more honest men who had served as a medic on Luzon in the Philippines said, "We dug in for the night, and lo and behold comes this Filipino with this girl and she's for sale—or, I should say, rent. I'd never had a girl and didn't want to die without knowing, so I asked him what the price was."[132]

In Germany at the end of the war, the men met some German women who had tried to live up to the Nazi creed of Aryan motherhood. The women informed some of the troops that they had slept with dozens of German soldiers in order to get pregnant faster. "I couldn't help but to think," one man remembered, "how proud their husbands would be upon returning from the war and learning how honorably their wives had also served their country."[133] One officer had the duty of keeping the watch out for venereal disease cases at the end of the war in Germany. He wrote to his wife, "As the boys say: 'This is a clapped-up goddamn country'—among other things. Prostitution is the rule—the *frauleins* having been so well indoctrinated on the subject by Hitler they don't seem to be able to get out of the habit."[134]

That sort of opinion was not limited to German women. In fact, many of the men held the women they found overseas in disdain, especially in comparison to American ladies. In turn many of the civilians in Europe and elsewhere looked askance at American troops. "Our soldiers returned the compliment and spoke of the loose morals of all European women," Chaplain Isaac Klein wrote. "They looked at every woman as an actual or potential harlot whose favors could be gotten for a price."[135] E. J. Kahn liked Australian women just fine but found them "neither as well dressed, nor as good-looking, nor as elaborately educated as American girls."[136] After seeing a couple of American Red Cross women, Raymond Gantter wrote, "I don't know *why* the sight of two American girls in slacks should be more exciting than the sight of equally attractive Belgian, French, or German girls in more feminine costume, but that's the way it was."[137]

While many soldiers found comfort or release in sex while overseas, the wives of married soldiers overseas sometimes did the same at home. Couples entered into many marriages during the war on a romantic whim—as an accelerated fulfillment of mutual attraction for young people who knew they might not have much time together. Still, when these hurried romances fell apart, so too did many soldiers. Nothing engendered more pain or rage then the infamous "Dear John" letters.[138] A chaplain in the Pacific wrote home of a soldier who visited him with a problem that was "typical of what too many men face out here." His wife wrote asking for a divorce; when he refused, she told him she was having a baby that was not his. "What a thing to learn," wrote the chaplain, "on the other side of the world! It crushes morale."[139] An infantry lieutenant in Europe saw a sergeant basically commit suicide in battle after receiving such a note, only this note also preyed on the prejudices of the time and place. The lieutenant recalled that the sergeant had shown him the letter: "It was the most wickedly cruel letter I had ever read. . . . He was from the south, and this little wench told him, among similar tidbits, that she had been sleeping with a Negro and that he was twice the man [the sergeant] was."[140]

The search for food and drink and the confusing sexual issues created by service in the army strengthened the exclusionary camaraderie of the military experience in World War II. They scrounged for food together and they drank whatever booze they could find together. They saw how people from all different backgrounds were subject to sexual urges, and to the extent that they felt guilty about fulfilling those urges, they projected that guilt onto the foreign women who would seemingly do anything. These activities reflected the growing list of differences upon which the men focused that had nothing to do with issues of American ethnicity or religion.

Some of these differences existed within the army itself. Pride for a unit could manifest itself in rivalries between divisions or branches. A man in the 101st Airborne Division found himself fighting alongside troops from the 82nd Airborne in the confusion after the Normandy invasion. He noted of the experience that even though he earned some respect, the "82nd and 101st Airborne had always had an intense rivalry towards each other. Men from the 82nd considered all members of the 101st to be second-class citizens."[141] Combat Engineer Robert Healey recalled that before D-Day, "while we were in England, we had been issued paratroop boots as an item of uniform. We were extremely proud of them although a few times when we ran into paratroopers, there were words and blows exchanged over what we were doing with paratroop boots on."[142]

The soldiers also harbored more generalized resentments that came from their specific position in the war. Front-line infantry men took exception to anyone to the rear of them. Front-line troops commonly called those behind them "rear echelon assholes." As one man said, "A staff weenie might be called a Triple A—for aides, adjutants, and assholes."[143] George Miller wrote to his mother, "It seems that we dig the foxholes for the supply units that follow us up—another Infantry gripe!"[144] A Mexican American soldier recalled a saying: "Mexicans, Oakies, Polacks, and Wops. That's all you see in the Infantry."[145] The rub was that just as combat infantry resented anyone to the rear of them, artillery men considered themselves at the front and they resented supply troops, just as all ground troops saw themselves as separate from the glamorous air forces. At the time, the men truly resented other groups in the military as not understanding what they saw as the real war, but the resentment did not last. Infantrymen would always be proud of the specific role they played in the war, but they did not carry resentment for other groups into their everyday peacetime lives. One soldier said that while the complaining about the rear echelon happened all the time, none "of the bitching was serious: we didn't really mean it, but it lent a bitter savor to our own misery."[146] All of these groupings had everything to do with position in the army and nothing to do with the key groupings of civilian life. They savored that misery together, across ethnic and religious boundaries.

The troops reserved a more lasting disdain for the home front, particularly when they felt the people at home were not doing their duty, including the duty of women to be faithful to their departed beaus. As a popular song from the era reminded the women, "Don't sit under the apple tree with anyone else but me." That thinking was part of why the men so reviled the Dear John letters. But the high expectation extended to all Americans. "Quite rightly, the boys can't understand a dual standard for service—one for soldiers, another for civilians," one officer wrote. "As I frequently hear: 'A few bombs dropped on the U.S.A. might wake people up, make them realize what war is all about.'"[147] Paratrooper Thomas Raulston wrote to his family from Europe, "How the guys at home can lift their heads is beyond me."[148] Klaus Huebner described being infuriated with a letter from home carrying the news that some workers feared the decline in war contracts. "It sounds as though some folks at home are enjoying this endless killing and are afraid that it may come to a sudden end and some may lose their well-paying jobs," he said. "Now I wish that some of these people were over here with us."[149]

The troops saved particular contempt for workers who went on strike. One veteran of the fighting in the Pacific recalled resenting work stoppages in defense plants at home.[150] Another wrote after the end of the war that the "boys are pretty mad about the stevedores going on strike in N.Y. This is really causing havoc in redeployment plans. . . . This is a kick in the back to the army. Here we are forced to stay overseas while money hungry chiselers who have fat bank accounts try to squeeze out a little fatter pay check at our expense."[151] Henry Novak told his family that "a lot of those strikers need to have a few G.I.'s around when they cause that kind of trouble. Then they would get their first taste of war and that's no kidding."[152] The United Mine Workers' strike of 1943 provoked one man to write, "All the soldier wants of labor is a hard day's work and I'm sure he deserves it. The striking miner surely will find little sympathy from my soldier friend, and if labor does let him down, Johnny will come home with a lot of anti-labor ideas which will be only the normal reaction."[153] Surely some of this resentment carried over into the postwar period, but the key fact at the time was that the soldiers were setting themselves apart from another group. In this case, American soldiers, all ethnically and religiously integrated American soldiers, saw themselves as a unified body in opposition to what they perceived as the slackers at home.

Above all, American soldiers set themselves apart from the people they met overseas. Even the Allies came under scrutiny, beyond the food and the women. Officer Jacob Belke wrote home, "The British people seem very queer to us, and I suppose we seem just as queer to them. . . . The whole U.S. now seems to be a highly desirable dream which is way out of reach. There are so many of the . . . ordinary everyday things of the American way of life that I miss a great deal. Funny papers, magazines, cokes, just any one of the million and one things that we accept as the usual thing are gone, and I have suddenly realized that I don't know when I'll see them again."[154] When his unit arrived in Scotland, Barnett Hoffner said, "We gaped at kids who were smoking who couldn't have been more than eight or nine years old in their tattered clothes, and then their strange accents." Later Hoffner added, "We got used to seeing the British land army girls in the countryside, some holding up huge rats by their tails, something you would never picture an American girl doing."[155] Even at the sharp end of war, they noted differences. When a British force relieved his unit on the line, an American soldier who happened to be a German immigrant, noted, "We have an excellent opportunity to observe their actions and manners. They are indeed different from us."[156] And on more than one occasion, the Americans found themselves infuriated that their British allies did not exhibit enough urgency to get into the fight.[157]

The Americans who expected an exotic land of kangaroos and boomerangs in Australia often found themselves in American-style camps in boring settings. With lowered expectations, the men began to notice the smaller peculiarities of Australia, not unlike those found by Americans in the British Isles. For men on leave from the front, Australia provided a welcome respite—so much so that some of the men took to calling it "the Land of

Oz"—but it still was not home.[158] One veteran of the Americal Division fighting in the Pacific remarked what a great country he had "compared to the Pacific islands—towns in Australia and New Caledonia."[159]

This process of comparing foreign lands to home became more pronounced as the men entered combat. In the entirely foreign locales in the African, Asian, and Pacific theaters, the distinctions were obvious. In North Africa the coarse language and poor manners of his fellow GIs embarrassed D. C. Perguson, but the filth, poverty, and lack of ambition among the natives—especially evident in the children begging for food and cigarettes—truly appalled him.[160] The same went for the Asian and Pacific theaters. Few, if any, of the men were descended from immigrants from New Guinea or Guadalcanal or any of the other Pacific Islands except the Philippines. So while the men might have friendly relationships with natives who wanted to stay out of the war or just get the Japanese out, there also was a note of condescension in how the Americans treated the natives. That condescension grew from both racial and cultural differences. On New Guinea, and elsewhere, soldiers called the natives with skin color and physical features they saw as black "fuzzy-wuzzies."[161] The Americans hated the unsanitary conditions they found from India to China to the South Pacific. The cultures there struck them as strange or barbaric. But the histories of those lands also engendered in Americans a newfound dislike for Europeans. The men saw firsthand the depredations of British, French, and Dutch colonialism, and their cultural disdain for rule imposed by strangers from afar led them to sympathize with natives they otherwise could not understand.[162] In such a situation, the only people who made any sense were other Americans, and the definition of American continued to broaden.

That process was most poignant when it involved ethnic soldiers returning to the lands of their parents or grandparents. Although some at the time and later believed that the army tacitly sent Italian Americans to the Pacific to avoid conflicts of interest, there were a lot of Italian Americans in the invasion of Italy. The Italians had been hit hard by the war. The fighting, poor weather conditions, and a massive refugee crisis created a situation in which people in the already impoverished southern part of the country went to the brink of starvation when the American troops began to tramp through in 1943.[163] Klaus Huebner said of the Italians in one village, "These people certainly are still primitive and seem years behind American civilization."[164] Some of the Italian American troops had romantic notions about the land of their ancestors, notions fed to them by enthusiastic parents and grandparents. Audie Murphy recounted the words of one such man in his unit: "All my life I wait to come to Italy, . . . and here I am buried like a goddam mole.

I write my old man that the country stinks. 'Wait'll you get to Rome,' he says. 'Wait'll you see your grandfather's place. Then you'll see the real Italy.' . . . The real Italy. Rome. In a pig's eye."[165] Italian Americans found a land very much different from what they expected, and their role in the invasion and occupation only made clear to them and their comrades how far they had come from their immigrant backgrounds.

They became the main deliverers of distinctly American ideals to these foreign lands. As veteran and combat correspondent Ralph Martin wrote of the invasion, "The Italian-speaking GI's (and there were plenty of them) were telling the people that we were going to help them, not hurt them. One of them, S/Sgt. Frank Sclafani, of the Bronx, N.Y., went around quoting Tom Paine in Italian. Something about, 'We Fight not to enslave, but to set a country free and make room upon the earth for honest men to live in.'"[166] Obviously, the ability to speak the language came in handy for such a mission. Journalist and combat correspondent John Hersey wrote about this phenomenon through the protagonist, Maj. Victor Joppolo, of his 1944 novel about the occupation of Italy, *A Bell for Adano*. In the foreword to the book Hersey wrote,

> America is the international country. Major Joppolo was an Italian-American going to work in Italy. Our Army had Yugoslavs and Frenchmen and Austrians and Czechs and Norwegians in it, and everywhere our Army goes in Europe, a man can turn to the private beside him and say: "Hey, Mac, what's this furriner saying? How much does he want for that bunch of grapes?" And Mac will be able to translate.
>
> That is where we are lucky. No other country has such a fund of men who speak the languages of the lands we must invade, who understand the ways and have listened to their parents sing the folk songs and have tasted the wine of the land on the palate of their memories. This is a lucky thing for America. We are very lucky to have our Joppolos. It is another reason why I think you should know the story of this particular Joppolo.
>
> America is on its way into Europe. You can be isolationist as you want to be, but there is a fact. Our armies are on their way in. Just as truly as Europe once invaded us, with wave after wave of immigrants, now we are invading Europe, with wave after wave of sons of immigrants.[167]

As Hersey wrote, the interaction of American ethnics with their distant cousins in the Old World did not stop in Italy.

"We could use the linguistic talents from a broad section of American troops who came from all over the country," one officer recalled. "We had men who spoke French, German, Russian, Polish, Yiddish, and Italian. It was such that even if one of our people could not speak a particular dialect, they could talk in such a way that most of the information would come out reasonably clear. We did this on many occasions during operations as we did not have the luck to have trained interrogators with us. We would only extract the immediate use of information and then send them back to the professionals."[168] George Madison found himself as part of an advanced reconnaissance team going into France. One of the men who went with him was Sgt. Harvey Gill: "Gill spoke French being from Louisiana and he was also an expert rifleman. He was a good fellow to have around."[169]

More and more American troops of all backgrounds found that these foreign lands offered little that they wanted. After talking about the French people he saw wearing wooden shoes to work and never carrying umbrellas or wearing raincoats, one man wrote home, "Gertrude Stein said 'The French are more spiritually minded' than the Americans—Actually they seem too stupid to realize there is no need to suffer the many inconveniences they contend with daily—Give a Frenchman a bar of soap, and he'll prob'ly set to work to carve a horse out of it—His dog eats the wasted chips—both are happy."[170] On leave in Paris, George Wilson took note of the way cleaning women came into men's public restrooms to do their work and everyone went about their business as usual. Men's relief stations on the streets were even more revealing, with barriers that hardly concealed the sights and sounds from within. Wilson appreciated their openness with a natural bodily function but also wrote that he could not "imagine any such device even in the worst slums of an American city."[171] Willard Fluck told a similar story about Paris in a letter home to his parents: "It seems to be a native custom when feeling the call of nature to find a side street, turn one's back to the lady friend (I don't believe it's considered polite to face her), and proceed to urinate against the side of the nearest building. And in one place I found a woman 'porter' cleaning the men's toilet. I didn't ask whether men cleaned the women's. Ah yes, Europe is a great place."[172] Children as young as seven smoking on the streets in Belgium engendered the same reaction in Raymond Gantter and his comrades.[173]

Generalized cultural lessons began to become clear. To the American soldiers, compared to home, people in foreign lands to one degree or another had nasty or scarce food, loose women, filthy habits, and weaker fundamental values.[174] No matter how friendly the local population, Felix Branham thought, "days in a foreign land never are happy ones."[175] Cletus Schwab said, "When you see what goes on in other countries, it makes you feel glad to be an American."[176] American soldiers found much strange about the foreign lands they visited during the world. Those places were not home; the people they met were clearly not American. That distinction made a lasting impression on the troops. They did not harbor an aggressive ill will toward the strangers, but they saw neutrals and even the Allies as different and in most cases inferior to Americans.

The same could not be said for America's enemies. American soldiers expressed a range of emotions that varied from distaste to disdain to outright hate for the people who made up the Axis powers. Not surprisingly, the troops reserved their most mild emotions for the weakest of the enemies. The soldiers generally treated the Italians with a combination of amusement and disdain. They had only met the Italians on the battlefield a few times before Italy got out of the war. As Italy withdrew from the fight, its people also became neutral in the eyes of the troops. The destruction to the Italian peninsula and the poverty of its people made it difficult for the Americans to hold strong negative emotions toward the Italians. For all intents and purposes, the average American soldier treated the Italians as they did any other civilians they encountered in nonbelligerent countries.

American soldiers also had a straightforward attitude toward the Japanese, but it was quite different from the feelings aimed at the Italians. Put simply, the troops reviled their Japanese enemy. A variety of factors intertwined and fed into this hatred. The Japanese had launched the sneak attack that brought the United States into the war—as President Roosevelt himself emphasized in his "Day of Infamy" speech—and Americans lusted for revenge against such treachery. At the same time, the conventional wisdom held that the Japanese were a strange and inferior race, part of the so-called yellow peril that was more akin to animals like rats than real thinking and feeling human beings. Cartoons, advertisements, propaganda, and literature all emphasized this theme. Its effects spread throughout the troops. One example, among many, was an officer in the Pacific who said fear could be combated by "knowing that the Jap is an animal to be ferreted out and killed."[177] It did not help that the war against Japan was fought in the unfamiliar geography and among the strange cultures of the Pacific and Asian theaters. That geography and those cultures resisted American efforts to tame them, so the Americans took out their frustration and fury on an equally stubborn and unknowable enemy. Most important, the Japanese soldiers refused to surrender for their own cultural reasons. They chose rather to die, and often to try to take as many Americans with them when they did. For all of these reasons, the Pacific war became a fight without rules and without restraint, with no quarter asked and none given.[178] And because the atomic bombs ended the war suddenly and before the invasion, most of the men never met Japanese civilians, especially the children, and thus never had the chance to soften their views.[179]

The Germans presented a much more complex problem. Wartime surveys queried the soldiers about hatred of the enemy. One question, "When the going was tough, how much were you helped by thoughts of hatred of the enemy?" found that 45 percent of infantrymen in Europe and 61 percent in the Pacific said "A lot" or "Some." More than a fifth of troops in both the Pacific and Europe who responded said that they would like to see the whole German nation wiped out. Most, over 65 percent, wanted to punish German leaders but not ordinary Germans. The question of postwar punishment for Japan received interesting responses. Of the troops in Europe who responded, only 29 percent said punish the leaders but not the ordinary Japanese, while over 58 percent said wipe out the whole Japanese nation. The Pacific troops who participated had a slightly less bloodthirsty view: 47 percent of them said punish the leaders but not the ordinary Japanese, while 42 percent wanted to wipe out the whole nation.[180] Whatever the broader conclusions to be drawn from the survey, the Americans clearly had a much more ambiguous view of the Germans, and it changed over time.

By the outbreak of the war, Americans despised Adolf Hitler and his band of tyrants. The very word "Nazi" became a serious insult.[181] The men carried these feelings into the service. The epithets for the enemy had none of the good-natured feelings of Americans kidding around with each other, even when the slurs were similar. That feeling perhaps explains why a German immigrant turned American combat doctor such as Klaus Huebner could without irony refer to Germans as "Krauts" and "Jerry."[182] Officers sometimes encouraged the men to hate the enemy in order to combat fear. One officer said he gave his troops "a brief talk about the Nazi bastards" to encourage them in the fighting.[183] On the other hand, Germans would, and did, surrender, and that made a world of difference from the Japanese. Although occasionally the Germans would feign surrender only to ambush American troops, and sometimes the Germans killed captured American soldiers, by and large the informal rules of war applied. The war in Europe, already brutal enough, did not turn into a fight to the last man. American soldiers hated the Germans but also respected them.

Even outside of combat many of the men found the German people not to their liking. Fighting in Germany at the end of the war, Dean Joy realized that he hated all adult Germans. He wrote home from the front in Germany about the necessity of war: "These German people do not think, talk, or understand the language of equality, kindness, generosity, compassion. All they understand is the language of cruel force. That's the language we must talk."[184] Such feelings spread and grew among the Americans later in the war, when they encountered displaced persons, prison, and concentration camps. These groups, and the war in Europe in general, proved a sobering reminder of how terrible ethnic and religious divisions could become.

Prior to encountering large numbers of displaced persons and the Nazi camps, the Americans had a general idea of what the Nazis were capable of, and they knew which groups of people the Nazis despised most. The men related this knowledge to their own comrades and country. Paratrooper William Guarnere remembered that in his unit, as in many others, "the Jewish G.I.'s took off the Star of David, for fear of retaliation from the Nazis."[185] At times, the Americans used the Nazis' anti-Semitism to gain an advantage. On such case happened on D-Day, as a Ranger interrogated an enemy on the battlefield. Victor Fast threatened the German, "If you . . . leave any doubt in my mind that you're telling the truth I'll turn you over to my Jewish buddy here standing next to me, Herb Epstein and he'll take you behind that bush over there—you get what I mean—He (Herb) nodded signifying to me he understood."[186] Yet even as the troops understood that Nazi Germany was hostile to Jews, the Americans had no idea how deep that hostility ran; they had no idea how far the Germans were willing to go.[187]

Although most American troops never made it to the full-scale extermination camps, what they did see was more than enough. Prison and concentration camps dotted the territories controlled by Nazi Germany, and the inmates of each suffered terrible horrors at the hands of the Germans. The Americans could not believe what they saw. Horace Evers wrote home about the camp at Dachau, "I previously had read about DACHAU and was glad of the chance to see for myself just to prove once and for all that what I had heard was propaganda. —But *no* it wasn't propaganda at all—if anything some of the truth had been held back. In two years of combat you can imagine I have seen a lot of death, furious death mostly. But nothing has ever stirred me as much as this." What Evers saw at Dachau gave him new reasons to fight. "I can't shrug off the feeling of utter hate I now hold for these people," he wrote. "I've shot at Germans with intent to kill before but only because I had to or else it was me—now I hold no hesitance whatsoever."[188]

The atrocities also gave the war new meaning for the American soldiers. The men already assumed that they were on the good side of the war, but the camps and refugees made that view all the more clear. The stark reality of the camps, the terrible stench, the emaciated bodies stacked in piles, the utter disregard for mercy and compassion, forced the Americans to wonder how anyone could perpetrate such horrors. More important, they also began to wonder if it all could happen at home in America. Some denied it outright.

Roscoe Blunt remembered talking to a German Jew who had been tortured in a camp. Blunt told the man that "in America, a Jew was treated as freely as any other citizen."[189] Others took a more mixed view. In a position along the Rhine, Kenneth Connelly met a German Jew who had been able to hide out for most of the war: "At last I had met one of the people in whose name we are waging this war—if we are waging this war in the name of justice. . . . Here was a living symbol of a philosophical stand, the stand that all men are brothers." Connelly expressed doubt that the German people he had encountered could participate in such cruelty, to which the man replied that such a thing could even happen in the United States. Connelly wrote, "I remembered a thousand and one remarks I had heard passed at cultured dinner parties, in class rooms, and among business men—and I didn't want to look that boy straight back in the eye."[190] The shock expressed by the Americans—even some who had anti-Semitic tendencies—at encountering the Holocaust, suggests that they could not even imagine such depravity happening in America. But more important, the Holocaust made them think about the possibility. It made them think about how it could happen, how all of the small prejudices could become horrible actions, and those small prejudices no longer seemed so small.

As horrified and angry as the men could be at the Germans for starting the war and committing those atrocities, they also could not hide a certain admiration for the German people. Long before the end of the fighting, the army invoked a policy of nonfraternization with the German enemy because, in General Eisenhower's words, the German people must not be "permitted to minimize the consequences of their defeat or to prepare the way for a resurgence of power by influencing the thoughts or actions of our troops."[191] The army had a serious problem enforcing this rule. "The American plan of Non Fratinization [sic] will prove to be one of our biggest mistakes," one man wrote home. "It can not be carried out. The American soldiers can not be cruel or brutal."[192] GIs were famous for having a soft spot toward the children they encountered all around the world. They passed out chewing gum, chocolate bars, candy, or even rations to kids who had never had such luxuries. At the very highest levels officers such as General Eisenhower agreed with this sentiment, especially toward children. Eisenhower worried about the breakdown of discipline because American troops would disobey any order to act cold or distant toward children. The truth was that the troops were just as likely to fraternize with German women, but the fact that the American men empathized with children as victims of the war indicates that they saw the foreign adults as guilty of causing all the trouble in the first place. It was yet another way the Americans showed their displeasure with the people in far-off lands. In any case it did not take too long after the war's end for the army to begin to relax its fraternization policies.[193]

Another soldier had a slightly different view: "Fraternization here is un-preventable—I see G.I.s bargaining with the heinies. . . . It's a sad state [that] G.I.s respect the Germans as soldiers. . . . The contrast between the sturdy Germans and the miserable French sort of hypnotizes the gullible American—he hates the 'Jigs'—he hates the 'Frogs'—he hates the 'Limeys' but I never hear him say anything against the Jerry."[194] Such a statement was an exaggeration. But part of the issue with the Germans was that as individuals they could not live up to the horrible regime to which they had been a party. Germany itself seemed a pleasant kind of place, full of neat and efficient people, not goose stepping madmen.[195] The contradictions they encountered in Germany left American soldiers with a more ambivalent view of the Germans than the Japanese. But in either case, the men did not have ambivalent views of the actions of their enemies in starting the war. For that, at least, the Americans despised the enemy.

The war dragged on, and the soldiers developed a much broader conception of what it meant to be an American. As the men tried to fill in the monotonous hours of everyday army life, they learned that their bonds as Americans were far greater than their ethnic or religious differences. The war, especially when it took them to foreign lands, made it perfectly clear how much they had in common with the men who served alongside them and how superficial their differences actually were. For one officer, the realization of the change came all at once, in a conversation with a French boy near his camp in 1944. "I told him we have many French and many Germans in America (his eyes widened), many Spanish, Italians, and Russians, but that they are all Americans," Robert Easton wrote. "This was a big idea for him and suddenly it was for me too."[196] That big idea became engrained in the American soldier in training and the long dull hours, days, and years of service in the U.S. Army in World War II. But that was not the end of it. The lesson of the war's hours of boredom would take on a much greater significance in its instants of excitement.

# 5

# INSTANTS OF EXCITEMENT AND TERROR

> Listen to the names at roll call, or read these names from
> a casualty list in the *New York Times* of 29 March 1945:
> Agostinello . . . Cohen . . . Curran . . . Grunwald . . . Hrubec . . .
> Ivanoski . . . Kuzian . . . Marshall . . . Thomas . . . Warblanski.
> Were any of these inferior?
>
> —"Prejudice," *Armed Forces Talk,* 1948

THE WORLD WAR II ARMY EXPERIENCE WAS MORE THAN A MASS EXCURSION of young Americans to visit distant lands and meet different people. All of the tedium of everyday military life—the drilling, routine, scrounging for food, waiting for letters—could make it easy to forget that the army had to attend to serious business. There was a war to be fought, a war on two broad fronts against determined and lethal foes. Even in the modern era of great air and sea power, fighting that war meant that American soldiers would have to close with their enemies on the ground. They would have to take and hold territory. They would have to sow destruction and death by their own hands. They, millions of them, would have to come under fire during World War II. That experience, more than anything else they faced in the military, would live on in them for the rest of their lives. The hatred, anticipation, terror, excitement, death, and destruction of battle gave powerful meaning to all that the soldiers had gone through in uniform. The blood and sacrifice made the war's lessons all the more powerful.

Whatever their general feelings toward the people of Italy, Japan, or Germany as a whole, American soldiers resented their enemies in uniform. It was the Italian, Japanese, and German militaries who had forced the Americans to go to war, forced them from their homes, forced them to fight and die on battlefields all over the world. This resentment for the enemy turned into dislike or hate, and it fed into the emotions of the men under fire. That emotion gave the men something on which to focus, something to take their minds off their own anxieties. It reinforced their belief that the Americans were on the good side in the war. That belief helped sustain the men in the overall fight; it helped them get from one day to the next. But while this disdain or hatred for the German and Japanese soldiers helped sustain the American fighting man, his emotions under fire on the actual battlefield in World War II did not really involve the enemy. Modern warfare and modern weapons stretched distances. Rarely did World War II soldiers kill at close range, looking into the other man's eyes as he died. Rarely did the fallen see their killers before they died. The enemy was a shadow, a silhouette, something distant and impersonal.

At the same time, combat in World War II acted to separate comrades from one another. In a general sense, the men already felt anonymous in the army. Soldiers in that greatest of all wars realized that they were part of something huge, and that there was certain obscurity about being just one among millions in modern war. To emphasize that feeling, they called themselves "GIs," an abbreviation of "government issue."[1] The implication of this nickname was obvious: When it came to combat, the average soldier was just another piece of expendable equipment. For a variety of reasons, that feeling of anonymity only intensified on the battlefield. For example, the thick jungles of Pacific islands such as New Guinea hid both friend and foe from the average soldier on the ground. Even in a hectic area a man could feel totally alone.[2] And when terrain did not separate the men, the realities of combat kept them apart. For much of the war the army had a real problem with American troops bunching together under fire, especially under artillery bombardment. The natural instinct of the troops was to find safety in numbers, but that instinct was wrong. Nothing was more dangerous than to present a bigger target to the enemy. Yet time and time again American troops fresh to the front lines gathered together and suffered terrible casualties from only one or two enemy weapons. As a result, the army made a special point of training men to keep their spacing under fire, and veterans learned to stay separated in combat zones.[3] The nature of modern war, the exigencies of the modern battlefield, meant that the instants of excitement were terrifyingly lonely.

Anxiety exacerbated the feelings of anonymity. The men began to feel the lonely dread of combat before they ever reached the battlefield. At first they experienced a more generalized anxiety. Veteran Franklin Gurley remembered the questions the men asked themselves before their first fight: "What will it be like? . . . How will I act under fire? . . . Will I still be around tomorrow night? . . . Will I chicken out . . . and shoot myself in the foot? . . . Will I see my girl and parents again? . . . Will I screw up and let [the captain] and the others down?"[4] Before D-Day one paratrooper grew pessimistic about his chances for survival and wrote, "What a lousy way to leave the world. Nobody to say good-bye. No friends or relatives at the bedside. How quiet it is—and godforsaken lonely."[5] Of the respondents of a wartime survey asking about fear symptoms in or before combat, more than 85 percent often or sometimes had violent pounding of the heart, 75 percent of enlisted men had a sinking feeling in the stomach, 56 percent of enlisted men shook all over, nearly a quarter of enlisted men vomited, a startling 18 percent admitted losing control of their bowels, and another 10 percent urinated in their pants.[6]

Anxiety manifested itself in more than physical symptoms. It affected the way the men dealt with one another. Individual troops understood that some American soldiers would die in the fight, but at first no individual believed he would be the one dying. Multiple soldiers told variations of the same story: When told by superior officers before their first combat that a certain percentage of the unit would not make it, each individual soldier looked around and thought, "Those poor bastards."[7] This mindset affected the way some of the men treated their comrades. One man recalled that before his unit's first combat an officer came by and told the men that some of them would most likely die. "We were all aware of that," Devon Larson said, "and no one tried to make close friends, not even with your partner."[8] Those who chose not to make close friends, like Larson, did so because they did not want to have to deal with the pain of losing that friend. They never assumed it would be their friend who would have to deal with the pain of losing them.

Later, when the men faced the fire and had spent more and more time in the lines, those feelings began to change. Most of the men went through variations of the same process. At first they felt bulletproof. If they survived a few engagements, they began to think that there was something special about them—a trinket they carried or a prayer they said protected them. But as they saw more and more of their comrades fall, they began to wonder when it would be their turn. The best soldiers and the worst soldiers were wounded or killed—with apparently no rhyme or reason. Veteran paratrooper Louis Simpson captured the feeling of resignation in a poem about combat in Normandy: "Everything's all right, Mother, / Everyone gets the same / At one time or another / It's all in the game."[9] Anxiety and resignation threatened to demoralize the troops. Describing combat to his younger brother, Paul Curtis wrote, "Take a combination of fear, anger, hunger, thirst, exhaustion, disgust, loneliness, homesickness, and wrap that all up in one reaction and you might approach the feelings a fellow has. It makes you feel mighty small, helpless and alone."[10]

The feeling was especially acute for replacement troops. Front-line combat units took heavy casualties during World War II, often at a turnover rate of well over 100 percent. Army policy dictated that whole units should not rotate out of the line to recuperate. Instead they stayed at the front to be replenished with fresh replacement troops. For a variety of reasons involving war planning, mobilization requests, and stiffening enemy resistance, the army faced a series of manpower shortages in the latter parts of the war. The replacement system accelerated, drawing soldiers from the army air and supply forces. The system had its advantages and drawbacks concerning overall combat effectiveness, but its effect on the actual replacements was pretty clear.[11]

The new men felt like strangers, even among their fellow soldiers. The army separated replacement troops from their training cohort, threw them together at replacement depots (the man called them Repple-Depples), and then distributed them to front-line units as needed. These men already faced all the normal fears and anxieties about combat, only they did so among people they had never met. Surveys found that recent transfers clearly had less pride in their new outfit.[12] The experience could be even more stark early on in the fighting in National Guard units that had kept some of their prewar local flavor. New Yorker John Barnes recalled just such an example: "The boys of A–Company came over 2 years earlier after being federalized from the National Guard. They were all in the Guard together from one town in Virginia, a town named Bedford. I felt a bit out of things as a New Yorker, except for about 15 of us new replacements. They all knew each other as old friends from home, and I felt lonelier than I had ever felt before in my life. My feelings didn't improve as the southern boys were bragging that their outfit was slated to be the assault unit in the landings to start a second front in France."[13]

Not all the men had a terrible time as a replacement. The men at the front generally did their best to get to know the new soldiers. The experience all depended on how long the men survived in their new units. Raymond Gantter recalled that he felt "kicked around" as a replacement until he got to the front. There the soldiers welcomed him: "The old men have been patient with our ignorance, kindly in their tutelage, and generous in the sharing of experience."[14] If a man could survive for a while he shed his replacement status and became part of the fraternity. After being in combat for a week as a replacement in the Battle of the Bulge, Preston Price wrote to his mother, "The dough boys here are certainly the best in the world. They are so generous and so awfully friendly. You all freeze alike. The war spares no rank here."[15] Still, if the replacements came in under fire, they did not have much of a chance to get to know the men next to them. Many veteran officers and enlisted men recalled seeing replacements killed before having ever learned their names. There at the front, in the worst of times, no soldiers felt more anonymous than the green replacement.

The soldiers tried to cope with the anxiety, loneliness, and terror in a variety of ways. In their darkest hours, coping with the idea that they might not survive, many men engaged religion in a way they had not before the war. The D-Day invasion of June 6, 1944, provided an especially strong example of this phenomenon. The men trained for months in preparation for the attack on the Normandy beaches, and they had been prepared to face strong defenses and to endure terrible casualties. They had a great deal of time to imagine what lay ahead. By the time they embarked on their ships for the voyage across the English Channel, many were prepared to find some solace in religion. "The day of the 5th of June was just another day aboard ship, resting in my bunk, and wondering what would happen next," one Ranger recalled of his lead up to the Normandy invasion. "We had this feeling that the 6th would be the day. Church services were held on deck, which I think we all attended."[16] Before D-Day Harry Bare also went to church. "We had religious services aboard ship at about 12:00 A.M.," he recalled. "I went to mass and received communion. I needed all the help I could get."[17] Not every preinvasion service carried the same solemnity. On one ship the duty fell to the senior officer, a captain described by one man as "a most blasphemous sinner." The services began, and the captain's "voice came booming solemnly over the loud speaker as he read the service. . . . We heard him announce a hymn, and he began singing with the men. . . . His singing dropped off and only the fainter sound of the men singing could be heard." The captain did not think the men put enough into their singing, so he yelled, "Sing, God-damn it, Sing!" The soldier who witnessed the whole affair recalled, "For all practical purposes the service ended there."[18] Despite such botched services, there was no denying the increased role of religion in the lives of the troops.

D-Day was just one example of combat or the anticipation of combat turning men toward religious faith. As Robert Easton wrote to his wife from Germany in January 1945, "The closer you get to the front, the more interest in religion there is."[19] Lloyd Dull also remembered that "friendly discussion of religion" increased on the front lines.[20] Even in areas that did not come under fire as frequently as the front lines, religion could play a significant role in the men's lives. A commander of a service base in North Africa wrote to the chief of chaplains to explain that in his opinion "a marked renewal of religious con-victions is occurring among our soldiers." The officer went on, "I believe that the chaplains of all denominations are rendering conspicuous service, and I am convinced that once these soldiers return to their homes, they are going to inject a new vitality into the religious forces of their communities."[21]

Not surprisingly, prayer increased in actual combat. Many of the troops had grown up in religious homes but had drifted away from religion. Many of the men never had much use for religion at all.[22] But the anxiety and fear of combat led most of the men at least to think about their religious convictions. When faced with their own mortality, they grasped for answers that only faith could provide. As a result, soldiers turned or returned to religion after facing combat. "Some of us got foxhole religion," said James McLeod, "and I went to confession and Mass after a long absence."[23] Franklin Gurley told the same to his parents: "Even our atheistic Sgts. [sergeants] have turned religious."[24] George Miller wrote home to his mother in Iowa from France in July 1944, "Believe me Mom, when I get home, you and I are going to church every Sunday and offer our thanks."[25] A particularly effective German gun led one man to joke, "It was rumored that there were more soldiers converted to Christianity by this 88 than by Peter and Paul combined."[26] One man who described himself as not particularly religious still carried around a small crucifix that he found in an abandoned apartment in Europe. "On many occasions," he wrote in his memoirs half a century later, "I pulled it out and looked at it for strength. I still have it today."[27]

Pvt. George Barrette recalled a particularly brutal artillery barrage: "Me and this buddy of mine were in the same hole with only a little brush on top, and I remember I was actually bawling. We were both praying to the Lord over and over again to please stop the barrage. We were both shaking and shivering and crying and praying all at the same time."[28] After an eighteen-day fight for an airfield on New Georgia in the Pacific, the men of one unit got out of the front lines and took the chance to bathe in the ocean. One of the soldiers went to the chaplain and said, "I never gave much thought to religion in my life, but during the battle I sure did a powerful lot of praying." The chaplain replied that they had all prayed a lot. "Well," the soldier replied, "I'm a changed man. There's a lot of water right here—how about baptizing me right now?"[29]

Because many of the troops returned to their religious background when they prayed in the service, their prewar religious differences came out in the open. It might have made sense for the men to fixate on those differences, to bring out all of their prejudices. But that did not happen. In fact, while the men noted denominational differences, the boundaries between various religions had less and less of a meaning to soldiers at the front. Paratrooper John Fitzgerald said that prior to beginning their mission on D-Day, all of the Catholics in his unit went to mass and took communion, and "the other denominations among us had made peace with their maker in their own way."[30] Hyman Haas saw a similar scene before D-Day: "There were religious services. (I am Jewish). I can remember being in some area. On one side of us, there was a Catholic priest holding mass. I had a rabbi who was holding [services] for the Jewish boys. There was a Protestant minister who was holding services for the Protestant boys. It was really strange; everyone praying in different religions and denominations. Each watching each other."[31]

A sergeant in a unit about to experience combat in Italy for the first time described the scene: "Our group was in the attic of one of these homes, and we all knelt together. We had people of various faiths, including this big Austrian who lost part of his family to the Nazis. We all just knelt there. Nothing was said."[32] Later on during the fighting, Roscoe Blunt and the fellow men in his mine-removal squad began to meet to read and discuss readings from the Bible. "We seemed to gain an inner strength, a peace of mind that pushed the war away for those few special minutes each night. The squad consisted of several Protestants, several Catholics and two Jews. None missed the nightly Scripture readings."[33] Some of the men explicitly prayed across denominational boundaries. Raymond Gantter recalled that he only went to a few religious services during his service in Europe, "and though I am not a Catholic, they were Catholic services that gave me a measure of serenity."[34] Francis Gigliotti said, "I'm Catholic, and when [we] were in a town with a church [of some] other denomination, [we] prayed their way."[35]

Not surprisingly, chaplains played a part in this process, and they lived up their army mandate to minister to all the men. "Our chaplains," one officer recalled, "particularly Father Maloney, were respected by all denominations and as such influenced all."[36] Paratrooper Carl Cartledge remembered that his unit's chaplain "was always moving around with us. I'm Presbyterian and he is Catholic and wonderful."[37] A Jewish officer wrote to a Protestant chaplain, "Chaplain, when I write home that my experiences in England have broadened my outlook on life, mostly I have you in mind. You've tempered my religious beliefs. You've taught me, albeit unknowingly, tolerance, compassion and a reverence for human values."[38] John Carey recalled, "We had a Catholic priest who conducted Jewish services as there was no Jewish chaplain on Guadalcanal."[39] Manny Krupin wrote home from France, "For Yom Kippur I was allowed to attend services at a nearby city. . . . No chaplain being available, a sergeant in the audience conducted the service. He did a fine job. The finishing touch was a short but very realistic talk by a Catholic priest. There were about five hundred or six hundred fellows present. The reception the priest received after his talk would have shaken any and all idiotic prattle that people of different faiths can't cooperate with one another. It was truly a heart-warming event."[40]

Some men felt that religion saved their lives. Lyle Groundwater was severely wounded in the fighting in Normandy. He recalled:

> The next thing that happened, there came this voice that I recognized, it was my good friend, Chaplain Kerns, a Catholic chaplain. I was not Catholic, but he and I were real good friends. He said, "Hello, Groundwater." And of course, I just laid there. And I heard a little noise and I thought he left, and then after a period of time, I could hear . . . again, and he said, "I've just said a little prayer over you, Groundwater." Well, I didn't think too much about it at the time. He left. Afterwards someone told me, he probably gave me the final rites of the church.
>
> Anyway, a week after that, I had finally reached Wales—we went right back to Abergavenny, Wales, where there was a station hospital. I was for a couple of weeks just kind of hovering between life and death, and shot in the lungs, and once, the first time, I started to die, and it was just as real an experience to me as if I had lit a cigarette. You know, if you light a cigarette, you know you've done it. I knew I was dying. And just before I finally went over the edge, I started to loosen my bowels, which I guess is one of the last things you do, and suddenly the recollection of that prayer came back to me, and it was just like turning on a light in a dark room, and I returned back to life.[41]

Max Feldman described religion playing a more unconventional role in his salvation. "One day my Army buddy Dominick was going to attend Mass being held somewhere in the rear," he recalled. "He reached down to me as I was in our foxhole. He wanted me to join him to attend the Mass. As he reached to pull me out of the foxhole we were arguing. I felt, being of the Jewish Religion, it was pointless for me to go to the Mass. But as we were arguing and walking away from the foxhole, a shell landed and hit our two man foxhole and blew it wide open. So Dominick DeLuca did save my life that day."[42]

Not all of the men practiced religion or put their faith in God to protect them. Not all men found God under fire. In fact, some came to believe that the horrors of war proved that there was no God, or at least no God that they could ever turn to for comfort.[43] Junior officer Charles Henne did not like the interference from chaplains or their interpretations about religion and war. "This business about no atheists in foxholes had to be fabricated by a chaplain," he said. "One of the men explained [it] this way, 'One day a chaplain happened to be on the line when the Japs shelled us. When the rounds hit he heard a GI scream, "Jesus Christ!" He went back to his clean sheets in the rear area declaring there were no atheists in foxholes.'"[44]

Whether or not the men found religion, they did not let religious differences stand in the way of camaraderie. In fact, quite the opposite—they came to respect the faith that got any man through. "We were comrades at arms and we were not based on religion," Murphy Foret said. "We believed in ourselves."[45] Paratrooper Donald Frederick had a similar experience: "Nobody tried to convert anyone. . . . It didn't make that much difference. We all seemed to pull together and beliefs didn't seem to matter."[46] As James Mayes put it, they "couldn't distinguish one person from another in combat. All seemed to do their best," regardless of religion.[47] E. J. Kahn described saying farewell to a close friend who was wounded on New Guinea: "'I know you don't believe in it much,' he said, 'but please pray for me.' I did."[48]

One man wrote home, "This war has done one thing . . . , it has made a lot of men think alike, men of all faiths are finding a brotherhood among themselves, they all believe in God without the rules that are supposed to go with it, Catholic kids are eating meat on Friday because they are hungry and need it, and the Jewish boys are eating non Kosher for the same reason, we are all equal, oh God, if they will only remember that when it is all over."[49] The war did not lead to a wholesale abandoning of religious backgrounds— most men returned home to the same faith they had left. But American religion did come to have a new meaning under fire. For the men, that religion would be tied up in what their war had meant. It would explain why they fought. It would create a new faith—a faith in one another. In times of peril, when modern war could make them feel utterly lonely, the presence of others provided some measure of comfort. If they had to be there, at least they were not totally alone.

When they turned to each other, when they looked at those who stood and fell beside them, they saw all kinds of Americans. That fact so struck them that later, when they could recall few specific details about the men around them in combat, they remembered regional background or ethnicity or religion. Recalling his experiences on D-Day among the units scattered along the beaches of Normandy, Theodore Aufort said he encountered one of the men in his unit: "I found one more fellow. I think of a Joe Porreca an Italian fellow from New Jersey."[50] Later he helped a wounded soldier: "He was a Jewish fellow but I can't recall his name."[51] Paratrooper Edward Boccafogli from New York City described scouting under fire in the fighting in Normandy with another soldier: "Mendez and myself—I'm pretty sure it was Patrico Mendez. It was a Mexican-American boy. Nice kid."[52] On D-Day, Felix Branham recalled, the "first man I saw from my company to die was a guy named Gene Ferrara. He was a little Italian boy out of Jersey City."[53] Ranger Sam Jacks from North Carolina remembered procuring some cider from a house in Normandy with a friend he described as a "Pollack . . . up out of the Bronx somewhere."[54] In the middle of a running battle Dean Joy met up with "Technical Sergeant Nero—a New York Italian."[55] Later Joy went on a patrol with a "Boston Irish kid we called Shaky Hayes."[56] Raymond Gantter witnessed the remains of a company that had been nearly wiped out in an attack: "I cannot forget one of them, an Italian boy."[57]

During a particularly intense period of shelling, Bob Woody described digging in with an Italian American fellow soldier: "The hole had the dimensions of a shallow grave—maybe three feet wide, three feet deep, and six feet long, just enough for two to cuddle and huddle in physical and psychological warmth."[58] Even Roscoe Blunt, who was not very close with most of his fellow soldiers, had one close buddy named Joe Everett, from Oklahoma. The self-professed loner needed the companionship in combat. As Blunt recalled, "Everett and I shared many foxholes and tried to maintain our sanity by arguing constantly whether older or younger women were more desirable."[59] When some Germans ambushed his company in the 90th Infantry Division in the later stages of the war, Carl Chumley recalled, "A big Jewish fellow named Friedman threw a couple of hand grenades toward them. That turned them back."[60] Roy Copeland recalled a good friend, "a Polish boy from Pennsylvania" who had a premonition he would be killed and then died that night when a German shell turned over his jeep.[61] Victor Fast noted that Dee Anderson, one of his two "very close buddies" who died on D-Day, was a Mormon from Salt Lake City.[62]

Sometimes background could matter to the men under fire. William Harness, who had the job of assigning litter bearers to carry wounded men back to the first aid station, said, "We had fellas from every state in the union. . . . Maybe I'm prejudiced because I'm from the south but, I preferred sending out at night and would rather risk some of the men from the south as those from the cities. The yankees from the cities didn't have the bird sense that most the fellas from the south that were raised in hill country or were hunters at night, they had a better sense of direction than people from the city."[63] Likewise, much as ethnically diverse soldiers who spoke the local language could be useful in dealing with civilians, getting food, and gathering intelligence, they could be helpful in combat. Joseph Blaylock described moving inland in Normandy with his buddy Mike Bieganski: "We ran into a sub-machine gun nest and they were looking right down our throat as we turned the curve. All of us just scooted down and threw our hands up. But they didn't fire; they came up with their hands up. They were Pollacks, and Bieganski being a

Pollack was able to talk to them a little bit."[64] Yet for the most part, ethnic or religious background did not matter to how the men performed in the war in the views of the other soldiers. All that mattered was that all varieties of men were there.

The horrors they shared created a level of understanding among the men that penetrated even the powerful notions of bravery and cowardice. Sustained combat eventually degraded the fighting effectiveness of even the most hardy soldier. The U.S. Army rotation system in World War II promised to keep men in the lines, with occasional respites to the rear or less active areas on the front, until the end of the war or the unit itself became too devastated to be effective. Studies during the war found that combat ability began to decline after six months in the line.[65] The men began to look for a way out besides death. Soldiers talked frequently among themselves about million dollar wounds—injuries that were serious enough to remove them from combat but would not permanently damage them.

But the million dollar wound often never came, and for some men the war became too much to handle. A few soldiers inflicted injuries on themselves in the effort to get out of the line of fire. Others just shut down mentally—either before, during, or after facing the enemy. In World War I, they called such cases shell shock; later generations would name the affliction post-traumatic stress disorder. In World War II, the army called it combat fatigue or combat exhaustion, but the effects were the same. Nearly all the men suffered from some form of combat fatigue at one time or another. Yet despite the horrors of the front lines and all the cases of combat fatigue, not every man tried to find a way out of combat duty. In fact, in quite a few cases wounded soldiers went out of their way, even going absent without leave, to get back to their units at the front. The bond proved that strong.

By and large, the troops did not judge between those who broke down and those who yearned to be with their buddies at the front. They understood both actions. They realized that every man, at his base, had a limit on the amount of pressure he could handle. They had little sympathy for those, as historian Peter Kindsvatter writes, "who had not first made a reasonable effort to cope and to do his share."[66] But as for the rest, they had seen what war could do to a man, and they respected that some men could only give so much. As one veteran of the 1st Infantry Division who fought all the way from North Africa to Czechoslovakia later said, "On two different occasions I was digging my foxhole and I drew that pick back to run in the thigh of my leg. So I could get out of it. But I couldn't do it. I hadn't quite reached that breaking point. It's hard to explain other than that. But I would never call another man a coward because I do believe in my own heart that a person who deliberately hurts himself has lost it at the time that he does. Regardless of how he tries. No man in his right mind, I don't believe, would ever deliberately hurt himself."[67]

American soldiers could forgive something they would have understood as weakness only a few years earlier, because in war groups of Americans became something more than their component parts. They had shared too much to be restricted by prejudices. E. J. Kahn described his fellow soldiers on New Guinea: "They were gaunt and thin . . . covered with tropical sores and had straggly beards . . . clothed in tattered stained jackets and pants. . . . Malaria, dengue fever, dysentery, and, in a few cases, typhus hit man after man. . . . Officers and men were equally bedraggled. They ran similar fevers, ate the same dreary rations, and wore the same shredded garments, without any insignia of rank."[68] Paratrooper David Jones explained the power of combat in creating unity:

> During our brief stay in Ireland and during one of our night training
> patrols, and after warming ourselves at a roadside pub, a fellow parachut-
> ist and I had gotten into a fairly good fistfight. After the rest of the group
> had separated us, this trooper had vowed that once we got into combat
> he was going to get my ass. Naturally you can guess who the first per-
> son was that I met while crawling along the edge of that causeway. Sure
> enough, the same trooper had me looking into the barrel of his Thompson
> machine gun. Well, after we hugged and slapped each other on the back
> telling each other how fortunate we were to have made it through this far,
> we started off together along the causeway toward a group of houses at the
> far end of the roadway.[69]

They could forgive each other for all of their differences because in the crucible of war they developed unique bonds of friendship the likes of which they had never experienced before and would never experience again. "Organization for a common and concrete goal in peacetime organizations does not evoke anything like the degree of comradeship commonly known in war," one veteran argued. "Evidently, the presence of danger is distinctive and important."[70] Ralph Burnett described his feelings the moments before his landing craft headed for Omaha Beach on D-Day: "Now, I had trained for six months with this squad, this company, this battalion, this division, and our squad had become very, very close. You really become close to somebody when you know you're going to be dependent on each other. We were all close and very good friends."[71] Salvatore DeGaetano, a son of immigrants, said combat "bound the units together—you depend on your buddy as he depended on you."[72] Dean Joy wrote home that the "thing that keeps us going, through it all, is just each other. We're all in it together, and we're all buddies."[73]

The bonds were so strong that some insisted that the word friendship did not suffice to describe their relationships—their feelings were better explained by words like family or love. In a scenario that may have seemed implausible when fictionalized in the movie *Saving Private Ryan,* Jack Burn, a veteran of the fight for Leyte in 1944, participated in a patrol to get a man named Jack Barker out of combat because Barker's sister and brother had both been killed in the war. After a short, intense firefight on the way to the beach, Burn recalled sitting down and having a drink with Barker, who "told me how much he didn't want to leave us since we were his brothers."[74] Ellis Laborde used similar language to describe one incident: "The truck right ahead of me had a direct hit. So, I got out of my truck and started pulling men that were burning alive. And a man pulled in a jeep, dressed in battle field fatigues, he came and complemented me on what I had done. Believe me, I was not seeking glory. Because to me, these men were like my brothers. We had been in the service together for several months."[75] Combat doctor Klaus Huebner explained why he ignored illness to stay with the men he worked with in the battalion aid station. "They have become a part of me," he said. "I trust them. They are reliable. They are faithful. They have been true comrades in misery. With them, I shall always share unforgettable memories, of danger, of humor, and of desperation. A romance such as this would be a pity to lose."[76]

William Walter from the 11th Airborne Division described the feeling in an interview: "There's a camaraderie; it's hard to explain. You've never been closer to anybody but your wife than you were with your army buddies. There was a bonding there that is hard to realize. Underneath, we were close as hell. That's why when you lose somebody, it really hits you hard."[77] The strength of the bond among the men also impressed Lyle Groundwater:

> One of the things that impressed me about as much as anything the only thing I can call it was love—that we had for each other. We'd all been indoctrinated where we all thought that infantry men were just head and shoulders above any common person such as a truck driver and a million times better than a civilian. But these men, we actually had times when men saved my life, and other times when I saved theirs. And golly, you just—well, as I say, it was just like a stronger love than what you feel for a woman.[78]

Paratrooper William Guarnere said of his company of paratroopers in the 101st Airborne Division, "It's a love and brother-ship that you can't achieve elsewhere . . . you can't explain it. You have to have been there to understand what—you know, my wife said I should have married the eagle. I'm not saying I care more for the guys in the Airborne than I do for my own wife and children. It's not that way. But sometimes it seems that way."[79]

That type of undying affection for fellow American soldiers created by the military experience brought into stark relief the missed opportunity created by racial segregation. The army's segregation meant white soldiers rarely saw black soldiers. They did not suffer through training together. They did not knowingly share a common resentment of officers, other branches, foreigners, and the enemy. Combat did not drive them to huddle together in fear or gather together in prayer. They missed a chance to learn that what they had in common far outstripped the superficial differences of skin color.

The few interactions between white and black troops hinted that a greater understanding was possible. Many African American soldiers served as truck drivers. One white soldier wrote, "I was impressed with the black drivers' bravery. . . . Some, in fact, even tried to wrangle ways to remain with us for a few days to join the actual fighting."[80] In fact, that same soldier said that in the fighting in Germany, he actually saw a black truck driver grab a Browning Automatic Rifle and some grenades and take out a German machine-gun nest that had held up a convoy. "Whoever this Quartermaster Corps driver was," he said, "he had earned the respect of an entire convoy of white GIs who were on their bellies observing the caper. He was one of the true heroes of the war and none of us ever found out his name."[81] William U'Ren of the 4th Infantry Division said, "While I was an MP in Cherbourg we walked town patrol with selected black MPs. We paired up—one black and one white. It worked fine for us."[82]

Two larger examples of wartime racial integration made the point. One came from officer training. Segregation was always expensive for the army for the obvious reason that separate facilities meant building two of everything. But in the case of training officers, segregation became too expensive, so the army quietly integrated the schools. A spokesman for the army wrote of the decision, "Our objection to separate schools is based primarily on the fact that black officer candidates are eligible from every branch of the Army . . . , and it would be decidedly uneconomical to attempt to gather in one school the material and instructor personnel necessary to give training in all these branches."[83] As a result, white and black officer candidates trained and lived together in the ground and service forces, with few problems.[84] A more salient example came in the winter of 1944–45, when personnel shortages compelled the army to allow some black troops in platoons or companies to integrate into battalions or companies. The experiment met with great success.[85] The integration of these units had a remarkable effect on the white soldiers. According to a survey that canvassed troops who had been in integrated companies, nearly two-thirds of white commissioned and noncommissioned officers were skeptical beforehand of the idea of companies made up of white and black platoons. After serving with black soldiers, 77 percent of those same men had a favorable view of the experiment. More than 98 percent thought black troops did well in combat, and more than 85 percent believed that black infantry soldiers were just the same or better than white troops.[86] White officer R. J. Lindo remembered:

> During the time I commanded the rifle company, I was given an experimental platoon of Black soldiers to fight in addition to my regular infantry company and attached tank destroyers and tanks. These were volunteers that had taken a bust from Master Sergeant, 1st Sergeant down to Private to prove themselves and they proved nothing but that a man is a man, because I could not keep these people from being heroes, and from killing Germans. Whether I had them in the attack or in the reserve, they were always up front. I was forced to assign a White platoon leader to them. These men were some of the most magnificent soldiers I had ever seen. But then, they were picked volunteers. They were out to prove something and they did.[87]

Other white soldiers who had occasion to fight alongside black troops came to similar conclusions. As Preston Price recalled thinking during the fighting around the Remagen bridgehead when some black soldiers arrived for the fight, "I am glad the colored men are here; we can use the help."[88] J. Kevin Hastings recalled, "In combat we worked once with a Black Tank Company. Even our red-necked Southerners appreciated them because they had 'Lib-er-ated a See-Gar factory,' and they were very generous to us Dogfaces. We also liked the way they handled their tanks."[89] Richard O'Brien agreed: "We had occasion to work with a colored tank battalion on [a] couple of attacks. They were terrific, they went in firing all guns and we took the towns with little resistance. They were as competent as the 4th and 6th armored units that we worked with later on."[90]

Unfortunately, such experiments remained relatively limited and their results largely unknown. White troops who did not serve alongside black soldiers did not have their prejudices challenged, and a survey of those men found that nearly two-thirds of the respondents "would dislike it very much" if their unit had a mix of black and white platoons.[91] Ignorance remained the greatest enemy to racial tolerance. As one man who served in the 101st Airborne explained when asked about ethnic, racial, or religious discrimination, "There seemed to be anti-black prejudice, as we had [no black troops]."[92]

Race did stand apart as a division in American society. A whole region of the country had its social structure built on the divisions between whites and blacks. The rest of the country had hardly thought to question such a structure. Ethnicity and religion mattered to Americans, but at the very least most accepted the idea that Italians and Irish and Jews were whites of some sort.[93] The discrimination against African Americans among white Americans did involve a unique animosity. One soldier claimed to have seen a horrifying incident in France: "I saw one man—I think from the 8th Infantry [Regiment, of the 4th Infantry Division]—shoot a black G.I. who was walking with a French woman down the street. He just shot him [with] his M-1. He was a southern soldier."[94] A letter from a nonveteran on the home front to a senator summed up the feelings of those who would not submit to any kind of racial integration:

> I hope that our Army "bigwigs" will not attempt to use the military as an instrument for experimenting with the race problem. Integration of the Negro into White regiments is the very thing for which the Negro intelligentsia is striving and such a move would serve only to lower the efficiency of the fighting units and the morale of the average white service man as well.
>
> I am a typical American, a southerner, and 27 years of age, and never in this world will I be convinced that race mixing in any field is good. All the social "do-gooders," the philanthropic "greats" of this day, the reds and the pinks . . . the disciples of Eleanor . . . the pleas by Sinatra . . . can never alter my convictions on this question . . . but I am loyal to my country and know but reverence to her flag, BUT I shall never submit to fight beneath that banner with a negro by my side. Rather I should die a thousand times, and see old Glory trampled in the dirt never to rise again, then to see this beloved land of ours become degraded by race mongrels, a throw back to the blackest specimen from the wilds.[95]

Such views toward race would prevail for the time being, and the racial segregation of the World War II army meant that most white soldiers did not have those views challenged. A one-time opportunity slipped away. Had there been racial integration, it stands to reason that racial bigotry would have been dealt a serious blow, if not a fatal one.

That lost opportunity was a shame—and the country would pay for the lost chance with the painful convulsions over race in the decades to come— but the opportunity lost should not obscure what did happen. Although not as bad as the racial divide, the ethnic and religious divisions in America up to the war had been serious and deep. That the military experience in World War II bridged those divisions among the troops was a testament to its power.

Nowhere was that power more evident than in the soldiers' understanding of the very meaning of the war. There can be no denying that the World War II generation struggled in applying significance to their war. Over and over, the soldiers denied that they fought for great causes. In fact, they were actively hostile to such ideas. When asked why they fought, they answered in banal terms: they said they wanted to finish the task and go home.[96] But their war did have a meaning; their fight did have a cause. That meaning, that cause, emerged in victory. It became clear in commemoration, especially for those who had been lost.

Veterans found that they became pretty immune to seeing enemy dead, and in fact they could become indifferent or worse. That lack of emotion could be seen in the wartime diary of one man fighting in Italy, who wrote, "Moved to a guard tunnel not far from Terraccina and saw my first Dead German soldier. Took a picture of him. There were also a lot of dead Italians in the tunnel, with many dead Krauts."[97] The annals of World War II are filled with examples of American troops rifling though the dead bodies of the enemy for souvenirs. Both the Germans and Japanese, especially the Japanese, took advantage of this American trait by setting up booby traps on the bodies of the fallen. In the war with Japan, the American lack of feeling toward enemy dead went so far as to manifest itself in the desecration of enemy bodies.[98] Some of the Americans could even ignore their dead comrades, in part because in horrible deaths, bodies seemed to lose their humanity.[99]

But most of the American soldiers men found that the sight of their dead countrymen affected them greatly, even when the bodies were strangers. As one man recalled, American dead "were dressed and looked like people you had been associated with even though you might not know them personally."[100] A veteran soldier told some new men at the front, "You know, seeing dead Krauts lying around don't make any more impression on me than leaves laying under the trees. But when I see one GI lying there cold, it really busts me up inside."[101] There was no image more powerful than American dead.

Americans, both at home and on the battlefield, valued that sacrifice more than any other. Above all, Americans treasured life. And as a result, they consecrated the fallen. The sacrifices made by the men who died took on a special importance. Most veterans would always argue that they were not heroes of World War II. The real heroes, they said, never came home. More than anything else, the deaths of their comrades made American fighting men reflect upon the meaning of their war.

The army gave the soldiers the context in which to reflect. Army commemorations of the victory did not favor one narrow group over another. Army services for the fallen made it clear that the sacrifices of the dead knew no ethnic or religious boundaries. Robert Easton described a regimental service to commemorate VE Day: "First a Protestant chaplain led us in a hymn, 3000 men standing with bowed heads. Then a Catholic chaplain led a prayer. Then a Jew recited the 23rd Psalm."[102] Gen. J. Lawton Collins sounded a similar theme at a memorial service on Guadalcanal two years earlier: "Without distinction as to creed or heritage we offer our united prayers in their behalf to their common maker."[103] An officer described the scene at another service to his wife:

> In front of me two boys shared the same hymn book. I saw them sharing the same frozen foxhole on an outpost along the Roer River, and when we jumped off and crossed the river they came one behind the other on the footbridge you saw pictured in *Life* which a mortar shell cut later and on which the dead floated all day. Those two men have eaten, slept, prayed, gotten drunk, argued, laughed, bitched about the Army and gone to the latrine together for six months and they've fought together, if there is such a thing. Actually nobody fights, you know. You just get up and go, scared to death, and hope you don't get killed this time, and then not *this* time, and so on through all the times. But if you have a buddy it isn't so bad and without ever saying it you cling to him and depend on him.[104]

Protestant chaplain Russell Stoup visited a cemetery and described it to his family: "Most of the graves are marked by white crosses, but there is the Star of David as well. I wish some of the anti-Semites at home could see them. I wish that they could know that their security and liberty have been bought for them at the price of the Jewish blood they despise."[105]

At the battle for Iwo Jima, a rabbi chaplain for the Marine Corps named Roland B. Gittelsohn gave a eulogy for the men who fell, a tribute consciously reflecting the words of Abraham Lincoln and so moving it was republished in several forms to be distributed among the American people. It read in part:

Star of David grave markers such as this one sit side-by-side with crosses in American World War II cemeteries around the world as a visible testament to the sacrifice of all Americans. Courtesy of the American Battle Monuments Commission, Arlington, Virginia.

This is perhaps the grimmest, and surely the holiest, task we have faced since D-day. Here before us lie the bodies of comrades and friends. Men who until yesterday or last week laughed with us, joked with us, trained with us. Men who were on the same ships with us, and went over the sides with us as we prepared to hit the beaches of this island. Men who fought with us and feared with us. Somewhere in this plot of ground there may lie the man who could have discovered the cure for cancer. Under one of these Christian crosses, or beneath a Jewish Star of David, there may rest now a man who was destined to be a great prophet—to find the way, perhaps, for all to live in plenty, with poverty and hardship for none. Now they lie here silently in this sacred soil, and we gather to consecrate this earth in their memory.

It is not easy to do so. Some of us have buried our closest friends here. We saw these men killed before our very eyes. Any one of us might have died in their places. Indeed some of us are alive and breathing at this very moment only because men who lie here beneath us had the courage and strength to give their lives for ours. To speak in memory of such men is not easy. Of them, too, can it be said with utter truth: "The world will little note nor long remember what we say here. It can never forget what they did here."

No, our poor power of speech can add nothing to what these men and the other dead of our division who are not here have already done. All that we can even hope to do is to follow their example. To show the same selfless courage in peace that they did in war. To swear that by the grace of God and the stubborn strength and power of human will, their sons and ours shall never suffer these pains again. These men have done their job well. They have paid the ghastly price for freedom. If that freedom be once again lost, as it was after the last war, the unforgivable blame will be ours, not theirs. So it is we, the living, who are here to be dedicated and consecrated.

We dedicate ourselves, first, to live together in peace the way they fought and are buried in this war. Here lie men who loved America because their ancestors generations ago helped in her founding, and other men who loved her with equal passion because they themselves or their own fathers escaped from oppression to her blessed shores. Here lie officers and men, Negroes and whites, rich and poor—together. Here are Protestants, Catholics, and Jews—together. Here no man prefers another because of his faith, or despises him because of his color. Here there are no quotas of how many from each group are admitted and allowed. Among these men there is no discrimination, no prejudice, no hatred. Theirs is the highest and purest democracy.

Any man among us, the living, who fails to understand that will thereby betray those who lie here dead. Whoever of us lifts his hand in hate against a brother, or thinks himself superior to those who happen to be in the minority, makes of this ceremony and of the bloody sacrifice it commemorates an empty, hollow mockery. Thus then, as our solemn sacred duty, do we, the living, now dedicate ourselves—to the right of Protestants, Catholics and Jews, of white men and Negroes alike, to enjoy the democracy for which all of them have here paid the price. . . .

. . . Thus do we memorialize those who, having ceased living with us, now live within us. Thus do we consecrate ourselves, the living, to carry on the struggle they began. Too much blood has gone into this soil for us to let it lie barren. Too much pain and heartache have fertilized the earth on which we stand. We here solemnly swear: This shall not be in vain. Out of this, and from the suffering and sorrow of those who mourn this, will come—we promise—the birth of a new freedom for the sons of man everywhere. Amen.[106]

Rabbi Gittelsohn could not give that speech at a general funeral because of politicking among chaplains, but he had expressed the sentiments of the soldiers.[107] Those sentiments, if not those exact words, became embedded in all commemoration of the war. More than just for the men on Iwo Jima, Rabbi Gittelsohn wrote a eulogy for the American war.

At the end of the war, most participants just wanted some kind of return to a normal life. They did not want to dwell on the war and all of the confusing and contradictory feelings service had created within them. But all of those emotions could not stay bottled up forever. Over time the veterans of World War II gave voice to what the war meant to them. Their reflections said everything. Dean Joy described his sixty days in combat as "by far the most profound of my life—they left deeper and more indelible scars on my psyche than any of the events that have happened to me since."[108] William Kennedy was asked during an exit interview about his feelings about his service: "My reply was that 'I would not have missed it for the world,' that I was extremely proud and relieved as to how it turned out, but 'if anyone has any ideas about me doing it again they may as well shoot me now.'"[109] Thomas Raulston said, "Of course there are a lot of things in combat that a man doesn't like, but . . . all in all my experience has been worth all the trouble and fears."[110] On the evening of D-Day Jack Ellery recalled, "I felt elated. It had been the greatest experience of my life, the greatest adventure. I was 10 feet tall. No matter what happened, I had made it off the beach, and reached the high ground. I was king of the hill, at least in my own mind, for a moment. My contribution to the heroic tradition of the United States Army might have been the smallest achievement in the history of courage, but at least, for a time, I had walked in the company of very brave men."[111]

In 1943, Lt. Walter Schuette wrote a letter to his newborn daughter to be given to her in the event that he should not make it back from the war. Indicating the bond among the soldiers, the letter included these statements:

"With this letter you will find a war bond . . . , and a list of names. A list of names to you, honey, buddies to me. Men of my company, who adopted you as their sweetheart when you came into the world. It is these men who bought you the bond as remembrance of when they were soldiers with your daddy." Schuette survived the war and read the letter to his daughter when she turned ten.[112]

What of those buddies? Some lessons were in part negative. Hawaiian William McGurn of the Eleventh Airborne said of his fellow Americans, "Not all of them are honest."[113] William Thibodeaux said he "learned both how great Americans can be—also being a country boy learned of some rotten Americans."[114] But for most of the men, familiarity did not breed contempt but quite the opposite. As they said over and over again, the main lesson they drew from the war was about unity. One Jewish soldier stationed in Ohio remembered an anti-Semitic Gerald L. K. Smith rally he saw during the war: "That rant hit the right buttons in that grievance-ridden crowd of losers, people to whom wartime prosperity had delivered nothing. How many of them had known any Jews? There surely were few if any Jews in Cedarville or the other little villages in southern Ohio, and, I doubted, many in Dayton or Springfield. But persons seeking others to blame for their own misfortune or incompetence don't need actual Jews. " He continued, "That Smith had a receptive audience here demonstrated the isolation, ignorance, and smoldering resentments of these farmers, who had no contact with the world beyond their own crops, pastures, and debts."[115] By 1945, the same could never again be said of the millions of Americans who had served in the wartime military, no matter their branch or area of service.

From the 11th Airborne Division, which saw service in the Pacific, Caesar Abate from California learned of "men from farms, coal mines, steel mills, and I'm a city boy."[116] William Weber from Alabama said, "We are, and remain, a great people. When united, we can achieve anything. Our diversity is both our greatest strength and weakness."[117] Ira Gross, from Ohio, wrote, "I learned to be appreciative of comrades, rest of U.S."[118] Newton Minow, who served in the China-Burma-India theater, wrote at the end of the war that "the greatest lesson I learned in the war; that the world is not large, but small; that peoples are not different, but the same; and that peace is the greatest gift of all."[119] Also from the Pacific theater, Missourian Floyd Todd of the 37th Infantry Division said, "We are a [diverse] lot and when we work together as we did in World War II we can accomplish almost anything."[120] Men of the Americal Division such as John Carey of Massachusetts recalled, "It showed that when you attack us watch as we get united as one."[121] George Christenson from North Dakota noted that "when there is a job to be done the Americans forgot about differences and did it."[122] Pennsylvanian Richard Cohen said, "Individuals of diverse backgrounds, location, etc. able to function as units toward a common goal."[123] According to William Shiepe, "No matter what our background we will succeed when we get together for a just cause."[124] North Dakotan John Stannard, who was a sergeant during the war but later rose to the rank of brigadier general, said, "Good combat Soldiers and poor combat Soldiers come in all sizes and shapes and often from unexpected sources, so don't prejudge an Infantry Soldier until you see his performance in battle. Infantry soldiers are team/family oriented. They are proud of their organization and themselves, and they will be as brave as they need to be."[125] And from the 1st Cavalry Division, John Sandidge of Texas wrote, "As combat soldiers we learn to respect others. American people are the best. Great[est] country in the world."[126] John Savarino from western Pennsylvania remembered of his countrymen, "They all served faithfully. We are all together and determined to prove it in the end."[127]

Those who served in the Mediterranean and European theaters told the same story. William Rape of the 2nd Armored Division said, "We were all one in World War II."[128] Also from the 2nd, Merritt Bragdon from Illinois wrote, "We are reasonably likeable and able people and can get along with each other well despite varied backgrounds,"[129] and Donald Eastlake recalled that "Americans from all walks of life came together and formed a great military machine."[130] Hollis Stabler, an Oklahoma Indian, learned that "America is made up of many different cultures and people, some good some bad."[131] Other men who fought in Europe agreed. From the 4th Infantry Division, William Lee of Pennsylvania said, "When America has to fight to protect its freedom and way of life we do it together regardless of color and race."[132] Lawrence Ostling of Illinois, from the 44th Infantry Division, said, "Americans are pretty much the same from all over the country. It's amazing how such an individualistic and independent people can band together in a single great effort."[133] New Yorker J. Kevin Hastings wrote, "We are a Joseph's Coat of ethnic, religious, language and national patches. But, my what a warm and beautiful coat!"[134]

From the 101st Airborne Division, southerner Carl Cartledge said, "No matter what our ethnic origins are, when we think as Americans we become a new nationality, a new breed that the centuries to come will be [as] blessed by its birth as we have been."[135] Salve Matheson of California stated, "Naturally it broadened one's viewpoints of our country and its people—favorably."[136] John Brandon Price, who lived in Michigan and Georgia, said, "When it comes down to the snortin' pole, we all come together in the common interest."[137] Tank operator William Preston wrote during the war, "I don't think there is much we won't be able to adjust to in the future. I think we've learned how important it is to be open minded, to ban silly prejudices which contribute greatly to warping your viewpoint on life."[138] From the 35th Infantry Division, James Graff of Illinois said that "it takes all kinds to make a country like ours."[139] Richard O'Brien noted, "We are a remarkably versatile and capable nation. We were absolutely united after Dec 7, 1941 and showed the world how a democratic country works when threatened. I enjoyed meeting and making friends with guys from every state."[140] Pennsylvanian Lloyd Dull, who became a prisoner of war, said of the United States, "I feel it was and still is the most wonderful country in the world. And that when there is a job to do Americans, whether race-creed or religion, get in and get the job done."[141] George Melochick said simply, "No flag waving. I love my county and its people."[142] James Bross wrote that he learned "how lucky I was to be born in America and how Americans became Americans when the chips were down."[143] When trying to come to grips with his war, Audie Murphy said he believed "in men like Brandon and Novak and Swope and Kerrigan; and in all the men who stood up against the enemy, taking their beatings without whimper and their triumphs without boasting."[144] Midwesterner Kensinger Jones concluded, "Our unit included Texans, Oklahomans, Mexicans, Arkansans, Missourians, urban, rural, rich, poor, educated, illiterate, a couple of gays. Under extremely difficult conditions, using our combined talents, we did fine. Isn't that what it's all about?"[145]

The overwhelming weight of these statements said something profound about the military experience in World War II. The war had changed the men. It had torn them from their homes, stripped them of their individuality, reformed them into new groups, shipped them to distant lands, and made them confront the most grand and terrible extremes of human existence. Despite their reluctance to say so, despite their unwillingness to go on as their Revolutionary and Civil War predecessors had about God and country, when they finally thought about it, when time made them reflect, it became all too clear that World War II did have a meaning for the soldiers. That meaning was each other, their fellow American soldiers, the men who had stood by them through the best and worst time of their lives—Americans, in all their regional, ethnic, and religious variety. In the end, after all that they had gone through, after all they had seen and done, after all they had won and lost, comrades became the cause. And they would not forget.

# 6

# COMING HOME, TAKING OVER

We left the other side of the tracks and began to move into
town. We moved to better neighborhoods and, thanks to the
GI Bill, we continued our education. We were able to buy new
homes. We began to go into business for ourselves, obtain
better positions of employment and some even managed to
get chosen, appointed or elected to public office.

—Raul Morin, *Among the Valiant,* 1963

AMERICA PREPARED FOR THE RETURNING VETERANS LIKE NO OTHER TIME IN
its history. For once the country sought to learn the lessons from the aftermath of its earlier wars, especially World War I. The veterans of that conflict
never felt they had been properly compensated for their efforts.[1] They organized and filled veterans' groups such as the American Legion and Disabled
American Veterans (DAV) in part because they believed that the country
had ignored their needs and wishes. When World War II came, many commentators invoked that earlier experience. "We must have no repetition of
the shabby chapter of ingratitude written in the government's treatment of
veterans of World War I," a 1943 editorial stressed. "We must have no jobless,
pitiful heroes selling apples or poppies on the streets; no homeless veterans
huddling under viaducts."[2] In the summer of 1945, a speaker at a Catholic War Veterans meeting said, "At present and for months to come, almost
ten percent of our total population and approximately twenty percent of our
electorate are absorbed in bringing the war to a victorious close. . . . Let us
not risk again the disillusionment experienced by the returning veteran of
World War I when upon his return he found the Prohibition Amendment
and the Volstead Act had been slipped over while he was absent from the
United States."[3]

The most salient example of earlier veteran discontent came from the
depths of the Great Depression. In 1932, thousands of veterans descended on

Washington, D.C., to ask the government to accelerate payment on bonuses they had been promised in 1924. They became known as the Bonus Army, and they shocked the whole country. Whether or not every American sympathized with their cause, and many did not, the image of destitute veterans organized and camped out in the nation's capital became tied to the failings of the Hoover administration. And when their effort to secure the bonus fell short, Hoover ordered the army to evict them from federal property. The ensuing violence was a sad testament to the country's failure to provide for those who had given so much in its defense.[4]

President Franklin Roosevelt understood the power of that image. In the frantic activity of the first one hundred days of his presidency, he found time to sign an executive order creating a temporary Veterans' Administration facility in Fort Hunt, Virginia. As the president himself wrote by hand on an early draft, "The sole purpose of this order is to take care of these veterans for a few days while they visit Washington for legitimate purposes."[5] He certainly did not want any "Rooseveltvilles" housed by veterans springing up around Washington, D.C., and his administration went to great pains to house and feed later marchers at a facility south of the city.

When World War II came, Roosevelt had already developed a broad conception of how to prepare the country for the return of peace and the reincorporation of the fighting men. One aide summed up Roosevelt's feelings toward the soldier: "The most important thing we can do for our veteran is to provide a sound economy for him when he comes home."[6] Roosevelt believed that the best way to provide a sound economy was to generalize the benefits for the whole population, veteran and nonveteran.[7] But he also recognized that soldiers made a unique sacrifice because the war interrupted their educational and career paths. So even the original Selective Service Act of 1940 included a provision for soldiers to return to preservice jobs.

However, that concession was not enough for the activist veterans of World War I. During the fighting, an undercurrent of dread about the postwar economy pervaded the country. Americans expected that the millions of returning servicemen would lead to high unemployment, and the high unemployment would lead to a return of the Depression. What is more, Americans expressed a widespread concern about whether or not the veterans would suffer from mental or emotional problems because of their wartime experiences. Study after study asked if they would be violent, surly, or uncontrollable. They questioned whether the troops would be able to adjust back to family life and if they would be able to recover their individualism.[8] Headlines in popular magazines told the families of vets to expect gloomy or moody behavior and suggested that they not try to sympathize or ask too many questions.[9]

The veterans of earlier wars, led by the American Legion and Veterans of Foreign Wars, did not want their World War II counterparts to suffer as they had. They used the fears about unemployment, depression, and potentially unstable veterans to lobby for a variety of special benefits for World War II servicemen. Their success was remarkable. Their pressure, and the increasingly obvious public will, changed the president's mind. One example illustrated the shift. In 1944, the president came out in support of preferences for veterans in hiring for the federal civil service. When an official from the Department of Commerce wrote to complain that such a measure would be unfair to civilian employees who had also sacrificed, one of the president's secretaries replied that the policy might be unfair to some. "If, however," he wrote, "we consider those who have entered the armed forces as a group in comparison with those who are given occupational preferences, I feel sure that you will agree with me that those who are a part of the armed forces have and will continue to be called upon to make far greater sacrifices than those who continue to hold civilian positions." He concluded the letter by pointing out "the current public attitude which is so sympathetic to the soldier that almost any preference legislation would be enacted if insisted on by veteran representatives."[10]

Armed with the belief that the veteran had sacrificed more than the civilian, and thus was due more from the government, Congress and the Roosevelt administration enacted an unprecedented series of legislation to benefit the returning fighting man. The Vocational Rehabilitation Act of 1943 provided for the training of disabled veterans. The Mustering-Out Pay Act of 1944 provided for a generous bonus for servicemen at their discharge. But their greatest success came in 1944 with the passage of the Servicemen's Readjustment Act, better known as the GI Bill. The bill provided for temporary readjustment unemployment payments (twenty dollars a week for up to fifty-two weeks), low-interest mortgage loans for buying homes, and grants for college or vocational training. Congress spent nearly fifteen billion dollars on the GI Bill by its first cut-off date in 1956. Over half of the sixteen million veterans of the war took advantage of the readjustment payments to one extent or another. The bill provided for over three and half million mortgagees. And roughly eight million of the veterans used the education and training benefits.[11] It was the most far-reaching social welfare bill in American history.[12] The advantages it provided the veterans were impossible to gauge.

And yet there were other trains of thought concerning benefits to veterans. Some individuals believed that veterans should be honored but should not get special treatment. Some of these people argued that the whole country had participated in the war, and the economic benefits should be distributed equally among all.[13] A few others expressed the point in a different way. Lawrence Westbrook, an army officer who served in the office of the chief of staff, gave a speech to the business leaders of the American Management Association in September 1944. He summed up the speech in a letter to President Roosevelt's aide and confidant, Harry Hopkins: "I have found the feeling generally prevalent that giving veterans jobs after the war is a problem that we must solve, no matter how difficult, because of our legal and moral justifications. . . . I don't think it is any such thing. These young men are the selected best of our entire population." The speech explained the point in more detail. The men, Westbrook told the audience, were in better physical shape, had more discipline, understood better how to work with others, had learned tolerance and understanding through travel, were more tempered and mature, and had been trained in a variety of specialized skills and trades. For these reasons, Westbrook concluded in his letter to Hopkins, "It is they who, in a few years, will really run this country, and there ought to be the keenest competition to obtain their services."[14]

The government, according to this line of thinking, had no special obligation to the veteran because the veterans already had the advantage of their military experiences. Westbrook had a point, but it was a cold, apolitical one that had no chance of turning into policy. The ideas of veterans groups and those sympathetic to the troops prevailed concerning public policy. Veterans received unique benefits as veterans. But it should not be forgotten that they also, as a group, had the advantages expressed by Westbrook in his speech. The combination of those benefits and those advantages combined to make World War II veterans one of the largest and most influential social groups in all of American history.

Their trek to greater influence in American society began at war's end. The atomic bombs that forced Japan to surrender and stunned the world with their terrifying power also shocked the army and its soldiers. In the months after Germany's surrender most of the troops celebrated, but they did so with a wary eye toward the future. They knew that the impending invasion of Japan would be a bloody and horrible affair; they feared nothing more than being the last casualty in a nearly completed fight. Then, suddenly, it was over. The bomb had ended the war, and for that the men were profoundly grateful and would ever remain so.[15]

All of the nervous energy that had been bent upon the fight in Japan turned to a new outlet—getting out of the military. Even earlier, much of their focus in uniform had been on issues at home and the end of the war.

Both officers and enlisted men in one survey listed among their top concerns "being a long way from home," "matters concerning my family or friends back home," and "what is going to happen to me after the war."[16] When the war ended, the men turned all their attention to getting home. To manage the process of demobilizing, the army developed a point system based on a variety of factors relating to service.[17] Although the system was generally fair, it pleased almost no one. Even among men not serving overseas, "commitment to duty quickly eroded into calculation of points earned toward discharge. . . . With no war to win, motivation faded; men went to their assignments impatiently, did them dutifully, without enthusiasm."[18] The men could not get home fast enough. In fact, thousands of soldiers demonstrated in January 1946 in both the Pacific and European theaters in an attempt to speed up demobilization.[19] The delays gave one man the opportunity to take yet another shot at the British and strikers on the American home front. An article indicating that the British had taken some ships out of the redeployment effort sparked his anger: "I don't know how much this is going to put us back if any but should it, I'll hate those Limeys as much as I do those striking bastards back at New York."[20]

For all of their impatience to get home, they did not really seem to have much of an idea of what they wanted to do once they got there. The men had generalized dreams of returning home. They imagined loving reunions with family and sweethearts. They envisioned taking some time off to explore their country and think about or forget what they had just experienced. Some had more specific ideas for their postwar life. For example, one man wrote, "After this war is over, I'd like to be a trucker. If I'm lucky maybe I can get a job trucking for the Pennsylvania Railroad and pull down fifty or sixty bucks a week."[21] But they often did not think in specific detail about what they would do for the rest of their lives once they returned home. Robert Peters recalled that he and his comrades rarely talked about the future, since few of them had goals in place.[22] One particularly astute soldier wrote from Germany of his trepidation about readjusting to civilian life: "I am impressed by the magnitude of the problem of readjustment for service men after the war. Many will certainly be very restless, and I am sure that all will have at least one good binge in them before settling down. Many who now think that they wish nothing more than to get out of the army, may find it very hard to become adjusted to civilian life, particularly to the routine of daily work on a job and to dull family life."[23]

The War Department worked with the American Historical Association to produce a series of pamphlets to help spark discussions among the troops about readjustment to civilian life. They ranged from straightforward issues of readjustment such as *What Will Your Town Be Like?*, *Shall I Go Back to School?*, and *Will There Be Work for All?* to specialized policy and personal questions such as *Why Do Veterans Organize?*, *Is Your Health the Nation's Business?*, *What Shall We Do With Our Merchant Fleet?*, and even *Will There Be a Plane in Every Garage?*[24] The topics of these pamphlets reflected the dichotomy between concerns and optimism the soldiers had for their lives in postwar America. They worried that they would not be able to find jobs, but they looked forward to experiencing steady employment in the new economy.

That dichotomy extended to their impressions of how the war had changed them personally. They wanted their friends and family at home to understand that they were both different and the same; that war had changed them, but they were still the same person deep down. Robert Easton described the car ride home with his parents and conversation about the weather and gasoline rationing and old friends. Wrote Easton, "They speak as if nothing has happened, as if everything will go on as before. . . . Deep inside I want to shout 'No, no, it can't!'—to try and tell them all that has happened to me, to the world; but know that I cannot, that it is impossible and probably always will be."[25] Mexican American veteran Raul Morin said, "For the returning Mexican-American veteran, things *were* different and furthermore he did not want to find things the way he had left them."[26] Many of the returning veterans echoed these feelings. At the same time, many of them resented the fact that family and friends acted as if they did not know them. They craved the stimulation of new experiences, but they worried when their hometowns did not match their memories.[27]

Every veteran faced his own issues and difficulties upon return from the war, and they all adjusted in their own way. "It was really some adjust[ment] to get readjusted, not knowing the price of cars, the price of land, the price of anything," William Harness said. "I'd been gone about three years and seven months. You lose track of the value of anything. I'd saved some money and I had to wait a while to get my bearing, get my head back on my shoulders before I would invest my money in anything."[28] Charles Sass said that when he returned home he found a sign on the door reading, "The rent is paid for a month. Good luck." So he headed to New York City and lived as a bum for a while, along with several other veterans. Eventually Sass took advantage of the money he had earned and the GI Bill, but for the time being he just had to adjust to peacetime.[29] Alfred Allred remembered, "I got out of the service in 1945. I went in civilian life, didn't work out too well. [I] Saw mills and farming as just too hard work. Well, it wasn't too hard work, but I wasn't happy. So, in 1948, I went back into the service."[30]

The return could be especially hard on the wounded. The permanently disabled had to rely on others, often the government, to get by.[31] Even before the war ended veterans wrote to the president of their situations. For example, Edward Myers of Evansville, Indiana, wrote that he was unable to walk due to injuries from the war and that he needed a pension badly in order to support his family.[32] Russell Thirlaway of Boulder, Colorado, noted that he did not even have enough money to fill the prescriptions given to him at the veterans' hospital. Thirlaway wrote that he had heard people say that nothing was too good for the veterans when they got back, but he had not seen it.[33]

The men struggled most with adjusting to the loss of the military social structure. Those who had seen up close what the war had done usually believed that those who had not been there would not be able to understand. The men who had been in combat did not want to relive their experiences, because it hurt to see friends die and they felt a certain guilt about surviving. And the men who had not seen combat felt a certain shame about not being tested. "I could not help but feel that my service in the Zone of the Interior had kept me from initiation into a maturity shared by some of my friends and many of my generation," one such man remembered.[34] So they did not want to talk about the war, either. The only comfortable place for these veterans was in the quiet company of others who had been through what they had been through.

Roscoe Blunt expressed the feeling of being separated from his buddies: "These wartime relationships were akin to family love and were nurtured by months of shared deprivation and hunger, of survival-threatening cold and excruciating anguish, of stark terror and sensitivity-shattering horror, crippling exhaustion and personal triumph. And never again would there be the nonsensical hilarity and crazy escapades that had forged bonds among us that would be emotionally difficult to break."[35] A few of the men did not make it, even if they survived the war. Pacific war veteran Max Kulick committed suicide in 1950. His friend Jack Herzig speculated as to why: "Perhaps, as the end of the unemployment program for GIs ran out after a year, he couldn't find any replacement program for the security of the company of fellow human beings who had shared the dangers of a shooting war and had even taught him to play double pinochle."[36] These veterans craved the camaraderie of their military service. Millions of them made up for the loss by joining veterans' organizations.

Veterans filled the rolls of literally hundreds of veterans' groups formed during and after World War II. Most of these were small organizations that catered to a specific group of veterans. Former members of specific units, usually divisions or regiments, organized societies exclusively for other former

This illustration comes from a 1946 pamphlet for the troops titled *Why Do Veterans Organize?* American Historical Association, *Why Do Veterans Organize?*

members. With their members spread all over the country, these organizations held periodic reunions and printed newsletters to keep their members abreast of the doings of their wartime buddies.[37] These groups acted as fraternal societies where the men could occasionally gather together, have a few drinks, and reminisce about their time together in the war.

Some organizations, usually left over from earlier wars, were built around specific ethnic or religious groups. The most prominent of these were the Catholic War Veterans and Jewish War Veterans. But Polish Americans, Italian Americans, Irish Americans, Greek Americans, Slovenian Americans, and others also had their own organizations. Most of these groups also focused on providing a continuation of the camaraderie among the men. And despite their ethnic or religious quality, they did not become especially provincial about their ethnicity or religion when it came to relations with other veterans' groups. None were exclusive; members of one group could be and often were members of another.[38] Most of these smaller groups focused primarily on providing a sense of fraternity for their members. Most of them had memberships that numbered only in the hundreds or low thousands, although the Jewish War Veterans and Catholic War Veterans claimed memberships that crept near or over one hundred thousand. For the men who wanted to belong to something bigger, there were other options.

The Veterans of Foreign Wars, American Legion, and Disabled American Veterans made up the "big three" of veterans groups—before, during, and after World War II. The VFW was the oldest, having formed after the Spanish American War as an organization specifically for veterans of overseas wars.[39] The VFW did not do a good job adjusting to the needs of World War I veterans, and as a result their membership did not grow much in the interwar period. To fill the gap, veterans of World War I formed both the American Legion and the DAV. The legion grew to over a million members in the interwar period. The more exclusive and necessarily smaller DAV made great use of the morality of its causes and maintained an active agenda that kept it in the national spotlight. All three opened their ranks to returning World War II servicemen, and all three grew precipitously after the war.

Many men joined the American Legion, VFW, and DAV for the same reasons they joined the smaller units: camaraderie. For example, veteran John Carey said that he joined and stayed in veterans groups specifically for comradeship.[40] The VFW and American Legion explicitly catered to the veteran's need for some kind of social structure and guidance. They recreated a more lax version of the military structure by having ranks and unit designations. Their popular organs, among them the *American Legion Monthly,* spent a great deal of time providing guidance on health, fashion, and leisure activities. Countless articles in the monthly, especially early on after the war, focused on hunting, fishing, and sports.

But the big three had other agendas, and their active members knew it. Former paratrooper William Weber joined all kinds of organizations. For him the smaller unit associations provided the comradeship he had experienced during the war, while the larger more generic associations gave veterans some influence on national issues.[41] William Lee joined for similar reasons, "to keep in contact with people I served with, and help further the cause of the veteran."[42] Beyond camaraderie, veterans' organizations represented the political needs and wants of veterans. The American Legion, VFW, and DAV especially fulfilled that mission, but they were not the only ones.

Although World War II veterans joined the American Legion, VFW, and DAV by the millions, some still believed that they needed their own organization to represent their own interests. A letter from a small veterans' group to President Truman in 1946 explained the thinking: "It is understandably impossible for the veterans of World War II to see eye to eye with veterans of World War I on current basic issues, so as a consequence would desire to have their own organizations. They are another generation living in an era of different ideals and principles. They, as a matter of fact, faced such vastly different, changed, and changing issues, even during their service, from those faced by veterans of World War I, that the veteran of World War I is unable to even vaguely understand the working of the minds of veterans of World War II."[43] Within the American Legion and VFW especially, the new generation of veterans clashed with the old over a variety of concerns. Some World War II veterans wanted their own national organizations.

A few of the servicemen had anticipated the potential political power of World War II veterans at war's end. Writing in September 1944 from France, one officer described a man in his unit who had great political ambitions: "He is warm, roly-poly, bright-eyed Irish and talks of a post-war organization of veterans of World War II similar to the American Legion but separate from it. Of course such an organization, 8 to 10 million strong, could rule the country."[44] The American Veterans of World War II (AMVETS) became the most prominent of such groups. Formed in late 1944, the AMVETS became the first World War II veterans' organization to receive a national charter from Congress. Early on in national politics, AMVETS leaned to more liberal policies than either the American Legion or VFW, but eventually it came to follow much the same path as those two groups.[45] Those who rejected the conservative message of the American Legion, VFW, and AMVETS formed their own organization around more liberal, and sometimes radical, principles. The American Veterans Committee (AVC) became the veterans' equivalent of the Americans for Democratic Action—a Left-leaning group that fractured over the issue of opposing communism and never had very high membership numbers.[46]

Although none of these groups ever enrolled anywhere near a majority of World War II veterans, millions did fill their ranks, and they served as some of the most important political voices for those millions. These groups represented a variety of concerns among the World War II veteran population, but economic issues in particular led them to become involved in the politics of the era.

For all the government's attempts at anticipating and dealing with demobilization and reconversion, some serious economic problems faced veterans upon their return.[47] Representative among these was housing. Eventually the

U.S. economy provided plenty of homes, but in the first year or two after the war that fact was small comfort to veterans without paying jobs and homes of their own.[48] The extent of the problem could be seen all over the country. In spring and summer 1946, 40 percent of the ninety-three hundred World War II veterans living in the area around Erie, Pennsylvania, lived with relatives or friends, and a quarter of them lived in homes without one or more standard facilities like central heat, electricity, running water, or a private bath. In Everett, Washington, nearly 20 percent of the twenty-six hundred recent veterans lived with family or friends and 10 percent lived without one or more of the facilities. In Madison, Wisconsin, 30 percent of the five thousand veterans lived with family or friends, and 20 percent went without standard facilities. One-third of the twenty-one thousand veterans living in San Antonio, Texas, shared homes with relatives, and 40 percent of them did not have all the standard facilities. Of the one thousand veterans in Henderson, Kentucky, the figures were 28 percent and 40 percent, respectively. None of these areas offered much by way of new housing, although anywhere from 30 percent to 40 percent of the veterans surveyed, many of them married and with families, planned on moving in the next twelve months.[49] The story was much the same all around the country. Of the respondents to a survey in April 1946, 19 percent of the total population said they had to double up because of the housing shortage. Of the homes with no veterans, only one in ten had to double up. Of the homes with veterans, the number was nearly 42 percent.[50]

The severity and immediacy of the problem ignited the passions of veterans, and they demanded action of their elected representatives. They complained to their representatives, and the representatives passed on the complaints to the president.[51] Delegate Bob Barlett from Alaska warned Truman, "We must protect, above all, the veterans from becoming a separate and discordant segment of our society."[52] The severity of the issue could be seen in President Truman's letter to Kentucky politician Wilson Wyatt requesting that he take the position of housing expediter in the Office of War Mobilization and Reconversion. "This country is faced by an acute shortage of housing," the president wrote. "Veterans are returning to homeless communities. . . . It is urgent that every available temporary living quarter be used in overcrowded communities, that the production of building materials be expedited, that the production of homes be hurried, that the cost of housing be protected from further inflation" with the goal of making "the peace production of homes equal to the task of housing our veterans and other civilians."[53] Truman released a statement a few months later about meeting with Catholic, Protestant, and Jewish leaders to discuss the housing shortage. Together they concluded that churches and synagogues could organize on a local level to help find housing for veterans and that such efforts would be especially effective with "community-wide cooperation in this effort among all religious and civic groups." After all, they reasoned, "surely no veteran who has served his country faithfully and well should now be left homeless on his return from service."[54]

The veterans turned up the pressure. An independent veterans' publication out of Philadelphia with a circulation of thirty thousand printed an open letter to President Truman demanding to know "Where are the Jobs?" and "Where are the Homes?" The author wrote, "You know, I didn't mind living in a tent for almost the whole time I was in uniform. . . . But my wife and kids aren't used to living under canvas, Harry."[55] Veterans held public meetings on the problem of housing. One man at such a meeting summed up his problem: "Look, we just got married a couple months ago and my wife has to sleep at the YWCA and me at the YMCA. What kind of marriage is that anyway?"[56]

President Truman and the Democratic majorities in Congress heard these complaints with the 1946 congressional elections looming on the horizon. The possibility of veterans uniting around an issue or two and voting as a bloc caused a great deal of anxiety and excitement for national politicians. As the 1946 elections approached, the potential power of that bloc became clear. One senator wrote to President Truman arguing that veterans were the key to saving Democratic majorities in both houses and assuring Truman's reelection in 1948. "Never before in American history have we had such a formidable group as our 20,000,000 living veterans," the senator wrote. "Even though some of the 20,000,000 veterans have not registered, their power can be felt in this election, as veterans and their families comprise nearly 60 per cent of the population in each community now."[57] The federal government was already pouring huge amounts of resources into compensating and reconverting veterans, but it was not enough. Even though both employment and housing conditions steadily improved after the war's end, veterans' groups kept up the pressure and the widespread individual cases of housing difficulties made news. In July 1946, a veteran from Milwaukee wrote a letter to the *American Legion Magazine* stating that Congress had done the job of mobilizing for the war emergency, "but if the same Congress doesn't think there is an emergency for a different kind of housing, then it should be voted into the political oblivion its disinterestedness merits."[58] The Republicans used such emotions to great effect in the campaign, asking the population, "Had Enough?" and mocking that one of the Democratic slogans should be "Two Families in Every Garage."[59] It worked. Truman's poll ratings plummeted. The party in power received the blame.

The 1946 election was a disaster for Truman's Democrats. Housing combined with other problems of reconversion, especially meat shortages, to cripple the Democrats' chances. For the first time since 1928, Republicans won majorities in both houses of Congress. The shocking victory for the Republicans did not represent a major shift in American electoral politics. It did not shatter Franklin Roosevelt's coalition. As a rule, Americans stayed with their party out of a sense of tradition or loyalty. Most prewar Republicans remained Republicans, just as most prewar Democrats remained Democrats.[60] The basic makeup of the party coalitions would not change until the 1960s and 1970s.[61] Still, the concerns of party members began to shift. New issues began to take precedence.[62]

The 1946 election introduced a new era in American politics, an era that could and would be dominated by the concerns of veterans. The housing issue in that election had shown that when veterans broadly agreed on a specific concern, they wielded remarkable power in shaping the outcome of national events. The first reason for their power was demographics. Veterans of World War II made up a greater proportion of the general population than veterans of any other war in American history. The population of the United States in 1950 was 150.7 million. World War II veterans that same year numbered over 15.4 million, or just over 10 percent of the total population. The civilian population of the United States over the age of eighteen was just over 100 million, of which World War II veterans constituted a little more than 15 percent. Even in 1950, they were relatively young.[63] More than 11 million of them were younger than thirty-four. The most common ages were twenty-eight and twenty-nine.[64]

It must also be kept in mind that women, who made up over half the total population, did not have much of a voice in postwar America. Men and women had an image of the role of women in society, and the war had only strengthened that image among the soldiers. No small amount of desperate romanticism went into many decisions to marry during the war. One soldier recalled that he proposed to no less than four women before going off to basic training.[65] Once overseas, most men thought only of coming home to get married and raise a family. Over and over again, soldiers during the war had said just that, whether they had a specific woman in mind or not. Gerald Herzfield wrote home to his parents, "I have every reason in the world to believe that I will return as I have a full life of peace to look forward to with the woman I will eventually marry."[66] "I will go back," Audie Murphy said at the end of the war. "I will find the kind of girl of whom I once dreamed."[67] George Wilson lived the dream, marrying within days of his return from Europe.[68] The result was a marriage boom during and after the war.[69]

Returning veterans had seen the seamier side of the rest of the world, especially when it came to what they believed was the fairer sex. As one soldier wrote home, "With the women of occupied countries it has often been a question of food or chastity, and they often found it necessary to choose the former."[70] In their dreams, home provided them something pure. They wanted their new wives, at least in appearance, not sullied by all the drinking, carousing, swearing, and whoring they saw during their service. One veteran described this worldview in relation to army nurses: "They found time all day long to walk up and down between the beds, talking to the men, joking with the boys and encouraging them to joke back as long as the G.I. humor wasn't too raw. . . . In our minds, they stood for some American girl we'd be out with having a good time if we were back home."[71] The imagined role they had for their wives in the home did not leave much room for expanded power and independence for women. And for their part, most of the women embraced the return to the home, at least initially.[72] With some notable exceptions, women stayed out of the national political picture in the immediate postwar era. Their absence made the demographic importance of male World War II veterans all the more clear. In 1950, there were roughly forty-nine million males over the age of nineteen in the United States. World War II veterans made up nearly a third of that population. They made up over half of the male population between the ages of twenty and forty-four.[73] If and when such numbers of people could agree anything, the weight of their numbers was bound to have great influence.

The raw numbers only told part of the story. The influence of veterans exceeded their proportion to the population, including in economics. For all of their initial concerns about jobs, housing, and a return of a depression, most of the veterans eventually did well for themselves. The U.S. economy continued to grow after the war, creating a great deal of consumer demand and more jobs. A report from the Labor Department's Veterans Employment Service claimed that by July 1948, more than 96 percent of the male veterans of World War II were employed in the civilian labor force.[74] Private enterprises made considerations for the returned fighting man. "For my money, the high point of my homecoming was when the Truck Drivers and Teamsters Union 249 gave me a life membership card," one veteran wrote. "Local 249 has a long waiting list. I'd tried to get in for two years before I joined up, but couldn't make it."[75] The American Guild of Variety Artists wrote to Truman in October 1945 requesting that he look into the issue of providing for returning actor-veterans.[76] Veteran Raul Morin recalled, "Never before had we been given preference over anyone in the purchase of goods, automobiles, new homes, homesteading, leases or rentals and employment in civil service. Now, as veterans, we had priority over non-veterans in all these shortages and it was something new to us."[77] One veteran wrote to President Truman in 1947 after reading in the newspaper that most of the president's mail came from people asking for favors. S. J. McGuinness did not want any favors; he only wanted to express his gratitude to his country and its president. "During the war . . . I lost my leg!" he wrote. "This at first was depressing. However since my return to civilian life the government has done so much for me that I often feel ashamed. First they have given me a pension that is more than just. Next, a gift of a new car was made. But the most important was the chance of educating myself."[78]

Much as Lawrence Westbrook had predicted, veterans already had important advantages over those who did not or could not serve. For example, soldiers had a head start in education. About twice as many veterans than nonveterans had finished eighth grade, and many more had gone on to some high school.[79] When they returned from the war, the educational provisions of the GI Bill gave the men a chance to broaden that gap. Fighting in Italy, Bud Winter wrote to his brother, "Found a couple of articles in *Yank* magazine which makes it look as if I won't have to worry about education expense. You don't have to worry about me studying when I get there. Since being over here, I realize how important education is!" Winter died in a German mortar attack, but the sentiment lived on in other veterans.[80] They went to college and enrolled in vocational programs by the millions. Bradford Perkins recalled that because of the GI Bill, "I completed my undergraduate and graduate education without having to work or draw heavily on family support."[81] They made good students. A veteran back in college noted, "Classes were filled with other returned servicemen, all older, more mature, more serious, more committed seminarians and discussants than we'd been in 1941 or '42."[82] One such student, Stuart Walzer, flunked out of the University of Wisconsin before serving in the army. When he returned, he graduated from UCLA and the Harvard Law School with honors.[83] A study of students at Columbia College showed that contrary to the popular opinion that veterans would be a "social and emotional problem," veterans outstripped both prewar students and nonveterans in a variety of mental, social, personality, and academic traits.[84] A variety of studies from schools all around the country concluded that veterans on average outperformed nonveterans in school.[85] By 1952, the average veteran between the ages of twenty-five and forty-four had about two more years of schooling than nonveterans of the same age. And nearly a quarter of all World War II veterans had gone to some college, compared to only 13 percent of nonveterans.[86]

In college, the veterans studied in programs that fed them into fields of prominence. One study of married vets at the University of Utah found that most aimed to become engineers, educators, doctors, and lawyers.[87] Later, the GI Bill administrators would claim that "450,000 engineers, 180,000 doctors, dentists, and nurses, 360,000 school teachers, 150,000 scientists, 243,000 accountants, 107,000 lawyers, [and] 36,000 clergymen" earned their degrees using the bill's benefits.[88] By 1952, a higher percentage of veterans than nonveterans already worked in professional and technical jobs, and the younger veterans were already catching up in management positions. Veterans began to take over occupations that required more education and that provided greater pecuniary benefits and leadership opportunities.[89] The last calendar year that veterans of World War II earned less than nonveterans was 1947. By 1948, they had pulled even. By 1949, they had pulled ahead.[90] And over the next five years, the gap only widened. In 1954, when the average nonveteran over the age of twenty-five made $3,087 a year, the average World War II veteran in the same age group made $4,039 a year.[91] The situation at elite schools was illustrative. Perkins claimed his class at Harvard contained 90 percent veterans.[92] When they entered the program in 1947, 91 percent of the Harvard Business School class of 1949 had served in World War II. By 1974, nearly half of the graduates of that class were chief executive or chief operating officers in some of the most important and prominent businesses in the country.[93]

World War II veterans constituted a large demographic bloc, had more education, made more money, and increasingly held positions of prominence in American business and industry, yet even those facts did not wholly explain the extent of their influence on the postwar period. Less evident statistically was the fact that the American people listened to what veterans had to say and looked to veterans for leadership. One study drawn from a survey in Washington state found that the VFW and American Legion had greater political influence among average citizens than all manner of voluntary associations, including both major political parties, churches, and labor unions.[94] Younger people looked up to them. For example, two fourteen year old boys wrote to President Truman in August 1945 to express their admiration of the veterans and to offer to help ensure that returning veterans had jobs.[95] Sheril Cunning grew up in Long Beach and recalled fondly the community of the war and the way everyone cheered on the troops.[96] Historians Stephen Ambrose and Edward Coffman were boys during the war, and both remembered looking to veterans as leaders and role models.[97] And generally, veterans, especially fathers, took on a sort of mystical quality for children in America. Their prolonged absence and sudden return created many difficulties within families, but there can be no doubt that children and teenagers reserved special romantic esteem for veterans of the war.[98] Veterans understood their role in relation to young people. The national commander of AMVETS wrote to

Truman in 1948 that they agreed that the veterans of World War II were "in a unique position to provide inspiring leadership to the young people of the country."[99]

The most obvious way veterans could provide leadership was through political office. The 1946 election did more than just indicate the influence of veterans as lobbyists for specific issues. The heated debates of that campaign helped to spark or respark an interest in politics for thousands of World War II veterans. They began to contemplate political careers of their own. They found that the public expected them to lead. And they found that the major political parties proved enthusiastic partners in launching those new careers.

There can be no doubt that veterans came to be overrepresented among political leadership. The famous examples started right at the top with Dwight D. Eisenhower, to whom both major parties offered their presidential nominations and who won widespread support from the American people in 1952 and 1956. Eisenhower had a special appeal among veterans. They connected with him in a way they rarely did with generals. Something about Ike resonated with people. As British field marshal Bernard Law Montgomery, a man not predisposed to giving compliments to rival generals, once said of Eisenhower, "He has the power of drawing the hearts of men towards him as a magnet attracts the bits of metal. He merely has to smile at you, and you trust him at once."[100] His natural leadership even extended to fashion. By the end of the war all the men in the army had even worn so-called Eisenhower jackets. According to one soldier, the switch to the "trim Eisenhower jacket with its broad chest and narrow waist greatly enhances the GI image."[101] The general's appeal extended beyond the dashing figure in the stylish jacket. In 1956, a local Republican official wrote to the president on behalf of a veteran to request a copy of the letter Eisenhower sent the men before D-Day. She quoted the veteran of Omaha Beach: "It really touched my heart, knowing that someone as big as a General in the Army was thinking of each individual in the Army. . . . He has a heart as big as the whole world."[102] M. D. Elevitch wrote that he restrained all of his emotions about the war: "They were stored up and broke loose finally in a torrent of tears some twenty-four years after the war. . . . It was the week . . . when my first child . . . was born, that in itself a cause for emotional unloading. Then at week's end General Eisenhower died, triggering those tears not for that worthy himself or his fatherly presence but, as I can make it out now, for my lost innocence, the lost years, the lost lives. Nothing like it since."[103] Election results reflected the widespread admiration for the general. Eisenhower won in 1952 and 1956 in large part due to his personal appeal as a candidate.[104]

Eisenhower recognized the importance of maintaining his appeal among veterans, and he could use his personal history to deal with their concerns. In 1952, he dismissed a whispering campaign among the troops and veterans' organizations that he planned to cut soldiers' pay: "What on Earth do they think I am—Soldiers that I have commanded on the battlefield and abroad—that I would come back here and say that I think their pay ought to be reduced? Someone ought to have his head examined and any soldier that has ever served with me knows better!"[105] He also knew when to cultivate the relationship. In the months approaching the 1956 election, he met with (and had publicity photos taken with) the leaders of the Jewish War Veterans, Disabled American Veterans, AMVETS, American Legion, Veterans of Foreign Wars, and Catholic War Veterans.[106]

His opponent in both elections, Illinois governor Adlai Stevenson, served for a short while in the navy in World War I. But his military experiences paled by comparison to Eisenhower's, and he did not ignite the passions of the veterans.[107] After Eisenhower, every American president until Bill Clinton was a veteran of the World War II era. John Kennedy and Richard Nixon entered national politics immediately after the war. Lyndon Johnson returned to politics after a brief stint in the service during the war. He ran in 1964 against Barry Goldwater, a veteran of the U.S. Army Air Forces. In 1972, Nixon beat George McGovern, another veteran of the U.S. Army Air Forces. Gerald Ford, Jimmy Carter, Ronald Reagan, and George H. W. Bush all became public figures and politicians in the decades after their service in the military during or shortly after World War II. Prominent postwar senators Bob Dole, Daniel Inouye, Strom Thurmond, William Knowland, Herman Talmadge, Paul Douglas, Fritz Hollings, Lloyd Bentsen, Jesse Helms, and Speakers of the House Carl Albert and James Wright all got their start in politics after serving in the military in World War II.[108]

The veterans' dominance in politics extended far beyond a few prominent examples. In 1946, 183 veterans of World War II ran in the primaries to represent the major parties in Congress. Eventually, sixty-nine veterans were elected, roughly 14 percent of the members of the new Congress.[109] The statistical domination only grew in the 1950s, especially within their age cohort. Between 1950 and 1954, veterans constituted 55 percent of those who won elections for the House of Representatives, even though veterans only made up 40 percent of all males over the age of twenty-five. In the general elections veterans did not necessarily have an advantage over nonveterans. However, both major political parties increasingly nominated veterans to run for political office, indicating that they believed the veterans had a better chance to win.[110] In the late 1950s, veterans made up half of the members of both the

House and the Senate. By 1969, according to one study, "over 90 percent of the members of Congress who were eligible for service in World War II or Korea were veterans."[111] Whether or not veterans disproportionately held political office because they had an advantage in elections or because both parties nominated mostly veterans was irrelevant. The effect was the same: veterans dominated national and local politics in the years after World War II. Veteran status had become an almost indispensable condition for political office.

The demographic, economic, and political power of World War II veterans was extensive and led to specific changes in American life. For example, in 1954 they used their clout to have Armistice Day officially changed into Veterans Day, so the national holiday did not celebrate exclusively the World War I generation.[112] This type of power to influence the mundane issue of a national holiday had many more serious ramifications, and those ramifications were well understood at the time. A 1951 book explained that veterans must be studied because "veterans of America's last two wars—among whom World War II veterans are fast achieving positions of leadership—must today be included among the major special interest groups of our society. The impact of their attitudes . . . will be among the determinants of American politics for many years."[113] President Truman said it better in a message to the American Legion in 1947: "Upon these veterans fall the heavy responsibility of maintaining the fruits of victory in the years ahead. . . . The future of this country is in the hands of the veterans."[114]

After the 1946 election, economic concerns continued to dominate the political efforts of the veterans and their organizations. For the next few years, many veterans expressed a concern that they would not be able to support their families. "As I am a World War 2 Vetteran and trying to farm until this year, times has got so hard and my health is Bad that I cant hold a job in the City," one Missouri farmer wrote to the president. "I owe a big Hospital and Dr. bill and Grocery Bill and no way to pay it. The Government taken away my pencion. No way to make a crop and my baby girl is bad sick and no funds to get hur doctored."[115] Roland Johnson of Massachusetts complained to his congressman and the president, "As a Veteran I consider it a CRIME that my wife and children must guess whether or not they are going to Eat, Have a roof over their Heads, Have Clothing, and Medical Care & Medicine."[116] In 1947, a group of Protestant, Catholic, and Jewish leaders joined together in New York to try to get action on housing. One of the members, a veteran chaplain, threatened, "I'm not ready to join the Communist party or to storm the Capitol at Albany—as yet."[117] Letters and veterans publications in these years sounded similar themes.[118] Veterans organizations also continued to work for increased benefits for their members, especially jobs and health benefits for disabled veterans.[119] One report noted that the first session of the Eightieth Congress saw introduced more than 1,100 bills concerning veterans benefits.[120] Between the end of the war and July 1948, the government passed some 225 laws dealing with veterans.[121]

The upkeep of veterans' hospitals and Veterans Administration facilities constituted the other great concern of the veterans' groups. For example, in 1947 the Truman administration asked former president Herbert Hoover to head up a commission to look into creating a more efficient organization of the executive branch. When the Hoover commission suggested reorganizing the Veterans Administration and reforming its control over hospitals as part of its recommendations, veterans strongly opposed the idea.[122] The veterans groups held fast to such positions, and spent the majority of their time as lobbyists arguing for the preservation or extension of VA benefits.[123]

In the meantime, their efforts for extended economic benefits for veterans without disabilities began to lose steam. In his first term, President Eisenhower ordered the creation of a commission under the leadership of Omar Bradley to look into the status of veterans pensions. A number of individual veterans and most of the veterans' groups railed against the convening of the commission because they assumed it meant a cut in benefits. They explicitly opposed any such cuts.[124] For its part, the Eisenhower administration believed that the Bradley commission proposals "would increase benefits for about 600,000 veterans, decrease benefits for about 350,000, and terminate benefits for about 150,000."[125] The professional wings of the veterans' organizations saw it as their job to fight for every last penny for veterans, but the improved conditions for veterans meant that on economic issues they had less and less enthusiastic support from the average members.[126] President Eisenhower had it right in a meeting with legislators in July 1954. "The President expressed the belief that the rank and file veterans of WW II and the Korean conflict were not clamoring for increases in pensions," an aide wrote, "and he believed that the professional veterans of high-pressure groups with the veterans' organizations were making these demands which has been the custom for thirty years."[127]

Eisenhower understood that on economic benefits in an era of general prosperity, World War II veterans did not constitute a single coherent interest group. In fact, on most specific issues, they did not constitute a single coherent interest group. Nor did they support one political party or the other exclusively. As one writer noted in 1948, the federal government spent about 20 percent of its budget on veterans, and most of those benefits had came about when Democrats controlled the government, "but that was only because the Democrats were in power. The veterans don't feel particularly obligated to the Democrats for these benefits; they feel they would have got them under any administration. . . . And so they would have."[128] Likewise, veterans as individuals experienced the full range of individual problems and entered into all manner of professions.[129] There was no such thing as the average veteran on most specific issues.

But there was an exception to this rule. There was such a thing as an average veteran on one issue especially: eliminating ethnic and religious intolerance in America. The soldiers had learned the lesson of tolerance and understanding. But when they looked home from the war they saw a society rent by ethnic and religious animosity. For all the efforts of right-minded people during the war years, despite even the horrifying example of the Hitler and his Nazis, the message of tolerance had not taken hold. One soldier wrote home from Europe that he and his fellow soldiers had just fought against Fascism and Nazism, but back home "we also have a Senator named Bilbo . . . who calls people wops, dagos, and hunkies. . . . My aching back, we sure are putting up with a lot."[130] In August 1946, one former serviceman warned in a letter to a veterans' group magazine that "certain malicious reactionaries are working to befuddle the veteran, to make him resent his neighbors and load him with prejudice against Americans of different races, religions, or national backgrounds. These wise guys have the Hitler line down pat."[131]

The veterans, as they spread around the country and entered positions of power, knew they had a job to do resisting intolerance. The individuals who would be more likely to be politically active—like those who would write in to magazines and organize veterans' groups—put special focus on the issue. When the soldiers magazine *Yank* asked the men what changes they would like to see made in postwar America, the respondents focused first and foremost on "the need for wiping out racial and religious discrimination." As one soldier said, "To make democracy work, many political and religious groups in the United States will have to believe in democracy for the first time and remove some of their discriminations and prejudices."[132] Daniel McGinnis and Robert Lasson wrote *Yank* magazine, "If from these years of toil and devastation and unlimited murder we have not learned to live with others, our fathers and brothers have died in the greatest farce in the history of this world."[133] The organizers of AMVETS included among the reasons they organized in the first place, "artificial barriers against our fellow men are crumbling under the impact of the war. Bullets do not distinguish between, color, race or creed. . . . These same democratic forces set in motion must be strengthened and reach their full function in peacetime."[134]

In the spring of 1946, celebrities and famous wartime leaders, including Spencer Tracy, Gen. Dwight Eisenhower, Adm. Chester Nimitz, and Bob Hope, contributed to a campaign to encourage tolerance among students of all ages. Courtesy of University of North Texas Libraries Digital Collections.

In order to combat prejudice, activist veterans applied the lessons of ethnic and religious tolerance they learned during the war to postwar politics, sometimes directly. Often invoking the Four Immortal Chaplains, they initiated a series of brotherhood days, weeks, and months to drum up support. They lobbied for fair hiring and employment practices. And the various veterans' groups even worked together on these efforts. One post of the Jewish War Veterans in Massachusetts wrote to President Truman in 1948 to announce that they met with members of the American Legion, Veterans of Foreign Wars, Italian-American Veterans, Disabled American Veterans, Amputee War Veterans, American Veterans Committee, and the United Veterans Progressive Association to celebrate the chaplains of the war and to sign a "Declaration of Brotherhood."[135] For Brotherhood Week in 1950, a legionnaire summed up what he believed to be the contributions of veterans since the war. Veterans, he wrote,

> all learned the same lesson and we're going to do our darndest to teach it to others. That lesson is the foxhole lesson—that you treat the other fellow right because he's your buddy and no questions asked. That's all there is to it. With the shells whining overhead, no one gives a hoot what church you go to or where your grandfather came from. Out there, the color of your liver is more important than the color of your skin. It ought to be more important at home too.
>
> But when our GI's came home, they found that everyone wasn't taking brotherhood quite so much for granted. Sometimes the vet couldn't find a place to live. And sometimes, when he did find a place, he couldn't move in because the neighborhood was barred to his race or religion. Or maybe a college or professional school would be closed to him for the same reason. Or perhaps he'd be turned down for a good job he could handle, simply because some bluenose didn't like the country his grandfather came from.
>
> That's when the vet took a long look around and decided there was plenty of work to be done on the home front. That's when we of the American Legion decided to see to it that the vet and his fellow-citizen got the full benefits of the American way of life we had fought for. . . .
>
> Many of the Legion members have been active also on the broader front of human rights for all Americans. In keeping with Legion resolutions opposing racial and religious discrimination in employment and education, our members have worked to implement these policies with legislation. And great progress has been made in the past few years. Already, eight states have passed Fair Employment laws to outlaw bias on

the job. The same number have outlawed discrimination in the National Guard. Six states have passed laws against discrimination in education. The Supreme Court has ruled that restrictive covenants, which bar racial or religious groups from owning property in certain areas, cannot be enforced by the courts.

And so it goes around the nation. . . . Yes, the results are showing. Vets have been thinking and acting in the past few years and America is a better nation for it.[136]

As this veteran indicated, their efforts met with political success. According to one historian, the years after the war saw "the movement against . . . religious prejudice advanced on every front. . . . Initiatives from the President and the Supreme Court . . . defended the rights of religious minorities, shattered quota systems in higher education, and made restrictive covenants unenforceable. In the decade beginning in 1945, ten states and more than thirty cities created fair employment practices commissions."[137] All of these were notable achievements, but they did not solve the larger problem. Unfortunately for the veterans of World War II, there was little to be achieved on the issues of ethnic and religious intolerance directly through political means. The veterans had enough political influence to handle legal intolerance directly. When it came to animosity among white ethnic and religious groups, the laws were not the problem.

In 1960, the American Legion released a statement for Brotherhood Month that cited an article by Omar Bradley from shortly after the war that had noted that in the armed forces there were 28,000 Kellys, 17,500 Cohens, 2,000 Kominskis, 16,000 Schultzes, and 1,200 Amatos:

It looks as though the General just pointed out these facts to make a very simple statement. THEY WERE ALL AMERICANS WHILE THEY WORE THE UNIFORM OF OUR COUNTRY, AND THEY WERE ALL AMERICANS WHEN THEY CAME HOME TO CIVILIAN LIFE. In fact, they were better Americans when they came home, because 28,000 Kellys got acquainted with 17,500 Cohens, and 16,000 Schultzes grew to know and respect 1,200 buddies named Amato. And some Kominskis remember some Kellys who did not come home, and some Cohens lie under Stars of David next to Schultzes under Crosses. And there is not a single Legionnaire who doesn't know some buddy named Kelly or Cohen or Kominski or Amato.

Well, I don't need to point out the moral to Legionnaires. But Legionnaires have to point out the moral to all other Americans. And the moral is that men are men. Regardless of differences in faith and race and color, men are men, and are created in God's image, and are equal to one another, both on the battlefield and here at home in America. That is our heritage, that is our hope. Let us not permit others to forget it.

Whether in our personal contacts or in our Legion program at the Post level, we ought to reemphasize this truth, so that Brotherhood Month can create a brotherly spirit throughout the year.[138]

The veterans of World War II were trying nothing less than to change the hearts and minds of their nation. It would take all of their formidable power in society to make that change happen.

# 7

# THE NEW CONSENSUS AND BEYOND

> We developed intense pride in America. . . . As veterans, we
> have become serious-thinking Americans. We have enlarged
> our circle of friends to include not only Mexican-Americans
> like ourselves, but Americans of many other nationalities.
> —Raul Morin, *Among the Valiant,* 1963

IF THE VETERANS OF WORLD WAR II WERE TO SPREAD THE LESSON OF TOL-
erance throughout the country, they had to do it within the framework of the
major events of the time. The Cold War, the great contest between the United
States and the Soviet Union, cast a shadow over what should have been jubi-
lant postwar years. World War II veterans had a strong group response to the
threat, which led to them having a key position in shaping Cold War foreign
policy and the role and nature of the postwar military. At the same time, their
shared worldview influenced the nature of the opposition to the Communist
threat at home. Because of the influence of veterans, both Cold War military
policy and domestic anticommunism, whatever their other traits, reflected the
World War II lessons of tolerance. But even more important than these concerns of high-level public politics and policy was the parallel effort of the veterans to spread the lessons of tolerance in everyday life, where, interestingly,
the actions of nonactivist and nonpolitical veterans spoke loudest of all.

Much to their dismay, the returned fighting men found that their country already faced another grave international threat. The spread of communism, orchestrated by the Soviet Union, haunted Americans. In its aggressive
takeover of war-weary Eastern Europe, this new totalitarianism—to which
the United States already had a strong ideological aversion—looked far too
much like the one that had just caused a world war. The more liberal American Veterans Committee did not represent the majority of veterans on most
issues, but they had one thing right in a memo from late 1945: "Above all
things World War II vets want no more shooting."[1] A War Department pamphlet for the troops put it another way: "Everybody has a stake in solving the

problem of how to prevent war—but nobody understands the need better than those now serving in the armed forces."[2]

The lesson they drew from World War II had been that aggression needed to be cut off early, before the aggressor became too strong. Japan, Italy, and Germany "went on to commit one aggression after another, and got away with them," the War Department pamphlet explained. "Finally, the situation became so threatening to the countries that remained unconquered that they (including the United States) were forced to unite for mutual defense. But by this time the aggressors had become so strong that they could only be defeated at an enormous expense of blood and treasure."[3] President Truman reiterated the point throughout the remainder of his presidency, including at the VFW's golden jubilee convention in August 1949. And the theme continued throughout the early part of the Cold War.[4] No group understood the expense of blood and treasure more viscerally than the veterans of World War II.

What they did not want, above all, was another world war that would require universal service in a mass army. The politically tone-deaf Henry Wallace summed up everything the veterans opposed when it came to military policy in a comment before the 1948 election: "If we need trained reserves, we now have 15 million veterans of World War II who constitute a reserve of trained personnel that will be available at least 10 more years."[5] That might have been true, but for those veterans, the idea of acting as a reserve ran counter to everything for which they thought they had been fighting. For that reason, pretty much any other option to halt the spread of communism was on the table for most veterans and their organizations. They backed a greater degree of internationalism for the United States than at any time in its history. They wanted an aggressive foreign policy to crush through economic aid, material support, or even small-scale military intervention any incipient Communist movements in the free world. They supported a strong stand against communism in China and in Korea, but not so much as to risk a world war. Even when they and the country turned against Truman when the Korean War dragged on, most still believed in the general principles of the fight.[6] In all of these positions, they fell directly in line with the emerging idea of containment.

The lengths they would go to avoid a mass army became clear in their specific recommendations for the implementation of containment. In order to stop the spread of communism before it started, the United States needed to display the deterring threat of a strong military. For the leadership of veterans' groups, one of the best ways to maintain a visibly strong and prepared military was through universal military training. In the years after the war, veterans organizations, especially the American Legion, led a vigorous campaign to require by law that all able-bodied males spend a significant time learning the basics of armed service.[7] They found allies in this effort in both President Truman and former army chief of staff George C. Marshall. For a decade after the end of World War II, various UMT legislative proposals bounced around Congress, but true universal training never happened. Other issues, like the immediate manpower needs of the Korean War, intervened. And while many Americans supported the idea in the abstract, the specifics of universal training sounded a little too much like universal military service, something anathema to the long standing American distrust of standing armies. Even the rank and file of the veterans groups could not get entirely behind the prospect. The mixed feelings could be seen in the back-and-forth argument of one veterans' group in 1948: "We are opposed to any plan for the disarmament of this country until the world is safe for democracy, yet we believe with the Secretary of State, General George Marshall, that this Nation should not at the present time be placed upon a complete war footing. However, we should maintain a strong national defense."[8] Instead of UMT, the country renewed and maintained Selective Service.[9] That action, in an era of general peace, reflected the strength of the veterans' support for a strong and flexible military in the face of the Communist threat.

Yet for most of the veterans of World War II, and increasingly most of the rest of the nation, strength needed not come from manpower. Technology, modern machines of war, could in large part replace the infantryman on the ground. As a result of this widespread belief veterans overwhelmingly supported a large U.S. Air Force and enlarged naval aviation.[10] Later, groups such as the VFW offered their backing for an expanded missile building program, while AMVETS set up fellowships for promising young scientists.[11] In this support for air power, improved missiles, and greater scientific achievement, veterans groups took their most radical position in the containment of communism overseas. Airplanes carried bombs, missiles delivered warheads; scientists made better planes, bigger bombs, and more accurate missiles. The effort to avoid a mass army led veterans to support even the proliferation of atomic weapons.

By and large, veterans of World War II looked at atomic power as a positive good, especially early on after the war. After all, the bomb had ended their war and saved thousands of lives. Initially, most Americans, especially veterans, looked at atomic power with great optimism. "The invention of the Atom Bomb is also causing quite a bit of talk today," one soldier wrote his father from Germany on August 8, 1945. "None of us understand it. I wonder if they are going to use atomic power in postwar industry?"[12] Atomic energy seemed to have the power to solve all of humankind's problems. In foreign policy, that meant using atomic weapons to act as a deterrent to further Communist expansion. Later, when the effects of radiation and the increased destructive power of the hydrogen bomb became widely known, and the Soviets procured a bomb of their own, Americans, including veterans, developed a healthy fear of the weapon.[13] They did not want a nuclear war any more than they wanted a large scale conventional war. Yet veterans' groups still backed atomic weapons as part of America's military power. The urgency to deter a nuclear war only increased the acceptance of militarism in the United States.

Yet there was another side to the veterans' strong militarism. They understood that the military as an institution in American life had its uses beyond just fighting wars. Later, when questioned about wartime draft policies and future recommendations, veteran after veteran expressed a belief that some sort of military service for the youth of the country would be of great benefit. Mark Durley said, "Every male and female should be drafted for universal service to the U.S.A."[14] William Shiepe agreed: "I believe that every teenager, male or female should be inducted into the service for at least 1 year and given strict basic training. Some have never been disciplined, but I guarantee that if I were a [drill instructor], each draftee would come out a much better person."[15]

All at once, as one historian has commented, the military became an institution that "taught youth democratic values and deference to authority and served the public as a large business—a place where youth could train for a good job, obtain fair pay and good benefits, and make the military a 'career.'"[16] The military establishment recognized the shift and adjusted, jettisoning its old image and reforming itself to appeal to the new thinking. The military became more democratic and tolerant within the framework of a specific worldview.[17] President Truman, hearkening back to his own military service in World War I, said it best when discussing UMT:

> I don't like to think of it as a universal military training program. I want it
> to be a universal training program, giving our young people a background
> in the disciplinary approach of getting along with one another, informing
> them of their physical make-up, and what it means to take care of this temple
> which God gave us. If we get that instilled into them, and then instill into
> them a responsibility which begins in the township, in the city ward, the
> first thing you know we will have sold our Republic to the coming genera-
> tions as Madison and Hamilton and Jefferson sold it in the first place.[18]

The veterans' support for universal military training always included this recognition that the military taught discipline. More than that, military service taught a particular kind of tolerant citizenship. Even while veterans supported extreme positions in foreign policy and national defense, they always kept in mind the ability of military service to teach tolerance. Such was the nature of the emerging postwar American worldview.

In the postwar environment, the veterans led the way in creating that worldview—one that represented a new consensus about America and Americans. Nothing illustrated that intellectual, ideological, and cultural perspective quite as well as the response to the threat of communism at home in the United States. Much like after World War I, a fear emerged within the United States after World War II that radicalism, especially communism, presented a grave threat to the country. Both the 1920s and the 1940s to 1950s became eras of intense antiradicalism. After World War I, the veterans' organizations had pushed for 100 percent Americanism. Their definitions of Americanism were primarily ideological, as they had seen a variety of people from a variety of backgrounds fight together in the Great War. But they got caught up in the times, and their definitions and actions drifted toward the racialized version of Americanism. The country split along ethnic and religious lines, and intolerance prevailed.

After World War II, veterans, along with most of the rest of the country, once again supported extreme measures to counter a radical threat. With the exception of a few smaller organizations, the veterans' groups wholeheartedly supported anti-Communist messages and actions. One group wrote to President Truman in 1948 that two of their key objectives were "active opposition to Communism or any other ideology that is foreign to our American way of life [and] the dissemination of information and the teaching of fundamental Americanism by precept to all persons living in this country whether or not they are citizens."[19] Later that same group would support the outlawing of the Communist party, denial of the right to vote and hold public office for those who opposed the American form of government, an expanded FBI, and the deportation of alien Communists.[20] The VFW supported similar measures, calling also for "a five-year time limit of residence in the United States of aliens who refuse to bear arms in defense of the Nation, or are criminals, or fail to file intention of becoming a citizen of the United States."[21] The American Legion supported any and all measures to expose Communists in America, including suggesting the use of wiretaps in treason trials.[22] The Catholic War Veterans held similar views. They resolved in 1955 that the Soviets could not be trusted in their campaigns for "peaceful co-existence," and they urged the president and State Department not even "to extend any invitation by our Government to any Communist leaders of U.S.S.R. to visit the United States at the current time."[23]

What the veterans did not support was using ethnicity or religion as an indicator of ideological purity. The leaderships of the American Legion and VFW struggled with the specifics of the definition of Americanism for a few years after the war, but the rank and file had pretty clear inclinations. By the early 1950s their view took firm root. In the words of one historian, "Action and good works defined 100 per cent Americanism for the V.F.W.," not, it should be noted, nationality or religion. At the same time, the official magazine of the American Legion sought to make clear that the concept of 100 percent Americanism was not "synonymous with zenophobia [sic] and isolation."[24] Much like after World War I, only to a greater degree, the definitions of Americanism for the veterans became solely ideological, abandoning every vestige of ethnic or religious bias.[25] Veterans, armed with this outlook, spread to their positions of power in American society.

Wider American society faced a Communist threat that was real but elusive. There was an inherent difficulty in distinguishing among spies, agents, fellow travelers, and the unwitting dupes of Soviet communism. As a result, panic, demagoguery, and extremism marked domestic anticommunism in the decade after World War II. More so than after World War I—because there was an actual, tangible foe in the Soviet Union—the threat was greater. As a result, nearly everyone appeared to become anti-Communist. Liberal groups such as the Americans for Democratic Action and, on a smaller scale, the Liberal party in New York had to be aggressively anti-Communist to have a voice in American politics.[26] The progressive American Veterans Committee followed a similar track, purging its Communist or fellow-traveling members in 1948.[27] In public affairs, anticommunism was open and virulent.

Such an environment invited a rise in ethnic and religious intolerance. And ethnicity and religion did make their way into the anti-Communist crusade, especially in the first few years after the war. Testimony before Congress in those years included warnings about southwestern Chicago, where the Communists could infiltrate the "Slavish nationalities, Italians, Jewish section." Another witness testified about the threat of "islands within this country . . . a little Poland, Russia, Hungary, Romania." Even President Truman's attorney general, Tom Clark, noted the potential for trouble from various eastern European nationalities, including Poles, Slavs, Bulgarians, and Ukrainians.[28] Jews working at an army research center in New Jersey probably faced special scrutiny as potential Communist subversives because of anti-Semitism.[29]

But these cases were the exception, not the rule. As nasty as the campaign against real and imagined Communists became, especially in the demagoguery of Joseph McCarthy, it never became ethnic or religious in any serious way. It helped that the Catholic Church in America bowed before no one when it came to opposing communism.[30] And it helped that most of the ethnic groups bought into the anti-Communist consensus wholeheartedly.[31] Although many ethnic groups continued on with their connections to the old world after the war, those connections were of a different nature than before. For example, eastern European ethnic groups mobilized to support resistance to communism in their ancestral lands.[32] Such efforts were a far cry from prewar immigrants and ethnics in the United States sympathizing with countries in conflict with America, such as Italian Americans supporting Mussolini before the war. The Italian-American War Veterans confirmed this impression. They noted that they had a potential membership of 1.5 million Italian American veterans from both world wars but added, "There is no question as to the loyalty and patriotism of this organization."[33] All of that said, most members of the various ethnic groups had professed their loyalty to the United States in the earlier period, too. Roman Catholics had always been anti-Communist, but that did not help in the 1920s.

More to the point, many members of the American Jewish community in the 1940s and 1950s sympathized with socialist reforms to one degree or another. Some prominent Jewish Americans openly sympathized with the Communist cause. Many of the leaders of the Communist party in the United States were Jews. Worst of all, a few American Jews actually worked for the Soviet Union. The most prominent spy case of the postwar period involved two Jewish Americans, Julius and Ethel Rosenberg. Still, the anti-Communist movement after World War II never incorporated anti-Semitism as an important factor.[34] In fact, not a single serious student of anticommunism in postwar America attributed the movement's rise or wide popularity to antiethnic or antireligious motivations.[35]

Even the worst demagogue of all, Joseph McCarthy (a Catholic), who would go to almost any extreme to further his personal cause, did not go after ethnic or religious minorities. In fact, when McCarthy began to go down, and some in his own party turned against him and accused him of appealing to anti-Semitism and hurting religious relations generally, McCarthy replied that his closest aides included Jews and Protestants, including counsel Roy Cohn, and that his opponents were inflaming "racial and religious bigotry."[36] As one biographer noted, unlike interwar anti-Communist figures such as Martin Dies, Charles Coughlin, and John Rankin, "Joe never engaged in anti-Semitic diatribes or made the loaded connection between Jews and left-wing radicalism. Despite the unrelenting hostility of organized Jewry to his crusade, McCarthy still praised the state of Israel, condemned Soviet persecution of Jews, and argued for retention of the Voice of America's Hebrew language desk. When asked why, he replied, 'I have many friends who are Jewish.'"[37]

Not only did anticommunism not lead to increased ethnic and religious animosity, it had the opposite effect. A student of the issue in the mid-1950s noted the page-one headline from the September 4, 1954, *New York Times:* "President Signs Bill to Execute Peacetime Spies; Also Bolsters Ban on Bias." The headline, he concluded, was indicative of a new trend: "Manifestations of ethnic intolerance today tend to decrease in proportion as ideological intolerance increases. In sharp contrast, both bigotries used to increase together."[38] A historian of the era put it another way, noting that "one of the appeals of McCarthyism was that it offered every American, however precarious his ancestry, the chance of being taken for a good American, simply by demonstrating a gut hatred for Commies."[39] Yet even those statements do not express the extent of the shift. At the Alfred E. Smith Memorial Foundation dinner in 1958, one speaker said that "the strongest ally of communism is a new type of traitor," a type that would deny rights to "men, women or children of a color or creed other than his own."[40] The logic had come to follow a new line: Ethnic and religious animosity weakened the nation. A weaker nation was more susceptible to communism. Therefore, intolerance actually helped the Communist cause; bigots were the traitors.

This type of Americanism was extreme. It was heavy-handed. It did not provide much room for the unique attributes of individual ethnic and religious groups to flourish. But compared to what had come before, it was a model of ethnic and religious tolerance. It was a pluralism that celebrated the contributions of any loyal ethnic or religious group. And in the midst of all of this, veterans' groups took the lead, initiating activities to reaffirm loyalty to their country. For example, in 1950, the VFW sponsored the Chicago demonstration of National Loyalty Day. The honorary chairmen included a Catholic cardinal, two Protestant ministers, and a rabbi.[41]

In the first decades after World War II, the United States accepted a more aggressive foreign policy and an increased militarism to fight the next great totalitarian threat. The country increasingly looked to this enlarged military as a positive social institution to build tolerance and understanding among Americans. In those same years, there developed the ethnically and religiously tolerant pluralism of postwar anticommunism. This was the Cold War consensus, and in every major way it fell exactly in line with the views and wishes of the veterans of World War II. The Cold War consensus, and all of the ethnic and religious tolerance therein, was the veterans' consensus.

The postwar consensus about the Cold War, communism, and what it meant to be American provided an intellectual framework for the era, but even it did

not explain the extent of the effect veterans had on ethnic and religious relations in American society. Outside of activist organizations and apart from
big events—such as the Berlin blockade, the launching of Sputnik, and the
U2 crisis—the Cold War and anticommunism did not intrude on the daily
lives of most Americans.[42] There, in everyday life, outside of organizations
and separate from the big issues of the Cold War, veterans had their most
subtle and profound effect on ethnic and religious relations in America. There
they lived the lessons of the World War II military experience. As the natural
leaders at every level of society, their actions and sometimes inaction set an
example that the whole country would follow.

Colleges were the one place where their leadership by example was most
apparent. No doubt the thought of barring veterans from schools revolted many
people and contributed in the postwar period to the widespread removal of
barriers against religious minorities in education. In 1946, President Truman
appointed the Commission on Higher Education to look at the problems of reforming schools to meet the needs of the influx of new students. As he wrote
to one veterans' group, "We have only recently completed a long and bitter
war against intolerance and hatred in other lands. A cruel price in blood and
suffering was paid by the American people in bringing that war to a successful
conclusion," and yet veterans faced a similar intolerance in finding jobs and
getting into schools.[43] The commission recommended that schools remove
ethnicity, religion, and race from the application process.[44] The states took
over the cause, led by New York. Beginning in 1948, New York, New Jersey,
Massachusetts, Oregon, and Pennsylvania all created commissions to pressure
universities and colleges to remove discriminatory barriers. New York even
established the State University of New York system that challenged Columbia
University by providing greater opportunities to minorities.[45]

The hundreds of thousands of men who took advantage of the educational
provisions of the GI Bill found that the crammed postwar schools provided
their own sense of camaraderie, only without the military's rigid structure or
all the explosions.[46] George Dingledy thought that adjustment to civilian life
was "very easy since the college class was composed of ex GI's and we had a
common bond and a common goal."[47] The student veterans carried on the
lessons of tolerance, many of them through activist channels. Some veteran
students at Northwestern University put together an organization dedicated
to world peace.[48] The veterans at Brooklyn College created their own organization and publication after the war with the expressed intent of destroying
"intolerance, misunderstanding, and 'griping.'" The April 9, 1946, issue of the
*Veterans in Brooklyn College Bulletin* editorialized about the threats of future
conflicts:

We ex-G.I.'s are pretty much concerned about the matter for we just coughed up the best years of our lives wading through the degeneration, filth, slime and guts of combat. We didn't realize that when men lose freedom anywhere in the world, in time it catches up with us.

Freedom doesn't depend on the shape of a nose, a different slant of the eyes or the sound of a name. It doesn't go with crushing and enslaving the spirit of the common man. If we only understood this, what misery and unnecessary suffering could have been prevented! As veterans, we have gone a long way in reaching this basic understanding. We've learned this bitter lesson the hard way: THERE IS NO COMPROMISE WITH FASCISM ANYWHERE; NO? NOT EVEN IN AMERICA!

When Bilbo, Rankin, Eastland and others get up in the halls of Congress and vilely spout the Nazi theme of race superiority while pigeon-holing the FEPC, we understand the nature of this venom. We understand this because we fought side by side with men of all racial and religious backgrounds. WE RECOGNIZE THE FUNDAMENTAL PRINCIPLE OF THE EQUALITY OF MAN![49]

The curriculum in the schools increasingly offered courses that reflected the veterans' worldview. In 1953 Harvard professor of psychology Gordon Allport celebrated the fact that people were beginning to apply scientific thought to "seek out the roots of prejudice and find concrete means of implementing men's affiliative values." He continued: "Since the end of the Second World War universities in many lands have given new prominence to this approach under various academic names: *social science, human development, social psychology, human relations, social relations.*"[50] Colleges and universities that had once been gentlemen's clubs for Anglo-Saxon Protestants developed into centers of diversity and tolerance.

In 1950, psychologists at Princeton University recreated a 1932 study of stereotyping among college students. The studies asked a sample of Princeton undergraduates to match attributes to Germans, English, Jews, Negroes, Turks, Japanese, Italians, Chinese, and Irish. The results were striking. In every instance—except the Germans and Japanese, for obvious reasons—negative stereotyping decreased. More important, nearly all of the students in the 1950 study objected to the process. They did not want to stereotype at all. The students wrote variations on the words of one respondent: "A whole race of people cannot be generalized as having common traits." Another even became hostile: "I refuse to be part of a childish game like this. It seems to me that the Psych. Dept. at Princeton, at least, ought to recognize the intelligence of students who choose courses in this department. As far as I have come in contact with these so-called ethnic groups I can think of no distinguishing characteristics which will apply to any group as a whole." The social scientists who ran the experiment struggled to explain the change, but did make the observation that "the post-war population has represented much more of a cross-section of American youth, as a result of the 'GI Bill.'"[51] Contact with veterans drastically increased the ethnic and religious tolerance in postwar schools.

In other areas of American society, the veterans had a more widespread and subtle effect. No area was more important than housing. The intense shortages of the postwar period did not lead to widespread government housing. Rather, government programs encouraged the growth of the private housing industry in America. The plan took some time to get started, but eventually it produced a housing boom. The year 1950 saw nearly 2 million housing starts, and the average per year for the rest of the decade was around 1.5 million. In 1940, just over 40 percent of Americans lived in homes they owned. By 1960, more than 60 percent of all Americans owned their homes. Veterans accounted for a significant proportion of the boom. Between 1945 and 1960, veterans took advantage of the home loan provisions in the GI Bill and the broader Federal Housing Administration to buy some 7.1 million homes, building at least 2.5 million new homes.[52]

This postwar building boom accounted for the precipitous growth of the American suburbs. Before the war, suburbs had been enclaves for the relatively few rich or upper middle classes who wanted a countrylike setting within easy reach of the cities. By 1955, at least thirty million Americans lived in the suburbs; by 1960, the number was fifty million.[53] The suburbs became the center of middle-class culture in America.[54] Two generalized trends converged in the growth of the suburbs. First, veterans made up a significant proportion of every new suburban community. For one thing, veterans tended to be more mobile than nonveterans within the same age cohort, even though both had access to loans through either the VA or FHA, or both.[55] The most basic reason for the disparity was need. As independent adults who increasingly had families, they needed homes of their own. The suburbs offered homes relatively cheap, so they moved.

However, other factors contributed to their moving to the suburbs. Many veterans struggled to move back to the relatively slow life of small towns and rural farms.[56] As one historian has written, "After meeting 'every kind of person' and seeing other parts of the world, . . . thousands of . . . vets had no wish to return to the 'farm.'"[57] Or as a popular song from World War I went, "How you gonna keep 'em down on a farm after they've seen Paree?"[58] The inclination to move off the farm combined with World War II deferments for agricultural workers so that by 1952, only 1.1 million World War II vets, slightly more than 8 percent of the total, lived on farms, while 3.5 million nonveteran males in the same age cohort, 17.6 percent, lived in rural farm areas.[59] On balance, more veterans left the South and the agricultural Midwest and Great Plains than entered.[60]

Veterans also moved out of cities in large numbers. Many veterans seemed to crave the more peaceful, bucolic life outside of the hustle and bustle of the cities. One soldier half-joked during the war, "When I return home, I then think I will be content with the serene simple life of a country squire, my wife, my home, a fireplace with a dog and a book by my side will then be my ultimate enjoyment from life."[61] Another said, "When the war is over we intend to buy a large ranch in Nevada. Lots of space, several children, simple living is our dream."[62] They also needed jobs. Suburbs offered them access to both. While most, about two-thirds, of the veterans who moved stayed within the same county, significant proportions moved to either suburbs just outside of their home cities, or to the new boom towns of the west. Most of the major prewar population centers saw a net loss of their veteran populations after the war. New York, Massachusetts, and Pennsylvania—read New York City, Boston, and Philadelphia, plus Washington, D.C.—lost veterans, while New Jersey, Connecticut, and Maryland showed gains in the veteran population. The only major region of the country to show a net gain in veteran migrants was the West, as veterans moved into the growing suburbs in California, Arizona, Colorado, Utah, Nevada, New Mexico, and Oregon. Suburban Florida with its mobile homes, the Milwaukee region, the Twin Cities in Minnesota, and the Cleveland-Akron metropolitan area also saw an increase in the veteran population.[63]

The second trend in the growth of the suburbs was the influx of large numbers of white ethnic and religious minorities from ethnic enclaves in the cities. The ethnic enclaves did not fade away overnight, or in some cases at all. The earlier generations of immigrants and their children did not disappear. The native population of white foreign or mixed parentage was 25.9 million in 1930, 23.1 million 1940, 23.5 million in 1950, and 24.3 million in 1960.[64] Of those with foreign or mixed parents, there were 2.3 million Irish in 1930, and 1.8 million in 1950; 888,000 Swedes in 1920, 832,000 in 1960; 700,000 Norwegians in 1920, 622,000 in 1960; 5.3 million Germans in 1920, 3.3 million in 1960; 1.3 million Poles in 1920, 2 million in 1960; 890,000 Czechs in 1930, 690,000 in 1960; 538,000 Hungarians in 1920, 456,000 in 1960; and 2.7 million Italians in 1930, 3.2 million in 1960.[65] These older generations, aided by their established community institutions, tended to stay in their ethnic and religious enclaves. Ethnic areas remained pretty stable even as individuals moved out of them after the war. And in some cases, the ethnic flight to the suburbs meant the creation of suburban ethnic communities.[66] "Nevertheless," two ethnic geographers have written, "population turnover and mixing, especially in the 20th century, have reduced the proportional strength of specific ancestry populations in most places."[67]

Italian Americans provided a good example. Early in the war, one Italian American intellectual said that "the war has given the final blow to the segregation of Italian communities in America."[68] Even as numerous Little Italys lived on in the cities, hundreds of thousands of Italian Americans of the younger generations moved into new houses in the suburbs.[69] Eventually the losses became so great that certain Italian American urban enclaves did disappear.[70] American Jews, Swedes, Slovaks, Norwegians, Hungarians, Czechs, Finns, and Greeks followed similar patterns.[71] Polish Americans did not move to the suburbs in huge numbers, but many did go.[72] Clearly, young ethnic and religious minorities moved to the suburbs in significant numbers in the late 1940s and 1950s.

Postwar suburbs such as Levittown, Pennsylvania, eventually came under criticism for their bland conformity, but under their uniform exterior the suburbs were remarkably ethnically and religiously diverse. National Archives and Records Administration.

The overlap of veterans and ethnic minorities moving to the suburbs was no coincidence. Many of the ethnic city dwellers who moved to the suburbs were veterans. Many of the veterans in the suburbs were ethnic and religious minorities, and many were not. To varying degrees and with varying ingredients, they mixed together in communities all over the country. And they did so with a remarkable lack of ethnic or religious animosity. Led by veterans, they left behind ethnically homogenous communities and came together in the suburbs. To be sure, some areas around the country, usually high-income communities such as Grosse Pointe, Michigan, maintained restrictions (against Jews especially), but these were typically preexisting policies and the states often stepped in to redress the problem.[73] In any case, such communities were the exception that proved the rule.

The veterans set the example. Wilson Wyatt, the housing expediter at the end of the war, received no correspondence from returning veterans that showed any concern about living among other ethnic or religious groups in new housing communities. Wyatt repeatedly met and corresponded with a Veterans Advisory Council, made up of members from the American Legion, VFW, Disabled American Veterans, AMVETS, and AVC. They never even brought up the issue. They just wanted sound, affordable homes.[74] Elsewhere the AVC, which was especially sensitive to issues of discrimination, claimed that housing problems were more severe for "the veteran of Negro, Jewish, Mexican, Japanese or Filipino ancestry . . . because of racial restrictive covenants designed to prevent the sale or occupancy of property to members of these groups," but did not list any examples aimed at anyone other than African Americans.[75]

Most studies of the suburbs in the 1950s and 1960s, critical and otherwise, found so little ethnic or religious animosity that they hardly saw fit to mention the subject.[76] *The Organization Man*, William Whyte's famous study of suburbia based on Park Forest, Illinois, echoed the findings of another study in saying he found no "appreciable anti-Semitism."[77] Of the sixty-five thousand residents of Levittown, New York, in 1960, more than twenty-one thousand were foreign-born or second-generation Americans—Italians, Germans, Poles, Czechs, Austrians, Russians, and more.[78] Another student of that town noted also a healthy mix of Catholics, Protestants, and Jews but added, "This heterogeneity does not mean that neighborhood relationships are less than warm and cordial. Common interests of home, car, and child care provide a strong basis for conventional 'give-and-take' in which personality affinities come to the fore."[79] Herbert Gans described some isolation for Japanese, Chinese, and Greek subcommunities, and only "rare" anti-Semitism in Levittown, New Jersey.[80] Indeed, the great criticism of the suburbs in the

1950s and 1960s was their conformity—their age, class, and ideological homogeny. Observers forgot to note, or did so as an aside, that the suburbs were not ethnically homogenous. Critics of the suburbs saw the variety and popularity of religion in the suburbs, but they only occasionally noted that the groups kept getting along.[81]

Americans of the postwar era, suburbanites and otherwise, did more than just move into ethnically and religiously diverse areas. They took advantage of the postwar prosperity to become serious consumers. Their choices in consumption reflected their tolerant postwar values. Popular movies, books, and television shows offered more human and complex versions of ethnic minorities, attacked even implicit bigotry, or presented an anodyne view of American life very much in line with the suburban environment. The multi-ethnic platoon continued to appear in popular World War II movies. Hollywood movies portrayed Catholics, Jews, and other minorities in a more favorable light.[82] Novels followed the same theme, especially war books written by veterans.[83] Several radio and television shows in the late 1940s and early 1950s dealt with ethnic issues, such as *The Goldbergs, Life with Luigi, Bonnino,* and *Mama,* and they fell in line with the general trends of the era. Eventually they would be replaced by suburban shows such as *Leave It to Beaver, Father Knows Best,* and *Ozzie and Harriet.*[84]

The war generation did more with its money than just provide conveniences or entertainment; veterans also had a sense of community in their consumerism. They did not build high fences around those homes; they tended to play an active role in the community. The World War II generation proved to be great joiners of all manner of formal and informal associations. The war had triggered a whole new level of civic and community participation. Veteran Robert Thobaben maintained that among the lessons he learned from his military service were "the importance of being part of a group—a family, church, university, social club—anything."[85] Most of the popular and less popular postwar groups—the veterans' organizations, Elks, Masons, Moose, Eagles, Shriners, AFL-CIO, Farm Bureau, Order of the Eastern Star, National Congress of Parents and Teachers, American Automobile Association, General Federation of Women's Clubs, YMCA, Anti-Profanity League, and so on—crossed over traditional ethnic and religious boundaries. Organizations tied to ethnicity or religion, like the Knights of Columbus and United Methodist Women, acted more as fraternal groups and did not engage in bigoted activities.[86] By 1960, Americans were spending $733 million a year on clubs and fraternal organizations, up from the 1941 level of

$203 million.[87] Bowling became one of the biggest shared recreational activities, as literally millions of Americans joined bowling leagues.[88] By 1960, there were 5.3 million bowlers in America and 858,000 men's bowling teams, up from the prewar levels of 684,000 bowlers and 132,000 teams.[89] By 1965, 8.1 percent of all American men were members of the American Bowling Congress and 1.3 percent of all American women were in the Women's International Bowling Congress.[90]

They did join organizations that had the potential to reignite tensions. The postwar period also saw a revival in religion. Millions of Americans joined or rejoined churches after the war.[91] Some observers ascribed the growth in American piety after World War II to a general anti-Soviet (and Soviet atheism) movement.[92] Veterans' groups such as the American Legion reflected that concern. Promoting increased church attendance in 1951, the legion listed as one of its issues the "continuous threat of Communism to freedom-loving countries throughout the world includes threats to both freedom of worship and religion."[93] Others noted the rise of revivalism as part of Americans trying to come to grips with a world where there could be a Holocaust or atomic bomb.[94] The American Legion also reflected this concern in a call for a religious emphasis week in 1958: "Today there is a greater need than ever before in our history for divine guidance in a world beset by threats of violence, by possibilities of unprecedented destruction, by the eroding influence of a cynical philosophy of materialism and opportunism, and by doubt, disunity, and fear."[95]

Of course the war itself probably convinced many Americans to go back to church. During the war, many people, including President Truman, noted an increase in religious participation. "Chaplains with our armed services report constantly on the increased interest in religion among our fighting men," he wrote one religious leader in July 1945. "Every American has seen photographs of our soldiers and sailors at devotions while on the battle line."[96] Plenty of men on the front lines made private deals with God that if they survived they would be regular churchgoers. The impulse to join organizations for social companionship also played a role in the rise in church membership, and helped to explain how Americans became increasingly secular theologically even as they flocked to churches.[97]

Whatever its origins, the rise in religious participation did not mean a rise in religious intolerance. Again, the general population followed the lead of the veterans. Religious days sponsored by veterans' groups explicitly crossed all boundaries. In 1950, the American Legion in Ohio passed out a guideline for celebrating a special religious holiday. The business portion of the letter reflected the tolerant nature of religiosity in the postwar period:

"The churches (Catholic, Greek Orthodox, and Protestant) are requested to observe Sunday, November 5, 1950, as *Veterans-Go-To-Church Day.* The Synagogues are requested to observe Friday evening, November 10th and Saturday morning, November 11th."[98] The great examples of interfaith cooperation and sacrifice used by veterans and nonveterans alike came from the war years. This time was when the Four Immortal Chaplains became the ultimate symbol of American unity and the centerpiece of many veterans' brotherhood celebrations.

Perhaps the most important postwar contribution to tolerance by the veteran-led communities came within the family. Ethnic and religious groups in the World War II generation intermarried at higher rates than in any earlier period. Just as important, they created an environment whereby the next half generation and next generation would intermarry at even higher rates without serious social reprobation.[99] Italians in Buffalo went from a 12 percent intermarriage rate in 1920 to 27 percent in 1950 to 50 percent in 1960.[100] As Arthur Mann has pointed out, the "phenomenon's sharp increase among Jews since the early 1960s . . . caused some Jewish leaders to fear for their group's survival."[101] Leaders and representatives from other smaller ethnic groups in America expressed similar fears in the same era.[102]

The World War II lessons of tolerance would not end with just the World War II generation. They passed on what they had learned to their children. In some ways, the transition was easy. Textbooks in schools eliminated many of the prejudiced views toward white ethnic groups and even pointed out the contributions of immigrants like Andrew Carnegie and Albert Einstein.[103] And just being in school and in the neighborhood in the ethnically and religiously integrated suburbs taught the baby boomers well. In her study of how Jews became white, Karen Brodkin recalled moving from an urban, predominantly Jewish neighborhood to suburban Long Island in 1949 when she was eight years old. In her new home, Brodkin wrote:

> Neither religion nor ethnicity separated us at school or in the neighborhood. Except temporarily. . . . Hostilities didn't last for more than a couple of hours and punctuated an otherwise friendly relationship. They [hostilities] ended by our junior high years, when other things became more important. Jews, Catholics and Protestants, Italians, Irish, Poles, "English" (I don't remember hearing WASP as a kid), were mixed up on the block and in school.[104]

Just in case the lesson did not come through in the normal course of hanging out on the block or mixing in school, the World War II generation passed their joining impulse on to their children. They encouraged their children to participate in a variety of activities for much the same reason they supported universal military training and joined postwar organizations themselves. As William McLaughlin said of his military experience, "All in all, I gained such a feeling of confidence in myself from all the situations which came up and confronted me that nothing in life has ever really fazed me since. I am sorry for the young lads today who do not have an opportunity to prove their manhood to themselves other than by drinking, driving fast and conquering women." McLaughlin credited the army with giving him the chance to learn how always to do his best and not shirk his duty. For that, he said, "I will always be grateful."[105] Donald Dehn also said that his military experience made him "think that all youth should have the experience to learn discipline."[106] For this reason, many boys and young men found themselves participating in organizations such as the YMCA and Boy Scouts in the 1950s and 1960s.[107]

For this reason also, organized participatory sports took off after the war. Of course the kids still played baseball in large numbers, but football grew by leaps and bounds after the war. The college game became more popular through the veterans and the Army-Navy game, and professional football took advantage of the dawn of television to begin its rise to the top of American spectator sports. But there was something else about football that gave it appeal as a participatory sport.[108] As a more martial game that required a great deal of discipline and teamwork, football hearkened to the military experience. Many of the men had played football either informally or on unit teams during their military service. One man remembered that at war's end he "had to pull some strings to be included on the team trip, for the 84th [Infantry Division] was in contention with the 82nd Airborne Division for the ETO football championship."[109] The men who had played football sometimes made the connection explicitly. Eugene Lawton assured his parents that "it takes team work between Infantry, Tanks, Artillery and Air Force. Perhaps I can give you a better understanding of what I mean. Football is a great game but it takes eleven players working together. One fellow moves under the protection of his team. Apply that to fighting over here and you have an idea of what I mean."[110] Having their kids participate in sports, football in particular, made veterans feel as if their kids were getting the discipline they needed when dad was not available.[111]

The veterans also saw to it that their children would not be as provincial as they had once been. A special war diary belonging to a Pvt. Horace Eakins, who served in the Pacific, asked the question of what the owner thought he would do when the war was over, and left room for his buddies to fill in their responses. One friend said he would "tour this my country for which I had given some good years of my life." Another said he wanted eventually to marry the right woman "and travel to all the towns I have been in while in the army on my honeymoon." A third said, "After a few years I want to travel with my wife and family and really see the good old U.S." A fourth wrote, "If my money holds out, I will hit some of the spots of interest which I liked while in the Army." Private Eakins himself said, "Someday, providing my wife has the money, we will travel to the spots where I spent my days in the Army. Of course, we will eat, and board, free, as I have the names of all my buddies in this book."[112]

In fact, vacationing within the United States increased dramatically in the postwar years. Total visits to national parks, monuments, and historical and military areas increased from 3.2 million in 1930 to 16.7 million in 1940, 21.7 million in 1946, 33.2 million in 1950, 56.5 million in 1955, and 79.2 million in 1960.[113] Total visits to national forest lands for camping and outdoor activities went from 4.6 million visits in 1924, to 18 million in 1941 and 1946, to 27 million in 1950, 45.7 million in 1955, and 92.5 million in 1960.[114] Veterans were aided in their travels by the development of the interstate highway system. Those servicemen who had made it into Europe had come to expect such a luxury. A soldier serving in the army during the war wrote back in wonder at the German highway system, "We've never seen anything like it. We don't have such freeways in the U.S. To our eyes it's a marvel of engineering—an elevated speedway atop an earthen fill, two lanes in either direction separated by a grass divider, underpasses for crossroads."[115] Roscoe Blunt recalled from his time in Germany, "We marveled at the autobahn highways that Hitler had built. . . . They were a welcome relief after being jounced around so roughly on the shell-pocked highways of France, Holland, Belgium and the Rhineland."[116] The experience in Germany raised their expectations of the capabilities of the nation's roads, and it was little wonder that President Eisenhower appointed Gen. Lucius Clay, the former commander in occupied Germany, to head up an investigation into the development of the system.[117] In any event, the smooth open roads made it that much easier for American families to travel the country by car and be exposed to all the different people and different locales, just as the veterans had during the war. Yet again, the military experience guided the teaching of open-minded tolerance.

What were the effects of the spread of the veterans' tolerance throughout society? It would be ridiculous to argue that all ethnic and religious animosity ceased in the postwar years. It would even be ridiculous to argue that all veterans had learned the folly of their ways and jettisoned the bigotry of their upbringing. Some prejudices ran too deep to just disappear. And it was not as if all of the intolerant members of ethnic and religious groups from earlier generations no longer existed either.

For example, in 1947 a small Methodist group in Kansas City attacked the Catholic church for curtailing religious freedom and urged the recall of the American envoy to the Vatican.[118] Two years later, *American Freedom and Catholic Power,* an anti-Catholic screed by Paul Blanshard, stayed on the best-seller list for six months.[119] When President Truman planned to appoint Gen. Mark Clark as ambassador to the Vatican in 1951, the move provoked a flood of protest from a variety of Protestant and some Jewish groups. The White House and State Department received some fifteen thousand telegrams and letters, most of them opposed to the idea of a formal connection with the Vatican. Clark withdrew from the job, and Truman never appointed an ambassador to the Vatican.[120] In 1948, voters in North Dakota narrowly voted in favor of barring teachers from wearing religious clothing to teach in public schools, a measure aimed at Catholic nuns and priests in some rural areas.[121] In 1949, the Anti-Defamation League reported that discrimination still existed in screening applicants for college, licensing for professions, and in vacation literature.[122] And isolated cases of violence against Jews and Mexicans continued in places like Florida and California.[123] Even veterans of the war participated in some of these activities. One scholar reported that a few American Legion and VFW posts excluded Mexican American veterans.[124] And veterans played a prominent role in the violent break-up of a Paul Robeson fund-raising concert in Peekskill, New York, in 1949. Although the violence broke out primarily over the Communist connections of the concert, some evidence suggested that the veterans were also enraged that most of the Communist spectators were also Jewish.[125] No doubt the first decades after World War II were filled with such local examples of everyday ethnic and religious intolerance.[126]

Despite these notable examples, nearly every other indicator—from anecdotes to educated impressions to polls and surveys—suggested a precipitous decline in ethnic and religious intolerance. Contemporary commentators marveled at the change. A study from 1948 designed to fight discrimination found "lesser fissure lines" concerning most white ethnic groups, because "members of these groups often break through the lines of discrimination, and when they do they have relatively little difficulty in attaining social acceptance in accord with the occupational status they win. Nor do they face under such conditions any formidable barrier to intermarriage on that level."[127] Jews in 1948 faced a "deeper fissure line" but at least were not a whole other caste, as were Asians, blacks, and some Latin Americans.[128] In the early 1950s, Samuel Lubell argued, "Of course, racial, religious and ethnic prejudices still burn fiercely in every part of the United States." Yet, he wrote, "I dare say that there are a few Americans who, in recent years, have not been on the verge of exploding, 'Why that ——,' only to check themselves and think, 'All —— are not like that.'" Lubell believed that "the American people were probably never more *consciously* tolerant than they are today."[129] In 1953, former vice president Alben Barkley spoke to the National Conference of Christians and Jews and reported that great gains had been made in interfaith tolerance. He told the audience that he could remember a time "when the Methodists would sing 'Will There Be Any Stars in My Crown?' and the Baptists would reply from across the street with the hymn, 'No Not One.'"[130] Popular Jewish theologian Will Herberg noted that it was not socially acceptable to be anti-Semitic anymore, even if he found some of the aspects of civic religion that reflected the change problematic.[131] Sociologist Digby Baltzell noted that the traditional power establishment of American society had begun to shift away from aristocratic Protestant classes and toward a more ethnically diverse meritocracy.[132]

Historian John Higham later reported that after the war "Anti-Catholic agitation virtually disappeared. . . . A close observer of southern life noted in 1955 that an anti-Catholic pronouncement on an editorial page of a southern newspaper, or even in the 'open forum' columns, had become 'absolutely unthinkable.'"[133] For example, the Columbians, Inc.—a racist, anti-Semitic, and nativist organization—was formed in Georgia at the end of the war and began to work alongside the Klan to terrorize racial, ethnic, and religious minorities. Their actions triggered widespread condemnation from a variety of newspapers, law enforcement agencies, religious groups, women's groups, the American Veterans Committee, Jewish War Veterans, and the Georgia Veterans of World War II. In 1947, the state of Georgia declared that the organization had "as its chief aims, the repression of the exercise of political and legal rights of Negroes, Jews, and persons not of Anglo-Saxon extraction—rights guaranteed to all persons who are citizens." The state revoked the Columbians' charter, and the House Un-American Activities Committee listed the Columbians as a subversive organization until 1961.[134]

Surveys and polls bore out similar conclusions. In 1951, the Anti-Defamation League of B'nai B'rith reported that after a steady increase in racial and religious prejudice from 1940 to 1946, the subsequent five years had seen a dramatic decrease in such feelings. Basing their information on a series of polls, the league noted that among the respondents, 67 percent "could find no threat at all to America among minority groups, whereas in 1946 only 25 per cent was free of such prejudice."[135] A series of studies in a variety of communities between 1948 and 1956 found only mild anti-Semitism based on some unclear questions and almost no negative stereotyping of Italian Americans.[136] A running opinion poll found that 64 percent of the respondents in 1946 had heard criticisms or talk against Jews. By 1950, the number was 24 percent, and in 1959, it was 12 percent.[137] A much later study of the public opinion polls on anti-Semitism in the postwar era confirmed that for all their flaws, the polls nevertheless indicated a pretty clear decline in anti-Semitism.[138]

The trend toward tolerance began to appear on the nation's biggest stage: national electoral politics. Over and over again, President Truman publicly celebrated the tolerance and diversity of America's religious and ethnic groups. He wrote to a Presbyterian assembly, "Religion in America is a supreme demonstration of unity in diversity. Significantly it is not uniformity. Ours is a religious unity without prejudice to any worthy loyalty of faith or creed." The president concluded, "What we have here achieved among different races, colors and faiths points the way and offers encouragement to all others."[139] He repeated the theme three years later in a radio address on religion in American life. He called on Americans to continue to embrace religion, because "it is this faith that makes us determined that every citizen in our own land shall have an equal right and an equal opportunity to grow in wisdom and in stature, and to play his part in the affairs of our nation."[140] Truman later wrote to a convention of the Catholic War Veterans, "By their leadership in home town affairs, veterans everywhere are continuing to render important peacetime service to the principles of democratic freedom. . . . It is heartening to know that veterans of all creeds and faiths are devoted to the task of maintaining our country's spiritual and material strength."[141] To the Conference of Christians and Jews in 1949, Truman said, "I have just come from the National Cemetery at Arlington, where I laid a wreath on the grave of an American hero. No American knows, no real American cares, whether that man was a Catholic, a Jew, or a Protestant, or what his origin and color were. That grave—the grave of the Unknown Soldier—symbolizes our faith in unity."[142]

More telling was the way that tolerance and the accusation of intolerance came to be used for gain in national politics. Truman kicked off his "Give 'em Hell, Harry" campaign in 1948 with his acceptance speech at the Democratic National Convention. He attacked the Republican-controlled Eightieth Congress as a do-nothing bunch. "I have discussed a number of these failures of the Republican 80th Congress," he said. "Every one of them is important. Two of them are of major concern to nearly every American family. They failed to do anything about high prices, they failed to do anything about housing."[143] Considering the results of the 1946 election, these criticisms might have been expected. In order to make it appear that high prices and housing shortages were the fault of the Republicans, he called the Congress back into session to redress their failings. What was more of a surprise was his next demand: the president wanted new legislation concerning displaced persons.

After the war, there were some one and a half million displaced persons in Europe, people driven from their homes by either the Nazis or the Soviets. Those who supported opening America's doors to these people explicitly avoided mentioning the fact that Jews made up most of the displaced persons, for fear that anti-Semitism would work against their efforts.[144] The situation grew more dire in 1946 and 1947. They needed homes, but in 1948 a bipartisan effort by restrictionists in Congress led to a bill that only allowed in 100,000 people over two years, and that insisted that nearly half be from the Protestant Baltic states. With Congress out of session Truman signed the bill, but he also saw a political opportunity.[145] In his nomination acceptance speech he stood at the podium and declared that this bill passed by the Republican-controlled Congress, was an "anti-Semitic, anti-Catholic law."[146] He repeated the charge throughout the campaign.[147]

The Republicans denied the claim even as they sought to reform the law. Republican senator Alexander Wiley of Wisconsin decried the efforts of what he called "smear experts" and denied the claims that the lawmakers were "prejudiced against any religion, race or group of people." Wiley concluded, "I personally have written to leaders of America's three great religious faiths—Protestant, Catholic and Jewish—inviting their suggestions on changes in the law."[148] Despite their efforts, Truman's grass-roots campaign and portrayal of an ineffective and bigoted Eightieth Congress resonated with enough Americans to win him a surprise victory in November.[149] The change in American national politics could not have been more clear: In 1939, President Roosevelt recognized the prevailing anti-Semitism in America and did not support a bill that would have let in twenty thousand German Jewish refugee children.[150] The bill did not pass. Nine years later, on the exact same issue of admitting Jewish refugees, President Harry Truman went before the American people and appealed to their sense of outrage over the bigotry of a bill that only let in one hundred thousand people. Truman won the election, and Congress amended the law to allow in more refugees.

After Truman's victory, the tone of American politics concerning ethnicity and religion continued to reflect the change. The debate over immigration reform and the resulting law, the McCarran-Walter Act of 1952, was indicative.

A variety of veterans' organizations initially opposed any attempts to open up immigration before the veterans were readjusted to society.[151] The commander of the Regular Veterans Association testified to that effect before the House Committee on Immigration and Naturalization in 1946. He added another concern: "I ask you not to permit the radicals, the subversive elements generally, their rabble-rousing radio mouthpieces, their gullible fellow-travelers, nor the credulous to stampede this country into blasting out of existence our immigration laws and policies of restriction."[152] Many individuals in positions of leadership, veterans organizations included, feared that open immigration would bring in radicals. They also worried about the influx of Asian immigrants from countries newly freed from colonial powers.

However, the senators and congressmen who supported restriction and the maintenance of the quotas, led by Senator Pat McCarran, by and large took great pains to avoid the race theories that had been so important to immigration restriction in the 1920s. Their words and actions hinted that they believed that among Europeans, those from the eastern and southern parts of the Continent tended more often toward radical or criminal behavior. They suggested that northwestern European culture was more compatible with American culture. But McCarran's subcommittee also explicitly denied "any theory of Nordic supremacy."[153] The subcommittee's bill maintained the national origins restrictions of the 1924 immigration act that provided higher quotas for northern and western Europeans. More liberal groups proposed compromise legislation that would also maintain the quota system that favored northwestern European countries, but shift any unfilled quotas (usually from Britain) to allow in more immigrants from southern and eastern European countries. These liberal groups hammered away at the idea that distinguishing among European nationalities would only divide the diverse ethnic population at home. When the McCarran-Walter bill passed both houses, President Truman sided with the liberals and vetoed the bill, calling it "a slur on the patriotism, the capacity, and the decency of a large part of the country."[154] Congress overrode the veto, and McCarran-Walter became law—eliminating racial distinctions but maintaining the quota system.[155]

Prominent ethnic organizations, led by Italian and Jewish groups, strongly opposed the continuation of the quotas because they believed them to be bigoted. But the evidence suggested that other issues drove the legislation, primarily a nonethnic and nonreligious consensus nationalism. As one historian has written, "Instead of viewing nationalism solely from the standpoint of ethnic composition of the population, the restrictionists, fearing the spread of Communism and Fascism to the United States, came to emphasize nationalism in the sense of loyalty to the nation."[156] The McCarran-Walter

Act tellingly included provisions for deportation of radicals, and it came on the heels of the McCarran Internal Security Act of 1950 that strictly excluded subversive aliens. It should be noted that after the war, aliens who had served in the United States Armed Forces made up one of the few groups that could be naturalized without meeting all of the usual requirements. And World War I, World War II, and Korean War veterans could be naturalized under a very simplified procedure.[157] Americanism in the law depended more on ideology than ethnicity. More important, elected representatives who thought otherwise could not say so publicly. Many national politicians who wanted to stay in office could no longer use ethnic arguments, even about non-Americans, that had been the norm only a few years earlier. As Senator Walter George of Georgia said on the floor of Congress with no small sense of exasperation, "I hope the time has not come when one must apologize for being a hateful Anglo-Saxon."[158]

The time had come. It became more and more clear that an accusation of ethnic or religious bigotry could damage the career aspirations of national political candidates. In the 1952 presidential election, politicians once again tried to gain an advantage by inserting religious or ethnic issues into campaigns. Late in the campaign between Eisenhower and Adlai Stevenson, after Eisenhower backed a Republican senatorial candidate who had supported the displaced persons bill, President Truman wrote to the National Jewish Welfare Board. He repeated his accusations of anti-Catholicism and anti-Semitism in the passage of the bill and then said, "The Republican candidate for the presidency cannot escape responsibility for his endorsements. He has had an attack of moral blindness, for today, he is willing to accept the very practice that identified the so-called 'master race,' although he took a leading part in liberating Europe from their domination."[159] The statement created an uproar. Republicans accused Truman of calling Eisenhower anti-Semitic and anti-Catholic, and Jewish and Catholic national leaders came to Eisenhower's defense. The pressure forced Truman to back off of his earlier statement, but several prominent Republicans did not think he went far enough. They publicly criticized Stevenson for not disassociating himself from Truman and the attempt to enflame religious and ethnic tensions.[160]

During the Eisenhower administration the focus on religion in American life intensified. In 1953, the American Legion staged a televised spiritual reawakening program called "Back to God." The program included statements from both President Eisenhower and Vice President Nixon. Protestant, Catholic, and Jewish religious leaders all played prominent roles in the program, and the affair was held on the anniversary of the sinking of the USS *Dorchester*. The legion built the program around the example set by the

Four Immortal Chaplains. During the invocation, Rabbi David Lefkowitz summed up the intent of the affair: "May our Program . . . be blessed with Holy strength and purpose and may it promote a spiritual reawakening in the hearts of our people, serving to symbolize for all nations and creed, the individual responsibility of free men—one to the other—in God."[161] In fact, it had become standard procedure for the major veterans groups to hear prayers from Jewish, Protestant, and Catholic clergy at their major meetings.[162] During the Eisenhower years, these veterans groups joined with religious bodies in giving their wholehearted support for the adoption of "In God We Trust" as a national motto and the inclusion of the phrase "under God" in the Pledge of Allegiance.[163]

Even the widely accepted terminology for American religious traditions included the lesson of religious tolerance. As a candidate in 1952, Eisenhower said, "Our Government has no sense unless it is founded in a deeply felt religious faith and I don't care what it is. With us of course it is the Judeo-Christian concept, but it must be a religion that all men are created equal."[164] Eisenhower repeated the theme of America's foundation in the Judeo-Christian tradition on several occasions, all with the intent of expressing tolerance among America's religious denominations.[165] When the idea of religion expanded beyond the United States, he even feared that the "Judeo-Christian" construction was too narrow. In 1957 he wrote to his brother Milton about a speech Milton had given to the Masons, "You speak of the 'Judaic-Christian heritage.' I would suggest that you use a term on the order of 'religious heritage'—this is for the reason that we should find some way of including the vast numbers of people who hold to the Islamic and Buddhist religions when we compare the religious world against the Communist world." Yet, the president continued, "I think you could still point out the debt we all owe to the ancients of Judea and Greece for the introduction of new ideas."[166]

The Judeo-Christian concept implied tolerance and unity among the major American religions. In fact, variations on the term itself had been used by activists for religious tolerance during the war. The fact that the president of the United States so readily used the term symbolized a shift in religious relations in the country as a whole. Although some opposed the idea of a Judeo-Christian tradition on theological grounds, the concept achieved widespread acceptance as a descriptive for the historical and social relationship among religions.[167] It was a concept practiced in the army and adopted by all of the major veterans' organizations after the war. It defined the religious relations of the era about as well as any other term.

The efforts of Presidents Truman and Eisenhower to attack bigotry and promote tolerance were more than just attempts to appeal to interest groups of ethnic and religious minorities, even if electoral politics played some part.

Both men were veterans. Truman often recalled fondly his military experiences and service in World War I, and remained in contact with the men of his battery for the rest of his life. Eisenhower spent the better part of a lifetime in the army, became thoroughly imbued with the value of camaraderie, and genuinely believed that belief in God should unite Americans, not divide them. But even more than that, both Truman and Eisenhower had a pulse on the American people. They openly expressed their values of tolerance in part because they understood that the broader public had changed. The American people, led by the veterans of World War II, were ready to embrace such ethnic and religious tolerance.

The intellectual consensus of the Cold War, the everyday life of postwar America, pronouncements of scholars, the polls and surveys, all pointed to the change. But no device measured the will of the people so well as the voting booth. The postwar period saw another new phenomenon: the presence of veterans in politics led to the widespread breaking of ethnic and religious electoral boundaries. In statewide elections, where it was much harder to get elected by the backing of just one ethnic or religious group, minority veterans emerged as viable candidates. They had an impressive effect.

In August 1946, a commentator noted that a Catholic would struggle to win a statewide primary in heavily Lutheran Wisconsin.[168] Marine Corps veteran and Catholic Joseph McCarthy won the Republican primary and then won election to senator later that year.[169] In 1949, Herbert Lehman, a World War I navy veteran and father to a pilot who was killed in World War II, became the first Jewish senator from New York. In 1956, World War II veteran Jacob Javits, who had been elected as a representative in 1946, became the second. In 1954, navy veteran Edmund Muskie became the first Catholic and first Polish American elected governor of Maine.[170] In 1954, army veteran Richard Neuberger became the first Jew elected senator from Oregon. In 1956, navy veteran Foster Furcolo became the first Italian American elected governor of Massachusetts. In 1956, U.S. Army Air Force veteran Stephen O'Connell became the first Catholic to win a statewide office in Florida when he was elected chief justice of the state supreme court. In 1956, navy veteran Steve McNichols became the first Catholic elected governor of Colorado. In 1958, World War I veteran David Lawrence became the first Catholic elected governor of Pennsylvania. Czech American and World War II veteran Otto Kerner became governor of Illinois in 1960.[171]

The ascension of ethnic and religious minorities to statewide offices began to extend beyond veterans. In 1945, Rhode Island's John Pastore became the state's first Italian American governor; five years later he became the country's first Italian American senator. In 1945, Slovenian American Frank Lausche became the first Catholic governor of Ohio. In 1954, Abraham Ribicoff became the first Jewish governor of Connecticut. In Washington state in 1956, Albert Rosellini became the first Catholic and first Italian American elected governor west of the Mississippi. In 1958, Michael DiSalle became the first Italian American governor of Ohio. In 1958, Eugene McCarthy, who served as a civilian in the War Department during the war, became the first Catholic elected senator from Minnesota.[172]

No doubt ethnic and religious minorities voted in high numbers for the candidates from their ethnic or religious group out of a sense of pride. Some probably even bolted from their parties to do so. But if the broader public of these various states cared about the national or religious background of these candidates, or disliked the idea of such people in statewide office, they did not do so in numbers that prevented the candidates from winning elections. Other issues became more important. Elections were yet another indicator that they had become ethnically and religiously tolerant. The country had changed, and veterans were squarely in the middle of that change. "The foolish old prejudices, many of them no more than myths and superstitions, are falling away from politics," one editorialist wrote of this issue in 1954. "We're a big country now!"[173] The roster of ethnic and religious firsts in statewide political offices would only continue to grow in the next few decades. But before that, the country had to hold another nationwide referendum on tolerance.

# CONCLUSION

When we became teenagers we fell away from the animosities of our parents. Our World War II Army dissolved the rem-
nants of active enmity between most ethnic groups.

— Bill Davis, quoted in *Payoff Artillery–WWII*

by Frank H. Armstrong, 1993

OBSERVANT AMERICANS IN THE 1950S NOTED THE TREND TOWARD ETHNIC
and religious tolerance, but they remained unsure of its depth and permanence. They knew the greatest possible test would be the nomination of a
minority candidate, probably a Catholic, for a national office. They looked to
that time with a mix of excitement and dread. Everyone who had any kind of
memory of the 1928 election paused at the idea of another Catholic candidate
for the presidency or vice presidency.[1] Polling indicated some general trends
but did not clear up the overall picture. In 1940, 62 percent of respondents in
a poll said they would vote for a Catholic for president; that number rose to
68 percent in 1958 and 71 percent in the summer of 1960.[2] The old questions
persisted. Some anti-Catholic writers revived the idea that Catholics could
not separate their religious beliefs from their political duties. But new trends
also emerged, such as anti-Catholic attacks in political campaigns beginning
to backfire against candidates.[3]

The issue also gained relevance in the 1950s because Catholics made up
roughly one-fifth of all American voters. Both parties understood the importance of the Catholic vote, even if it was not totally monolithic. Because many
national political leaders believed that a Catholic could help a national ticket,
the movement to nominate a Catholic for the vice presidency became pretty
strong in 1956.[4] Political pundits for leading newspapers pushed the issue
throughout the decade.[5] Even President Eisenhower, who ran pretty well
with Catholics due to personal appeal, briefly toyed with the idea of drop-
ping Nixon from the ticket and replacing him with a Catholic.[6] Neither party
nominated a Catholic for the vice presidency that year, but a very visible

candidate emerged from the fray. In 1956, John F. Kennedy, then a young senator from Massachusetts, actively campaigned for the vice presidency. He did so as a Catholic, with the expressed intent of drawing the Catholic vote. Though his attempt failed, he made a name for himself in national politics and emerged as a potential candidate for the Democratic nomination in 1960.

The Catholic issue continue to loom. The Catholic vote had power, but so did the fear of an anti-Catholic vote. Kennedy recognized the problem, and when he became a candidate for president in 1960 he changed his tactics. His candidacy was not about adding the vote of a particular interest group to a larger ticket; it was about heading the ticket. Kennedy needed to get votes from a cross-section of the American people. Running as a Catholic candidate who could draw Catholic votes risked alienating Protestant voters. So he no longer advertised his ability to draw the Catholic vote. In fact, he even denied or publicly ignored the idea of such a thing as the Catholic vote. As he wrote to an aide, "Once we get into the argument . . . about there being a Catholic vote, we are on very treacherous grounds, indeed."[7]

For this reason, Kennedy would have rather ignored the religion issue altogether, and at first he had some success. When he officially began his campaign in January 1960, he dealt with the religious question by affirming his belief in the First Amendment and the separation of church and state. "When the candidate gives his views on that question," he said, "and I think I have given my views fully, I think the subject is exhausted."[8] But the events of the following months brought the issue to the fore. His main opponent in the primaries was Hubert Humphrey of Minnesota. Their first major contest came in Wisconsin, where Kennedy won a solid victory.[9] Unfortunately for him, the victory came in large part due to the support of the predominantly Catholic districts in the state. He had not run nearly as well in the Protestant areas. As the page-one headline of the *New York Times* declared, "Religion Big Factor in Kennedy Victory."[10] Suddenly the argument about the Catholic vote became "The 'Catholic Vote': How Important Is It?"[11] To add to the problem, overwhelmingly Protestant West Virginia hosted the next major primary. As the media and candidates discussed the religious issue in Wisconsin, Kennedy's religion became more widely known in West Virginia, and his poll numbers began to drop. Most observers predicted that the anti-Catholic vote would give Humphrey the win in West Virginia. As the candidate feared, the debate over the Catholic vote put his campaign on treacherous ground.

Kennedy decided to face the religious issue more directly, though he still avoided the idea of a Catholic vote. "Even if such a vote exists—which I doubt," he said in a speech, "I want to make one thing clear again: I want no votes solely on account of my religion."[12] He reaffirmed his belief in the separation of church and state by telling a television audience that a president swore on a Bible to uphold the principle: "And if he breaks his oath, he is not only committing a crime against the Constitution . . . but he is committing a sin against God." He continued, "A sin against God, for he has sworn on the Bible."[13] But in facing religion, he also began to appeal to the voters' sense of fairness and tolerance. In so doing, he alluded to the great example in the recent American past of fairness and tolerance, the World War II military experience. The Kennedy campaign made a huge issue in West Virginia out of its candidate's World War II service as a naval officer on PT boats in the Pacific. As he told the Protestant crowds, "Nobody asked me if I was a Catholic when I joined the United States Navy." And he went further, saying the United States should not be a place that excluded people from office because of religion: "That wasn't the country my brother [Joseph Kennedy Jr.] died for in Europe, and nobody asked my brother if he was a Catholic or a Protestant before he climbed into an American bomber plane to fly his last mission."[14]

The implication was clear, a vote against him because of his religion was a vote against all the country had fought for in World War II. One voter told an observer she would now vote for Kennedy: "We have enough trouble in West Virginia, let alone to be called bigots, too."[15] On May 10, West Virginians voted, and Kennedy won a resounding victory. The Kennedys poured huge amounts of money into the contest, used volunteers to great effect, and campaigned intensely. They tied their candidate's name to popular local tickets all around the state. John Kennedy used his immense personal charisma to connect with crowds and audiences. Through it all, the anti-Catholic factor did not matter enough to change the outcome.[16] Humphrey dropped out of the campaign for the nomination, and Kennedy went on to win the rest of the major primaries and the Democratic nomination.

The religion issue did not die with Kennedy's victory in West Virginia. For a year and a half up to election day, leaders from various Protestant denominations and branches all over the country issued statements either questioning the fitness of a Catholic to be president or outright declaring that a Catholic president would mean the end of the United States as a free nation.[17] The old fake Knights of Columbus oath reappeared.[18] As the election approached, some individuals and groups organized mass mailing campaigns for anti-Catholic propaganda.[19] Two of the most prominent Protestant ministers in the country, Norman Vincent Peale and Billy Graham, both expressed strong concerns about a Catholic president, Peale publicly, Graham privately.[20]

Where the anti-Catholic propaganda most decidedly did not come from was the Republican party or its candidate, Richard Nixon. Throughout the campaign, the Republicans repeatedly decried the use of the religious issue. At the Republican convention in July, the Subcommittee on Civil Rights and Immigration of the platform committee issued an official statement under the heading "Religious Freedom": "Ours is a religious nation. Every faith has contributed to our national sense of duty and high moral purpose. Because every form of private religious practice is welcome here, there can be no such thing as a 'religious issue' in an American political campaign."[21] They focused on Kennedy's youth and inexperience, his poor voting record in the Senate, but not his religion. And none of the issues they went after Kennedy for could even be considered proxies for religion, like Prohibition or schools.[22] President Eisenhower spoke out on the issue on multiple occasions. In April 1960, he actually read from the Constitution, which stated that "no religious Test shall ever be required as a Qualification to any Office or public Trust under the United States" and "Congress shall make no law respecting an establishment of religion, or prohibiting the free exercise thereof."[23] Later he acknowledged that religion would be an issue in some areas of the country, but that it should not be. As he stated, "I don't think I would ever admit that it is really a legitimate question."[24]

All of Nixon's comments on the issue followed the same line. In August, Nixon's campaign actually issued a gag order on religion. The order "warned campaign staff against contact with any individual or group that offered support on religious grounds. No Republican volunteers, party organization, or campaign headquarters were to distribute literature addressing Catholicism. Even jokes or allusions to Kennedy's religion were off-limits."[25] A few weeks later, Nixon went on *Meet the Press* and asked Kennedy to agree to a cut-off date, after which there would be absolutely no talk of religion in the campaign. Nixon went on to affirm, "I have no doubt whatever about Senator Kennedy's loyalty to his country."[26] In all of these efforts, the Republicans insisted that a Catholic could be perfectly qualified to be president of the United States. They were, in effect, giving Kennedy something of an endorsement.

In the meantime, the Kennedy campaign built upon the strategies from the primaries. Kennedy presented his religion as entirely separate from his public life. He maintained that nothing about Roman Catholicism conflicted with the duties of the presidency. He publicly opposed sending an ambassador to the Vatican. On September 12, he even went before a large meeting of influential Protestant ministers to share his views: "I believe in an America where the separation of church and state is absolute. . . . I believe in an America that is officially neither Catholic, Protestant nor Jewish. . . . Finally, I believe in an America where religious intolerance will someday end. . . . This is the kind of America I believe in—and this is the kind of America I fought for in the South Pacific and the kind my brother died for in Europe."[27] Once again Kennedy implied that anti-Catholicism, or any kind of bigotry, went against the defining ideals of Americanism that the country had fought so hard for in World War II.

The Democrats took that theme on the campaign trail. For the rest of the campaign, Kennedy's supporters either implied or outright accused the Republicans of using religious bigotry to stir up support. African American congressman Adam Clayton Powell said Nixon represented "the worst forces of bigotry in America."[28] Later, Powell said that "all bigots will vote for Nixon and all right-thinking Christians and Jews will vote for Kennedy rather than be found in the ranks of the Klan-minded."[29] Former President Truman repeatedly accused the Republicans of engaging in anti-Catholic propaganda. Robert Kennedy and Democratic National Chairman Henry "Scoop" Jackson declared that anti-Catholic propaganda in various states was tied directly to the Nixon campaign.[30] Jackson insisted that Nixon explicitly repudiate the anti-Catholic statements of prominent Protestant leaders like Peale.[31] When Nixon followed his own order not to discuss religion as an issue in the campaign, the Democrats accused him of backing the bigotry.

In the third presidential debate, a moderator asked the candidates about the purpose of such accusations. Kennedy took the opportunity to get in another shot at Nixon by association: "Mr. Griffin, I believe, who is the head of the Klan, who lives in Tampa, Florida, indicated a—in a statement, I think, two or three weeks ago that he was not going to vote for me, and that he was going to vote for Mr. Nixon." Yet, he added, "I do not suggest in any way, nor have I ever, that . . . Mr. Nixon has the slightest sympathy, involvement, or in any way imply any inferences in regard to the Ku Klux Klan. That's absurd. I don't suggest that, I don't support it. I would disagree with it."[32] Nixon again stated that religion should not be an issue in the campaign: "I repudiate anybody who uses the religious issue; I will not tolerate it, I have ordered all of my people to have nothing to do with it and I say—say to this great audience, whoever may be listening, remember, if you believe in America, if you want America to set the right example to the world, that we cannot have religious or racial prejudice. We cannot have it in our hearts. But we certainly cannot have it in a presidential campaign."[33] Eventually Nixon began to grow weary of the accusations. At the Alfred E. Smith Memorial dinner in late October, yet another tribute to the idea of a Catholic president, he decried the efforts to paint him as a bigot.[34]

The use of the religious issue by the two campaigns had become pretty clear. The best historian of the election described the differences: "Kennedy's supporters promoted the idea that pluralism required aggressive repudiation of religious and racial bigotry. Republican Party leaders portrayed ignoring and ostracizing anti-Catholic critics as the best means of defending pluralist ideals."[35] Something else was going on in the 1960 election besides a reprise of the animosities of the 1928 election. For all of the individual church leaders and anti-Catholic bigots who said a Roman Catholic should not be president of the United States, there were an equal or greater number who declared that bigotry had no place in an American election. For example, the North Carolina AMVETS condemned "all appeals based on religious bigotry, racial prejudices or any other appeal made to pit class against class as un-American and un-democratic" and sent the resolution to both political parties and all the candidates running in North Carolina.[36] Religious leaders representing Judaism and a wide variety of Protestant denominations came out in support of similar positions.[37]

A contemporary observer summed up the concerns of both sides. The Democrats worried that voters would go into the booth leaning toward Kennedy and then decide they really could not handle a Catholic in the White House. "For the Republicans," he wrote, "it is: will any large number of voters now leaning toward Vice President Nixon suddenly decide 'I can't be on the side of bigots' when they come to cast their votes?"[38] The Kennedys were banking on the hope that those who opposed bigotry, Catholics and Protestants, outnumbered those who did not. They were banking on tolerance.[39]

John Kennedy won what was then the closest presidential election ever. Richard Nixon gave his assessment of the 1960 election in his memoirs:

> Kennedy had two principal liabilities. In my judgment one was only apparent—his Catholicism; the other was real—his lack of experience. The religion issue would cut several ways and would probably end up as an advantage for Kennedy. The pockets of fundamentalist anti-Catholic prejudice that still existed were concentrated in states that I stood to win anyway. But many Catholics would vote for Kennedy because he was Catholic, and some non-Catholics would vote for him just to prove they were not bigoted.[40]

Catholics did vote for Kennedy in large numbers, and no doubt some non-Catholics voted for him to avoid looking like bigots. Many Protestants did vote against him, but not in large enough numbers to change the outcome.[41]

In 1928, Al Smith lost overwhelmingly to Herbert Hoover. He lost his home state. He even lost some of the Solid South. And the defeat came at the end of a campaign where bigots at every level of American society openly reveled in their bigotry. Only thirty-two years later, John Kennedy won a plurality of the popular vote and a majority of the electoral vote by winning in states all over the country. He held the Solid South. And the victory came at the end of a campaign where almost all of those who openly distrusted the Catholic church claimed they did not do so out of bias—a campaign where the greatest slur of all was the word "bigot" itself. The 1960 campaign and the election of a World War II veteran as the first Catholic president indicated the level to which the veterans had spread the lessons of their war throughout American society.

The 1960 campaign drew out some of the problems with the inclusive pluralism of the postwar years. About 70 percent of all African Americans voted for John Kennedy, in part at least, because they sympathized with the fight against bigotry.[42] The ethnic and religious tolerance of the veterans' consensus after the war put a strain on the issue of race. The fighting men had been racially segregated during the war. They did not develop widespread tolerance across racial lines. As a result, the role of veterans in postwar racial relations was not as straightforward as their position on ethnicity and religion.

As a general rule, white World War II veterans fell into three broad groups when it came to race relations in the United States.[43] The first group, mostly from the South, actively opposed any expansion of the civil rights of African Americans. They became reactionary on issues of race in their fear of blacks challenging them both economically and socially. Some veterans in New Orleans wrote to President Truman in March 1948 that they resented the recently introduced civil rights bill.[44] In 1954, the local VFW post in Indianola, Mississippi, resolved "to aid all Races but not at each others expense. To provide equal but separate schools for the Black and White Races. To prevent mongrelization of our nation by avoiding conditions that foster and promote intermarriage of the races. To uphold Segregation in the states that desire it and whose social structure requires it."[45] Some of these reactionaries joined the resurgent Klan and even took part in some of the postwar lynchings of black veterans. The revived Klan of the postwar period, while still rhetorically nativist, anti-Semitic, and anti-Catholic, focused almost all of its attention on terrorizing African Americans and opposing the expansion of their civil rights.[46]

The second group was made up of veterans who had taken the lessons of ethnic and religious tolerance and expanded them to race. As one historian has written, "The ability of these whites to overcome prejudices toward Jews, Catholics, and other groups whom they had feared or despised may also have allowed them to question the validity of prejudice applied to any group, blacks included, in ways they had not been able to before."[47] Not surprisingly, the American Veterans Committee was the most active within this group. For example, in 1947 it submitted a memorandum to the President's Committee on Civil Rights expressing its support for equal rights, especially in regard to race, in voting, the armed forces, education, employment, and housing.[48]

After the war, organizations such as Jewish War Veterans promised to use their reputations to combat anti-Semitism and other forms of discrimination at home in the United States.[49] When they found that anti-Semitism had decreased precipitously after the war, these organizations turned their attention to the plight of blacks in America. There were other examples. Members of the Pittsburg (California) Veterans Committee wrote to President Truman in 1948 stating that they fought in two world wars for the freedom of oppressed people yet the war continued at home. They urged the president to end segregation in the armed forces.[50] A group of white veterans elected to the Mississippi state senate in 1948 pushed for more progressive policies toward African Americans.[51] In Georgia, progressive white veterans tried to work with black leaders to enact reforms after the war, with only mixed success.[52]

The third group constituted the majority of veterans. They focused on getting on with their own lives, and on developing the economic wealth of the country so they could live and work in peace. They tried to ignore issues of race. When blacks moved into their city neighborhoods, they moved out for fear of declining property values. They became detached from social justice movements, even if those movements had resonated with them before the war. For example, as the NAACP worked to get a permanent FEPC after the war, they found that some of their traditional allies had abandoned them. The wartime economy meant Catholics as a group no longer had a distinct economic problem, and many of them, according to one newspaperman, resented "being lumped with colored people in America's thinking." Similarly, wrote a historian of the FEPC, "Jews were also pulling back in the belief that their minority troubles were social, rather than economic, in origin." Neither group wanted published FEPC statistics indicating that they had been helped by the committee.[53] When it came to black civil rights, apathetic best described most World War II veterans. They did not live postwar lives of racial tolerance. They chose not to deal with the great American dilemma.[54] The costs of not integrating the men along race lines in World War II stand out in even more stark contrast when put up against the results of mixing white ethnic and religious soldiers.[55]

For their part, black veterans used the war as a jumping off point in the civil rights movement. They came back less willing to accept the racist and segregated system at home. Many joined the growing efforts on behalf of civil rights. They began to participate in the grassroots part of the civil rights movement. The actions of that grassroots movement made it so that by the end of the 1950s, the majority of apathetic white veterans who were just living their lives would not be able to ignore issues of race for too much longer.

By the late 1960s, the discontent fostered by the civil rights movement, the emergence of feminism, and the difficulties of the Vietnam War created an environment that led many Americans to question the assumptions of the white male veterans' postwar consensus. The idea of a common Judeo-Christian faith came under attack from all quarters as the various American religions sought to set themselves apart.[56] In regard to race and ethnicity in the new view, as one historian has written, the "traditional American values of freedom and equality were to be achieved not by disregarding race and treating everyone the same but by taking race and group belonging into positive account in social policy."[57] Even at the height of the postwar consensus, every specific ethnic and religious group experienced their increased contact with the rest of society in their own way. As one student of the process emphasized, "What was actually occurring was a complex multi-part process of negotiation within the group and between the group and the larger society."[58] For example, for many Jewish American veterans the war had triggered a greater pride in their American-ness and Jewish-ness, at the same time.[59] In the late 1960s and early 1970s, many of the groups began to symbolically pull back from the rest of society. The era saw a rise in ethnic pride movements, as various groups celebrated what made them unique in American society, not what made them the same.[60] At the same time, new groups of immigrants flooded into the country from Latin America and Asia and developed their own unique concerns to add to the mix.

The trend toward celebrating diversity caused, and continues to cause, consternation on the part of many observers. The next thirty years saw no small amount of ink spilled on such topics as "The Rise of the Unmeltable Ethnics," "The Disuniting of America," and "Reinventing the Melting Pot."[61] Many feared that the different cultural values of the newest immigrants and the rise of ethnic pride movements would mean that the country could no longer share the ideals that had once made it great. They assumed that the postwar consensus had been lost. But its most important aspect survived. For all the tensions among America's many peoples, the country has never returned to the levels of ethnic and religious intolerance and hostility that marked the time before the veterans of World War II came home. That legacy lives on.

In every measurable way, the United States faced real and serious ethnic and religious intolerance up until the end of World War II. In every measurable way, ethnic and religious intolerance decreased in the first decade and a half after the end of the war. This study has sought to explain why.

The horrifying example of the Nazi persecution of minorities did not cause Americans at home to abandon their prejudices during the war. In fact, the last years of the war saw a jump in ethnic and religious animosity at home, until the veterans came back. Besides, the Holocaust simply did not resonate in American life to a large degree in the first two decades after the war, when tolerance expanded the most.[62] And when and where the lessons of Nazi atrocities did trigger a backlash against discrimination, it was only to the extent that the Holocaust was made an American memory by the veterans who had witnessed its effects.[63] Nor did the postwar Communist threat alone trigger the era of ethnic and religious tolerance. Only twenty-five years earlier, the threat of radical communism had led to one of the worst eras of ethnic and religious strife in American history. Insomuch as the threat of communism united Americans of various ethnicities and religions after World War II, it was under a single ideology of Americanism—an ideology dictated verbatim by the veterans. Similarly, while consumerism and mass culture after World War II increasingly saw Americans desiring and purchasing similar products, the uniformity of consumerism and mass culture had not created tolerance in the prosperous 1920s.

Nor did generational differences wholly explain the change. The closing off of immigration in the 1920s meant a sharp decrease in the number of new first-generation immigrants, allowing the more Americanized third-generation ethnic minorities to rise to prominence. But the speed of the decline of intolerance after the war belied the generational explanation. The first-generation immigrants and less-Americanized second-generation ethnics at home in America did not disappear at the end of the war. However, their provincialism became less of a factor and animosity toward and among them decreased. Insomuch as generational differences explained this shift, it was because the World War II generation rose to prominence so rapidly after the war. The veterans led that movement, too.

By the time the United States had entered World War II, the country's military had developed personnel policies that actively and completely mixed America's diverse white ethnic and religious population. The sudden removal from the comforts of home, the often degrading and humiliating experiences of military life, and the unit- and friendship-building of training leveled the men. The activities meant to fill times of boredom in the military reminded the men of all that they had in common as Americans, especially in comparison to the foreign nationals they encountered overseas. Under fire, the men survived by leaning on buddies, regardless of their ethnicity or religion. And the dead of all backgrounds offered an undeniable testament to their sacrifices as Americans. When they came home from the war, they found a country willing to hand them all manner of advantages and looking to them for leadership. As a result, World War II veterans played the prominent role in the shaping of postwar American society. At every turn, they used their positions of power—in law, in intellectual matters, in culture, in the community, in politics—to increase ethnic and religious tolerance. The sea change in ethnic and religious relations in the United States came from the military experience in World War II. The war remade the nation. The nation was forged in war.

One thing remained undone. Enraged by the McCarran-Walter Immigration Act of 1952, President Truman set up a commission to look into immigration and naturalization. The commission issued its final report the following year. The report condemned the national quota system as a total failure and called for its abolition. According to the report, the quotas had hurt the work force, damaged America foreign policy with a variety of countries around the world, and had failed to change the proportion of immigrants to get a more favorable racial mix, as had been the original intent. Most important, the quota system had violated the nation's founding principles in applying "discriminations against human beings on account of national origin, race, creed and color."[64] The report noted, "American unity has been achieved without national uniformity."[65] The Regular Veterans Association, now with an Italian American national commander, wrote to Truman commending him for setting up the commission.[66]

In the mid fifties, as legislators began to introduce legislation to eliminate the national origins quotas, President Eisenhower suggested to Congress that they at least amend the system. As a candidate in 1952, Eisenhower had said, "No man's race or creed or color should count against him in his economic or civil or other rights. Only second-class Americanism tolerates second-class citizenship. It's time to get rid of what remains of both, and that includes rewriting the unfair provisions of the McCarran Immigration Act."[67] Politicians sought to make friends with principled stands on the issue. In 1955, New York senator Irving Ives told an audience of Italian American Republicans that the 1952 act was "based on callous discrimination" and had been the work of "a Democrat-led group in a Democrat Congress."[68] Despite the politicization by Ives, a student of the issue noted in 1956, "A vital change . . . seems to have taken place in the last four years in the status of the immigration issue. From a somewhat partisan, relatively localized issue, it appears to have become a nonpartisan national issue."[69] In his state of the union address that same year, Eisenhower once again called for Congress to revise immigration laws.[70] In the following years, the government looked the other way while people from all over the world immigrated to the United States in numbers exceeding their quotas.[71]

By the early 1960s, Congress was finally ready to act. The quota system had become a social, intellectual, and moral anachronism—a testament to a bygone era of bigotry and intolerance. One year after the Civil Rights Act of 1964, and the same year as the Voting Rights Act, the Congress passed a third great law for group relations in America. The Immigration Act of 1965 once and for all removed national origin quotas from immigration law. President Lyndon Johnson signed the bill at the base of the Statue of Liberty.[72]

In the course of the debate, one resident of Louisville, Kentucky, wrote to his senator asking that he fight "tooth and toe nail" any proposed changes to the laws that would allow immigrants to enter on a "first come–first serve basis." The problem, as he saw it, were the large number of Italians backlogged to immigrate to the United States:

President Lyndon Johnson speaks at the ceremony for the signing of the Immigration Act of 1965. Courtesy of Lyndon Baines Johnson Presidential Library.

I have nothing personal against the Italians as a race except they are responsible for the deaths of many thousands of Americans in two wars. They are very brave until the hail of hell hits them and then they are our "friends." Newspaper accounts of the hoodlums gathering in the Appalachians gave their number as 60 men, all Italians, who are the heads of all the gangsterism in this country. We don't need to go back to Capone days to say the majority of our hoodlums are Italians.[73]

Acknowledging the power of being accused of being an anti-Catholic bigot, the writer continued:

Senator Kennedy might try to counter by saying that since I am a Protestant I am fighting Catholicism. If such were the case I could write protesting the immigration to this country of Irish, French[,] Spaniards, etc. I just don't want any more people in this country who can't seem to be deported regardless of what laws they break, and judging from past history, seem to regard lawlessness as the proper way to make a living in this country.

He then promised to follow the senator's "efforts in this fight" and promised to take up the issue with the American Legion, which he assumed would support his position.[74]

The senator who had been warned of the threat of Italians was Kentucky Republican John Sherman Cooper. "I was very interested in your comments about the immigration legislation proposed by Senator Kennedy," Cooper wrote back to his constituent. But, he went on, "it seems to me that it is very difficult to assign to a whole nation the misdoings of individuals of that group. I think a sounder approach would be to screen very carefully all applicants for admission to this country, regardless of the nation of their birth."[75]

It should come as no surprise that John Sherman Cooper had served as a captain in Gen. George S. Patton's Third Army in World War II.[76] How fitting a veteran should write those words to a potential voter. How clearly the country had changed.

# ACKNOWLEDGMENTS

I ACCUMULATED A GREAT MANY PERSONAL DEBTS IN THE COURSE OF WRITING this book. A number of archivists and librarians made the process much easier with their hard work on my behalf. Especially helpful were Mark Renovitch and Alycia Vivona at the Franklin D. Roosevelt Presidential Library; Randy Lee Sowell and Dennis Bilger at the Harry S. Truman Presidential Library; Chelsea Millner, Tom Branigan, and Michelle Kopfer at the Dwight D. Eisenhower Presidential Library; Ken Schlessinger and Don Singer at National Archives and Records Administration II; Kevin Flanagan at the American Legion Archives National Headquarters; Bill Marshall and Jeff Suchanek at the Margaret I. King Library, University of Kentucky; and R. L. Baker and Stephen M. Bye at the U.S. Army Military History Institute/Army Heritage Center. Martin Morgan at the Eisenhower Center in New Orleans generously shared electronic copies of their extensive oral history collection. Finally, the staffs at Alden Library at Ohio University and the Combined Arms Research Library at Fort Leavenworth, especially Renee Geary, Sharon Strein, and Heather Turner, tracked down innumerable interlibrary loans, without which this book could not have been written.

A number of individuals contributed directly to the finished product. Doug Mundy lent me his father's unpublished memoir. Joshua Brown generously let me use an image from his father's sketchbook. The American Battle Monument Commission shared some photographs with me. T. David Curp offered much-needed advice with some of the international aspects of the study, and Donald Jordan let me borrow some family materials. Shae Davidson took time from his own work to point out, and often copy, a variety of interesting sources that hopefully helped give life to this study. Likewise, Brent Geary paused his own research to dig up a document for me at the National Archives.

Several friends patiently listened and provided important feedback as I prattled along about this topic. First among equals in this regard stands Ren Lessard, an expert in military affairs and great friend to boot. My colleagues at the Center of Military History, Combat Studies Institute, and the School of Advanced Military Studies also deserve mention, especially Tim Challans, Dan Cox, Robert Epstein, John Frappier, Candi Hamm, Jacob Kipp, Stephen

Lofgren, Rob McClary, Michael Mosser, Jim Schneider, and Michael Swanson. I also have to mention the remarkable men and women of Seminar 6 (2007– 8), who graciously let me spend a class period discussing my book topic. They are all bravely serving our country in its current war, and I admire them all more than they can know.

J. D. Wyneken and James Waite read some of the early chapters and offered thoughtful advice. Alonzo Hamby, Charles Alexander, Richard Vedder, John Bodnar, Edward M. Coffman, and a number of other anonymous readers looked at parts or all of the manuscript, and all of their comments and criticisms helped make for a better final product. The same goes for all of the folks at the University of Tennessee Press, especially director Scot Danforth, manuscript editor Gene Adair, and freelance copyeditor Karin Kaufman. Marvin Fletcher and G. Kurt Piehler deserve special mention in this respect, as they both put in more effort making this book work than I hoped for (or deserved). Even without such aid, I would like to thank all of them for their friendship. I hope the final product—including its inevitable flaws, which are mine alone—lives up to their expectations.

This book began as a historian's exploration into how World War II changed the United States, an enormous topic. I needed some small slice of the issue, and that came on a long drive to a library book sale with my friend Robert T. Davis II. Amid my ramblings about the war and all the ways it changed the country, I mentioned something about how in their surveys at Carlisle, multiple veterans mentioned the joking nature of ethnic slurs in their units in the army. Robert had been reading wartime letters from his grandfather to his grandmother, and one of those letters included a note about how he had been working with a Jewish soldier. He was the first Jew Robert's grandfather had ever met, and he was a good guy. So I have Robert T. Davis, and his grandson and namesake, to thank for giving me my angle on World War II and two of the photographs in this book.

Robert T. Davis and his wife came from Kansas. They were Presbyterians of English and German descent. Their son Norman married Tina Blackmor, a German Methodist from Texas and daughter of a World War II–era veteran. I met their oldest son Robert in graduate school at Ohio University, and I am honored to call him one of my closest friends.

I also met Derek C. Catsam and Stephen K. Tootle at Ohio University. Derek comes from New Hampshire—his Native American and French Canadian maternal grandfather served in World War II, and his Romanian paternal grandfather had an injury that kept him out of the service. He lives in

Texas now, with his wife Ana Martinez, whose family comes from Mexico. Stephen is from California's Central Valley. His grandparents were Okies who moved to California during the Depression, and both his grandfathers served in World War II. He is married to Erica Lutterbein, an Ohio native descended from German and Swiss Methodists. They live back in California. Even though we all live far apart now and come from very different places and backgrounds, I consider Derek and Stephen to be the brothers I never had.

Where I came from we had a lot of experience getting along with people from different backgrounds. I spent most of my youth in Brunswick, Ohio, a suburb of Cleveland. My best friend then, as now, was Ryan Neumeyer. His mom's parents were Slovaks, and the Neumeyers were German Catholic. Julius Neumeyer served in the Marines in World War II; Steve Gabre (his maternal grandfather) landed in Normandy with the U.S. Army on D Day. I never knew Gabre, but I have plenty of memories of Mr. Neumeyer. They are both gone now, but certainly not forgotten. Our friends in Ohio were like the Neumeyers. In my parents' generation, the baby boomers, Gnews had married Smiths, Jefferses had married Fredmonskis, Steblinskis had married Giulianos, Pezzulos had married Stautihars—and they pretty much all came from veterans of World War II. We all lived in the suburbs together.

My family was no different. Henry R. Bruscino and Violet (Vivolo) Bruscino were both children of Italian immigrants. Henry never finished high school; during the Depression his father sent him to work as a carpenter. When the war broke out, he joined the U.S. Navy and became a carpenter's mate in a naval construction battalion—the famed Seabees—and saw more of the Pacific than he ever wanted to. He came home, married my grandmother, and they had five children, including my father, Thomas Anthony Bruscino. William Jones, my maternal grandfather, was a bit younger. He graduated from high school in 1945 and joined the U.S. Navy. He was a crack shot from his days hunting in southwestern Pennsylvania, and he became a rear seat machine gunner in the navy's aviation branch. The war ended before he could leave the United States. He married Wilma Phillips, and my mother, Nancy Louise Jones, came along a few years later, the second of three children. The Jones and Phillips families came from old stock English, Scots Irish, Welsh, and German descent; we have tracked my grandfather's side to their arrival in South Carolina in 1648.

The postwar years eventually led the Bruscino and Jones families to Middleburg Heights, Ohio, the archetypal postwar suburb (it had been a farming village south of Cleveland up until the war). My parents met in high school and got married after graduation. My sister Sheri came along first, then me. We moved to Colorado in 1989, to a different kind of suburb, one that had been built to absorb the technological boom of the 1980s and 1990s. There people were more likely to live alongside Mormons or Hispanics than Irish or Polish, but the ethnic diversity was still there, just faded into the background, as I happily found out.

I met my future wife, Terrie Lynn Overmyer, at Adams State College in Alamosa, Colorado. In the 1970s, her parents, Steven and NancyJo Overmyer, met in Colorado through mutual friends and decided to settle there permanently. Steve came from Michigan, the son of Vernon and Virginia Overmyer. Vernon served in the Army in World War II. NancyJo came from Bristol, Rhode Island. Her maiden name was Nenna, and she's the daughter of Frederick and Mary Nenna, children of Italian immigrants. Fred also served in the U.S. Army in World War II as an artilleryman fighting in Europe. By the time I met him, senile dementia had left him with hardly any memories, but he could recall—he could not help but recall—one war story. One time, as his unit was traveling in trucks near the front, they came under German artillery fire. The trucks stopped and the men jumped out, but one of them got caught up on a truck by his wedding band and was killed when a shell hit. From that day forward, Fred's sergeant would not let any of his men wear any rings. I was honored to be a pall bearer at Papa Nenna's funeral. He is on the cover of this book, third from the left in the back row.

Terrie and I live in Kansas now. The flag that was draped over Henry Bruscino's coffin sits on the mantle over our fireplace; pictures of all our grandparents from the war years hang on the walls. They are steady reminders of where we come from, of who we are. That is even more true for our children, Dominic, Anthony, and Mariana. They do not know it yet, they are still too young, but someday they will look at those pictures and at that flag and realize that they are Italian, German, Irish, English, Welsh, and French. They will realize that they are American, and all that means.

To my family this book is dedicated, because this book is all about them. Great world-changing events are great and world changing because of the accumulation of effects they have on a host of individual lives. World War II, as great and terrible as it was, touched millions of individual Americans in ways that would eventually bring them together as a new, stronger nation. The people in Brunswick, Ohio, and Bristol, Rhode Island, at Adams State College and Ohio University, my friends and family, and especially, for me, my beautiful wife and children, are the parts that make that story whole.

They are all here, all of them, in these pages, in spirit if not always in word. It is said that you write what you know. I am so lucky, so blessed, to know such a great story.

# NOTES

## Abbreviations

| | |
|---|---|
| AL | American Legion National Headquarters, Indianapolis, Ind. |
| DDE | Dwight D. Eisenhower Presidential Library and Museum, Abilene, Kans. |
| EC | Eisenhower Center, University of New Orleans, New Orleans, La. |
| FDR | Franklin D. Roosevelt Presidential Library and Museum, Hyde Park, N.Y. |
| HEAEG | Thernstrom, Orloy, and Handlin, Harvard Encyclopedia of American Ethnic Groups |
| HST | Harry S. Truman Presidential Library and Museum, Independence, Mo. |
| HSUS | Bureau of the Census, Historical Statistics of the United States: Colonial Times to 1970 |
| KL | Margaret I. King Library, University of Kentucky, Lexington |
| NARA II | National Archives and Records Administration II, College Park, Md. |
| NYT | New York Times |
| USAMHI | U.S. Army Military History Institute/Army Heritage Center, Carlisle Barracks, Carlisle, Pa. |
| WDAR | War Department Annual Report |
| YSOH | Youngstown State University Oral History Program, William F. Maag Jr. Library, Youngstown State University, Youngstown, Ohio |

## Introduction

1. Dan Kurzman, *No Greater Glory: The Four Immortal Chaplains and the Sinking of the Dorchester in World War II* (New York: Random House, 2004); and Francis Beauchesne Thornton, *Sea of Glory: The Magnificent Story of the Four Chaplains* (New York: Prentice Hall, 1953).

2. G. Kurt Piehler, *Remembering War the American Way* (Washington, D.C.: Smithsonian Institution Press, 1995), 126–153; and Nicholas Mills, *Their Last Battle: The Fight for the National World War II Memorial* (New York: Basic Books, 2004).

3. "Pool Honors Heroism," *NYT,* Feb. 4, 1947, 27; and "Pool Is Dedicated," *NYT,* July 28, 1947, 17.

4. Maurine McCarthy, "Chapel of 3 Faiths Honors 4 Heroes," *Washington Post,* Dec. 21, 1947, B1; "Truman to Speak," *Washington Post,* Jan. 30, 1951, 4; "Aides to Join Truman," *NYT,* Feb. 2, 1951, 29; William G. Weart, "Donors View Rites," *NYT,* Feb. 4, 1951, 61; and Harry S. Truman, "Address in Philadelphia at the Dedication of the Chapel of the Four Chaplains," Feb. 3, 1951, *Public Papers of the Presidents of the United States,* American Presidency Project online, http://www.presidency.ucsb.edu/ws/, hereafter cited as American Presidency Project.

5. Kurzman, *No Greater Glory,* 184; "Stamp Honors Memory," *Los Angeles Times,* May 29, 1948, 5; and "4 Chaplains to Be Honored," *Washington Post,* May 22, 1948, 12. Quotation in "Truman Says Deaths," *NYT,* May 29, 1948, 17. See also Harry S. Truman, "Informal Remarks in San Francisco," June 13, 1948, *Public Papers,* American Presidency Project online.

6. "Four Chaplains Honored," *NYT,* May 26, 1952, 20; "Brotherhood Month Opens," *Hartford Courant,* Feb. 11, 1951, 10; "Spiritual Rebirth Is Urged by Legion," *NYT,* Feb. 4, 1952, 7; "Ike Supports Back to God Legion Campaign," *Christian Science Monitor,* Feb. 2, 1953, 3; "Gen. Ridgway to Preach at Cathedral," *Washington Post,* Sept. 14, 1953, 15; "President Urges Commemoration of Ship Sinking," *Hartford Courant,* Feb. 3, 1957, 14A.

7. "Text of President's Talk on Faith," *NYT,* Feb. 8, 1954, 11. See also Dwight D. Eisenhower, "Remarks Recorded for the American Legion "Back to God" Program," Feb. 1, 1953; and Dwight D. Eisenhower, "Remarks Broadcast as Part of the American Legion "Back to God" Program," Feb. 7, 1954, both in *Public Papers,* American Presidency Project online.

8. "Fountain Honors Four Chaplains," *Washington Post,* Sept. 24, 1955; "Sand Sculptor," *Time,* Oct. 10, 1955.

9. Kurzman, *No Greater Glory,* 184–185; "Senate Votes Medals," *NYT,* May 2, 1958, 16; "Heroic Chaplains Voted Medals," *Hartford Courant,* June 6, 1960; "Kin of Hero Chaplains Get Medals," *Washington Post,* Jan. 19, 1961, B8.

10. John Higham, *Send These to Me: Immigration in Urban America* (1975; rev. ed., Baltimore: Johns Hopkins Univ. Press, 1984), 15; Robert A. Divine, *American Immigration Policy, 1924–1952* (New Haven, Conn.: Yale Univ. Press, 1957), 192; Roger Daniels, *Coming to America: A History of Immigration and Ethnicity in American Life* (New York: HarperCollins, 1990), 122–125, 127, 146, 165; and Roger Daniels, *Not Like Us: Immigrants and Minorities in America, 1890–1924* (Chicago: Ivan R. Dee, 1997), 3–19.

11. Ray Allen Billington, *The Protestant Crusade, 1800–1860: A Study of the Origins of American Nativism* (New York: Macmillan, 1938); Michael F. Holt, *The Rise and Fall of the American Whig Party* (New York: Oxford Univ. Press, 1999), 844–850, 963–981; Sean Wilentz, *Chants Democratic: New York City and the Rise of the American Working Class, 1788–1850* (New York: Oxford Univ. Press, 1984), 344–345; John D. Hicks, *The Populist Revolt: A History of the Farmers' Alliance and the People's Party* (Univ. of Minnesota Press, 1931); C. Vann

Woodward, *Tom Watson: Agrarian Rebel* (1938; reprint, New York: Oxford Univ. Press, 1963); Lawrence Goodwyn, *Democratic Promise: The Populist Movement in America* (New York: Oxford Univ. Press, 1976); Norman Pollack, *The Humane Economy: Populism, Capitalism, and Democracy* (New Brunswick, N.J.: Rutgers Univ. Press, 1990); Michael Kazin, *The Populist Persuasion: An American History* (New York: Basic Books, 1995); Richard Hofstadter, *The Age of Reform: From Bryan to F.D.R.* (New York: Alfred A. Knopf, 1955), 77–81; and Higham, *Send These to Me,* 95–116.

12. Daniel J. Kevles, *In the Name of Eugenics: Genetics and the Uses of Human Heredity* (Cambridge: Harvard Univ. Press, 1985, 1995); Stefan Kuhl, *The Nazi Connection: Eugenics, American Racism, and German National Socialism* (New York: Oxford Univ. Press, 1994); Edward Alsworth Ross, "The Old World and the New: Racial Consequences of Immigration," *Century Illustrated Magazine* 87 (Feb. 1914): 615–616, 618, 619, 621, 622; Edward Alsworth Ross, "The Celtic Tide," *Century Illustrated Magazine* 87 (Apr. 1914): 952–955; Robert Hunter, *Poverty: Social Conscience in the Progressive Era* (New York: Macmillan, 1904; reprint, ed. Peter d'A. Jones, New York: Harper Torchbooks, 1965), 268–269, 270, 302, 313–314.

13. Israel Zangwill, *The Melting-Pot* (New York: Macmillan, 1909), 198–200. See also Arthur Mann, "The Melting Pot," in *Uprooted Americans: Essays to Honor Oscar Handlin,* ed. Richard L. Bushman, Neil Harris, Barbara Miller Solomon, and Stephan Thernstrom (Boston: Little, Brown, 1979), 289–318; and Arthur Mann, *The One and the Many: Reflections on the American Identity* (Chicago: Univ. of Chicago Press, 1979), chap. 5. Nor were they simply, in Oscar Handlin's phrase, "the uprooted," universally ignorant and powerless peasants who had no choice but to travel to unknown futures in the United States. Oscar Handlin, *The Uprooted: The Epic Story of the Great Migrations that Made the American People* (Boston: Little, Brown, 1951).

14. Rudolph J. Vecoli and Suzanne M. Sinke, eds., *A Century of European Migrations, 1830–1930* (Urbana: Univ. of Illinois Press, 1991), especially Frank Thistlethwaite, "Migration from Europe Overseas in the Nineteenth and Twentieth Centuries," Ewa Morawska, "Return Migrations: Theoretical and Research Agenda," and Walter D. Kamphoefner, "The Volume and Composition of German-American Return Migration." See also Camille Guerin-Gonzales, *Mexican Workers and American Dreams: Immigration, Repatriation, and California Farm Labor, 1900–1939* (New Brunswick, N.J.: Rutgers Univ. Press, 1994); Ewa Morawska, "Immigrants, Transnationalism, and Ethnicization: A Comparison of This Great Wave and the Last," in *E Pluribus Unum? Contemporary and Historical Perspectives on Immigrant Political Incorporation,* ed. Gary Gerstle and John Mollenkopf (New York: Russell Sage Foundation, 2001),175–199; Mark Wyman, *Round-Trip to America: The Immigrants Return to Europe, 1880–1930* (Ithaca, N.Y.: Cornell Univ. Press, 1993); Hunter, *Poverty,* 264; and Salvatore LaGumina, ed., *Wop!* (San Francisco: Straight Arrow Books, 1973), 161.

15. Even if they tried to assimilate into the dominant culture, that assimilation seemed to entail adopting prejudices of their own. Noel Ignatiev, *How the Irish Became White* (New York: Routledge, 1995); David R. Roediger, *The Wages of Whiteness: Race and the Making of the American Working Class* (New York: Verso, 1991); Thomas A. Guglielmo, *White on Arrival: Italians, Race, Color, and Power in Chicago, 1890–1945* (New York: Oxford Univ. Press, 2003), 6–9; Jennifer Guglielmo and Salvatore Salerno, eds., *Are Italians White? How Race Is Made in America* (New York: Routledge, 2003); Karen Brodkin, *How Jews Became White Folks: And What that Says about Race in America* (New Brunswick, N.J.: Rutgers Univ. Press, 1998), 35–52; and Eric L. Goldstein, *The Price of Whiteness: Jews, Race, and American Identity* (Princeton, N.J.: Princeton Univ. Press, 2006).

16. Such enclaves were not ghettos; ethnic neighborhoods were rarely demographically pure, but the ethnic cultural cohesiveness remained strong. David R. Roediger, *Working Toward Whiteness: How America's Immigrants Became White* (New York: Basic Books, 2005), 133–169. On chain migration, see Reino Kero, "Migration Traditions from Finland to North America"; Robert P. Swierenga, "Local Patterns of Dutch Migration to the United States in the Mid-Nineteenth Century"; Jon Gjerde, "Chain Migrations from the West Coast of Norway"; June Granatair Alexander, "Moving into and out of Pittsburgh: Ongoing Chain Migration"; Julianna Puskas, "Hungarian Overseas Migration: A Microanalysis"; and Franco Ramella, "Emigration from an Area of Intense Industrial Development: The Case of Northwestern Italy," in Vecoli and Sinke, *Century of European Migrations.* See also Yaroslav J. Chyz, *225 Years of the U.S. Foreign Language Press: Notes on Its Influence, History and Present Status* (New York: American Council for Nationalities Service, 1959), 7.

17. Alan Dawley, *Struggles for Justice: Social Responsibility and the Liberal State* (Cambridge, Mass: Belknap Press, 1991), 87–89; Eric Rauchway, *Murdering McKinley* (New York: Hill and Wang, 2003), 14–20, 113–131; and E. P. Hutchinson, *Legislative History of American Immigration Policy, 1798–1965* (Philadelphia: Univ. of Pennsylvania Press, 1981), 127–133.

18. Daniels, *Not Like Us*, 93–95.

19. David Kennedy, *Over Here: The First World War and American Society* (New York: Oxford Univ. Press, 1980), 63–69; Ronald Schaffer, *America in the Great War: The Rise of the War Welfare State* (New York: Oxford Univ. Press, 1991), 20–28; William E. Leuchtenburg, *The Perils of Prosperity, 1914–1932,* 2nd ed. (1958; reprint, Chicago: Univ. of Chicago Press, 1993), 42–44; Michael McGerr, *A Fierce Discontent: The Rise and Fall of the Progressive Movement in America, 1870–1920* (New York: Free Press, 2003), 288–292; Daniels, *Not Like Us*, 79–83, 96–99; John Higham, *Strangers in the Land: Patterns of American Nativism, 1860–1925* (New York: Atheneum, 1967), 242–250, 278–280, 300–301; David E. Kyvig, *Repealing National Prohibition* (Chicago: Univ. of Chicago Press, 1979), 10–13.

20. Frank Hoffmann, Dick Carty, and Quentin Riggs, *Billy Murray: The Phonograph Industry's First Great Recording Artist* (Lanham, Md.: Scarecrow Press, 1997), 203–204.

21. Nancy Gentile Ford, *Americans All! Foreign-born Soldiers in World War I* (College Station: Texas A&M Univ. Press, 2001), 3, 147–148 fn. 1; and Christopher M. Sterba, *Good Americans: Italian and Jewish Immigrants during the First World War* (New York: Oxford Univ. Press, 2003).

22. African Americans were segregated into their own divisions; Asian Americans on Hawaii also served in a segregated unit. The small number of Asian Americans in the U.S. Army were integrated into the larger force. Lucy E. Salyer, "Baptism by Fire: Race, Military Service, and U.S. Citizenship Policy, 1918–1935," *Journal of American History* 91 (Dec. 2004): 854; and Richard Slotkin, *Lost Battalions: The Great War and the Crisis of American Nationality* (New York: Henry Holt, 2005).

23. See John Keegan, *The Face of Battle* (New York: Penguin Books, 1976); Victor Hicken, *The American Fighting Man* (New York: Macmillan, 1969); Peter S. Kindsvatter, *American Soldiers: Ground Combat in the World Wars, Korea, and Vietnam* (Lawrence: Univ. Press of Kansas, 2003); and Nancy Gentile Ford, "'Mindful of the Traditions of His Race': Dual Identity and Foreign-born Soldiers in the First World War American Army," *Journal of American Ethnic History* 16 (Winter 1997): 35–57.

24. U.S. Senate, Committee on Veterans' Affairs, *Medal of Honor Recipients, 1863–1978* (Washington, D.C.: GPO, 1979), 465–466.

25. Quoted in Ford, *Americans All!* 142. Of course not all of the men got along; see Jennifer D. Keene, *Doughboys, the Great War, and the Remaking of America* (Baltimore: Johns Hopkins Univ. Press, 2001), 33–34.

26. Ford, *Americans All!* 144–145.

27. Chellis V. Smith, *Americans All: Nine Heroes Who in the World War Showed that Americanism Is Above Race, Creed, or Condition* (Boston: Lothrop, Lee and Shepard, 1925), 11–22.

28. Bill Bottoms, *The VFW: An Illustrated History of the Veterans of Foreign Wars of the United States* (Rockville, Md.: Woodbine House, 1991), 64.

29. Thomas A. Rumer, *The American Legion: An Official History, 1919–1989* (New York: M. Evans, 1990), 7.

30. Ibid., 70–71, 91–92.

31. Bottoms, *VFW,* 64–65.

32. Quoted in Rumer, *American Legion,* 51.

33. Including Asian immigrants. See Salyer, "Baptism by Fire," 866–874. On this point I am indebted to Melissa Kuhn for sharing her research on the American Legion.

34. Slotkin, *Lost Battalions,* 364–521; Rodney G. Minott, *Peerless Patriots: Organized Veterans and the Spirit of Americanism* (Washington, D.C.: Public Affairs Press, 1962), 45–89; William Pencak, *For God and Country: The American Legion, 1919–1941* (Boston: Northeastern Univ. Press, 1989); Raymond Moley Jr., *The American Legion Story* (New York: Dell, Cloan and Pearce, 1966); and Cherep-Spiridovich to John R. Quinn, 1923, Americanism-Propaganda, microfilm, AL.

35. Walter Millis, *Road to War: America 1914–1917* (Boston: Houghton Mifflin, 1935).

36. Alonzo L. Hamby, *For the Survival of Democracy: Franklin Roosevelt and the World Crisis of the 1930s* (New York: Free Press, 2004), 93.

37. The average duration of service in the World War I armed services was twelve months, in World War II it would be thirty-three months. *HSUS,* pt. 2, 1140. See also Keene, *Doughboys,* 161–178; Donald J. Lisio, "United States: Bread and Butter Politics," in *The War Generation: Veterans of the First World War,* ed. Stephen R. Ward (Port Washington, N.Y.: Kennikat Press, 1975), 38–55; and Richard Severo and Lewis Milford, *The Wages of War* (New York: Simon and Schuster, 1989), 247–263.

38. Gary Gerstle, *American Crucible: Race and Nation in the Twentieth Century* (Princeton, N.J.: Princeton Univ. Press, 2001), 102–103; and Leuchtenburg, *Perils of Prosperity,* 81–83. A more detailed account is Paul Avrich, *Sacco and Vanzetti: The Anarchist Background* (Princeton, N.J.: Princeton Univ. Press, 1991).

39. Quoted in Philip Perlmutter, *Divided We Fall: A History of Ethnic, Religious, and Racial Prejudice in America* (Ames: Iowa State Univ. Press, 1992), 222.

40. Although agriculture continued to suffer throughout the decade.

41. Frederick Lewis Allen, *Only Yesterday: An Informal History of the Nineteen-Twenties* (New York: Blue Ribbon Books, 1931), 62.

42. Warren G. Harding, *Our Common Country: Mutual Good Will in America* (Columbia: Univ. of Missouri Press, 2003), 111

43. Ibid., 132.

44. Kristi Anderson, *After Suffrage: Women in Partisan and Electoral Politics before the New Deal* (Chicago: Univ. of Chicago Press, 1996), 71–75.

45. Oscar Handlin, *Al Smith and His America* (Boston: Little, Brown, 1958), 79, 83.

46. Constantine Panunzio, "The Foreign Born's Reaction to Prohibition," in *The Politics of Moral Behavior: Prohibition and Drug Abuse,* ed. in K. Austin Kerr (Reading, Mass: Addison-Wesley, 1973), 120–124.

47. Kyvig, *Repealing National Prohibition,* 23–28.

48. Officially, the second Ku Klux Klan came to being in Georgia in December 1915. See David M. Chalmers, *Hooded Americanism: The First Century of the Ku Klux Klan, 1865–1965* (Garden City, N.Y.: Doubleday, 1965), 22–33; Charles C. Alexander, *The Ku Klux Klan in the Southwest* (1965; reprint, Norman: Univ.

of Oklahoma Press, 1995), 1–19; Kenneth T. Jackson, *The Ku Klux Klan in the City, 1915–1930* (New York: Oxford Univ. Press, 1967), xi–8; Wyn Craig Wade, *The Fiery Cross: The Ku Klux Klan in America* (New York: Simon and Schuster, 1987), 119–139; Nancy MacLean, *Behind the Mask of Chivalry: The Making of the Second Ku Klux Klan* (New York: Oxford Univ. Press, 1994), 3–11.

49. Alexander, *Ku Klux Klan in the Southwest,* 19. See also Chalmers, *Hooded Americanism,* 291–299; Wade, *Fiery Cross,* 239–254; MacLean, *Behind the Mask,* 177–188; and Jackson, *Ku Klux Klan,* 254–255.

50. Hutchinson, *Legislative History,* 180–181; Daniels, *Not Like Us,* 132–134; Divine, *American Immigration Policy,* 5–10; and Higham, *Strangers in the Land,* 314.

51. Divine, *American Immigration Policy,* 14.

52. The 1924 act also excluded Asians *entirely.* Divine, *American Immigration Policy,* 14–19; Hutchinson, *Legislative History,* 187–194.

53. See Reed Ueda, "Historical Patterns of Immigrant Status and Incorporation in the United States," in *E Pluribus Unum? Contemporary and Historical Perspectives on Immigrant Political Incorporation,* ed. Gary Gerstle and John Mollenkopf (New York: Russell Sage Foundation, 2001), 310, 315; Thomas Sowell, *Ethnic America: A History* (New York: Basic Books, 1981); and Brodkin, *How Jews Became White Folks,* 35–52. Because of the improvement of ethnic and religious relations in the country at midcentury, most of the studies of intergroup tensions in America turned their attention away from ethnicity and religion and toward race—sometimes Asian Americans but almost always African Americans. Ronald Takaki, *A Different Mirror: A History of Multicultural America* (Boston: Little, Brown, 1993), 373–402; and Donald R. McCoy and Richard T. Ruetten, *Quest and Response: Minority Rights in the Truman Administration* (Lawrence: Univ. Press of Kansas, 1973).

54. Classic versions of this model are Marcus L. Hansen, *The Problem of the Third Generation Immigrant* (Rock Island, Ill.: Augustana Historical Society, 1938); Margaret Mead, *And Keep Your Powder Dry: An Anthropologist Looks at America* (New York: William Morrow, 1942), especially chap. 3; and Will Herberg, *Protestant—Catholic—Jew: An Essay in American Religious Sociology* (Garden City, N.Y.: Doubleday, 1955). For more recent commentary, see Joel Perlmann and Roger Waldinger, "Second Generation Decline? Children of Immigrants, Past and Present—A Reconsideration," *International Migration Review* 31 (Winter 1997): 893–922; and Deborah Dash Moore, "At Home in America?: Revisiting the Second Generation," in *Immigration, Incorporation, and Transnationalism,* ed. Elliot R. Barkan (New Brunswick, N.J.: Transaction Publishers, 2007), 143–154.

55. Gary Gerstle and John Mollenkopf, "The Political Incorporation of Immigrants, Then and Now," in *E Pluribus Unum? Contemporary and Historical Perspectives on Immigrant Political Incorporation,* ed. Gary Gerstle and John Mollenkopf (New York: Russell Sage Foundation, 2001), 5. See also Michael Denning, *The*

*Cultural Front: The Laboring of American Culture in the Twentieth Century* (London: Verso, 1996), 448.

56. Lizabeth Cohen, *Making a New Deal: Industrial Workers in Chicago, 1919–1939* (Cambridge: Cambridge Univ. Press, 1990); and Roediger, *Working Toward Whiteness*. See also Mike Davis, *Prisoners of the American Dream: Politics and Economy in the History of the Working Class* (London: Verso, 1986).

57. Lary May, *The Big Tomorrow: Hollywood and the Politics of the American Way* (Chicago: Univ. of Chicago Press, 2000), 262.

58. Philip Gleason, "Americans All: World War II and the Shaping of American Identity," *Review of Politics* 43 (Oct. 1981): 511.

59. See the introduction to Higham, *Send These to Me*; Rudolph Vecoli, "From *The Uprooted* to *The Transplanted*: The Writing of American Immigration History, 1951–1989," in *From "Melting Pot" to Multiculturalism,* ed. Valeria Gennaro Lerda (Rome: Bulzoni Editore, 1990), 25–53; Kathleen Neils Conzen, David A. Gerber, Ewa Morawska, George E. Pozetta, and Rudolph J. Vecoli, "The Invention of Ethnicity: A Perspective from the U.S.A.," *Journal of American Ethnic History* 12 (Fall 1992): 3–42; Russell A. Kazal, "Revisiting Assimilation: The Rise, Fall, and Reappraisal of a Concept in American Ethnic History," *American Historical Review* 100 (Apr. 1995): 437–471; Arthur M. Schlesinger Jr., *The Disuniting of America: Reflections on a Multicultural Society* (Knoxville, Tenn.: Whittle Direct Books, 1991); Mann, *One and the Many.*

60. Elliot R. Barkan, "Immigration, Incorporation, Assimilation, and the Limits of Transnationalism," in *Immigration, Incorporation, and Transnationalism,* ed. Elliot R. Barkan (New Brunswick, N.J.: Transaction Publishers, 2007), 1–23; and Elliot R. Barkan, *And Still They Come: Immigrants and American Society, 1920 to the 1990s* (Wheeling, Ill.: Harlan Davidson, 1996), 55–109.

61. Roediger, *Wages of Whiteness*; Roediger, *Working Toward Whiteness*; Ignatiev, *How the Irish Became White*; Matthew Frye Jacobson, *Whiteness of a Different Color: European Immigrants and the Alchemy of Race* (Cambridge: Harvard Univ. Press, 1998), 91–135; Matthew Pratt Guterl, *The Color of Race in America, 1900–1940* (Cambridge: Harvard Univ. Press, 2001); David A. Gerber, "Caucasians Are Made and Not Born: How European Immigrants Became White People," *Reviews in American History* 27 (Sept. 1999): 437–443; Thomas A. Guglielmo and Earl Lewis, "Changing Racial Meanings: Race and Ethnicity in the United States, 1930–1964," in *Race and Ethnicity in America: A Concise History,* ed. Ronald H. Bayor (New York: Columbia Univ. Press, 2003), 167–192; and Jennifer L. Hochschild, *Facing Up to the American Dream: Race Class and the Soul of the Nation* (Princeton, N.J. : Princeton Univ. Press, 1995).

62. Richard M. Dalfiume, *Desegregation of the United States Armed Forces* (Columbia: Univ. of Missouri Press, 1969); Neil A. Wynn, *The Afro-American and the Second World War* (New York: Holmes and Meier, 1975); Morris J. MacGregor Jr., *Integration of the Armed Forces, 1940–1965* (Washington, D.C.: Center of

Military History United States Army, 1981); Nicholas Lemann, *The Promised Land: The Great Black Migration and How It Changed America* (New York: Vintage Books, 1991); and Merl E. Reed, *Seedtime for the Modern Civil Rights Movement: The President's Committee on Fair Employment Practice, 1941–1946* (Baton Rouge: Louisiana State Univ. Press, 1991).

63. Robin M. Williams Jr., *American Society: A Sociological Interpretation* (New York: Alfred A. Knopf, 1951), 527.

64. John Morton Blum, *V Was for Victory: Politics and American Culture During World War II* (New York: Harcourt Brace Jovanovich, 1976), 147–155, 172–175.

65. George E. Pozzetta, "From Rustbelt to Sunbelt: Patterns of Ethnic Migration and Integration in America, 1940–1989," in *From "Melting Pot" to Multiculturalism,* ed. Valeria Gennaro Lerda (Rome: Bulzoni Editore, 1990), 263–279; and George E. Pozzetta, "'My Children Are My Jewels': Italian-American Generations during World War II," in *The Home-Front War: World War II and American Society,* ed. Kenneth Paul O'Brien and Lynn Hudson Parsons (Westport, Conn: Greenwood Press, 1995). See also Gary R. Mormino, "Little Italy Goes to War: Italian Americans and World War II," in *Italy and America, 1943–44: Italian, American and Italian American Experiences of the Liberation of the Italian Mezzogiorno* (Naples, Italy: La Citta Del Sole, 1997).

66. Gerstle, *American Crucible,* 220–237. See also Thomas Guglielmo, *White on Arrival,* 172–176.

67. Deborah Dash Moore, *GI Jews: How World War II Changed a Generation* (Cambridge: Belknap Press of Harvard Univ. Press, 2004). See also Goldstein, *Price of Whiteness,* 189–208.

68. For an introduction into the debates over these terms, see the various discussions in *HEAEG.*

69. The same rules apply to other, smaller Latino groups.

70. *HSUS,* pt. 1, 116.

71. Asian Americans and the World War II military, including the segregated Japanese Americans and the integrated Chinese, Korean, and Filipino Americans, is a fascinating topic and will be touched on briefly, but it is outside the main thrust of the book. For more detail on those groups, see K. Scott Wong, *Americans First: Chinese Americans and the Second World War* (Cambridge: Harvard Univ. Press, 2005); Bill Yenne, *Rising Sons: The Japanese American GIs Who Fought for the United States in World War II* (New York: Thomas Dunne, 2007); and Robert Asahina, *Just Americans: How Japanese Americans Won a War at Home and Abroad* (New York: Gotham, 2006). Likewise, American Indians in the World War II military are generally outside the purview of this study and are the subject of an excellent book by Alison R. Bernstein, *American Indians in World War II* (Norman: Univ. of Oklahoma Press, 1991).

72. Even specialized units like the 10th Mountain Division had their own diversity, as many of its men were European skiers who immigrated from Norway, Switzerland, Austria, and elsewhere. Furthermore, the Tenth eventually filled about half of its ranks with transfers from infantry divisions. Peter Shelton, *Climb to Conquer: The Untold Story of World War II's 10th Mountain Division Ski Troops* (New York: Scribner, 2003), 25, 31–34, 67–68.

73. Daniel Hoffmann, *Zone of the Interior* (Baton Rouge: Louisiana State Univ. Press, 2000), x.

74. Michael D. Gambone, *The Greatest Generation Comes Home: The Veteran in American Society* (College Station: Texas A&M Univ. Press, 2005); Robert Francis Saxe, *Settling Down: World War II Veterans' Challenge to the Postwar Consensus* (New York: Palgrave Macmillan, 2007); Mark D. Van Ells, *To Hear Only Thunder Again: America's World War II Veterans Come Home* (Lanham, Md.: Lexington Books, 2001); Jennifer E. Brooks, *Defining the Peace: World War II Veterans, Race, and the Remaking of Southern Political Tradition* (Chapel Hill: Univ. of North Carolina Press, 2004); Keith W. Olson, *The G.I. Bill, the Veterans, and the Colleges* (Lexington: Univ. Press of Kentucky, 1974); Davis R. B. Ross, *Preparing for Ulysses: Politics and Veterans during World War II* (New York: Columbia Univ. Press, 1969); Michael J. Bennett, *When Dreams Came True: The G.I. Bill and the Making of Modern America* (Washington, D.C.: Brassey's, 1996); Suzanne Mettler, *Soldiers to Citizens: The G.I. Bill and the Making of the Greatest Generation* (New York: Oxford Univ. Press, 2005); Kathleen J. Frydl, "The G.I. Bill" (Ph.D. diss., Univ. of Chicago, 2000); and David H. Onkst, "'First a Negro . . . Incidentally a Veteran': Black World War Two Veterans and the G.I. Bill of Rights in the Deep South, 1944–1948," *Journal of Social History* 31 (Spring 1998): 517–543.

75. Mary Dudziak, *Cold War Civil Rights: Race and the Image of American Democracy* (Princeton, N.J.: Princeton Univ. Press, 2000), 15; and John Fousek, *To Lead the Free World: American Nationalism and the Cultural Roots of the Cold War* (Chapel Hill: Univ. of North Carolina Press, 2000), 7.

76. Lizabeth Cohen, *A Consumer's Republic: The Politics of Mass Consumption in Postwar America* (New York: Knopf, 2003); William H. Whyte, *The Organization Man* (New York: Simon and Schuster, 1956); Richard H. Pells, *The Liberal Mind in a Conservative Age* (New York: Harper and Row, 1985); and George Lipsitz, *Rainbow at Midnight: Labor and Culture in the 1940s* (Urbana: Univ. of Illinois Press, 1994), chap. 11.

# 1. The America They Left Behind

1. Racism against African Americans was a given; it was other prejudices that the 1928 election exposed. See Allan J. Lichtman, *Prejudice and the Old Politics: The Presidential Election of 1928* (Chapel Hill: Univ. of North Carolina Press, 1979), 147–159.

2. Charles C. Marshall, "An Open Letter to the Honorable Alfred E. Smith," *Atlantic Monthly* 139 (Apr. 1927): 540–549.

3. Alfred E. Smith, "Catholic and Patriot: Governor Smith Replies," *Atlantic Monthly* 139 (May 1927): 721–729.

4. Ibid., 721.

5. "Above All Else America! A Plea for Religious Tolerance and American Fair Play in Considering the Candidacy of Gov. Alfred E. Smith," Political File Series, 1928 Presidential Election—Campaign Literature, Box 8, Alben Barkley Papers, KL.

6. Lichtman, *Prejudice and the Old Politics,* 62–64; and Joan Hoff Wilson, *Herbert Hoover: Forgotten Progressive* (Boston: Little, Brown, 1975), 122–133. For a more sympathetic view to Hoover on this issue, see his own memoirs, Herbert Hoover, *The Memoirs of Herbert Hoover: The Cabinet and the Presidency* (New York: Macmillan, 1952), 207–209; and Edmund A. Moore, *A Catholic Runs for President: The Campaign of 1928* (New York: Ronald Press, 1956), 145–152. For examples of Republicans playing on the religious issue, see Michael Williams, *The Shadow of the Pope* (New York: Whittlesey House, 1932), 199; Lichtman, *Prejudice and the Old Politics,* 63–67; and Robert A. Slayton, *Empire Statesman: The Rise and Redemption of Al Smith* (New York: Free Press, 2001), 306–308.

7. Williams, *Shadow of the Pope,* 176–182.

8. McKeage to Barkley, July 19, 1928, Political File Series, 1928 Presidential Election—Correspondence July–August, Box 8, Alben Barkley Papers, KL.

9. Smith to Barkley, July 5, 1928, Political File Series, 1928 Presidential Election—Correspondence July–August, Box 8, Alben Barkley Papers, KL.

10. Williams, *Shadow of the Pope,* 226–277.

11. Roy V. Peel and Thomas C. Donnelly, *The 1928 Campaign: An Analysis* (New York: R. R. Smith, 1931), 99–100.

12. David Burner, *The Politics of Provincialism: The Democratic Party in Transition, 1918–1932* (New York: Alfred A. Knopf, 1968), 201–204.

13. Williams, *Shadow of the Pope,* 199.

14. Fountain Avenue M.E. Church, South, "Weekly Bulletin," Sept. 16, 1928, Political File Series, 1928 Presidential Election—Campaign Literature, Box 8, Alben Barkley Papers, KL.

15. Williams, *Shadow of the Pope,* 198. On the various editorials, see 194–205.

16. Quoted in Slayton, *Empire Statesman,* 311.

17. Quoted in Burner, *Politics of Provincialism,* 204.

18. Slayton, *Empire Statesman,* 309–310.

19. "Facts Gathered by Knights of Luther from Washington Bureau of Statistics," Political File Series, 1928 Presidential Election—Campaign Literature, Box 8, Alben Barkley Papers, KL.

20. Williams, *Shadow of the Pope,* 174, 215.

21. "30 Reasons Why Protestants Should Vote for Alcohol Smith," Political File Series, 1928 Presidential Election—Campaign Literature, Box 8, Alben Barkley Papers, KL.

22. "Who Was the Unknown Soldier?" Political File Series, 1928 Presidential Election—Campaign Literature, Box 8, Alben Barkley Papers, KL.

23. Even his own account of the campaigning noted the lukewarm reception. Alfred E. Smith, *Up to Now: An Autobiography* (New York: Viking, 1929), 394–402.

24. Frances Perkins, *The Roosevelt I Knew* (New York: Viking, 1946), 46.

25. Ernie Pyle, "Maria Pyle," in *Ernie's America: The Best of Ernie Pyle's 1930s Travel Dispatches,* ed. David Nichols (New York: Random House, 1989), 14.

26. Handlin, *Al Smith,* 117–121.

27. Smith, *Up to Now,* 413.

28. Burner, *Politics of Provincialism,* 199.

29. Ever since the election there has been an active debate about the role religion played in the outcome. For various views, see Peel and Donnelly, *1928 Campaign;* Williams, *Shadow of the Pope;* Moore, *Catholic Runs;* Ruth C. Silva, *Rum, Religion, and Votes: 1928 Re-examined* (University Park: Pennsylvania State Univ. Press, 1962); Burner, *Politics of Provincialism;* Paul A. Carter, *Politics, Religion, and Rockets: Essays in Twentieth-Century American History* (Tucson: Univ. of Arizona Press, 1991), 25–61; Lichtman, *Prejudice and the Old Politics;* Slayton, *Empire Statesman,* 322–324; and Anderson, *After Suffrage,* 71–75.

30. Perlmutter, *Divided We Fall,* 222; Allen, *Only Yesterday,* 62; and Harding, *Our Common Country,* 111.

31. Higham, *Send These to Me,* 25. Immigrants and their children also became engaged in politics through unions and other civic institutions, especially the Roman Catholic Church. Evelyn Savidge Sterne, "Beyond the Boss: Immigration and American Political Culture from 1880 to 1940," in *E Pluribus Unum? Contemporary and Historical Perspectives on Immigrant Political Incorporation,* ed. Gary Gerstle and John Mollenkopf (New York: Russell Sage Foundation, 2001), 33–66.

32. John D. Buenker, *Urban Liberalism and Progressive Reform* (New York: Charles Scribner's Sons, 1973).

33. Arthur S. Link, *Woodrow Wilson and the Progressive Era, 1910–1917* (New York: Harper and Brothers, 1954), 60–61, 223–230, 234–251; Burner, *Politics of Provincialism,* 28–32.

34. Burner, *Politics of Provincialism;* Douglas Craig, *After Wilson: The Struggle for the Democratic Party, 1920–1934* (Chapel Hill: Univ. of North Carolina Press, 1992). See also Richard K. Vedder and Lowell E. Gallaway, *Out of Work: Unemployment and Government in Twentieth-Century America,* updated ed. (New York: New York Univ. Press, 1993, 1997), 67–71; Robert K. Murray, *The Politics of Normalcy:*

*Governmental Theory and Practice in the Harding-Coolidge Era* (New York: Norton, 1973); Donald R. McCoy, *Calvin Coolidge: The Quiet President* (New York: Macmillan, 1967); Robert Sobel, *Coolidge: An American Enigma* (Washington, D.C.: Regnery, 1998); and Wilson, *Herbert Hoover,* 79–133.

35. Sterne, "Beyond the Boss," 57–60.

36. Handlin, *Al Smith,* 142–143.

37. See Frank Freidel, "The Election of 1932," in *The Coming to Power: Critical Presidential Elections in American History,* ed. Arthur M. Schlesinger Jr. (New York: Chelsea Hill, 1971), 322–354. See also the party papers, Box 404, Religion, Library and Research Branch, 1928–1933, Democratic Party National Committee Papers, FDR.

38. See, for example, Roediger, *Working Toward Whiteness,* 199–207; George Q. Flynn, *American Catholics and the Roosevelt Presidency, 1932–1936* (Lexington: Univ. of Kentucky Press, 1968); Higham, *Send These to Me,* 169–170; and the correspondence in the Roosevelt Library under President's Personal File 2525, Religious Freedom, FDR. See also Joe Marcus interview, in Studs Terkel, *Hard Times: An Oral History of the Great Depression* (New York: Pantheon Books, 1970) (hereafter cited as Terkel, *Hard Times*), 266.

39. See James T. Patterson, *Congressional Conservatism and the New Deal: The Growth of the Conservative Coalition in Congress, 1933–1939* (Lexington: Univ. of Kentucky Press, 1967); James MacGregor Burns, *Roosevelt: The Lion and the Fox* (New York: Harcourt, 1956); and Hamby, *For the Survival,* 345–346.

40. See William E. Leuchtenburg, *Franklin D. Roosevelt and the New Deal* (New York: Harper and Row, 1963), 96–106, 179–183; and Alan Brinkley, *Voices of Protest: Huey Long, Father Coughlin, and the Great Depression* (New York: Alfred A. Knopf, 1982).

41. Rexford G. Tugwell, *The Democratic Roosevelt* (Garden City, N.Y.: Doubleday, 1957), 342–343.

42. Moses to Franklin Roosevelt, Mar. 24, 1933, President's Official File 75, Box 1, Prohibition (in favor of) 1933–37 J–R, Franklin D. Roosevelt Papers, FDR; President's Official File 75, Box 1, Franklin D. Roosevelt Papers, FDR. Box 2 in the same location includes the fewer letters in support of repeal.

43. Harry De Vore to Eleanor Roosevelt, Dec. 17, 1932, Prohibition Correspondence, Anti ER Jan–Feb 1933, Box 12, Eleanor Roosevelt Papers, FDR.

44. Graves was referring to Eleanor Roosevelt endorsing Ponds Extract Company before becoming first lady. Perhaps the best part of the correspondence was that Roosevelt responded, apologizing for offending the Ohioan but informing him that she "did not advocate girls drinking all the 'synthetic gin they can carry.'" W. E. Graves to Eleanor Roosevelt, Jan. 14, 1933, and Eleanor Roosevelt to W. E. Graves, Jan. 25, 1933, Prohibition Correspondence, Pro ER Jan–Feb 1933, Box 12, Eleanor Roosevelt Papers, FDR.

45. See *Public Papers and Addresses of Franklin D. Roosevelt,* vol. 1 (New York: Random House, 1938), 684–692, 810, 839–840.

46. Kyvig, *Repealing National Prohibition;* and Craig, *After Wilson.* See also Stephen Early to R. J. Turner, Dec. 14, 1936, President's Personal File 244, Prohibition Matters, Franklin D. Roosevelt Papers, FDR. See also Early to Fred D. Fant, Mar. 22, 1938, in the same file.

47. Hamby, *For the Survival,* 278–280; "President Roosevelt's Address to Relief Chiefs," *NYT,* June 18, 1935, 2.

48. Divine, *American Immigration Policy,* 88–89.

49. Harold L. Ickes, *The Secret Diary of Harold Ickes: The Inside Struggle, 1936–1939* (New York: Simon and Schuster, 1954), 342–343.

50. Divine, *American Immigration Policy,* 92–104.

51. John M. Allswang, *The New Deal and American Politics* (New York: John Wiley and Sons, 1978), 25. See also Holt Correspondence, May, 1939, President's Personal File 2525, Religious Freedom, FDR.

52. William E. Leuchtenburg, "The Election of 1936," in *The FDR Years: On Roosevelt and His Legacy,* by William E. Leuchtenburg (New York: Columbia Univ. Press, 1995); Kristi Anderson, *The Creation of a Democratic Majority, 1928–1936* (Chicago: Univ. of Chicago Press, 1979); Flynn, *American Catholics;* Walter Dean Burnham, *Critical Elections and the Mainsprings of American Politics* (New York: W. W. Norton, 1970), 57–60; Samuel Lubell, *The Future of American Politics* (New York: Harper and Brothers, 1951), 31–50; James Boylan, *The New Deal Coalition and the Election of 1946* (New York: Garland, 1981), 1–18.

53. John W. Jeffries, *Testing the Roosevelt Coalition: Connecticut Society and Politics in the Era of World War II* (Knoxville: Univ. of Tennessee Press, 1979), 44–48; Allswang, *New Deal,* 1–6; "Hannegan and Brownell Pledge to Keep Campaign Free of Bias," *NYT,* Sept. 14, 1944, 17.

54. Roosevelt Correspondence with the Finnish-American Religious Union, Aug. 1940, and the American Slav Congress, Apr. 1942, President's Personal File 2525, Religious Freedom, FDR.

55. Marcus L. Hansen, "The Third Generation in America," reprinted in *Commentary* 14 (Nov. 1952): 492–500. Roediger, *Working Toward Whiteness,* 133–156; and Benjamin L. Alpers, "This Is the Army: Imagining a Democratic Military in World War II," *Journal of American History* 85 (June 1998): 143–145.

56. Philip Gleason, "American Identity and Americanization," in *HEAEG,* 47.

57. Cohen, *Making a New Deal;* Roediger, *Working Toward Whiteness,* 207–224; and David E. Kyvig, *Daily Life in the United States, 1920–1939: Decades of Promise and Pain* (Westport, Conn.: Greenwood Press, 2002), 159–176.

58. Williams, *Shadow of the Pope,* 293–298.

59. Which later became the National Conference of Christians and Jews.

60. Paul J. Weber and W. Landis Jones, *U.S. Religious Interest Groups: Institutional Profiles* (Westport, Conn.: Greenwood Press, 1994), 18–20.

61. Quotation from "Enriching America," *NYT,* Feb. 5, 1932, 20. See also "Letters to the Editor," *NYT,* Sept. 12, 1934, 22. See also David Tyack, "School for Citizens: The Politics of Civic Education from 1790 to 1990," in *E Pluribus Unum? Contemporary and Historical Perspectives on Immigrant Political Incorporation,* ed. Gary Gerstle and John Mollenkopf (New York: Russell Sage Foundation, 2001), 352–357.

62. David M. Kennedy, *Freedom from Fear: The American People in Depression and War, 1929–1945* (New York: Oxford Univ. Press, 1999), 761.

63. As compared to the approximately 32 percent first and second generation in 1930. *HSUS,* pt. 1, 116–117.

64. Morawska, "Immigrants, Transnationalism, and Ethnicization," 188–189.

65. A headline from a 1932 Chicago Slovak paper read, "Patronize the Stores of Your Countrymen." Tracey Deutsch, "Untangling Alliances: Social Tensions Surrounding Independent Grocery Stores and the Rise of Mass Retailing," in *Food Nations: Selling Taste in Consumer Societies,* ed. Warren Belasco and Philip Scranton (New York: Routledge, 2002), 160–161, 180 fn. 30. See also Morawska, "Immigrants, Transnationalism, and Ethnicization," 189. See also Mark Villchur, "The Immigrant Press," in *Our Racial and National Minorities: Their History, Contributions, and Present Problems,* ed. Francis J. Brown and Joseph Slabey Roucek (New York: Prentice Hall, 1937), 584–589.

66. Chicago Public Library Omnibus Project, *The Chicago Foreign Language Press Survey: A General Description of its Contents* (Chicago: Works Project Administration, 1942), 1–5, 17–20; and East Side Italiano Club Memo, Nov. 2, 1935, Box 48, Ethnic Studies, Ethnic Groups—Materials, Caroline Ware Papers, FDR.

67. Gary R. Mormino and George E. Pozzetta, "Ethnics at War: Italian Americans in California during World War II," in *The Way We Really Were: The Golden State in the Second Great War,* ed. Roger W. Lotchin (Urbana: Univ. of Illinois Press, 2000), 144–145; and John Patrick Diggins, *Mussolini and Fascism: The View from America* (Princeton, N.J.: Princeton Univ. Press, 1972), pt. 2.

68. George Q. Flynn, *Roosevelt and Romanism: Catholics and American Diplomacy, 1937–1945* (Westport, Conn.: Greenwood Press, 1976); Frederick Lewis Allen, *Since Yesterday: The Nineteen-Thirties in America* (New York: Harper and Brothers, 1939), 302; Hamby, *For the Survival,* 394. Quotation in Ickes, *Inside Struggle,* 390. See also Blanche Weisen Cook, *Eleanor Roosevelt,* vol. 2, *1933–1938* (New York: Viking, 1999), 453–455, 504–5, 521–522; Kenneth J. Heineman, *A Catholic New Deal: Religion and Reform in Depression Pittsburgh* (University Park: Pennsylvania State Univ. Press, 1999), xiv; Cohen, *Making a New Deal;* and David J. O'Brien, *American Catholics and Social Reform: The New Deal Years* (New York: Oxford Univ. Press, 1968).

69. Roediger, *Working Toward Whiteness*, 173.

70. Quoted in "Population Shifts Held New Problem," *NYT*, July 23, 1933, N1. For the statistics, see *HSUS*, pt. 1, 116–117. See also Thomas Jackson Woofter, *Races and Ethnic Groups in America* (New York: McGraw Hill, 1933); the general report "President's Research Committee on Social Trends," in *Recent Social Trends in the United States* (New York: McGraw Hill, 1933); and Francis J. Brown, "Minority Communities," in *Our Racial and National Minorities: Their History, Contributions, and Present Problems*, ed. Francis J. Brown and Joseph Slabey Roucek (New York: Prentice Hall, 1937), 567–568.

71. Louis Adamic, *From Many Lands* (New York: Harper and Brothers, 1940), 295–297.

72. Willard L. Sperry, *Religion in America* (Boston: Beacon Press, 1946, 1963), 227. See also Roediger, *Working Toward Whiteness*, 167; and Ronald H. Bayor, *Neighbors in Conflict: The Irish, Germans, Jews, and Italians of New York City, 1929–1941* (Baltimore: Johns Hopkins Univ. Press, 1978).

73. Michael J. Patrone Interview, Oral History 1402, YSOH, 9. See also U.S. House, Select Committee Investigating National Defense Migration, *Hartford Hearings*, 77th Cong., 1st sess., 1941 (hereafter cited as *Hartford Hearings*), United States Citizens of German and Italian Descent, pt. 13, 5254–5255; and Raul Morin, *Among the Valiant: Mexican Americans in WW II and Korea* (Alhambra, Calif.: Borden, 1963), 29–33.

74. Deborah Dash Moore, *At Home in America: Second Generation New York Jews* (New York: Columbia Univ. Press, 1981), 30–31.

75. Roediger, *Working Toward Whiteness*, 224–234; and James Paul Allen and Eugene James Turner, *We the People: An Atlas of America's Ethnic Diversity* (New York: Macmillan, 1988).

76. Perlmann and Waldinger, "Second Generation Decline?" 893–922. See also Leonard Covello, "Language as a Factor in Social Adjustment"; and Clara A. Hardin and Herbert A. Miller, "The Second Generation," in *Our Racial and National Minorities: Their History, Contributions, and Present Problems*, ed. Francis J. Brown and Joseph Slabey Roucek (New York: Prentice Hall, 1937), 681–696. On Italian immigrants specifically, see Leonard Covello, *The Social Background of the Italo-American School Child*, ed. Francesco Cordasco (Leiden, Netherlands: E. J. Brill, 1967), 360–371, 398–402.

77. Joel Perlmann, *The Romance of Assimilation? Studying the Demographic Outcomes of Ethnic Intermarriages in American History*, Working Paper no. 230 (New York: Jerome Levy Economics Institute of Bard College, June 2001); and Roediger, *Wages of Whiteness*, 196–198.

78. Samuel C. Krincheloe, *Research Memorandum on Religion in the Depression* (New York: Social Science Research Council, 1937), 53.

79. Adamic, *From Many Lands*, 295–297.

80. A counter to class identity is Hamby, *For the Survival,* 212.

81. MacLean, *Behind the Mask,* 186.

82. E. George Payne, introduction to *Our Racial and National Minorities: Their History, Contributions, and Present Problems,* ed. Francis J. Brown and Joseph Slabey Roucek (New York: Prentice Hall, 1937), xxi.

83. Francis J. Brown and Joseph Slabey Roucek, "The Meaning of Minorities," in *Our Racial and National Minorities: Their History, Contributions, and Present Problems,* ed. Francis J. Brown and Joseph Slabey Roucek (New York: Prentice Hall, 1937), 17.

84. Frederic M. Thrasher, "Are Our Criminals Foreigners?" in *Our Racial and National Minorities: Their History, Contributions, and Present Problems,* ed. Francis J. Brown and Joseph Slabey Roucek (New York: Prentice Hall, 1937), 697.

85. Newton Diehl Baker, Carlton Joseph Huntley Hayes, and Roger Williams Straus, eds., *The American Way: A Study of Human Relations Among Protestants, Catholics, and Jews* (Chicago: Wilett, Clark, 1936), 34–38; and National Conference of Jews and Christians, *Public Opinion in a Democracy* (New York: National Conference of Jews and Christians, 1937), 4. See also Krincheloe, *Research Memorandum,* 99; Gleason, "Americans All," 492; and Gordon M. Ridenour and Francis J. Brown, "Religion and Minority Peoples," in *Our Racial and National Minorities: Their History, Contributions, and Present Problems,* ed. Francis J. Brown and Joseph Slabey Roucek (New York: Prentice Hall, 1937), 609.

86. Higham, *Send These to Me,* 169; "Says Bias Dictates Choice of Teachers," *NYT,* Aug. 16, 1931, 19.

87. Correspondence, Oct. 14, 1938, President's Personal File 2525, Religious Freedom, FDR

88. Donald S. Strong, *Organized Anti-Semitism in America: The Rise of Group Prejudice During the Decade 1930–1940* (Washington, D.C.: American Council on Public Affairs, 1941), 146, 175.

89. Scott M. Beekman, "Silver Shirts and Golden Scripts: The Life of William Dudley Pelley" (Ph.D. diss., Ohio Univ., 2003).

90. Strong, *Organized Anti-Semitism,* 70–75, quotation on 165.

91. Richard Polenberg, *One Nation Divisible: Class, Race, and Ethnicity in the United States since 1938* (New York: Viking, 1980), 40–41.

92. Strong, *Organized Anti-Semitism,* 172; Adamic, *From Many Lands,* 295; Allen, *Since Yesterday,* 329–330; and Brinkley, *Voices of Protest,* 269–273.

93. Adamic, *From Many Lands,* 347.

94. J. Morris Jones, *Americans All . . . Immigrants All: A Handbook for Listeners* (Washington, D.C.: United States Office of Education, n.d.), iii, 21–91.

95. Jones, *Americans All,* 4–5.

96. Robert Spiers Benjamin, ed., *I Am an American: By Famous Naturalized Americans* (Freeport, N.Y.: Books for Libraries Press, 1941, 1970), vii; and Monroe E. Deutsch, *Our Legacy of Religious Freedom* (New York: National Conference of Christians and Jews, 1941), 29.

97. Francis Biddle, *In Brief Authority* (Garden City, N.Y.: Doubleday, 1962), 118–119.

98. Raymond Fielding, *The March of Time, 1935–1951* (New York: Oxford Univ. Press, 1978), 266.

99. Historian Robert L. Fleegler argues that the outbreak of the war led to a change in these programs from an emphasis on minority contributions to an emphasis on fostering tolerance. See Fleegler, "'Forget All Differences Until the Forces of Freedom Are Triumphant': The World War II–Era Quest for Ethnic and Religious Tolerance," *Journal of American Ethnic History* 27 (Winter 2008): 59–84.

100. Quoted in Kennedy, *Freedom from Fear*, 760.

101. Gleason, "Americans All," 499–511.

102. J. P. Shalloo and Donald Young, foreword to *Minority Peoples in a Nation at War*, ed. J. P. Shalloo and Donald Young, American Academy of Political and Social Science *Annals* 223 (Sept. 1942): vi.

103. Alfred McClung Lee, "Subversive Individuals of Minority Status," in *Minority Peoples in a Nation at War*, ed. J. P. Shalloo and Donald Young, American Academy of Political and Social Science *Annals* 223 (Sept. 1942): 162–172; and Clyde R. Miller, "Foreign Efforts to Increase Disunity," in *Minority Peoples in a Nation at War*, ed. J. P. Shalloo and Donald Young, American Academy of Political and Social Science *Annals* 223 (Sept. 1942) 173–181.

104. Everett V. Stonequist, "The Restricted Citizen," in *Minority Peoples in a Nation at War*, ed. J. P. Shalloo and Donald Young, American Academy of Political and Social Science *Annals* 223 (Sept. 1942): 155; see especially the following in the same *Annals*: Donald R. Perry, "Aliens in the United States," 1–16; H. M. Kallen, "National Solidarity and the Jewish Minority," 17–28; Carl Wittke, "German Immigrants and Their Children," 85–91; George L. Warren, "The Refugee and the War," 92–99; Edward Corsi, "Italian Immigrants and Their Children," 100–106; Shotaro Frank Miyamoto, "Immigrants and Citizens of Japanese Origin," 107–113; Maurice R. Davie, "Immigrants from Axis-Conquered Countries," 114–122; W. Rex Crawford, "The Latin-American in Wartime United States," 123–131; and Marian Schibsby, "Private Agencies Aiding the Foreign-Born," 182–189. See also Mead, *Keep Your Powder Dry*; and David F. Bowers, ed., *Foreign Influences in American Life* (Princeton, N.J.: Princeton Univ. Press, 1944).

105. *Knute Rockne, All American*, directed by Lloyd Bacon, Warner Brothers, 1940.

106. Richard Slotkin, "Unit Pride: Ethnic Platoons and the Myths of American Nationality," *American Literary History* 13 (Autumn 2001): 469–498; May, *Big*

*Tomorrow,* 144–145; Jeanne Basinger, *The World War II Combat Film: Anatomy of a Genre* (New York: Columbia Univ. Press, 1986), 61–66; Gerstle, *American Crucible,* 204–206.

107. Hasia R. Diner, *Hungering for America: Italian, Irish, and Jewish Foodways in the Age of Migration* (Cambridge: Harvard Univ. Press, 2001).

108. Leon Rappoport, *How We Eat: Appetite, Culture, and the Psychology of Food* (Toronto: ECW Press, 2003), 72. For examples, see Charles C. Alexander, *Our Game: An American Baseball History* (New York: MJF Books, 1991), 177; and Charles C. Alexander, *Breaking the Slump: Baseball in the 1930s* (New York: Columbia Univ. Press, 2002), 193. The list could go on. In 1944, psychologist A. A. Roback had published his *Dictionary of International Slurs,* a fairly exhaustive list of common and less common racial and ethnic slurs and proverbs in English and other languages. Of course many of the most popular slurs had nothing to do with food: "heeb," "kike," "yid," and "sheeny" for Jews; "bohunk" for Czechs or other Slavs; "dago," "eyetie," "wop," and "guinea" for Italians; "spick" and "greaser" for Mexicans or other Latin Americans; "mick" for the Irish; and "polack" for Poles. But a whole series of terms did reflect cuisine: "kraut" for Germans; "limey" for the English, "frogeater" for the French; "butter-box" or "butter-mouth" for the Dutch (more common in England); "goulash" for Hungarians; "macaroni" for Italians; and "chili-eater" for Mexicans. A. A. Roback, *A Dictionary of International Slurs* (Cambridge, Mass: Sci-Art Publishers, 1944). See also Roediger, *Working Toward Whiteness,* 37–45.

109. Common Council for American Unity, *What's Cooking in Your Neighbor's Pot* (New York: Common Council for American Unity, 1944), 1.

110. Benjamin Fine, "Tolerance Study Urged for Nation," *NYT,* Mar. 16, 1944, 21.

111. Arnold Herrick and Herbert Askwith, eds., *This Way to Unity: For the Promotion of Good Will and Teamwork among Racial, Religious, and National Groups* (New York: Oxford Book, 1945). The quotation is from Arnold Herrick, "Filtrable Virus," 177–178.

112. Frank Sinatra, "People are Human Beings," in Herrick and Askwith, *This Way to Unity,* 179–182.

113. *The House I Live In,* directed by Mervyn Leroy, RKO, 1945; and Roediger, *Working Toward Whiteness,* 235–244. See also Leonard Mustazza, "Frank Sinatra and Civil Rights," in Stanislao G. Pugliese, ed., *Frank Sinatra: History, Identity, and American Culture* (New York: Palgrave Macmillan, 2004), 36–37.

114. Wallace Stegner, *One Nation* (Boston: Houghton Mifflin, 1945), v, 290–299, 308–317; Willard Sperry, John LaFarge, John T. McNeill, Louis Finkelstein, and Archibald MacLeish, *Religion and Our Divided Denominations* (Cambridge: Harvard Univ. Press, 1945); and Willard Sperry, ed., *Religion and Our Racial Tensions* (Cambridge: Harvard Univ. Press, 1945).

115. Fielding, *March of Time,* 280.

116. Francis J. Brown and Joseph Slabey Roucek, eds., *One America: The History, Contributions, and Present Problems of Our Racial and National Minorities* (New York: Prentice Hall, 1945), v–vii; emphasis added.

117. See also W. Lloyd Warner and Leo Srole, *The Social Systems of American Ethnic Groups* (New Haven, Conn: Yale Univ. Press, 1945), 286–293; and Gardner Murphy, ed., *Human Nature and Enduring Peace* (Boston: Houghton Mifflin, 1945), 43–44, 254–259, 348–356.

118. Arnold M. Rose, *Studies in Reduction of Prejudice: A Memorandum Summarizing Research on Modification of Attitudes* (Chicago: American Council on Race Relations, 1948), 1–24.

119. Alexander added an important qualification: "For both servicemen and civilians, however, the vicissitudes of war enlarged contacts and undoubtedly helped improve relations between the nation's Protestants, Catholics, and Jews." Charles C. Alexander, *Nationalism in American Thought, 1930–1945* (Chicago: Rand McNally, 1969), 223.

120. Roger Daniels, *Prisoners Without Trial: Japanese Americans in World War II* (New York: Hill and Wang, 1993); and Peter Irons, *Justice at War* (New York: Oxford Univ. Press, 1983).

121. Rose D. Schlerini, "When Italian Americans Were 'Enemy Aliens,'" in *Una Storia Segreta: The Secret History of the Italian American Evacuation and Internment during World War II*, ed. Lawrence DiStasi (Berkeley, Calif.: Heydey Books, 2001), 16.

122. See Schlerini, "When Italian Americans"; Stephen Fox, "The Relocation of Italian Americans in California during World War II," in *Una Storia Segreta: The Secret History of the Italian American Evacuation and Internment during World War II*, ed. Lawrence DiStasi (Berkeley, Calif.: Heydey Books, 2001); and two other works by Stephen Fox: *America's Invisible Gulag: A Biography of German American Internment and Exclusion* (New York: Peter Lang, 2000) and *The Unknown Internment: An Oral History of the Relocation of Italian Americans during World War II* (Boston: Twayne, 1990).

123. Fair Employment Practice Committee (FEPC), *First Report, July 1943–December 1944* (Washington, D.C.: GPO, 1945), 37–38. See also Andrew Edmund Kerston, *Race, Jobs, and the War: The FEPC in the Midwest, 1941–46* (Urbana: Univ. of Illinois Press, 2000).

124. Reed, *Seedtime*, 251–266.

125. "Job Agency Aides Tell of Wide Bias," *NYT*, May 14, 1943, 21. Another almost 10 percent of the claims filed to the FEPC between from 1943 to 1944 focused on discrimination because of national origin or alien status. The majority came from Mexicans in the Southwest, but also some from Italians, Germans, Chinese, and Japanese Americans. FEPC, *First Report*, 37–38. For a closer look at the Hispanic experience with the FEPC, see Clete Daniel, *Chicano Workers and*

*the Politics of Fairness: The FEPC in the Southwest, 1941–1945* (Austin: Univ. of Texas Press, 1991).

126. U.S. House, Select Committee Investigating National Defense Migration, *San Diego Hearings,* 77th Cong., 1st sess., 1941, letter from the National Congress of the Spanish Speaking People of the U.S.A., pt. 12, 5010.

127. *Hartford Hearings,* testimony of Major Leonard J. Maloney, pt. 13, 5115. See also *Hartford Hearings,* testimony of Nicholas Tomassetti, pt. 13, 5297; and *Hartford Hearings,* Connecticut Industrial Activity and the Need for Works Projects Administration Employment, May 1941, pt. 13, 5456–5459.

128. U.S. House, Select Committee Investigating National Defense Migration, *Trenton Hearings,* 77th Cong., 1st sess., 1941 (hereafter cited as *Trenton Hearings*), testimony of Vincent Parsonnet, pt. 14, 5601. See also *Trenton Hearings,* testimony of H. J. Lepper, pt. 14, 5643.

129. "Bias Seen Barring Many from Jobs," *NYT,* May 17, 1941, 9.

130. *Hartford Hearings,* United States Citizens of German and Italian Descent, pt. 13, 5254–5255.

131. In case there was any doubt about how pervasive such stereotypes were during the early 1940s, the representative continued: "We do know they are temperamental. Nevertheless, some of the finest workers we had have been Italian, and in some places we would like to have more of them." *Trenton Hearings,* testimony of H. J. Lepper, pt. 14, 5643.

132. *Hartford Hearings,* testimony of Major Leonard J. Maloney, pt. 13, 5115.

133. "10 Holders of Big War Contracts Ordered to Cease Discrimination," *NYT,* Apr. 13, 1942, 1.

134. Robert Moses, "What's the Matter With New York?" *NYT,* Aug. 1, 1943, SM8.

135. Sperry, *Religion in America,* 235.

136. Higham, *Send These to Me,* 171.

137. William A. Lydgate, *What America Thinks* (New York: Thomas Y. Crowell, 1944), 60–62.

138. Lydgate, *What America Thinks,* 160.

139. Rose, *Studies in Reduction of Prejudice,* 59–61.

140. Tyack, "School for Citizens," 357; and Stuart J. Foster, "The Struggle for American Identity: Treatment of Ethnic Groups in United States History Textbooks," *History of Education* 28 (Sept. 1999): 260–262.

141. Alexander, *Breaking the Slump,* 5, 10, 117, 191–195; and John Kieran, "Sports of the Times," *NYT,* Dec. 2, 1936, 39. See also "Topics of the Times," *NYT,* Oct. 18, 1938, 24.

142. Phyllis Lorimer interview, in Terkel, *Hard Times,* 103.

143. John E. Bistrica Oral History, EC, 1.

144. Dean P. Joy, *Sixty Days in Combat* (New York: Presidio Press, 2004), xiii.

145. Joseph P. Barrett Oral History, EC, 3.

146. Robert Easton and Jane Easton, *Love and War: Pearl Harbor Through V-J Day* (Norman: Univ. of Oklahoma Press, 1991), 41–42.

147. Carl M. Becker and Robert G. Thobaben, *Common Warfare: Parallel Memoirs by Two World War II GIs in the Pacific* (Jefferson, N.C.: McFarland, 1992), 107.

148. Samuel Hynes, *The Growing Season: An American Boyhood Before the War* (New York: Viking, 2003), 7, 72–73, 124–126.

149. Ibid., 80–81, 114.

150. Quoted in Kurzman, *No Greater Glory,* 38.

151. Frank F. Mathias, *The GI Generation: A Memoir* (Lexington: Univ. Press of Kentucky, 2000).

152. Mario Puzo, *The Godfather Papers: And Other Confessions* (London: Heinemann, 1972), 13.

153. Robert Peters, *For You, Lili Marlene* (Madison: Univ. of Wisconsin Press, 1995), 29.

154. Becker and Thobaben, *Common Warfare,* 30.

155. "The Stab of Intolerance," *NYT,* July 10, 1941, 18.

156. Stegner, *One Nation,* 1–2, 318–319. The idea that Jews were sitting out the fight came up many times during the war. Note the Irish versus Jewish theme of one particular piece of wartime doggerel: "First man killed—Mike Murphy / First man to sink a Jap warship—Colin Kelly / First man to down five Jap planes— Eddie O'Hara / First man to get four new tires—Abie Cohen." Quoted in Henry L. Feingold, *A Time for Searching: Entering the Mainstream, 1920–1945* (Baltimore: Johns Hopkins Univ. Press, 1992), 257–258. See also "End to Prejudice Urged by Mayor," *NYT,* Sept. 26, 1943, 13. One scholar of the subject called the war years "high tide" for anti-Semitism in the United States. Leonard Dinnerstein, *Antisemitism in America* (New York: Oxford Univ. Press, 1994), 128–149.

157. George E. Sokolsky, "Holy Ground," in Herrick and Askwith, *This Way to Unity,* 83–85.

## 2. The Ethnic Army

1. Russell F. Weigley, *History of the United States Army* (New York: Macmillan, 1967), 167–168; and Edward M. Coffman, *The Old Army: A Portrait of the American Army in Peacetime, 1784–1898* (New York: Oxford Univ. Press, 1986), 137–141, 180–182.

2. William L. Burton, *Melting Pot Soldiers: The Union's Ethnic Regiments,* 2nd ed. (New York: Fordham Univ. Press, 1998); Ella Lonn, *Foreigners in the Union Army and Navy* (Baton Rouge: Louisiana State Univ. Press, 1951); Margaret S.

Creighton, *The Colors of Courage: Gettysburg's Forgotten History—Immigrants, Women, and African Americans in the Civil War's Defining Battle* (New York: Basic Books, 2005); and James M. McPherson, *Battle Cry of Freedom: The Civil War Era* (New York: Oxford Univ. Press, 1988), 606–607. See also Ella Lonn, *Foreigners in the Confederacy* (1940; reprint, Chapel Hill: Univ. of North Carolina Press, 2002); Richard J. Jensen, "'No Irish Need Apply': A Myth of Victimization," *Journal of Social History* 36 (Winter 2002): 405–429; and Christian Keller, *Chancellorsville and the Germans: Nativism, Ethnicity, and Civil War Memory* (New York: Fordham Univ. Press, 2007).

3. See, for example, *WDAR* (1890), 67; *WDAR* (1891), 80–81; *WDAR* (1892), 198; and *WDAR* (1893), 73–75.

4. Of the 9,585 accepted recruits in the 1893 report, most listed their occupations as laborers, soldiers, or farmers. *WDAR* (1893), 415.

5. Marvin E. Fletcher, "The Army and Minority Groups," in *The United States Army in Peacetime,* ed. Robin Higham and Carol Brandt (Manhattan, Kans.: Military Affairs/Aerospace Historian, 1975), 107–109; Robert M. Utley, *Frontier Regulars: The United States Army and the Indian, 1866–1891* (Bloomington: Indiana Univ. Press, 1973), 22–24; and William Bruce White, "The Military and the Melting Pot: The American Army and Minority Groups, 1865–1924" (Ph.D. diss., Univ. of Wisconsin, 1968), 303–304.

6. White, "Military and the Melting Pot," 303–330.

7. *WDAR* (1899), 702; *WDAR* (1900), 915; *WDAR* (1901), 606–607.

8. The overall numbers of foreign-born recruits hovered about 12 percent. *WDAR* (1910), 362; *WDAR* (1913), 592; *WDAR* (1914), 171–172, 439; *WDAR* (1915), 549; *WDAR* (1917), 189.

9. Edward M. Coffman, *The Regulars: The American Army, 1898–1941* (Cambridge: Belknap Press of Harvard Univ. Press, 2004), 97–98.

10. Ford, *Americans All!*

11. Morris Janowitz, *The Professional Soldier: A Social and Political Portrait* (New York: Free Press, 1960), 79–101; C. Wright Mills, *The Power Elite* (New York: Oxford Univ. Press, 1956), 180; Richard C. Brown, "Social Attitudes of American Generals, 1898–1940" (Ph.D. diss., Univ. of Wisconsin, 1951), 3.

12. Quoted in White, "Military and the Melting Pot," 305–306.

13. Quoted in ibid., 309. See also Joseph W. Bendersky, *The "Jewish Threat": Anti-Semitic Politics of the U.S. Army* (New York: Basic Books, 2000), 15–32.

14. Quoted in Bendersky, *"Jewish Threat,"* 32.

15. Coffman, *Regulars,* 96. See also Alfred Reynolds, *The Life of the Enlisted Soldier in the United States Army* (Washington, D.C.: GPO, 1904), 8; White, "Military and the Melting Pot," 306–313; and Coffman, *Old Army,* 330–331.

16. Bendersky, *"Jewish Threat,"* 35–46.

17. Coffman, *Regulars,* 124–125.

18. Reynolds, *Life of the Enlisted Soldier,* 7.

19. Ibid., 11–12.

20. Fletcher, "Army and Minority Groups,"107–109; and White, "Military and the Melting Pot," 303–304.

21. James B. Jacobs and Leslie Anne Hayes, "Aliens in the U.S. Armed Forces: A Historico-Legal Analysis," *Armed Forces and Society* 7 (Winter 1981): 187.

22. See the essays in N. F. Dreisziger, ed., *Ethnic Armies: Polyethnic Armed Forces from the Time of the Habsburgs to the Age of the Superpowers* (Waterloo, Ont.: Wilfrid Laurier Press, 1990).

23. Quoted in Joseph J. Ellis, *Founding Brothers: The Revolutionary Generation* (New York: Vintage Books, 2000), 154.

24. "The Germans in Hooker's Battles—The National Spirit of our Adopted Citizens," *NYT,* June 4, 1863, 4. See also Creighton, *Colors of Courage,* chap. 1.

25. Ronald J. Barr, *The Progressive Army: US Army Command and Administration, 1870–1914* (New York: St. Martin's Press, 1998); Michael Pearlman, *To Make Democracy Safe for America: Patricians and Preparedness in the Progressive Era* (Urbana: Univ. of Illinois Press, 1984); Samuel P. Huntington, *The Soldier and the State: The Theory and Politics of Civil-Military Relations* (Cambridge, Mass: Belknap Press, 1957), 237–288; Weigley, *History,* 313–341; Peter Karsten, "Armed Progressives," in *The Military in America,* ed. Peter Karsten (New York: Free Press, 1980), 246–260; Jerry M. Cooper, *The Army and Civil Disorder: Federal Military Intervention in Labor Disputes, 1877–1900* (Westport, Conn.: Greenwood Press, 1980); Carol Reardon, *Soldiers and Scholars: The U.S. Army and the Uses of Military History, 1865–1920* (Lawrence: Univ. Press of Kansas, 1990); Lori Lyn Bogle, *The Pentagon's Battle for the American Mind: The Early Cold War* (College Station: Texas A&M Press, 2004), 21–39; and Martha Derthick, *The National Guard in Politics* (Cambridge: Harvard Univ. Press, 1965), 15–44.

26. John Garry Clifford, *The Citizen Soldiers: The Plattsburg Training Camp Movement, 1913–1920* (Lexington: Univ. of Kentucky Press, 1972).

27. Pearlman, *To Make Democracy Safe,* 11–144; John Whiteclay Chambers II, *To Raise an Army: The Draft Comes to Modern America* (New York: Free Press, 1987), 73–101, 243; Keene, *Doughboys,* 19–21; Brown, "Social Attitudes," 84–116; Bruce White, "War Preparations and Ethnic and Racial Relations in the United States," in *Anticipating Total War: The German and American Experiences, 1971–1914,* ed. Manfred F. Boemeke, Roger Chickering, and Stig Förster, eds. (New York: Cambridge Univ. Press, 1999), 97–124.

28. Quoted in William Henry Harbaugh, *The Life and Times of Theodore Roosevelt* (1961; reprint, New York: Collier Books, 1963), 451–452.

29. Quoted in Kennedy, *Over Here,* 17.

30. Leonard Wood, "Heat Up the Melting Pot," *Independent* 87 (July 3, 1916): 15. See also Bendersky, *"Jewish Threat,"* 30; and Slotkin, *Lost Battalions,* 12–34.

31. For a fuller discussion of exemptions and the processes of Selective Service, see Weigley, *History,* 356–357; Ford, *Americans All!* 52–55; and especially Chambers, *To Raise an Army,* 179–204.

32. Ford, *Americans All!;* Sterba, *Good Americans.* For the practical results of this mixing in two individual units, see Slotkin, *Lost Battalions,* 72–111, 153–212, 241–271, 305–363; and James J. Cooke, *The All-Americans at War: The 82nd Division in the Great War, 1917–1918* (Westport, Conn.: Praeger, 1999), 1–38.

33. On high illiteracy rates and lack of assimilation among immigrants, see U.S. Bureau of Education, *Report of the Commissioner of Education, 1919* (Washington, D.C.: GPO, 1919), 42–46.

34. White, "Military and the Melting Pot," 326–327. See also Bruce White, "The American Military and the Melting Pot in World War I," in *The Military in America,* ed. Peter Karsten (New York: Free Press, 1980), 301–310, and Ford, *Americans All!*

35. Ford, *Americans All!* 13, 67–111; and White, "The American Military and Melting Pot in World War I," 304–305.

36. Chambers, *To Raise an Army,* 229–231; White, "Military and the Melting Pot," 336.

37. Quoted in Brown, "Social Attitudes," 121.

38. White, "Military and the Melting Pot," 342–348. See also *Principles, Plans and Purposes of the Educational Program* (Camp Upton, N.Y.: Recruit Educational Center, 1920); Ford, *Americans All!* 144–145; and White, "American Military and the Melting Pot," 305–310.

39. *Army Lessons in English,* bk. 1 (Camp Upton, N.Y.: Recruit Educational Center, 1920), 4–17.

40. *Army Lessons in English,* bk. 5 (Camp Upton, N.Y.: Recruit Educational Center, 1920), 20–21.

41. *Army Lessons in English: Military Stories* (Camp Upton, N.Y.: Recruit Educational Center, 1920), 6–7.

42. Ibid., 7.

43. On the Slavic Legion, see Ford, *Americans All!* 62–63. On the Polish Legion, see Joseph T. Hapak, "Selective Service and Polish Army Recruitment during World War I," *Journal of American Ethnic History* 10 (Summer 1991): 38–61; Ford, *Americans All!* 36–37; and Chambers, *To Raise an Army,* 229–230. For a similar story of Jewish Americans joining a Jewish Legion that fought in the British army, see Martin Watts, *The Jewish Legion and the First World War* (New York: Palgrave Macmillan, 2004).

44. Weigley, *History,* 395–403, 568–569; Coffman, *Regulars,* 227–235; and Robert K. Griffith Jr., *Men Wanted for the U.S. Army* (Westport, Conn.: Greenwood Press, 1982).

45. Peyton C. March, *The Nation at War* (Garden City, N.Y.: Doubleday, 1932), 340–341. At the same time, not all of the army's officers embraced the idealism of Roosevelt and Wood. See Brown, "Social Attitudes," 3–5, 15, 213; "U.S. Army: Who's in the Army Now?" *Fortune* 12 (Sept. 1935), 43; Carl Brigham, *A Study of American Intelligence* (Princeton, N.J.: Princeton Univ. Press, 1923); White, "Military and the Melting Pot," 358–375; Bendersky, *"Jewish Threat"*; and Milton Goldin, review of *The "Jewish Threat": Anti-Semitic Politics of the U.S. Army,* by Joseph W. Bendersky, H-Net, H-Antisemitism, Feb. 2001, http://www.h-net.org/reviews/; Coffman, *Regulars,* 237.

46. John W. Killigrew, *The Impact of the Great Depression on the Army* (New York: Garland, 1979).

47. William O. Odom, *After the Trenches: The Transformation of U.S. Army Doctrine, 1918–1939* (College Station: Texas A&M Univ. Press, 1999), 199–220.

48. Griffith, *Men Wanted,* 111–129; and Douglas MacArthur, *Reminiscences* (New York: McGraw Hill, 1964), 100.

49. Brown, "Social Attitudes," 383. See also John W. Thomason, "The Case for the Soldier," *Scribner's Magazine* 97 (Apr. 1935), 211.

50. Coffman, *Regulars,* 298.

51. Griffith, *Men Wanted,* 104.

52. Quoted in Coffman, *Regulars,* 237.

53. Ibid., 238–239.

54. Quoted in Donald M. Kington, *Forgotten Summers: The Story of the Citizens' Military Training Camps* (San Francisco: Two Decades, 1995), 91. See also Pearlmann, *To Make Democracy,* 189–191; and George F. James, *Eleven Years of the CMTC: A Brief Account of the Citizens' Military Training Camps, 1921–1931* (Chicago: Military Training Camps Association, n.d), 1–22.

55. Kington, *Forgotten Summers,* 151–152.

56. *CMTC: Memoirs of the Citizens Military Training Camps* (Chicago: Military Training Camp Association, 1935), 32.

57. John A. Salmond, *The Civilian Conservation Corps, 1933–1942: A New Deal Case Study* (Durham, N.C.: Duke Univ. Press, 1967). See also Brown, "Social Attitudes," 320–324; Killigrew, *Impact of the Great Depression,* XII-1–XIII-41; Griffith, *Men Wanted,* 132–133, 158–160; Pearlmann, *To Make Democracy,* 230–233; Weigley, *History,* 402; and Forrest C. Pogue, *George C. Marshall: Education of a General, 1880–1939* (New York: Viking, 1963), 274–280, 300–311.

58. The CCC did lean toward rural communities: 56 percent of the enrollees came from farms, 28 percent from small towns, and 16 percent from larger cities.

Marjorie A. O'Brien, "An Evaluation of the Civilian Conservation Corps as an Educational Institution" (master's thesis, Ohio Univ., 1970), 40; Kenneth Holland and Frank Ernest Hill, *Youth in the CCC* (Washington, D.C.: American Council on Education, 1942), 61. See also Miles Whaley Interview, Oral History 1318, YSOH, 3.

59. U.S. Department of Labor, *Handbook for Agencies Selecting Men for the Civilian Conservation Corps* (Washington, D.C.: GPO, 1936), 5–10, 34. African Americans were segregated and faced difficulties even trying to sign up for the program. Charles W. Johnson, "The Army, the Negro and the Civilian Conservation Corps: 1933–1942," *Military Affairs* 36 (Oct. 1972): 82–88.

60. Holland and Hill, *Youth in the CCC*, 60–62. In 1930, 21 percent of the overall population had foreign or mixed parentage, in 1940 the number was 17.5 percent. *HSUS*, pt. 1, 116–117. See also Frank Ernest Hill, *The School in the Camps: The Educational Program of the Civilian Conservation Corps* (New York: American Association for Adult Education, 1935), 4–6; and Helen M. Walker, *The CCC Through the Eyes of 272 Boys* (Cleveland: Western Reserve Univ. Press, 1938), 11.

61. Educational Policies Commission, *The Civilian Conservation Corps, the National Youth Administration, and the Public Schools* (Washington, D.C.: GPO, 1941), 17.

62. Olaf Steiglitz, "'. . . very much an American life': The Concept of 'Citizenship' in the Civilian Conservation Corps, 1933–1942," in *The American Nation, National Identity, Nationalism,* ed. Knud Krakau (New Brunswick, N.J.: Transaction Publishers, 1997), 185–195. See George C. Marshall, "Comments on Vancouver Barracks District C.C.C.," Oct. 1937, in *The Papers of George Catlett Marshall,* vol. 1, ed. Larry I. Bland (Baltimore: Johns Hopkins Univ. Press, 1981), 561–562; and Pogue, *Education of a General,* 308–309.

63. Walker, *CCC Through the Eyes,* 54.

64. James Allen Interview, Oral History 1311, YSOH, 3.

65. Raymond James Shuster Interview, Oral History 1317, YSOH, 8.

66. Frank Delgenio Interview, Oral History 1419, YSOH, 25; Walker, *CCC Through the Eyes,* 53–55, 72–74; Holland and Hill, *Youth in the CCC,* 235–240; Blackie Gold interview, in Terkel, *Hard Times,* 58; and Alfred C. Oliver and Harold M. Dudley, *This New America: The Spirit of the Civilian Conservation Corps* (London: Longmans, Green, 1937), 65–110.

67. "No More Aliens in Army," *Army & Navy Register* 58 (Aug. 28, 1937): 5; "Lets Aliens Reenlist," *NYT,* Aug. 25, 1937, 11; and Jacobs and Hayes, "Aliens in the U.S. Armed Forces," 189.

68. Selective Service would eventually register and induct men ranging from age eighteen to forty-five, and even older men could and did enlist in small numbers. But the structure of Selective Service deferments and the nature of enlistments (young men wanting to get into the fight) skewed the figures toward those born 1910 and after. The result was that the average age of a soldier in World War II was

the mid-twenties. Therefore, almost all who were first-generation immigrants would have arrived in the United States when they were still young and became citizens in the meantime. *Selective Service in Wartime: The Second Report of the Director of Selective Service, 1941–1942* (Washington, D.C.: GPO, 1943), 55–57. See also Mapheus Smith, "Populational Characteristics of American Servicemen in World War II," *Scientific Monthly* 65 (Sept. 1947): 247. In any case, of the 6.1 million foreign born males living in the United States in 1940, more than 4 million were forty-five years old or older and only about 400,000 were between the ages of ten and thirty. Campbell J. Gibson and Emily Lennon, "Historical Census Statistics on the Foreign-born Population of the United States: 1850–1990," U.S. Bureau of the Census, http://www.census.gov/population/www/documentation/twps0029/twps0029.html.

69. *Selective Service and Victory: The Fourth Report of the Director of Selective Service* (Washington, D.C.: GPO, 1948), 205–209.

70. On the higher education levels, see Smith, "Populational Characteristics," 250–251; Samuel A. Stouffer, Edward A. Suchman, Leland C. DeVinney, Shirley A. Star, and Robin M. Williams Jr., eds., *Studies in Social Psychology in World War II*, vol. 1, *The American Soldier: Adjustment during Army Life* (Princeton, N.J.: Princeton Univ. Press, 1949), 57–65; and *What the Soldier Thinks*, 15 vols. (Washington, D.C.: Morale Services Division, Army Services Forces, 1943–45), 1, 12–13. On the problem of illiteracy in World War II, see Selective Service System, *Problems of Selective Service: Special Monograph No. 16* (Washington, D.C.: GPO, 1952), 157–168; Selective Service System, *Special Groups: Special Monograph No. 10.* (Washington, D.C.: GPO, 1953),143–167; and Samuel Goldberg, *Army Training of Illiterates in World War II* (New York: Teachers College, Columbia Univ., 1951). For a brief example of World War II–era U.S. Army special language instruction to non-English speakers, see "The Alphabet and the Army," *Washington Post,* Sept. 19, 1943, L5. For an exception, see Morin, *Among the Valiant,* 59–61.

71. From 1940 to 1945, Selective Service would register over forty-six million American men and induct nearly ten million of the sixteen million who served. *Selective Service and Victory,* 262–269; J. Garry Clifford and Samuel R. Spencer Jr., *The First Peacetime Draft* (Lawrence: Univ. Press of Kansas, 1986); John O'Sullivan, *From Voluntarism to Conscription: Congress and Selective Service, 1940–1945* (New York: Garland, 1982); George Q. Flynn, *The Draft, 1940–1973* (Lawrence: Univ. Press of Kansas, 1993), 1–52; George Q. Flynn, *Lewis B. Hershey, Mr. Selective Service* (Chapel Hill: Univ. of North Carolina Press, 1985), 66–102; Forrest C. Pogue, *George C. Marshall: Ordeal and Hope, 1939–1942* (New York: Viking, 1965), 56–63, 145–156; Marvin A. Kreidberg and Merton G. Henry, *History of Military Mobilization in the United States Army, 1775–1945* (Washington, D.C.: Department of the Army, 1955), 541–653; Chambers, *To Raise an Army,* 255–275; and Robert E. Summers and Harrison B. Summers, comps., *Universal Military Service,* Reference Shelf, vol. 15, no. 2 (New York: H. W. Wilson, 1941).

72. Feingold, *Time for Searching,* 257–258; Isidor Kaufman, *American Jews in World War II: The Story of 550,000 Fighters for Freedom* (New York: Dial Press, 1947); *In the Nation's Service: A Compilation of Facts Concerning Jewish Men in the Armed Forces During the First Year of the War* (1942; reprint, New York: National Jewish Welfare Board, 1943).

73. James H. Tashjian, *The Armenian American in World War II* (Boston: Hairenik Association, 1953), vii–xii.

74. Guglielmo, *White on Arrival,* 237, fn. 2.

75. Memo from [Frank Stanton] to Archibald MacLeish, May 25, 1942, p. 5, Entry 171, Folder 2, Box 1848, RG 44, NARA II.

76. Gary Mormino draws on newspapers to provide some figures on Italian American service in various localities but was unable to confirm any totals offered by some less reliable sources. Mormino, "Little Italy Goes to War," 365. Raul Morin's history of Mexican Americans in World War II did not even try to come up with a number but discussed the numbers of Mexican Americans in the United States in the 1940s. Morin, *Among the Valiant,* 1–33.

77. Quoted in Flynn, *Lewis B. Hershey,* 103.

78. Smith, "Populational Characteristics," 246–252; Flynn, *Draft,* 85–87. Army personnel policies ended up being remarkably fair even to conscientious objectors. O'Sullivan, *From Volunteerism to Conscription,* 201–202; and Selective Service System, *Conscientious Objection: Special Monograph No. 11* (Washington, D.C.: GPO, 1950).

79. "Table VII—Enlisted composition of National Guard divisions, June 30, 1941," Entry 188, "The Procurement of Military Personnel," vol. 3, RG 160, NARA II.

80. *HSUS,* pt. 1, 116–117.

81. The army did divide the men based on the Army General Classification Test. Robert R. Palmer, Bell I. Wiley, and William R. Keast, *The Procurement and Training of Ground Combat Troops* (Washington, D.C.: GPO, 1948), 3–47. However, the effect that AGCT distribution had on the ethnic and religious diversity of units throughout the army seemed to be negligible if the memory of the men was any indication.

82. Quoted in *The Officers' Guide,* 9th ed. (Harrisburg, Pa.: Military Service Publishing, 1942), 452.

83. "A Polyethnic Panel," *Selective Service,* IV (Mar. 1944), 1, National Headquarters of Selective Service, RG 407, NARA II.

84. *The Soldier's Handbook* (New York: Thomas Y. Crowell, 1941), 36. On training, see also *Officers' Guide,* 203–221, 445–484; U.S. War Department, *Military Training,* Field Manual 21–5 (Washington, D.C.: GPO, July 1941); Palmer et al., *Procurement and Training;* and Dinnerstein, *Antisemitism,* 137.

85. Quotation in Andrew Klavan, "The Lost Art of War," *City Journal* 18 (Winter 2008), http://www.city-journal.org/ (accessed Feb. 5, 2008). See also May, *Big Tomorrow,* 144; Gerstle, *American Crucible,* 204–206; and Clayton R. Koppes and Gregory D. Black, *Hollywood Goes to War: How Politics, Profits and Propaganda Shaped World War II Movies* (Berkeley and Los Angeles: Univ. of California Press, 1987). See also Alpers, "This Is the Army," 129–163; Kreidberg and Henry, *History of Military Mobilization,* 614–617; and Bogle, *Pentagon's Battle,* 40–47.

86. Stephen Vincent Benét, "Dear Adolf," in *We Stand United and Other Radio Scripts,* by Stephen Vincent Benet (New York: Farrar and Rinehart, 1945), 49–58.

87. Stephen Vincent Benét, "Your Army," in *We Stand United and Other Radio Scripts,* by Stephen Vincent Benét (New York: Farrar and Rinehart, 1945), 185–202.

88. Alpers, "This Is the Army," 145–146.

89. Thomas William Bohn, *An Historical and Descriptive Analysis of the "Why We Fight" Series* (New York: Arno Press, 1977), 136–138.

90. Emily S. Rosenberg, *A Date Which Will Live: Pearl Harbor in American Memory* (Durham, N.C.: Duke Univ. Press, 2003), 21–22.

91. Clifford and Spencer, *First Peacetime Draft,* 1.

92 Coffman, *Old Army,* 178–180, 390–392; Roy J. Honeywell, *Chaplains of the United States Army* (Washington, D.C.: Department of the Army, 1958), 1–202; Earl F. Stover, *Up from Handymen: The United States Army Chaplaincy, 1865–1920* (Washington, D.C.: Department of the Army, 1977); Robert L. Gushwa, *The Best and Worst of Times: The United States Army Chaplaincy, 1920–1945* (Washington, D.C.: Department of the Army, 1977), 4–10; Weigley, *History,* 403.

93. On the CMTC, see Kington, *Forgotten Summers,* 148, 152–153; and Gushwa, *Best and Worst of Times,* 35–38. On the CCC, see Gushwa, *Best and Worst of Times,* 58–68; Honeywell, *Chaplains,* 210–212; Oliver and Dudley, *This New America,* 111–131; Holland and Hill, *Youth in the CCC,* 213–215; and Walker, *CCC Through the Eyes,* 50.

94. Coffman, *Regulars,* 237–238; Adjutant General to Edward M. Lahley, Feb. 15, 1924, Legislative and Policy Precedent File 1943-1975, Chaplains 61, RG 407, NARA II. For the statistical religious breakdown of the United States in the twentieth century, see *HSUS,* pt. 1, 391–392. See also Radio Address Press Release, Nov. 9, 1936, Decimal File 1920–1945 080, Ind. Fundamental Churches of America to Jewish Welfare Board, vol.1, RG 247, NARA II.

95. *Officers' Guide,* 195.

96. Army Regulations 60–5, Chaplains, Feb. 1941, Decimal File 1920–1945, 337 Miscellaneous Correspondence on Conference, RG 247. NARA II.

97. *The Chaplain,* Technical Manual No. 16–205 (Washington, D.C.: War Department, Apr. 1941). The chief of chaplains repeated the theme in some of his wartime correspondence. See William R. Arnold to Reverend Walter Mitchell, Dec. 27, 1943, Decimal File 1920–1945, 000.3 Religion, RG 247, NARA II.

98. William R. Arnold to Chaplain Clarence Reese, Mar. 20, 1944, Decimal File 1920–1945, 000.3 Religion, RG 247, NARA II.

99. Honeywell, *Chaplains,* 247–252; Deborah Dash Moore, "Worshipping Together in Uniform," paper presented at the Swig Lecture, Univ. of San Francisco, Sept. 2001, 8, http://www.usfca.edu/judaicstudies/lectures.html.

100. Isaac Klein, *The Anguish and the Ecstasy of a Jewish Chaplain* (New York: Vantage Press, 1974), 22–29.

101. Honeywell, *Chaplains,* 252.

102. See Klein, *Anguish and the Ecstasy,* 20–22.

103. William P. Smith to William R. Arnold, Jan. 31, 1945, Decimal File 1920–1945, 000.3 Religion, RG 247, NARA II.

104. Morris A. Gutstein to William R. Arnold, Mar. 10, 1943, Decimal File 1920–1945, 000.3 Religion, RG 247, NARA II. On interfaith services, see also Headquarters S.S. Mariposa, Office of the Transport Chaplain, Schedule of Religious Services, Decimal File 1920–1945, 000.3 Religion, RG 247, NARA II; and Memorial Day Service, 25th Infantry Division, Apr. 20, 1943, and Memorial Service, 25th Infantry Division, Oct. 17, 1943, both in Entry 360, Decimal File 1943–1945, 000.3, RG 407, NARA II.

105. See correspondence concerning Seventh-Day Adventists and with the National Jewish Welfare Board in Entry 360, Decimal File 1943–1945, 000.3, RG 407, NARA II.

106. John F. O'Hara to George C. Marshall, Oct. 25, 1941, Entry 363, Decimal File 1940–1945, 000.34 Services in the Army, RG 407, NARA II.

107. Memorandum to Secretary, General Staff from William R. Arnold, Nov. 6, 1941, Entry 353, Decimal File 1940–1945, 000.34 Services in the Army, RG 407, NARA II.

108. William R. Arnold to J. Oliver Buswell, Nov. 3, 1942, Decimal File 1920–1945 080, American Bible Soc. to American Legion, RG 247, NARA II. Arnold made similar points in responding to requests from individual denominations to send auxiliary civilian chaplains to minister to their adherents overseas. See Frank F. Bunker Correspondence (Concerning Christian Scientist Chaplains), August 1944, Entry 363, Decimal File 1940–1945, 000.3 Churches, RG 407, NARA II.

109. Memorandum concerning the Reverend Ben F. Wyland, Oct. 8, 1945, Decimal File 1920–1945, 056 Army Statistics, RG 247, NARA II.

110. William R. Arnold to Philip S. Bernstein, June 9, 1943, Decimal File 1920–1945, 000.3 Religion, RG 247, NARA II; Honeywell, *Chaplains,* 214–215. The Bureau of the Census ran four complete surveys of the religious breakdown of the country from 1906 to 1936. The fourth was somewhat underfunded and some of the numbers were no doubt off, but it did provide a baseline for the World War II Chaplain Corps. U.S. Bureau of the Census, *Census of Religious Bodies, 1936, Part I: Summary and Detailed Tables* (Washington, D.C.: GPO, 1940).

111. Albert Wedemeyer was the main author of the so-called Victory Program. In its final form in the summer of 1941, it called for 8.79 million troops divided into 213 divisions. The actual strength of the army in May 1945 was 8.29 million, but they were divided into only 89 divisions. See Kreidberg and Henry, *History of Military Mobilization,* 620–625.

112. The chief of chaplains never completely filled the quotas for Roman Catholics, Jews, or especially Colored Baptists. Conversely, all of the other major denominations listed above were overrepresented to varying degrees because those denominations dominated the prewar regular army, National Guard, and reserve chaplaincy, and because of the earlier quota system favored them too heavily. Honeywell, *Chaplains,* 214–218.

113. Klein, *Anguish and the Ecstasy,* 115; Moore, "Worshipping Together," 5–6; Abron Opher and Louis Gales Correspondence, Jan. 1945, Decimal File 1920–1945, 000.3 Religion, RG 247, NARA II. See chapters 5 and 6 for more examples from the perspectives of the men.

114. *Battleground,* directed by William Wellman, MGM, 1949.

115. Adjutant General Edward Witsell to Reverend Patrick M. Crowley, Oct. 1, 1946, Legislative and Policy Precedent File, Religion in the Army 64, RG 407, NARA II. See also Witsell to Hagan correspondence in the same file. The policy continued for years after the war. See "Non-Military Sources Denied Statistical Data of Discriminatory or Prejudicial Nature," May–June 1948, Legislative and Policy Precedent File, 1943–1975, Jews 63, RG 407, NARA II, and the correspondence between Adjutant General R. V. Lee and Elmer Brecker, Oct. 1959, in the same file.

116. J. Demos Kakridas to Franklin D. Roosevelt, Sept. 1, 1944, Entry 363, Decimal File 1940–1945, 000.3 Churches, RG 407, NARA II; William C. Tyirin to the Office of War Information, Apr. 26, 1943, Decimal File 1920–1945, 000.3 Religion, RG 247, NARA II.

117. J. A. Ulio to J. Demos Kakridas, Sept. 1, 1944, Entry 363, Decimal File 1940–1945, 000.3 Churches, RG 407, NARA II. The military began to spell out religions on identification tags in 1955. "Armed Forces Identification Tags to Spell out Religious Faiths," July 28, 1955, Legislative and Policy Precedent File, Religion in the Army 64, RG 407, NARA II. See also Hobson-Stimson Correspondence, April–May 1942, Entry 363, Decimal File 1940–1945, 000.3 Religion, RG 407, NARA II.

118. Roy J. Honeywell to Ralph Vander Pol, Feb. 17, 1943, Decimal File 1920–1945, 000.3 Religion, RG 247, NARA II.

119. Memorandum from William R. Arnold to Chief of Staff, Aug. 1, 1944, Decimal File 1920–1945, 032 Letters to Congress, RG 247, NARA II.

120. Ray A. Truitt to Chief of Chaplains, June 5, 1944, Decimal File 1920–1945, 000.3 Religion, RG 247, NARA II.

121. Roy J. Honeywell to Ray A. Truitt, June 22, 1944, Decimal File 1920–1945, 000.3 Religion, RG 247, NARA II.

122. Ray A. Truitt to Roy J. Honeywell, Aug. 14, 1944, Decimal File 1920–1945, 000.3 Religion, RG 247, NARA II.

123. Roy J. Honeywell to Ray A. Truitt, Aug. 26, 1944, Decimal File 1920–1945, 000.3 Religion, RG 247, NARA II.

124. Robert S. Wakefield to the Chief of Chaplains, Apr. 6, 1945, and Roy J. Honeywell to Robert S. Wakefield, Apr. 14, 1945, Decimal File 1920–1945, 000.3 Religion, RG 247, NARA II.

## 3. Introduction to the Army

1. See, for example, Raymond Gantter, *Roll Me Over: An Infantryman's World War II* (New York: Ivy Books, 1997), 7.

2. Richard Grondin Oral History, EC, 1–2.

3. Puzo, *Godfather Papers,* 25–26.

4. Louis Banks interview, in Terkel, *Hard Times,* 43.

5. Leonard Herb interview, EC, 2. Lloyd Dull said something similar: "I was 18 at the time and I don't think I really thought too much about it. I did feel it was my duty to the country." Lloyd Dull Questionnaire, 35th Infantry Division, USAMHI, 1.

6. John D. Kenderdine, *Your Year in the Army: What Every New Soldier Should Know* (New York: Simon and Schuster, 1940), 6.

7. Gene Coughlin, *Assistant Hero* (New York: Thomas Y. Crowell, 1944), 15.

8. Frank Ehrman Oral History, EC, 1–2.

9. Robert F. Dove, "Off to War," in *The Purple Testament,* ed. Don M. Wolfe (Garden City, N.Y.: Doubleday, 1947), 35–36.

10. The same man said that "last battalion short-arm inspection of eight hundred men was completed in two hours." Klaus H. Huebner, *Long Walk Through War: A Combat Doctor's Diary* (College Station: Texas A&M Univ. Press, 1987), 5–6.

11. See also Jack Gray Oral History, EC, 2; Charles E. Kelly, *One Man's War* (New York: Alfred A. Knopf, 1944), 128–129; Gantter, *Roll Me Over,* 2; Peters, *For You,* 16; Robert Kotlowitz, *Before Their Time* (New York: Anchor Books, 1997), 87–91; Sidney Bowen, *Dearest Isabel: Letters from an Enlisted Man in World War II* (Manhattan, Kans.: Sunflower Univ. Press, 1992), 2.

12. Franklin L. Gurley, *Into the Mountains Dark: A WWII Odyssey from Harvard Crimson to Infantry Blue* (Bedford, Pa.: Aberjona Press, 2000), 65.

13. John Jenkins to Miss Foster, Sept. 27, 1942, in *Letters from the Front, 1898–1945,* ed. Michael E. Stevens (Madison: State Historical Society of Wisconsin, 1992), 78–79.

14. M. D. Elevitch, *Dog Tags Yapping: The World War II Letters of a Combat GI* (Carbondale: Southern Illinois Univ. Press, 2003), 11.

15. Peters, *For You,* 21.

16. Quoted in John Costello, *Virtue Under Fire: How World War II Changed Our Social and Sexual Attitudes* (Boston: Little, Brown, 1985), 76.

17. Matthew B. Ridgway, *Soldier: The Memoirs of Matthew B. Ridgway* (New York: Harper and Brothers, 1956), 3.

18. Kenderdine, *Your Year in the Army,* 14.

19. Russell Cartwright Stoup, *Letters from the Pacific: A Combat Chaplain in World War II* (Columbia: Univ. of Missouri Press, 2000), 165.

20. Gurley, *Into the Mountains,* 33.

21. Warren Lloyd Oral History, EC, 1.

22. Quoted in Annette Tapert, ed., *Lines of Battle: Letters from American Servicemen, 1941–1945* (New York: Times Books, 1987), 64.

23. Kelly, *One Man's War,* 10.

24. Ibid., 8.

25. Stoup, *Letters from the Pacific,* 27.

26. John Hinton Oral History, EC, 1.

27. Audie Murphy, *To Hell and Back* (New York: MJF Books, 1949), 8.

28. Maynard Marquis Oral History, EC, 1.

29. George Wilson, *If You Survive* (New York: Ivy Books, 1987), 2.

30. Kelly, *One Man's War,* 10.

31. Hoffmann, *Zone of the Interior,* 40.

32. Wayne Colwell Questionnaire, 2nd Armored Division, USAMHI, 5.

33. Richard O'Brien Questionnaire, 35th Infantry Division, USAMHI.

34. Lee Kennett, *G.I.: The American Soldier in World War II* (New York: Charles Scribner's Sons, 1987), 34.

35. For a more detailed description of the breakdown and distribution from the AGCT, see Palmer et al., *Procurement and Training,* 3–47.

36. Lawrence Dowler Oral History, EC, 1.

37. Andrew George Nelson Questionnaire, 11th Airborne Division, USAMHI, 18.

38. On the differences between civilian and U.S. Army life, see Stouffer et al., *Studies in Social Psychology* 1:54–104; Arnold Rose, "The Social Structure of the Army," *American Journal of Sociology* 51 (Mar. 1946): 361–364; Howard Brotz and Everett Wilson, "Characteristics of Military Society," *American Journal of Sociology* 51 (Mar. 1946): 371–375.

39. J. Glenn Gray, *The Warriors: Reflections on Men in Battle* (Lincoln: Univ. of Nebraska Press, 1959, 1998), 15.

40. Hoffmann, *Zone of the Interior,* 48–49.

41. Robert Healey Oral History, EC, 6.

42. Perguson quoted in Nancy Disher Baird, "An Opportunity to Meet 'Every Kind of Person': A Kentuckian Views Army Life during World War II," *Register of the Kentucky Historical Society* 101 (Summer 2003): 302.

43. Kelly, *One Man's War,* 22.

44. Hoffmann, *Zone of the Interior,* 76.

45. Roscoe C. Blunt Jr., *Foot Soldier: A Combat Infantryman's War in Europe* (Cambridge, Mass.: De Capo, 2002), 124.

46. Gurley, *Into the Mountains,* 14.

47. Hyman Haas Oral History, EC, 6.

48. Easton, *Love and War,* 75–77.

49. Quoted in Mark P. Parillo, ed., *We Were in the Big One: Experiences of the World War II Generation* (Wilmington, Del.: Scholarly Resources, 2002), 18.

50. Joy, *Sixty Days,* 23.

51. Angus Nott Questionnaire, Americal Division, USAMHI, 5, 7.

52. Gerald Kelsey, "As the Motors Slowed Down," in *The Purple Testament,* ed. Don M. Wolfe (Garden City, N.Y.: Doubleday, 1947), 49. Other soldier descriptions of multiethnic units include Baird, "Opportunity to Meet," 303–305, 309–310, 313; Gantter, *Roll Me Over,* 64–65, 163; Harold Leinbaugh and John D. Campbell, *The Men of Company K* (New York: William Morrow, 1985); and Becker and Thobaben, *Common Warfare,* 30 (for Becker), 115 (for Thobaben).

53. Carwood Lipton Questionnaire, 101st Airborne Division, USAMHI, 5.

54. Gordon Carson Questionnaire, 101st Airborne Division, USAMHI, 5.

55. Jarrold A. Davis Questionnaire, 11th Airborne Division, USAMHI, 5.

56. William Guarnere Interview, EC, 13.

57. Moore, *GI Jews,* 80.

58. Frank H. Armstrong, *Payoff Artillery–WWII* (Burlington, Vt.: Bull Run, 1993), 28–29.

59. Hollis Stabler Questionnaire, 2nd Armored Division, USAMHI, 5. For more examples of joking along ethnic lines, see Murphy, *To Hell and Back.*

60. Charles Henne Questionnaire, 37th Infantry Division, USAMHI, 10.

61. Bailey Tyre Questionnaire, 11th Airborne Division, USAMHI, 5.

62. James Sammons Questionnaire, 2nd Armored Division, USAMHI, 5.

63. Alexander Davit Questionnaire, 4th Infantry Division, USAMHI, 5.

64. James Manning Questionnaire, 35th Infantry Division, USAMHI, 5.

65. Merritt Bragdon Questionnaire, 2nd Armored Division, USAMHI, 7.

66. Tom Rounsaville Questionnaire, 11th Airborne Division, USAMHI, 7.

67. Albert Schantz Questionnaire, 4th Infantry Division, USAMHI, 5–7.

68. Jack Foley Questionnaire, 101st Airborne Division, USAMHI, 5.

69. Richard O'Brien Questionnaire.

70. Even close studies of religion and chaplains did not produce a lot of examples of religious animosity among the men. For example, Donald F. Crosby, *Battlefield Chaplains: Catholic Priests in World War II* (Lawrence: Univ. Press of Kansas, 1994), 66–67.

71. The experiences of Jewish Americans in the World War II military are best recounted in Moore, *GI Jews.*

72. James R. Jones Questionnaire, 37th Infantry Division, USAMHI, 5; William U'Ren Questionnaire, 4th Infantry Division, USAMHI, 5.

73. Donald Dehn Questionnaire, 44th Infantry Division, USAMHI, 5.

74. Nicholas Scotto Questionnaire, Americal Division, USAMHI, 5.

75. Klein, *Anguish and the Ecstasy,* 40.

76. Werner Kleeman Questionnaire, 4th Infantry Division, USAMHI, 5.

77. Andrew George Nelson Questionnaire, 5.

78. James Graff Questionnaire, 35th Infantry Division, USAMHI, 5.

79. Joseph P. Barrett Oral History, EC, 3.

80. On the issue of anti-Semitism in the ranks, see Bendersky, *"Jewish Threat,"* 295–301; and Dinnerstein, *Antisemitism,* 137–142.

81. Edwin A. Mann Questionnaire, 2nd Armored Division, USAMHI, 5.

82. Gurley, *Into the Mountains,* 16–21. A couple more examples can be seen in Rowland Berthoff, "A Rejoinder on Wartime Anti-Semitism," *Journal of American History* 77 (Sept. 1990): 590.

83. Eli D. Bernheim Jr. Questionnaire, 11th Airborne Division, USAMHI, 5.

84. The most direct question is on U.S. Army Military History Institute's World War II questionnaire: Question 21: "Did you note any instances of ethnic, racial or religious discrimination? Please explain." The racial part of the question is dealt with below.

85. Kensinger Jones Questionnaire, 35th Infantry Division, USAMHI, 5.

86. Kenneth Lytton Questionnaire, 101st Airborne Division, USAMHI, 5.

87. Paul Miller Questionnaire, 101st Airborne Division, USAMHI, 5.

88. William McLaughlin Questionnaire, Americal Division, USAMHI, 5.

89. Fred Martin Questionnaire, 1st Cavalry Division, USAMHI, 5.

90. William A. Bonds Questionnaire, 101st Airborne Division, USAMHI, 5.

91. Joel Thomason Questionnaire, 4th Infantry Division, USAMHI, 5.

92. Eugene McConachie Questionnaire, 44th Infantry Division, USAMHI, 5.

93. Charles Henne Questionnaire, 10.

94. William Lessemann Questionnaire, 44th Infantry Division, USAMHI, 5.

95. Caesar Abate Questionnaire, 11th Airborne Division, USAMHI, 5.

96. Lloyd Magee Questionnaire, 1st Cavalry Division, USAMHI, 5.

97. Quoted in Baird, "Opportunity to Meet," 300.

98. Christopher E. Mauriello and Roland J. Regan Jr., *From Boston to Berlin: A Journey through World War II in Images and Words* (West Lafayette, Ind.: Purdue Univ. Press, 2001), 20.

99. Nap Glass quoted in Parillo, *We Were in the Big One,* 20–21.

100. Kenderdine, *Your Year in the Army,* 153.

101. For sample breakdowns of training schedules and details, see War Department, *Military Training; Soldier's Handbook* (1941); Kenderdine, *Your Year in the Army,* 46–47; Kennett, *G.I.,* 46–53; and Brotz and Wilson, "Characteristics of Military Society," 371.

102. Kennett, *G.I.,* 52.

103. Carl I. Hovland, Arthur A. Lumsdaine, and Fred D. Sheffield. *Studies in Social Psychology in World War II,* vol. 3, *Experiments on Mass Communication* (Princeton, N.J.: Princeton Univ. Press, 1949), 182–200.

104. Gurley, *Into the Mountains,* 22.

105. Kenderdine, *Your Year in the Army,* 81–82.

106. Hoffmann, *Zone of the Interior,* 40–41. See also William H. McNeill, *Keeping Together in Time: Dance and Drill in Human History* (Cambridge: Harvard Univ. Press, 1997).

107. Quoted in Stouffer et al., *Studies in Social Psychology* 1:76–79. See also *What the Soldier Thinks,* 3, 13; and Brotz and Wilson, "Characteristics of Military Society," 372–373.

108. Quoted in Parillo, *We Were in the Big One,* 45.

109. Coughlin, *Assistant Hero,* 56–57. For other examples, see Becker and Thobaben, *Common Warfare,* 17.

110. O. A. Kennerly, "Five A.M.," in *The Purple Testament,* ed. Don M. Wolfe (Garden City, N.Y.: Doubleday, 1947), 37–38.

111. Shelton, *Climb to Conquer,* 36–37.

112. *What the Soldier Thinks,* 3, 13.

113. *What the Soldier Thinks,* 4, 2.

114. See the drawings "Blisters" and "Chigger Bites" by Sgt. Wallace Brodeur in Fort Custer Army Illustrators, *As Soldiers See It* (New York: American Artists Group, 1943).

115. George J. Veach, "The Second Jump," in *The Purple Testament,* ed. Don M. Wolfe (Garden City, N.Y.: Doubleday, 1947), 46.

116. Elevitch, *Dog Tags,* 46.

117. Becker and Thobaben, *Common Warfare*, 19.

118. An excellent example is Peters, *For You*.

119. See Henry Elkins, "Aggressive and Erotic Tendencies in Army Life," *American Journal of Sociology* 51 (Mar. 1946): 408–413; Margot Canaday, "Building a Straight State: Sexuality and Social Citizenship under the 1944 G.I. Bill," *Journal of American History* 90 (Dec. 2003), 935–957; Costello, *Virtue Under Fire*, 101–119; and Allan Berube, *Coming Out Under Fire: The History of Gay Men and Women in World War Two* (New York: Free Press, 2000).

120. Brotz and Wilson, "Characteristics of Military Society," 374–375; Kennett, *G.I.*, 58–62.

121. Andrew George Nelson Questionnaire, 18.

122. Elevitch, *Dog Tags*, 17.

123. Brotz and Wilson, "Characteristics of Military Society," 375.

124. Lloyd Dull Questionnaire, 5.

125. Kensinger Jones Questionnaire, 5.

126. Morin, *Among the Valiant*, 90–93.

127. Kelly, *One Man's War*, 10.

128. Kelsey, "As the Motors Slowed," 49.

129. Fairview Reformed Presbyterian Church to Franklin Roosevelt, May 10, 1942, President's Official File 75, Box 2, Prohibition Petitions 1942–1944 A–H, Franklin Roosevelt Papers, FDR. See in same file the correspondence from constituents forwarded in Louis Johnson to Franklin Roosevelt, Jan. 29, 1942; Wright Patman to Franklin Roosevelt, Mar. 13, 1943; and Paul Brown to E. M. Watson, May 18, 1943. Members of the Mormon church also complained about this issue. Office of the First President, Church of Jesus Christ of Latter Day Saints to Franklin Roosevelt, Oct. 28, 1942.

130. O'Donnell, *Into the Rising Sun*, 166–167.

131. Gantter, *Roll Me Over*, 55.

132. Maynard Marquis Oral History, EC, 2.

133. Quoted in O'Donnell, *Into the Rising Sun*, 108.

134. Blunt, *Foot Soldier*, 22, viii.

135. Alfred Allred Oral History, EC, 3.

136. Easton, *Love and War*, 75–77.

137. Becker and Thobaben, *Common Warfare*, 115.

138. "The Last Battle," Morris Pockler File, Box 49, Cornelius Ryan Collection, Alden Library, Ohio Univ., Athens.

139. Thomas A. Bruscino Jr., "The Greatest and the Toughest: American Rifle Company Commanders and the War Against Germany, 1942–1945" (master's thesis,

Ohio Univ., 2002), 89–94, 164–168. See also Stouffer, *Studies in Social Psychology* 2:138.

140. *What the Soldier Thinks,* 6, 7.

141. Ibid., 13, 1.

142. Leinbaugh and Campbell, *Men of Company K,* xiv.

143. Jack Gray Oral History, EC, 20.

144. Gurley, *Into the Mountains,* 60–61.

145. More than half the men in all branches but the Medical Corps (48%), Cavalry (37%), and Infantry (28%) liked their own branch the best. Less than 10 percent of the men in every branch but the Infantry (25%), liked their own branch the least. *What the Soldier Thinks,* 1, 23. For example, Carl Becker was quite pleased to find himself in the antiaircraft artillery. Becker and Thobaben, *Common Warfare,* 10.

146. For the pride in those units, see, for example, Shelton, *Climb to Conquer;* Stephen E. Ambrose, *Band of Brothers* (New York: Simon and Schuster, 1992); William O. Darby and William H. Baumer, *Darby's Rangers: We Led the Way* (San Rafael, Calif.: Presidio Press, 1980); and Arthur Miller, *Situation Normal . . .* (New York: Reynal and Hitchcock, 1944), 29.

147. Eli D. Bernheim Jr. Questionnaire, 5.

148. *What the Soldier Thinks,* 1, 23.

149. "The Making of the Infantryman," *American Journal of Sociology* 51 (Mar. 1946): 376–379; *What the Soldier Thinks,* 2, 8.

150. Kennett, *G.I.,* 87; *What the Soldier Thinks,* 9, 9.

151. Kenderdine, *Your Year in the Army,* 49–50.

152. Brotz and Wilson, "Characteristics of Military Society," 373.

153. Kindsvatter, *American Soldiers,* 56–59.

154. John Hooper Oral History, EC, 8.

155. Walter Scott Gordon Questionnaire, 101st Airborne Division, USAMHI, 5.

156. See Ambrose, *Band of Brothers,* 21–25.

157. Clarence Hester Oral History, EC, 4.

158. "Making of the Infantryman," 376–377 fn.

159. Paul Fussell, *Wartime: Understanding and Behavior in the Second World War* (New York: Oxford Univ. Press, 1989), 80.

160. *What the Soldier Thinks,* 14, 9.

161. Bruscino, "Greatest and the Toughest."

162. Quoted in Parillo, *We Were in the Big One,* 46.

163. Warren Fitch Questionnaire, 37th Infantry Division, USAMHI, 5.

164. Klein, *Anguish and the Ecstasy,* 23.

165. Banks interview, in Terkel, *Hard Times,* 43.

166. Robert Lekachman interview, in Studs Terkel, *"The Good War": An Oral History of World War II* (New York: New Press, 1984) (hereafter cited as Terkel, *Good War*), 66.

167. Becker and Thobaben, *Common Warfare,* 115.

168. Easton, *Love and War,* 89.

169. Morin, *Among the Valiant,* 87–88.

# 4. Hours of Boredom

1. On boredom as a topic in World War II, see Bradford Perkins, "Impressions of Wartime," *Journal of American History* 77 (Sept. 1990): 564–565.

2. In April 1945, ground combat units made up about 37 percent of the ground army, but even that number included thousands of men who were in noncombat roles within the combat forces. Kent Roberts Greenfield, Robert R. Palmer, and Bell Irvin Wiley, *The Organization of Ground Combat Troops* (Washington, D.C.: GPO, 1947), 189–25.

3. Ulysses Lee, *The Employment of Negro Troops* (Washington, D.C.: GPO, 1966), passim; Wynn, *Afro-American,* 21–38.

4. For an example of a black soldier from Wyoming making the transition to service, see Vernon Baker, *Lasting Valor* (Columbus, Miss: Genesis Press, 1997).

5. Herbert Garris Questionnaire, 101st Airborne Division, USAMHI, 5.

6. For their part, the newly inducted black troops in one survey also had a generally negative view toward whites. Harry V. Roberts, "Prior-Service Attitudes Toward Whites of 219 Negro Veterans." *Journal of Negro Education.* 22 (Autumn 1953): 455–465.

7. Easton, *Love and War,* 112.

8. Ibid., 190.

9. Edward Tipper Questionnaire, 101st Airborne Division, USAMHI, 5.

10. Gail Thomas Questionnaire, 35th Infantry Division, USAMHI, 5.

11. Richard Winters Questionnaire, 101st Airborne Division, USAMHI, 5.

12. Palmer et al., *Procurement and Training,* 5.

13. E. B. Sledge, *With the Old Breed* (New York: Oxford Univ. Press, 1981), 27.

14. William Brant Jones, interview with author, Oct. 11, 2003, Pittsburgh, PA.

15. Huebner, *Long Walk,* 159.

16. See Lars Anderson, *The All-Americans* (New York: St. Martin's Press, 2004); Jack Clary, *Army vs. Navy: Seventy Years of Football Rivalry* (New York: Ronald Press,

1965), 138–187; James A. Blackwell, *On Brave Old Army Team* (Novato, Calif.: Presidio Press, 1996), 152–171; and Henry E. Mattox, *Army Football in 1945: Anatomy of a Championship Season* (Jefferson, N.C.: McFarland, 1990).

17. Quoted in Carlo D'Este, *Patton: A Genius for War* (New York: HarperCollins, 1995), 604.

18. Becker and Thobaben, *Common Warfare*, 56.

19. *What the Soldier Thinks*, 13, 7.

20. James Russell Major recalled that despite the cramped conditions, "on the whole, it was a pleasant voyage." *The Memoirs of a Forward Artillery Observer* (Manhattan, Kans.: Sunflower Univ. Press, 1999), 57.

21. Greenfield, Palmer, and Wiley, *Organization of Ground Combat Troops*, 194.

22. Shelton, *Climb to Conquer*, 70.

23. Kelly, *One Man's War*, 24.

24. Blunt, *Foot Soldier*, 5.

25. Joseph P. Barrett Oral History, EC, 11.

26. Bowen, *Dearest Isabel*, 44–48.

27. Joy, *Sixty Days*, 50.

28. Quoted in Kurzman, *No Greater Glory*, 55–56.

29. Gurley, *Into the Mountains*, 72. Robert Peters remembered "perpetual crap and poker games" on his trip over to Europe. Peters, *For You*, 32.

30. Kelly, *One Man's War*, 18–19.

31. Baird, "Opportunity to Meet," 304.

32. John Jamieson, "A History of Armed Services Editions," in *Editions for the Armed Services: A History*, by John Jamieson (New York: Editions for the Armed Services, 1948), 1–31; and John Y. Cole, "The Armed Services Editions: An Introduction," in *Books in Action: The Armed Services Editions*, ed. John Y. Cole (Washington, D.C.: Library of Congress, 1984), 1–11.

33. John Jamieson, *Editions for the Armed Services: A History* (New York: Editions for the Armed Services, 1948), 26–27.

34. Joseph P. Barrett Oral History, EC, 10.

35. Kotlowitz, *Before Their Time*, 55–56.

36. William V. O'Connor interview, Chaplains Oral Histories, Box 3, p. 16, USAMHI.

37. Jamieson, *Editions for the Armed Services*, 27.

38. John L. Ahearn Oral History, EC, 5. Joel Thomason of the Fourth Infantry Division also read *A Tree Grows in Brooklyn* prior to the invasion. Joel Thomason Questionnaire, 5.

39. Quoted in John Y. Cole, ed., *Books in Action: The Armed Services Editions* (Washington, D.C.: Library of Congress, 1984), viii.

40. Quoted in Jamieson, *Editions for the Armed Services,* 29–30. Raymond Gantter also wrote about how much he enjoyed the ASE in *Roll Me Over,* 16, as did Robert Peters, *For You,* 32.

41. Kenneth C. Davis, *Two-Bit Culture: The Paperbacking of America* (Boston: Houghton Mifflin, 1984), 56–82.

42. Michael Hackenberg, "The Armed Services Editions in Publishing History," in Cole, *Books in Action,* 19–20.

43. Christopher P. Loss, "Reading Between Enemy Lines: Armed Service Editions and World War II," *Journal of Military History* 67 (July 2003): 829.

44. Cole, "Armed Services Editions," 6.

45. Examples of rumors and actual attacks can be found in John Brawley, *Anyway, We Won* (Marceline, Mo.: Walsworth, 1988), 69–74; Wilson, *If You Survive,* 5; and Bowen, *Dearest Isabel,* 46–47.

46. Kennett, *G.I.,* 117–118. See also Dan van der Vat, *The Atlantic Campaign: World War II's Great Struggle at Sea* (New York: Harper and Row, 1988), and the essays in Timothy J. Runyan and Jan M. Copes, eds., *To Die Gallantly: The Battle of the Atlantic* (Boulder, Colo.: Westview Press, 1994).

47. Peter Schrijvers, *The GI War Against Japan: American Soldiers in Asia and the Pacific during World War II* (New York: New York Univ. Press, 2002), 7, 27–28.

48. E. J. Kahn, *G.I. Jungle: An American Soldier in Australia and New Guinea* (New York: Simon and Schuster, 1943), 1–7; Becker and Thobaben, *Common Warfare,* 25–26, 54.

49. Quoted in Kurzman, *No Greater Glory,* 56.

50. Sam Daugherty Oral History, EC, 4.

51. Roger Brugger Oral History, EC, 1.

52. John E. Bistrica Oral History, EC, 1.

53. Felix Branham Oral History, EC, 2–3.

54. John Hooper Oral History, EC, 3.

55. Huebner, *Long Walk,* 30.

56. Isadore E. Cutler Oral History, EC, 3.

57. Huebner, *Long Walk,* 11.

58. Kelly, *One Man's War,* 25.

59. See for example Joy, *Sixty Days,* 70; Kindsvatter, *American Soldiers,* 34; and Kelly, *One Man's War,* 31.

60. Kindsvatter, *American Soldiers,* 35.

61. Blunt, *Foot Soldier,* 96.

62. Joy, *Sixty Days,* 56–57.

63. Kelly, *One Man's War,* 128.

64. Kahn, *G.I. Jungle,* 63.

65. Schrijvers, *GI War Against Japan,* 46.

66. Kahn, *G.I. Jungle,* 88.

67. Wilson, *If You Survive,* 208.

68. A. Preston Price, *The Last Kilometer: Marching to Victory in Europe with the Big Red One, 1944–1945* (Annapolis, Md.: Naval Institute Press, 2002), 33.

69. Kelly, *One Man's War,* 66.

70. Leo Lick Oral History, EC, 2.

71. See William Manchester, *Goodbye Darkness: A Memoir of the Pacific War* (Boston: Little, Brown, 1979).

72. Schrijvers, *GI War Against Japan,* 101–134. See also Eric Bergerud, *Touched with Fire: The Land War in the South Pacific* (New York: Viking, 1996), 55–103.

73. Edward McLogan in Patrick K. O'Donnell, *Into the Rising Sun* (New York: Free Press, 2002), 96.

74. Herbert Campbell Oral History, EC, 1.

75. Gantter, *Roll Me Over,* 97–98.

76. Wilson, *If You Survive,* 208.

77. Blunt, *Foot Soldier,* 117.

78. Herbert Campbell Oral History, EC, 1.

79. John J. Barnes Oral History, EC, 4.

80. See Kurzman, *No Greater Glory,* 5–6.

81. In so doing they discovered a new ethnic American star. After doing hundreds of interviews with GIs, one historian has concluded that "they all came back loving Frank Sinatra." On D-Day a group of soldiers used as a code phrase "Who's the great American singer?"—to which the correct reply was "Frank Sinatra." Douglas Brinkley, "Frank Sinatra and the American Century," in Pugliese, *Frank Sinatra,* 20.

82. Barnett Hoffner Oral History, EC, 10.

83. Blunt, *Foot Soldier,* 168.

84. Joseph P. Barrett Oral History, EC, 2.

85. Jerry Kimball Oral History, EC, 5.

86. Easton, *Love and War,* 128.

87. Mauriello and Regan, *From Boston to Berlin,* 75–76.

88. Ibid., 77, 79. Certain ethnic groups, especially Italians, seemed to value food more. Puzo, *Godfather Papers,* 17–18.

89. Norman Longmate, *The G.I.s: The Americans in Britain, 1942–1945* (New York: Charles Scribner's Sons, 1975); Juliet Gardiner, *"Overpaid, Oversexed, and Over Here": The American GI in World War II Britain* (New York: Canopy Books, 1992); and David Reynolds, *Rich Relations: The American Occupation of Britain, 1942–1945* (New York: Random House, 1995). On Americans in Australia, see John Hammond Moore, *Over-Sexed, Over-Paid, and Over Here: Americans in Australia, 1941–1945* (St. Lucia: Univ. of Queensland Press, 1981); and E. Daniel Potts and Annette Potts, *Yanks Down Under, 1941–45: The American Impact on Australia* (New York: Oxford Univ. Press, 1985).

90. August Bruno Oral History, EC, 2.

91. Peters, *For You,* 39–40.

92. Ray Aebischer Oral History, EC, 2.

93. Kahn, *G.I. Jungle,* 14–20, 27.

94. Ibid., 107.

95. Kelly, *One Man's War,* 44. See also Mormino, "Little Italy Goes to War," 360–361, 366.

96. Shelton, *Climb to Conquer,* 124.

97. Joy, *Sixty Days,* 66. See also Edward G. Jones Jr. Oral History, EC, 26.

98. Alfred Allred Oral History, EC, 5–6. George Wilson also remembered a lot of wine and cider in France. *If You Survive,* 55–56.

99. Price, *Last Kilometer,* 9.

100. Robert Crousore Oral History, EC, 1–2.

101. Kelly, *One Man's War,* 93.

102. Kennett, *G.I.,* 119–120.

103. Schrijvers, *GI War Against Japan,* 202–203.

104. Richard Cherney Questionnaire, 11th Airborne Division, USAMHI, 5.

105. Bergerud, *Touched with Fire,* 484–486.

106. Schrijvers, *GI War Against Japan,* 202.

107. Eli D. Bernheim Jr. Questionnaire, 5.

108. Gordon Carson Interview, EC, 10.

109. Blunt, *Foot Soldier,* 230.

110. Mauriello and Regan, *From Boston to Berlin,* 76.

111. Joy, *Sixty Days,* 261–264.

112. Costello, *Virtue Under Fire,* 149, 132–155. See also Robert B. Westbrook, *Why We Fought: Forging American Obligations in World War II* (Washington, D.C.: Smithsonian Books, 2004), 67–91.

113. Easton, *Love and War,* 170.

114. Quoted in Costello, *Virtue Under Fire*, 7.

115. See Gantter, *Roll Me Over*, 215–217, 393.

116. Klein, *Anguish and the Ecstasy*, 221.

117. Costello, *Virtue Under Fire*, 81–89.

118. See Reynolds, *Rich Relations*; Longmate, *G.I.s*; Gardiner, *"Overpaid, Oversexed, and Over Here"*; Graham Smith, *When Jim Crow Met John Bull: Black American Soldiers in World War II Britain* (New York: St. Martin's Press, 1987); and Costello, *Virtue Under Fire*, 229–243.

119. Elevitch, *Dog Tags*, 78.

120. Russell Barr to Mr. and Mrs. Elmer Barr, Oct. 26, 1944, in Stevens, *Letters from the Front*, 87.

121. Costello, *Virtue Under Fire*, 210–228.

122. Jack Gray Oral History, EC, 5.

123. Quoted in Shelton, *Climb to Conquer*, 122.

124. Elevitch, *Dog Tags*, 114–115.

125. Sam Jacks Oral History, EC, 13. See also Huebner, *Long Walk*, 119–121, 164–165.

126. Victor Fast Oral History, EC, 3.

127. Lekachman interview, in Terkel, *Good War*, 67.

128. Ralph G. Martin, *The GI War, 1941–1945* (Boston: Little, Brown, 1967), 267.

129. Kahn, *G.I. Jungle*, 20, 32; Costello, *Virtue Under Fire*, 239–240.

130. Ibid., 60–61, 102–103. See also Schrijvers, *GI War Against Japan*, 151–152.

131. "Ross Back in U.S.; Tells of Fight with Japs," *Chicago Tribune*, Feb. 26, 1943, 21.

132. Jack McGrath quoted in O'Donnell, *Into the Rising Sun*, 188. See also Martin, *GI War*, 317.

133. Blunt, *Foot Soldier*, 255.

134. Easton, *Love and War*, 362.

135. Klein, *Anguish and the Ecstasy*, 222.

136. Kahn, *G.I. Jungle*, 136–137.

137. Gantter, *Roll Me Over*, 147. See also Schrijver, *GI War Against Japan*, 151–152.

138. Costello, *Virtue Under Fire*, 8, 16, 192–203.

139. Stoup, *Letters from the Pacific*, 142, 158.

140. Wilson, *If You Survive*, 96–97.

141. John Fitzgerald Oral History, EC, 10.

142. Robert Healey Oral History, EC, 6.

143. Charles Henne Questionnaire, 10.

144. George Miller to Mrs. Miller, July 29, 1944, George Miller File, 35th Infantry Division, USAMHI.

145. Morin, *Among the Valiant,* 84.

146. Gantter, *Roll Me Over,* 159.

147. Easton, *Love and War,* 292.

148. Quoted in Tapert, *Lines of Battle,* 156–157.

149. Huebner, *Long Walk,* 59.

150. W. Mark Durley Questionnaire, Americal Division, USAMHI, 17.

151. Mauriello and Regan, *From Boston to Berlin,* 82.

152. Quoted in Parillo, *We Were in the Big One,* 245.

153. Ron Bergengren to Don Anderson, July 2, 1943, in Stevens, *Letters from the Front,* 146–148. Other examples can be found in Tapert, *Lines of Battle,* 25;

154. Quoted in Tapert, *Lines of Battle,* 147.

155. Barnett Hoffner Oral History, EC, 2.

156. Huebner, *Long Walk,* 154.

157. For example, during Operation Market-Garden in Holland, some British troops stopped for tea at a crucial point. See Stephen E. Ambrose, *Citizen Soldiers* (New York: Simon and Schuster, 1997), 129.

158. Bergerud, *Touched with Fire,* 494–499.

159. William J. Hoelzel Questionnaire, Americal Division, USAMHI, 17.

160. Baird, "Opportunity to Meet," 310.

161. Martin, *GI War,* 260.

162. On this situation, see Schrijvers, *GI War Against Japan,* 49–59, 135, 144–146, 73–76.

163. George F. Botjer, *Sideshow War: The Italian Campaign, 1943–1945* (College Station: Texas A&M Univ. Press, 1996), 116–122.

164. Huebner, *Long Walk,* 38. See also Robert M. Hill and Elizabeth Craig Hill, *In the Wake of War: Memoirs of an Alabama Military Government Officer in World War II Italy* (Tuscaloosa: Univ. of Alabama Press, 1982).

165. Murphy, *To Hell and Back,* 27–28.

166. Martin, *GI War,* 71.

167. John Hersey, *A Bell for Adano* (New York: Alfred A. Knopf, 1944, 1967), vi–vii.

168. Edward G. Jones Jr. Oral History, EC, 10–11.

169. George Madison Oral History, EC, 4.

170. Elevitch, *Dog Tags,* 84–85.

171. Wilson, *If You Survive,* 225–226.

172. Quoted in Parillo, *We Were in the Big One,* 246–247.

173. Gantter, *Roll Me Over,* 71.

174. One postwar study found statistical evidence of the veterans' disdain for other countries and happiness with home. Robert J. Havighurst, Walter H. Eaton, John W. Baugham, and Ernest W. Burgess, *The American Veteran Back Home* (New York: Longmans, Green, 1951), 221–222, 227–228.

175. Felix Branham Oral History, EC, 3.

176. Cletus Schwab Questionnaire, 37th Infantry Division, USAMHI, 17.

177. *What the Soldier Thinks,* 6, 8.

178. Rosenberg, *Date Which Will Live;* Schrijvers, *GI War Against Japan;* Bergerud, *Touched with Fire;* Gerald F. Linderman, *The World Within War: America's Combat Experience in World War II* (New York: Free Press, 1997), chap. 4; John W. Dower, War *Without Mercy: Race and Power in the Pacific War* (New York: Pantheon Books, 1986) ; George Feifer, *Tennozan: The Battle of Okinawa and the Atomic Bomb* (New York: Ticknor and Fields, 1992); Richard B. Frank, *Downfall: The End of the Imperial Japanese Empire* (New York: Random House, 1999); and John A. Lynn, *Battle: A History of Combat and Culture* (Boulder, Colo.: Westview Press, 2003), chap. 7.

179. The view became more muddy for the troops who participated in the occupation. See, for example, H. Stanley Huff, *Unforgettable Journey: A World War II Memoir* (Fort Wayne, Ind.: Bridgeford Press, 2001), 189–237. See also John W. Dower, *Embracing Defeat: Japan in the Wake of World War II* (New York: W. W. Norton, 1999).

180. *What the Soldier Thinks,* 7, 8–9.

181. For example, Sinatra used "Nazi" as an insult when he was convincing the children not to be bigots in *The House I Live In.*

182. Huebner, *Long Walk.*

183. *What the Soldier Thinks,* 6, 8.

184. Joy, *Sixty Days,* 130–131, 186.

185. William Guarnere Questionnaire, 101st Airborne Division, USAMHI, 5.

186. Victor Fast Oral History, EC, 2.

187. See Deborah E. Lipstadt, *Beyond Belief: The American Press and the Coming of the Holocaust, 1933–1945* (New York: Free Press, 1986).

188. Horace Evers to "Mom and Lou," May 2, 1945, in *War Letters: Extraordinary Correspondence from American Wars,* ed. Andrew Carroll (New York: Scribner, 2001), 275. Other examples are Huff, *Unforgettable Journey,* 242; Parillo, *We Were in the Big One,* 238–240, 252–253; and Perkins, "Impressions of Wartime," 567. The best overall study of American reactions to the camps is Robert H. Abzug, *Inside the Vicious Heart: Americans and the Liberation of Nazi Concentration Camps* (Oxford: Oxford Univ. Press, 1985).

189. Blunt, *Foot Soldier,* 246.

190. Quoted in Tapert, *Lines of Battle*, 239–240.

191. Dwight D. Eisenhower to Bernard Law Montgomery et al., Sept. 12, 1944, SHAEF AG 091-2 (Germany), in Dwight D. Eisenhower, *The Papers of Dwight David Eisenhower: The War Years*, ed. Albert D. Chandler Jr. (Baltimore: Johns Hopkins Univ. Press, 1970), 4:2131–2132. See also Eisenhower to George C. Marshall, Sept. 22, 1944, and Eisenhower to Walter Bedell Smith, Sept. 22, 1944, in Eisenhower, *Papers*, 4:2176–2177; and Earl F. Ziemke, *The U.S. Army in the Occupation of Germany, 1944–1946* (Washington, D.C.: GPO, 1975), 97.

192. Mauriello and Regan, *From Boston to Berlin*, 72.

193. Ziemke, *U.S. Army in the Occupation*, 321–327.

194. Elevitch, *Dog Tags*, 159.

195. See Kennett, *G.I.*, 216–217; and Ziemke, *U.S. Army in Occupation*, 139.

196. Easton, *Love and War*, 224.

# 5. Instants of Excitement and Terror

1. On this phenomenon, see Kindsvatter, *American Soldiers*, 54–55.

2. Kahn, *G.I. Jungle*, 118–119.

3. Bruscino, "Greatest and the Toughest," 56–59.

4. Gurley, *Into the Mountains*, 96.

5. Daniel Webster quoted in John C. McManus, *The Americans at D-Day* (New York: Forge, 2004), 124.

6. *What the Soldier Thinks*, 6, 11.

7. See, for example, Moore, *GI Jews*, 84; and Linderman, *World Within War*, 8.

8. Devon Larson Oral History, EC, 2.

9. Louis Simpson, "Carentan O Carentan," in *The Norton Book of Modern War*, ed. Paul Fussell (New York: W. W. Norton, 1991), 517–519.

10. Paul Curtis to Mitchell Curtis, May 28, 1944, in *War Letters: Extraordinary Correspondence from American Wars*, ed. Andrew Carroll (New York: Scribner, 2001), 233.

11. For the American replacement system, see Greenfield, Palmer, and Wiley, *Organization of Ground Combat Troops*, 189–195; Ambrose, *Citizen Soldiers*, 273–289; Martin van Creveld, *Fighting Power* (Westport, Conn.: Greenwood Press, 1982); Michael D. Doubler, *Closing with the Enemy: How GIs Fought the War in Europe, 1944–1945* (Lawrence: Univ. Press of Kansas, 1994); Russell F. Weigley, *Eisenhower's Lieutenants* (Bloomington: Indiana Univ. Press), 370–373; and Peter R. Mansoor, *The GI Offensive in Europe: The Triumph of American Infantry Divisions* (Lawrence: Univ. Press of Kansas, 1999).

12. *What the Soldier Thinks*, 5, 4–6.

13. John J. Barnes Oral History, EC, 1.

14. Gantter, *Roll Me Over,* 44–45.

15. Price, *Last Kilometer,* 29.

16. Francis W. Dawson Oral History, EC, 2.

17. Harry Bare Oral History, EC, 2.

18. Ralph Eastridge Oral History, EC, 11.

19. Easton, *Love and War,* 290.

20. Lloyd Dull Questionnaire, 5.

21. Warren E. Pugh to Chief of Chaplains, Mar. 14, 1943, Entry 363, Decimal File 1940–1945, 000.3 Religion, RG 407, NARA II.

22. For a statistical breakdown of the American population by denomination in 1940 and 1945, see *HSUS,* pt. 1, 391–392.

23. James McLeod Questionnaire, 44th Infantry Division, USAMHI, 7.

24. Gurley, *Into the Mountains,* 154.

25. George D. Miller to Mrs. Miller, July 30, 1944, George D. Miller File, 35th Infantry Division, USAMHI.

26. John Fitzgerald Oral History, EC, 7.

27. Blunt, *Foot Soldier,* 74.

28. Martin, *GI War,* 191.

29. William R. Arnold to Aime J. Forand, May 4, 1944, Decimal File 1920–1945, Letters to Congress 032, RG 247, NARA II. Klaus Huebner also came to describe himself as a "superstitious foxhole Christian." Huebner, *Long Walk,* 130.

30. John Fitzgerald Oral History, EC, 1.

31. Hyman Haas Oral History, EC, 7.

32. Quoted in Shelton, *Climb to Conquer,* 132.

33. Blunt, *Foot Soldier,* 88.

34. Gantter, *Roll Me Over,* 52.

35. Francis Gigliotti Questionnaire, 4th Infantry Division, USAMHI, 7.

36. Salve Matheson Questionnaire, 101st Airborne Division, USAMHI, 7.

37. Carl Howard Cartledge Questionnaire, 101st Airborne Division, USAMHI, 7.

38. Quoted in Chaplain Sterling Wheeler to William Arnold, May 8, 1944, Decimal File 1920–1945, 000.3 Religion, RG 247, NARA II. The officers involved in this particular letter were from the Army Air Forces.

39. John Carey Questionnaire, Americal Division, USAMHI, 5.

40. Quoted in Tapert, *Lines of Battle,* 182.

41. Lyle Groundwater Oral History, EC, 7.

42. Max Feldman Oral History, EC, 2. Both Feldman and DeLuca survived the war and remained friends.

43. Kindsvatter, *American Soldiers,* 113–117.

44. Charles Henne Questionnaire, 13. The figures were no doubt skewed by the reporting, but chaplains reported that the attendance for religious services during the war topped two hundred million men. See "Report on Conditions of Military Service, Religious Services, World War II," Section VII Special Services (5), Box 60, President's Commission on Veterans' Pensions Papers, DDE.

45. Murphy Foret Questionnaire, 37th Infantry Division, USAMHI, 7.

46. Donald Frederick Questionnaire, 101st Airborne Division, USAMHI, 7.

47. James Mayes Questionnaire, 35th Infantry Division, USAMHI, 7.

48. Kahn, *G.I. Jungle,* 132–133.

49. Quoted in Morale Report, Church and Religion, Office of the Chief Base Censor, Dec. 1, 1943, Decimal File 1920–1945, 000.3 Religion, RG 247, NARA II.

50. Theodore Aufort Oral History, EC, 5.

51. Ibid., 6.

52. Later on Boccafogli said the other soldier's name may have been Hernandez. Edward Boccafogli Oral History, EC, 6.

53. Felix Branham Oral History, EC, 14.

54. Sam Jacks Oral History, EC, 11.

55. Joy, *Sixty Days,* 105.

56. Ibid., 245.

57. Gantter, *Roll Me Over,* 137.

58. Quoted in Shelton, *Climb to Conquer,* 162.

59. Blunt, *Foot Soldier,* 79.

60. Donald Carl Chumley Oral History, EC, 3.

61. Willie Roy Copeland Oral History, EC, 6.

62. Victor Fast Oral History, EC, 3.

63. William Harness Oral History, EC, 6.

64. Joseph S. Blaylock Oral History, EC, 6.

65. *What the Soldier Thinks,* 15, 1–2.

66. Kindsvatter, *American Soldiers,* 175. See his chapter 6 on this point.

67. Jack Gray Oral History, EC, 20.

68. Kahn, *G.I. Jungle,* 121–122.

69. David Jones Oral History, EC, 3.

70. Gray, *Warriors,* 43.

71. Ralph R. Burnett Oral History, EC, 2.

72. Salvatore DeGaetano Questionnaire, 1st Cavalry Division, USAMHI, 7.

73. Joy, *Sixty Days,* 160.

74. O'Donnell, *Into the Rising Sun,* 164.

75. Ellis Laborde Interview, EC, 1.

76. Huebner, *Long Walk,* 148–149.

77. O'Donnell, *Into the Rising Sun,* 166.

78. Lyle Groundwater Oral History, EC, 8.

79. William Guarnere Interview, EC, 14.

80. Blunt, *Foot Soldier,* 176.

81. Ibid., 231.

82. William U'Ren Questionnaire, 5.

83. Quoted in MacGregor, *Integration of the Armed Forces,* 50–51.

84. Ibid., 51.

85. See Greenfield, Palmer, and Wiley, *Organization of Ground Combat Troops,* 243–244; Weigley, *Eisenhower's Lieutenants,* 568–571; Lee, *Employment of Negro Troops,* 688–704; MacGregor, *Integration of the Armed Forces,* 51–56; and Marvin E. Fletcher, *America's First Black General: Benjamin O. Davis, Sr., 1880–1970* (Lawrence: Univ. Press of Kansas, 1989), 137–141. A useful study of one such integrated platoon is David P. Colley, *Blood for Dignity: The Story of the First Integrated Combat Unit in the U.S. Army* (New York: St. Martin's Press, 2003).

86. Army Information and Education Division Report No. B-157, "Opinions About Negro Infantry Platoons in White Companies of 7 Divisions," July 3, 1945, 1–3, HST, online at http://www.trumanlibrary.org.

87. R. J. Lindo Oral History, EC, 3.

88. Price, *Last Kilometer,* 131.

89. J. Kevin Hastings Questionnaire, 44th Infantry Division, USAMHI.

90. Richard O'Brien Questionnaire.

91. "Opinions About Negro Infantry Platoons," 6.

92. Donald Malarkey Questionnaire, 101st Airborne Division, USAMHI, 5.

93. One example of this sort of thinking can be found in Moore, *GI Jews,* 72–73.

94. John F. Huntley Questionnaire, 4th Infantry Division, USAMHI, 5.

95. Robert C. Byrd to Theodore Bilbo, Dec. 11, 1945, quoted in Smith, *When Jim Crow,* 225.

96. Thomas A. Bruscino Jr., "The Analogue of Work: Memory and Motivation for World War II Soldiers," paper presented at the Society for Military History Conference, The Citadel, Charleston, S.C., Feb. 24–27, 2005; and Thomas E. Rodgers, "Billy Yank and G.I. Joe: An Exploratory Essay on the Sociopolitical Dimensions of Soldier Motivation," *Journal of Military History* 69 (Jan. 2005): 93–121.

97. Casimer Prunchunas quoted in Parillo, *We Were in the Big One,* 81.

98. See Dower, *War Without Mercy,* 64–66.

99. Kindsvatter, *American Soldiers,* 47–54.

100. Lindley R. Higgins Oral History, EC, 8.

101. Gurley, *Into the Mountains,* 102.

102. Easton, *Love and War,* 312.

103. Memorial Day Service, 25th Infantry Division, Apr. 20, 1943, Entry 360, Decimal File 1943–1945, 000.3, RG 407, NARA II.

104. Easton, *Love and War,* 313–314.

105. Stoup, *Letters from the Pacific,* 79.

106. Roland B. Gittelsohn, "Memorial Address on Iwo Jima," in Herrick and Askwith, *This Way to Unity,* 359–361. For a slightly different version, see Dudziak, *Cold War Civil Rights,* 10.

107. See Moore, "Worshipping Together"; and Deborah Dash Moore, "Jewish GIs and the Creation of the Judeo-Christian Tradition," *Religion and American Culture* 8 (Winter 1998): 44–46.

108. Joy, *Sixty Days,* xi.

109. William Kennedy Questionnaire, 35th Infantry Division, USAMHI, 18.

110. Quoted in Tapert, *Lines of Battle,* 156–157.

111. John B. Ellery Oral History, EC, 6. See also Gray, *Warriors,* 44.

112. Walter Schuette to Anna Mary Schuette, Dec. 21, 1943, in *War Letters: Extraordinary Correspondence from American Wars,* ed. Andrew Carroll (New York: Scribner, 2001), 227.

113. William McGurn Questionnaire, 11th Airborne Division, USAMHI, 17.

114. William Thibodeaux Questionnaire, 2nd Armored Division, USAMHI, 17.

115. Hoffmann, *Zone of the Interior,* 84–86.

116. Caesar Abate Questionnaire, 17.

117. William Weber Questionnaire, 11th Airborne Division, USAMHI, 17.

118. Ira Gross Questionnaire, 11th Airborne Division, USAMHI, 17.

119. Quoted in Tapert, *Lines of Battle,* 295.

120. Floyd Todd Questionnaire, 37th Infantry Division, USAMHI, 17.

121. John Carey Questionnaire, 17.

122. George Christenson Questionnaire, Americal Division, USAMHI, 17.

123. Richard Cohen Questionnaire, Americal Division, USAMHI, 17.

124. William Shiepe Questionnaire, Americal Division, USAMHI, 17.

125. John Stannard Questionnaire, Americal Division, USAMHI, 17.

126. John Sandidge Questionnaire, 1st Cavalry Division, USAMHI, 17.

127. John Savarino Questionnaire, 1st Cavalry Division, USAMHI, 17.

128. William L. Rape Questionnaire, 2nd Armored Division, USAMHI, 5.

129. Merritt Bragdon Questionnaire, 17.

130. Donald Eastlake Questionnaire, 2nd Armored Division, USAMHI, 17.

131. Hollis Stabler Questionnaire, 17.

132. William Lee Questionnaire, 4th Infantry Division, USAMHI, 17.

133. Lawrence Ostling Questionnaire, 44th Infantry Division, USAMHI, 17.

134. J. Kevin Hastings Questionnaire.

135. Carl Howard Cartledge Questionnaire, 17.

136. Salve Matheson Questionnaire, 17.

137. John Brandon Price Questionnaire, 101st Airborne Division, USAMHI, 17.

138. Quoted in Tapert, *Lines of Battle,* 164.

139. James Graff Questionnaire, 17.

140. Richard O'Brien Questionnaire.

141. Lloyd Dull Questionnaire, 17.

142. George Melochick Questionnaire, 35th Infantry Division, USAMHI, 17.

143. James Bross Questionnaire, 35th Infantry Division, USAMHI, 17.

144. Murphy, *To Hell and Back,* 273.

145. Kensinger Jones Questionnaire, 17.

## 6. Coming Home, Taking Over

1. Severo and Milford, *Wages of War,* 229–279; and William Pyrle Dillingham, *Federal Aid to Veterans, 1917–1941* (Gainesville: Univ. of Florida Press, 1952).

2. Quoted in Van Ells, *To Hear Only Thunder Again,* 28.

3. Edward T. McCaffrey Talk, June 3, 1945, President's Personal File 1577, Box 528, Harry S. Truman Papers, HST.

4. Roger Daniels, *The Bonus March: An Episode in the Great Depression* (Westport, Conn: Greenwood Press, 1971); and Donald J. Lisio, *The President and Protest: Hoover, Conspiracy, and the Bonus Riot* (Columbia: Univ. of Missouri Press, 1974). A newer study must be used with care: Paul Dickson and Thomas B. Allen, *The Bonus Army: An American Epic* (New York: Walker, 2004). See also Keene, *Doughboys,* 179–198; and Stephen R. Ortiz, "The 'New Deal' for Veterans: The Economy Act, the Veterans of Foreign Wars, and the Origins of New Deal Dissent," *Journal of Military History* 70 (Apr. 2006): 415–438.

5. Executive Order, May 1933, Veterans, Box 54, Louis Howe Papers, FDR.

6. Samuel I. Rosenman, *Working with Roosevelt* (New York: Harper and Brothers, 1952), 394.

7. Throughout the 1930s, Roosevelt opposed the paying out of bonuses early. Ross, *Preparing for Ulysses,* 17–33.

8. Dixon Wecter, *When Johnny Comes Marching Home* (Cambridge, Mass: Riverside Press, 1944), 477–558; Willard Waller, *The Veteran Comes Back* (New York: Dryden Press, 1944); Alanson H. Edgerton, *Readjustment or Revolution?* (New York: McGraw-Hill, 1946); Edward A. Strecker and Kenneth E. Appel, *Psychiatry in Modern Warfare* (New York: Macmillan, 1945), 59–82; Walter H. Eaton, "Research on Veterans' Readjustment," *American Journal of Sociology* 51 (Mar. 1946): 483–487; John F. Cuber, "Family Readjustment of Veterans," *Marriage and Family Living* 7 (May 1945): 28–30; Arthur E. Easterbrook, "Reconversion of Men: Restoring the Veteran's Individuality," *Vital Speeches of the Day* 11 (Aug. 1, 1945): 610–612; and Wilbur B. Brookover, "The Adjustment of Veterans to Civilian Life," *American Sociological Review* 10 (Oct. 1945): 579–586.

9. Joseph C. Goulden, *The Best Years, 1945–1950* (New York: Atheneum, 1976), 38–39; and Jack Goodman, ed., *While You Were Gone: A Report on Wartime Life in the United States* (New York: Simon and Schuster, 1946).

10. Correspondence among the president, Congressman Robert Ramspeck, Malcolm Kerlin, and William McReynolds, Feb.–Apr. 1944, quotation from McReynolds to Kerlin, Apr. 7, 1944, Veterans Preferences, Box 9, William McReynolds Papers, FDR.

11. Ross, *Preparing for Ulysses;* Gambone, *Greatest Generation Comes Home;* Olson, *G.I. Bill,* 3–24; Bennett, *When Dreams Came True,* 1–180; Mettler, *Soldiers to Citizens;* Theodore R. Mosch, *The G.I. Bill: A Breakthrough in Educational and Social Policy in the United States* (Hicksville, N.Y.: Exposition Press, 1975); Theda Skocpol, "The G.I. Bill and U.S. Social Policy, Past and Future," *Social Philosophy and Policy* 14 (Summer 1997): 95–115; Lisio, "United States," 38–55; Keene, *Doughboys,* 205–214; and Milton Greenberg, *The GI Bill: The Law that Changed America* (New York: Lickle, 1997).

12. Kathleen Frydl maintains that the decentralized administration of the bill—what she calls its "congressional federalism"—led to some localities denying benefits to African Americans. Frydl, "G.I. Bill." See also Onkst, "First a Negro," 517–543. Margot Canaday argues that consistent pressure from the VA led to the denial of GI bill benefits to those discharged from the military for homosexuality. With the GI bill such a key federal policy for rewarding those who fulfilled their civic duty by serving, the blatant omission of this one group explicitly made it the position of the federal government that homosexuality and American citizenship were not compatible. Canaday, "Building a Straight State," 939. On that point she is correct. The importance of excluding the relatively small numbers of individuals discharged for homosexuality only reinforces the idea that to define oneself as an American meant one needed to be included under the GI bill (veteran)

tent. Despite the exclusion of homosexuals, that tent was remarkably broad and inclusive.

13. David Saposs to Samuel Rosenman, Oct. 10, 1944, Seniority Rights for Veterans, Box 16, Samuel Rosenman Papers, FDR.

14. Lawrence Westbrook to Harry Hopkins, Sept. 25, 1944, Veterans, Box 229, Harry Hopkins Papers, FDR. See also Cyril O. Houle, Elbert W. Burr, Thomas H. Hamilton, and John R. Yale, *The Armed Services and Adult Education* (Washington, D.C.: American Council on Education, 1947); and Robert E. Sherwood, *Roosevelt and Hopkins: An Intimate History* (New York: Harper and Brothers, 1948), 75–76, 86–87.

15. See the responses to question 49b, "What was your opinion in August, 1945, on the use of the Atomic Bomb?" and 49c, "Has that opinion since changed? If so, how?" of the USAMHI World War II questionnaire. Overwhelmingly the men responded that the bomb ended the war and saved lives, and their opinion had not really changed. For a frank and somewhat crass version of this view, see Paul Fussell, *Thank God for the Atom Bomb, and Other Essays* (New York: Summit Books, 1988).

16. *What the Soldier Thinks*, 5, 11. See also Saxe, *Settling Down*, 12–51.

17. R. Alton Lee, "The Army 'Mutiny' of 1946," *Journal of American History* 53 (Dec. 1966): 556–557.

18. Hoffmann, *Zone of the Interior*, 109.

19. Lee, "Army 'Mutiny,'" 562–571.

20. Henry Novak quoted in Parillo, *We Were in the Big One*, 244–245.

21. Kelly, *One Man's War*, 179.

22. Peters, *For You*, 76.

23. Quoted in Tapert, *Lines of Battle*, 232–233.

24. American Historical Association, *What Will Your Town Be Like?* EM 33, GI Roundtable (Washington, D.C.: AHA, 1945); American Historical Association, *Shall I Go Back to School?* EM 34, GI Roundtable (Washington, D.C.: AHA, 1945); American Historical Association, *Will There Be Work for All?* EM 22, GI Roundtable (Washington, D.C.: AHA, 1944); American Historical Association, *Why Do Veterans Organize?* EM 6, GI Roundtable (Washington, D.C.: AHA, 1946); American Historical Association, *Is Your Health the Nation's Business?* EM 29, GI Roundtable (Washington, D.C.: AHA, 1946); American Historical Association, *What Shall We Do with Our Merchant Fleet?* EM 25, GI Roundtable (Washington, D.C.: AHA, 1946); and American Historical Association, *Will There Be a Plane in Every Garage?* EM 37, GI Roundtable (Washington, D.C.: AHA, 1945).

25. Easton, *Love and War*, 370.

26. Morin, *Among the Valiant*, 277.

27. Van Ellis, *To Hear Only Thunder,* 57–83.

28. William Harness Oral History, EC, 13.

29. O'Donnell, *Into the Rising Sun,* 290.

30. Alfred Allred Oral History, EC, 9.

31. David A. Gerber, "Heroes and Misfits: The Troubled Social Reintegration of Disabled Veterans of World War II in *The Best Years of Our Lives,*" in *Disabled Veterans in History,* ed. David A. Gerber (Ann Arbor: Univ. of Michigan Press, 2000), 70–91.

32. Edward Myers to the President, July 22, 1945, Official File 190-A 1945, Box 801, Harry S. Truman Papers, HST.

33. Russell Thirlaway to the President, July 17, 1945, Official File 190-A 1945, Box 801, Harry S. Truman Papers, HST.

34. Hoffmann, *Zone of the Interior,* 115.

35. Blunt, *Foot Soldier,* 259.

36. Quoted in O'Donnell, *Into the Rising Sun,* 173.

37. Examples include the China-Burma-India Veterans Association, which put out a monthly magazine called *Ex-CBI Roundup.* The Flying Tigers of the 14th Air Force Association published the *Jing Bao Journal.* Professor Donald Jordan generously shared private copies of these two publications from his family records. A less professional but very thorough example was the homemade newsletter of the Twenty-seventh Cavalry Reconnaissance Troop, *Troop Revue,* included in Arnold Gates to the President, Feb. 17, 1952, Official File 190-A 1948–1953 (2 of 3), Box 803, Harry S. Truman Papers, HST.

38. When representatives of the Jewish War Veterans met with President Eisenhower in 1958, they said that most of their 102,000 members were also members of the other major groups. Earle Chesney to Ann Whitman, May 28, 1958, Ann Whitman File, DDE Diary Series, May 1958 Staff Notes (1), Box 32, Dwight D. Eisenhower Papers, DDE.

39. As opposed to the still dominant northern veterans of the American Civil War and their major organization, the Grand Army of the Republic.

40. John Carey Questionnaire, 17.

41. William Weber Questionnaire, 17.

42. William Lee Questionnaire, 17.

43. Columbia Chapter, United Negro and Allied Veterans of America to the President, July 22, 1946, Official File 190-A Aug–Dec 1946 (1 of 2), Box 802, Harry S. Truman Papers, HST.

44. Easton, *Love and War,* 249.

45. A celebratory in-house history is Richard W. Flanagan, *AMVETS: 50 Years of Proud Service to America's Veterans* (Lanham, Md.: AMVETS National Headquarters, 1994).

46. Robert L. Tyler, "The American Veterans Committee: Out of the Hot War and into the Cold," *American Quarterly* 18 (Autumn 1966): 419–436; and Robert Francis Saxe, "'Citizens First, Veterans Second': The American Veterans Committee and the Challenge of Postwar 'Independent Progressives,'" *War and Society* 22 (Oct. 2004): 75–94. On the AVC and some of its early debates about direction, see the correspondence in American Veterans Committee, Box 1, Joseph Lash Papers, FDR. For the general background on the VFW, American Legion, DAV, AVC, and AMVETS, see Minott, *Peerless Patriots;* Van Ellis, *To Hear Only Thunder,* 83–89; Rumer, *American Legion;* Bottoms, *VFW;* and Sam Savisky, "Where Does the Veteran Stand Today?" American Academy of Political and Social Science *Annals* 259 (Sept. 1948): 128–135.

47. Herman Miles Somers, *Presidential Agency: Office of War Mobilization and Reconversion* (Cambridge: Harvard Univ. Press, 1950); and Jack Stokes Ballard, *The Shock of Peace: Military and Economic Demobilization after World War II* (Washington, D.C.: Univ. Press of America, 1983).

48. Charles Abrams, *The Future of Housing* (New York: Harper and Brothers, 1946); and Robert Lasch, *Breaking the Building Blockade* (Chicago: Univ. of Chicago Press, 1946).

49. "Surveys of Housing of World War II Veterans and Dwelling Unit Vacancy and Occupancy in the Erie Area, Pennsylvania," "Everett Area, Washington," "Madison Area, Wisconsin," Greater San Antonio, Texas," and "Henderson, Kentucky," compiled by the Bureau of the Census, Housing for Vets, Box 52, Isidor Lubin Papers, FDR.

50. "This Quarter's Polls," *Public Opinion Quarterly* 10 (Summer 1946): 257.

51. See correspondence with Congressmen Jerry Voorhis of California, George H. Fallon of Maryland, and John Lesinski of Michigan, Nov.–Dec. 1945, Official File 190-A 1945, Box 801, Harry S. Truman Papers, HST; and Correspondence with Congressman John McMillan of South Carolina, and general correspondence from January–July 1946, Official File 190-A Jan–July 1946 (3 of 3), Box 801, Harry S. Truman Papers, HST.

52. E. L. Bartlett to the President, Dec. 21, 1945, Official File 190-A Jan–July 1946 (1 of 3), Box 801, Harry S. Truman Papers, HST.

53. Harry S. Truman to Wilson Wyatt, Dec. 12, 1945, Official File 190-A 1945, Box 801, Harry S. Truman Papers, HST.

54. Statement by the President, Feb. 28, 1946, Official File 190-A Jan–July 1946 (1 of 3), Box 801, Harry S. Truman Papers, HST.

55. *Veterans Journal,* May 15, 1946, Official File 190-A Jan–July 1946 (2 of 3), Box 801, Harry S. Truman Papers, HST.

56. Stuart Chase, *For This We Fought* (New York: Twentieth Century Fund, 1946), 5.

57. Tunnell-Truman Correspondence, September–November 1946, Official File 190-A Aug–Dec 1946 (1 of 2), Box 802, Harry S. Truman Papers, HST. See also James McCaffrey, "State Democrats Offer Housing Aid," *NYT,* Sept. 3, 1946, 9.

58. "Memo to Congress," *American Legion Magazine,* July 1946, 6.

59. Robert J. Donovan, *Conflict and Crisis: The Presidency of Harry S. Truman, 1945–1948* (New York: W. W. Norton, 1977), 230.

60. On the election of 1946 and the Roosevelt coalition, see Boylan, *New Deal Coalition,* 71–190; Jeffries, *Testing the Roosevelt Coalition,* 206–258; Lubell, *Future of American Politics;* Burnham, *Critical Elections,* 54–70; Allswang, *New Deal,* 128–131; Alonzo L. Hamby, *Man of the People: A Life of Harry S. Truman* (New York: Oxford Univ. Press, 1995), 381–386; Donovan, *Conflict and Crisis,* 229–238. See also the useful statistics in Paul T. David, *Party Strength in the United States, 1872–1970* (Charlottesville: Univ. Press of Virginia, 1972).

61. "Five 'Imponderables' That Keep Experts Guessing," *NYT,* Oct. 26, 1952, E3.

62. Alan Brinkley, *The End of Reform: New Deal Liberalism in Recession and War* (New York: Alfred A. Knopf, 1995). See also Edwin Amenta and Theda Skocpol, "Redefining the New Deal: World War II and the Development of Social Provision in the United States," in *The Politics of Social Policy in the United States,* by Margaret Weir, Ann Shola Orloff, and Theda Skocpol (Princeton, N.J.: Princeton Univ. Press, 1988), 81–122.

63. Men who entered the service at a younger age, regardless of socioeconomic background, tended to readjust easier than veterans who entered the service later in life. Glen H. Elder Jr., "War Mobilization and the Life Course: A Cohort of World War II Veterans," *Sociological Forum* 2 (Summer 1987): 449–472.

64. *HSUS,* pt. 2, 1145; and *Historical Statistics of the Veteran Population, 1865–1960—A Compendium of Facts About Veterans* (Washington, D.C.: GPO, 1961).

65. Peters, *For You,* 4.

66. Quoted in Tapert, *Lines of Battle,* 17. On a later survey, many of the men answered the question of what they wanted to do when they came home with some variation of "expected to get married." Question 58a, World War II Questionnaire, USAMHI.

67. Murphy, *To Hell and Back,* 273.

68. Wilson, *If You Survive,* 266.

69. Robert D. Grove and Alice M. Hetzel, *Vital Statistics Rates in the United States, 1940–1960* (Washington, D.C.: GPO, 1968), 59, 102–109. Surprisingly, one study found that the hasty marriages of veterans during the war years lasted about as well as the marriages of nonveterans in the same time frame. The postwar marriages of World War II veterans had significantly lower divorce rates than nonveterans. For reasons that are as yet unclear, Korean war veterans had much higher divorce rates. See William Ruger, Sven E. Wilson, and Shawn L. Waddoups, "Warfare and Welfare: Military Service, Combat, and Marital Dissolution," *Armed Forces and Society* 29 (Fall 2002): 85–107.

70. Quoted in Tapert, *Lines of Battle,* 232–233.

71. Kelly, *One Man's War,* 132.

72. See Karen Anderson, *Wartime Women: Sex Roles, Family Relations, and the Status of Women during World War II* (Westport, Conn: Greenwood Press, 1981); Doris Weatherford, *American Women in World War II* (New York: Facts on File, 1990); Susan M. Hartmann, *The Home Front and Beyond: American Women in the 1940s* (Boston: Twayne, 1982); and Elaine Tyler May, *Homeward Bound: American Families in the Cold War Era* (New York: Basic Books, 1988).

73. *Historical Statistics of the Veteran Population,* 25.

74. Veterans Employment Service, *Keeping Pace with Veteran Employment,* U.S. Department of Labor, July 1948–June 1949, Official File 15m, Veterans Employment Service, Box 115, Harry S. Truman Papers, HST.

75. Kelly, *One Man's War,* 179.

76. Ted Claire to the President, Oct. 22, 1945, Official File 190-A 1945, Box 801, Harry S. Truman Papers, HST.

77. Morin, *Among the Valiant,* 278.

78. S. J. McGuinness to the President, Apr. 25, 1947, Official File 190-A 1947 (1 of 3), Box 802, Harry S. Truman Papers, HST.

79. President's Commission on Veterans' Pensions (Bradley Commission), *Veterans in Our Society: Data on the Conditions of Military Service and on the Status of the Veteran* (Washington, D.C.: GPO, 1956), 105.

80. Shelton, *Climb to Conquer,* 155–156, 183.

81. Perkins, "Impressions of Wartime," 564.

82. Hoffmann, *Zone of the Interior,* 121.

83. Harry Stein, *The Girl Watchers Club: Lessons from the Battlefields of Life* (New York: HarperCollins, 2004), xxv.

84. Norman Alexandroff, "A Comparison of World War II Veterans and Nonveterans in Social and Personal Adjustment," June 1945, Official File 190-A 1945, Box 801, Harry S. Truman Papers, HST.

85. A limited study at the University of Wisconsin was Svend Riemer, "Married Veterans Are Good Students," *Marriage and Family Living* 9 (Feb. 1947): 11–12. The most important and widespread study was Norman Frederiksen and W. B. Schrader, *Adjustment to College: A Study of 10,000 Veteran and Nonveteran Students in Sixteen American Colleges* (Princeton, N.J.: Educational Testing Service, 1951).

86. Bradley Commission, *Veterans in Our Society,* 105. There is a debate about how many of these men would have attended college without World War II service and the GI bill. The consensus seems to be most of them, but that debate is irrelevant to the straightforward point here that veterans had on average more education than nonveterans. See Olson, *G.I. Bill,* 101–111; and Frederikson and Schrader, *Adjustment to College,* 321.

87. Rex A. Skidmore, Therese L. Smith, and Delbert L. Nye, "Characteristics of Married Veterans," *Marriage and Family Living* 11 (Aug. 1949): 102–104.

88. Quoted in Olson, *G.I. Bill,* 109.

89. Bradley Commission, *Veterans in Our Society,* 106.

90. The details varied from locale to locale—one comparison of veterans and nonveterans from the Midwest in 1949 found very little difference in earnings—but the overall trend was clearly in favor of the veterans. Havighurst et al., *American Veteran Back Home,* 235–264.

91. Bradley Commission, *Veterans in Our Society,* 100–101. In 1994, economists Joshua Angrist and Alan B. Krueger used "an implemented variables strategy that exploits the relationship between date of birth and veteran status" to come to the conclusion that "World War II veterans earn no more than comparable nonveterans, and may well learn less." "Why Do World War II Veterans Earn More than Nonveterans?" *Journal of Labor Economics* 12 (Jan. 1994): 74–97. The modifier "comparable"—including the statistical gymnastics used to get a specific group of nonveterans to "comparable" status—and the use of census data beginning with 1960 (after the large earnings disparities of the 1950s) discredit that conclusion. World War II veterans earned more than nonveterans, in part because they were a selected group (albeit a huge one), in part because of their service, and in part because of the benefits they received after the war.

92. Perkins, "Impressions of Wartime," 564.

93. David Callahan, *Kindred Spirits: Harvard Business School's Extraordinary Class of 1949 and How They Transformed American Business* (Hoboken, N.J.: John Wiley and Sons, 2002).

94. Howard E. Freeman and Morris Showel, "Differential Political Influence of Voluntary Associations," *Public Opinion Quarterly* 15 (Winter 1951–52): 703–714.

95. Donald Jackson and Billy Walker to the President, Aug. 26, 1945, Official File 190-A 1945, Box 801, Harry S. Truman Papers, HST.

96. Terkel, *Good War,* 238–239.

97. Stephen E. Ambrose, *To America: Personal Reflections of an Historian* (New York: Simon and Schuster, 2002); Ambrose, *Citizen Soldiers,* 470–471; Edward M. Coffman, "A Younger Brother of the Greatest Generation," *Register of the Kentucky Historical Society* 100 (Spring 2002): 129–38.

98. William M. Tuttle, *"Daddy's Gone to War": The Second World War in the Lives of America's Children* (New York: Oxford Univ. Press, 1993).

99. Edgar Corry to the President, Feb. 24, 1948, Official File 190-A 1948–53 (2 of 3), Box 803, Harry S. Truman Papers, HST.

100. Bernard Law Montgomery, *The Memoirs of Field-Marshal Montgomery* (Cleveland: World Publishing, 1958), 484.

101. Peters, *For You,* 45.

102. Mrs. Bob Stephenson to the President, Oct. 13, 1956, White House Central Files, General File 125-E World War II (1), Box 926, Dwight D. Eisenhower Papers, DDE.

103. Elevitch, *Dog Tags,* xii.

104. Paul T. David, Malcolm Moos, and Ralph M. Goldman, eds., *The National Story: Presidential Nominating Politics in 1952* (Baltimore: Johns Hopkins Univ. Press, 1954); Angus Campbell, Gerald Gurin, and Warren E. Miller, *The Voter Decides* (Evanston, Ill.: Row, Peterson, 1954); and Alfred De Grazia, *The Western Public: 1952 and Beyond* (Stanford, Calif.: Stanford Univ. Press, 1954). See also Heinz Eulau, *Class and Party in the Eisenhower Years: Class Roles and Perspectives in the 1952 and 1956 Elections* (New York: Free Press, 1962).

105. Reference to telegram of Sept. 10, 1952, Ann Whitman File, Campaign Series–Veterans, Box 7, Dwight D. Eisenhower Papers, DDE.

106. See the memos of meetings from Earle Chesney to Ann Whitman, Oct. 3–24, 1956, Ann Whitman File, DDE Diary Series, October 1956 Diary Staff Memos, Box 19, Dwight D. Eisenhower Papers, DDE.

107. See, for example, the comparison of the appearances of Stevenson and Eisenhower before the American Legion in 1952 in James Hagerty, "Stevenson Denounces Use of 'Patriotism' as a Club," *NYT,* Aug. 28, 1952, 1.

108. *Biographical Dictionary of the United States Congress, 1774–Present,* http://bioguide.congress.gov/. On Kennedy, see Saxe, *Settling Down,* 53–82.

109. Goulden, *Best Years,* 229.

110. Those who gathered these statistics recognized that women were eligible for political office but chose to acknowledge the reality that men dominated national political office at the time. As the source of this statistic noted, "If women were included among those eligible, the disproportion [in favor of veterans] would be even more striking." Albert Somit and Joseph Tanenhaus, "The Veteran in the Electoral Process: The House of Representatives," *Journal of Politics* 19 (May 1957): 184–201.

111. William T. Bianco and Jamie Markham, "Vanishing Veterans: The Decline of Military Experience in the U.S. Congress," in *Soldiers and Civilians: The Civil Military Gap and American National Security,* ed. Peter D. Feaver and Richard H. Kohn (Cambridge, Mass: MIT Press, 2001), 275–287.

112. See the correspondence in White House Central Files, General File 132 Veterans Day, Box 1035, Dwight D. Eisenhower Papers, DDE.

113. Havighurst et al., *American Veteran Back Home,* 2.

114. Memo for Gen. Vaughn, July 16, 1947, Official File 190-A 1947 (3 of 3), Box 803, Harry S. Truman Papers, HST.

115. Clyde Steelman to the President, Apr. 7, 1948, Official File 190-A 1948–53 (1 of 3), Box 803, Harry S. Truman Papers, HST (typos in the original).

116. Roland Johnson to the President, Apr. 18, 1949, Official File 190-A 1948–53 (1 of 3), Box 803, Harry S. Truman Papers, HST.

117. "U.S. 'Phony' Excuses on Housing Decried," *NYT*, Feb. 26, 1947, 34.

118. See the correspondence in Official File 190-A 1947, 1948–1953, Boxes 802–803, Harry S. Truman Papers, HST; and the letters in D. M. Giangreco and Kathryn Moore, *Dear Harry . . . : Truman's Mailroom, 1945–1953* (Mechanicsburg, Pa.: Stackpole Books, 1999), 102–104.

119. See the correspondence in Official File 3144, Regular Veterans Association, Box 1750, Harry S. Truman Papers, HST; Clarence Adamy (AMVETS) to the White House, Mar. 16, 1953, White House Central Files, General File 80 Veterans Administration 1952–53 (1), Box 443, Dwight D. Eisenhower Papers, DDE; Omar Ketchum (VFW) to the White House, May 13, 1953, White House Central Files, General File 80 Veterans Administration 1952–53 (1), Box 443, Dwight D. Eisenhower Papers, DDE; and Lewis Gough (American Legion) to the President, Mar. 13, 1953, White House Central Files, General File 20-D-2 Veterans Employment Service, Box 346, Dwight D. Eisenhower Papers, DDE.

120. Memorandum from James Rowe to the Commission on Organization of the Executive Branch of the Government, June 1, 1948, Commission on Organization of the Executive Branch of the Government—Veterans Affairs, Box 65, James Rowe Papers, FDR.

121. Van Ells, *To Hear Only Thunder Again,* 31.

122. The report is abbreviated in *The Hoover Commission Report* (New York: McGraw Hill, n.d.), 359–363. Veterans especially opposed the idea of combining and closing VA hospitals. See correspondence and notes in Ann Whitman File, Ann Whitman Diary Series–January 1955 (3), Box 4, Dwight D. Eisenhower Papers, DDE.

123. Gambone, *Greatest Generation Comes Home,* 38–62. See also Rumer, *American Legion,* and Bottoms, *VFW.*

124. See George Pickett, Albany County Veterans Service Officer to the President and Congress, Jan. 3, 1956, White House Central Files, General File 125-I-I Bradley Commission, Box 932, Dwight D. Eisenhower Papers, DDE; Memo for General Brannon, May 20, 1955, Veterans Letters–Statistics, Box 6, President's Commission on Veterans' Pensions Papers, DDE; Resolutions of the Catholic War Veterans, November 1955, White House Central Files, General File 120 Catholic War Veterans, Box 704, Dwight D. Eisenhower Papers, DDE; and "Analysis of Comments Submitted by Veterans' Organizations and Other Groups in Answer to General Bradley's Letter of March 29, 1955," Indexed Replies Copy 1 (1), Box 8, President's Commission on Veterans' Pensions Papers, DDE.

125. Legislative Leadership Meeting Supplementary Notes, June 27, 1957, Ann Whitman File, DDE Papers as President, Legislative Meetings Series 1957 (3), Box 2, Dwight D. Eisenhower Papers, DDE.

126. See the statements of the American Legion and the VFW in U.S. Senate, Committee on Banking and Currency, *Housing Act of 1954–Hearings* (Washington, D.C.: GPO, 1954), 351–364, 1121–1122.

127. Memorandum from Earle Chesney to Ann Whitman, July 21, 1954, Ann Whitman File, Ann Whitman Diary Series–July 1954 (3), Box 2, Dwight D. Eisenhower Papers, DDE. See also "This Quarter's Polls," *Public Opinion Quarterly* 10 (Winter 1946–47): 642–643; 11 (Spring 1947): 166–167; 11 (Winter 1947–48): 646; and Severo and Milford, *Wages of War,* 283–297.

128. Savisky, "Where Does the Veteran Stand," 135.

129. Leo P. Crespi and G. Schofield Shapleigh, "'The' Veteran—A Myth," *Public Opinion Quarterly* 10 (Aug. 1946): 361–372.

130. Henry Novak quoted in Parillo, *We Were in the Big One,* 245–246.

131. "Operation Veteran," *American Legion Magazine,* Aug. 1946, 6.

132. Joe McCarthy, "GI Vision of a Better America," *NYT,* Aug. 5, 1945, 74.

133. *Yank: The Army Weekly* 2 (Feb. 4, 1944): 14.

134. Statement of Purpose and Aims, Veterans of World War II, Inc., Box 18, Joseph Lash Papers, FDR.

135. Abraham Hertzkl to the President, Mar. 2, 1948, Official File 190-A 1948–53 (1 of 3), Box 803, Harry S. Truman Papers, HST.

136. George Fredman to William Mayer, Jan. 21, 1950, Americanism-Religion-National Conference of Christians and Jews, Microfilm, AL.

137. Higham, *Send These to Me,* 171. See also Nathan Glazer and Reed Ueda, "Prejudice and Discrimination, Policy Against," in *HEAEG,* 853–855.

138. Rabbi Robert Kahn, "Brotherhood Month and the Four Chaplains," Jan. 8, 1960, Americanism-Religion-National Conference of Christians and Jews, Microfilm, AL.

# 7. The New Consensus and Beyond

1. Memo from the AVC, Dec. 24, 1945, Correspondence Veterans, Box 183, James Roosevelt Papers, FDR.

2. American Historical Association, *Can We Prevent Future Wars?* EM 12, GI Roundtable (Washington, D.C: AHA, 1944), 1.

3. Ibid., 13.

4. Harry S. Truman, "An Investment for Peace: Military Program Is a Bulwark Against Communism," *Vital Speeches of the Day* 15 (Sept. 1, 1949): 674–676.

5. Quoted in Savisky, "Where Does the Veteran Stand," 134.

6. For example, John L. Smith (former National Commander of AMVETS) to President-Elect Eisenhower, Nov. 21, 1952, White House Central Files, General File 125-4 Korean Emergency, Box 927, Dwight D. Eisenhower Papers, DDE.

7. On the legion's campaign for UMT, see Rumer, *American Legion,* 289–375 and passim.

8. Regular Veterans Association to the President, Dec. 16, 1948, Official File 190-A 1948–53 (1 of 3), Box 803, Harry S. Truman Papers, HST. See also Regular Veterans Association to U.S. Congress, Nov. 3, 1947, President's Personal File 564, Box 488, Papers of Harry S. Truman, HST.

9. On UMT and Selective Service, see Flynn, *Lewis B. Hershey,* 162–189; Hamby, *Man of the People,* 340, 368–369; Melvyn P. Leffler, *A Preponderance of Power: National Security, the Truman Administration, and the Cold War* (Stanford, Calif.: Stanford Univ. Press, 1992), 209, 223–224; and Walter Millis, ed., *The Forrestal Diaries* (New York: Viking Press, 1951).

10. See the national resolutions in the VFW National Headquarters to the President, Sept. 8, 1949, Sept. 12, 1950, Sept. 27, 1951, and Oct.13, 1952, Official File 84 1949–1953, Boxes 520–521, Harry S. Truman Papers, HST. See also "Resolutions of the 82nd Airborne Division Association," July 4, 1955, White House Central Files, General File 125-C-1 Veterans, Box 927, Dwight D. Eisenhower Papers, DDE; Savisky, "Where Does the Veteran Stand," 131; and the shifting opinion polls on the subject in "This Quarter's Polls," *Public Opinion Quarterly* 9 (Winter 1945–46).

11. Earle Chesney to Ann Whitman, Mar. 20, 25, 1958, Ann Whitman File, DDE Diary Series, Staff Notes March 1958(1), Box 31, Dwight D. Eisenhower Papers, DDE.

12. Mauriello and Regan, *From Boston to Berlin,* 75.

13. See Paul Boyer, *By the Bomb's Early Light: American Thought and Culture at the Dawn of the Atomic Age* (New York: Pantheon Books, 1985); and Allan M. Winkler, *Life Under a Cloud: American Anxiety About the Atom* (New York: Oxford Univ. Press, 1993).

14. W. Mark Durley Questionnaire, 1.

15. William Shiepe Questionnaire, 1.

16. Mark R. Grandstaff, "Making the Military American: Advertising, Reform, and the Demise of an Antistanding Military Tradition, 1945–1955," *Journal of Military History* 60 (Apr. 1996): 299.

17. Ibid., 299–323.

18. Harry S. Truman, *Memoirs,* vol. 2, *Years of Trial and Hope* (Garden City, N.Y.: Doubleday, 1956), 54.

19. Regular Veterans Association to the President, Dec. 16, 1948, Official File 190-A 1948–53 (1 of 3), Box 803, Harry S. Truman Papers, HST.

20. Regular Veterans Association to the Secretary to the President, July 11, 1951, Official File 3144, Box 1750, Harry S. Truman Papers, HST. See also Program, 1953–1954, and Resolutions, 1959–1960, White House Central Files, General

File 120 Regular Veterans Associations, Box 711, Dwight D. Eisenhower Papers, DDE.

21. See the national resolutions in the VFW National Headquarters to the President, Sept. 8, 1949, Sept. 12, 1950, Sept. 27, 1951, and Oct.13, 1952 (the quotation is from the 1952 letter), Official File 84 1949–1953, Boxes 520–521, Harry S. Truman Papers, HST.

22. American Legion Digest of Resolutions for the President, 1954, White House Central Files, General File 120 American Legion 1954, Box 700, Dwight D. Eisenhower Papers, DDE.

23. Resolutions of the Catholic War Veterans, November 1955, White House Central Files, General File 120 Catholic War Veterans, Box 704, Dwight D. Eisenhower Papers, DDE. See also "Catholics to Train Own 'Officer' Unit," *NYT*, July 17, 1948, 28.

24. Minott, *Peerless Patriots*, 70–71.

25. See also Moley, *American Legion Story*, 289–376.

26. On the Liberal Party in New York, see Adolf Berle Speech to Catholic War Veterans, May 6, 1948, Speeches 1948, Box 147, Adolf Berle Papers, FDR.

27. Tyler, "American Veterans Committee," 430–436.

28. David Caute, *The Great Fear: The Anti-Communist Purge Under Truman and Eisenhower* (New York: Simon and Schuster, 1978), 224–226, 586–587 fn. 2; and Polenberg, *One Nation Divisible*, 115–117.

29. David M. Oshinsky, *A Conspiracy So Immense: The World of Joe McCarthy* (New York: Free Press, 1983), 330–332.

30. For a critical view of anticommunism in the Catholic church, see Caute, *Great Fear*, 108–110.

31. Mormino, "Little Italy Goes to War," 378–379.

32. Morawska, "Immigrants, Transnationalism, and Ethnicization," 189–190.

33. Italian-American War Veterans to John W. McCormack, Aug. 15, 1950, President's Personal File 3398, Box 571, Harry S. Truman Papers, HST.

34. Higham, *Send These to Me*, 171–172; Dinnerstein, *Antisemitism*, 164. Only marginalized extremists such as Gerald L. K. Smith persisted in equating anticommunism with anti-Semitism. Oshinsky, *Conspiracy So Immense*, 203–205.

35. See, for example, Daniel Bell, ed., *The Radical Right* (Garden City, N.Y.: Doubleday, 1963); Michael Paul Rogin, *The Intellectuals and McCarthy*; Robert Griffith, *The Politics of Fear: Joseph R. McCarthy and the Senate* (Lexington: Univ. Press of Kentucky, 1970); and Richard M. Fried, *Nightmare in Red: The McCarthy Era in Perspective* (New York: Oxford Univ. Press, 1990). For obvious reasons, Russian Americans remained a quiet group in the 1940s and 1950s and did not seem to suffer any special persecution for their national background. Paul Robert Magocsi, "Russians," in *HEAEG*, 893.

36. William S. White, "Flanders Likens M'Carthy, Hitler," *NYT,* June 2, 1954, 1.

37. Oshinsky, *Conspiracy So Immense,* 205 fn.

38. Peter Viereck argued that McCarthyism was an heir to the anti-elite, anti-intellectual intolerance of the populists of earlier generations; only the latest version proved more ethnically, religiously, and regionally diverse. McCarthy himself served as a conduit between the "sticks," the "hick-Protestant mentalities of the west (Populist-Progressive on the Left, Know-Nothing on the Right)," and the "slums," the "South Boston mentalities in the east," by which Viereck meant immigrants, Catholics, and Jews in the cities. Attempts to understand the trends of the postwar era while ignoring the wartime experience often led to such mental gymnastics. Peter Viereck, "The Revolt Against the Elite," in Bell, *Radical Right,* 135–154. The essay was originally published in 1955 in the earlier edition of the book, *The New American Right.*

39. Caute, *Great Fear,* 21. See also Samuel A. Stouffer, *Communism, Conformity, and Civil Liberties: A Cross-section of the Nation Speaks Its Mind* (Garden City, N.Y.: Doubleday, 1955).

40. Peter Kihss, "Harriman Finds Bias Decreasing," *NYT,* Oct. 31, 1958, 20.

41. "First Chicago Demonstration," 1950, Official File 84 Jan–Aug 1950, Box 521, Harry S. Truman Papers, HST.

42. Peter Filene, "'Cold War Culture' Doesn't Say It All," in *Rethinking Cold War Culture,* ed. Peter J. Kuznick and James Gilbert (Washington, D.C.: Smithsonian Institution Press, 2001), 156–170.

43. Harry S. Truman, "Letter to the Chairman, American Veterans Committee, Concerning Discrimination on Campus," Sept. 4, 1946, *Public Papers,* American Presidency Project online.

44. President's Commission on Higher Education, *Higher Education for American Democracy,* vol. 2, *Equalizing and Expanding Individual Opportunity* (Washington, D.C.: GPO, 1947).

45. "Prejudice and Discrimination, Policy Against," in *HEAEG,* 854; Dinnerstein, *Antisemitism,* 158–159; Perlmann and Waldinger, "Second Generation Decline?" 907.

46. For pictures, see Greenberg, *GI Bill,* 35–59.

47. George Dingledy Questionnaire, Americal Division, USAMHI, 16.

48. Students for Federal World Government to the President, Apr. 27, 1946, Official File 190-A Jan–July 1946 (3 of 3), Box 801, Harry S. Truman Papers, HST.

49. V.B.C. Bulletin, Apr. 9, 1946, Official File 190-A Jan–July 1946 (1 of 3), Box 801, Harry S. Truman Papers, HST.

50. Gordon W. Allport, *The Nature of Prejudice* (Cambridge, Mass: Addison-Wesley, 1954), xiv.

51. G. M. Gilbert, "Stereotype Persistence and Change Among College Students," *Journal of Abnormal and Social Psychology* 46 (1951): 245–254.

52. Van Ellis, *To Hear Only Thunder,* 232–233; Bennett, *When Dreams Came True,* 284–287; *Veterans in the United States—1960* (Washington, D.C.: GPO, 1967), 348–350.

53. Scott Donaldson, *The Suburban Myth* (New York: Columbia Univ. Press, 1969), 3–4.

54. See for example Bennett M. Berger, *Working-Class Suburb: A Study of Auto Workers in Suburbia* (Berkeley and Los Angeles: Univ. of California Press, 1960); and Polenberg, *One Nation Divisible,* 140–145.

55. From May 1951 to April 1952, 28 percent of male veterans moved, while only 14 percent of male nonveteran did. Bradley Commission, *Veterans in Our Society,* 112. Between 1955 and 1960, almost exactly half of the thirteen million World War II veterans moved to new homes. *Veterans in the United States—1960,* 250.

56. Van Ellis, *To Hear Only Thunder,* 60.

57. Baird, "Opportunity to Meet," 318.

58. Bradley Commission, *Veterans in Our Society,* 111.

59. Ibid., 110.

60. *Veterans in the United States—1960,* 249.

61. Horace G. Eakins Diary, 2nd Armored Division Questionnaire Files, USAMHI.

62. Quoted in May, *Homeward Bound,* 141.

63. *Veterans in the United States—1960,* 249. On those areas as centers of suburban growth after the war, see Kenneth T. Jackson, *Crabgrass Frontier: The Suburbanization of the United States* (New York: Oxford Univ. Press, 1985), 231–284.

64. *HSUS,* pt. 1, 116.

65. Ibid.

66. See Lubell, *Future of American Politics,* chap. 4.

67. Allen and Turner, *We the People,* 22.

68. Max Ascoli quoted in Blum, *V Was for Victory,* 154.

69. Mormino, "Little Italy Goes to War," 370–371. For the example of California, see Mormino and Pozzetta, "Ethnics at War," 158; and for the example of Tampa, Florida, see Gary R. Mormino and George E. Pozzetta, *The Immigrant World of Ybor City: Italians and Their Latin Neighbors in Tampa, 1885-1985* (Urbana: Univ. of Illinois Press, 1987), 298–301. For an Italian American urban community that survived suburbanization through this period, see Herbert J. Gans, *The Urban Villagers: Group and Class in the Life of Italian-Americans* (New York: Free Press, 1962); for an Italian and Jewish community, see Jonathan Rieder, *Canarsie: The Jews and Italians of Brooklyn against Liberalism* (Cambridge: Harvard Univ. Press, 1985).

70. Humbert S. Nelli, "Italians," in *HEAEG,* 559.

71. Arthur A. Goren, "Jews," 592–593; Ulf Beijbom, "Swedes," 980; M. Mark Stolarik, "Slovaks," 934; Peter A. Munch, "Norwegians," 760; Paula Benkart, "Hungarians,"

470–471; Karen Johnson Freeze, "Czechs," 270–272; and Theodore Saloutos, "Greeks," all in *HEAEG,* 438–440.

72. Victor Greene, "Poles," in *HEAEG,* 802.

73. Dinnerstein, *Antisemitism,* 157.

74. See Housing Expediter records, Boxes 49–52, 58, 61 Political Series, Wilson Wyatt Papers, KL.

75. Robert Carr to the President's Committee on Civil Rights, June 13, 1947, Correspondence with American Veterans Committee, Box 10, Records of the President's Committee on Civil Rights, HST.

76. A later study did find social divisions, but not animosity, between Catholics and Protestants in one suburb. Andrew M. Greeley, *Why Can't They Be Like Us? America's White Ethnic Groups* (New York: E. P. Dutton, 1971), 103–119. See also Polenberg, *One Nation Divisible,* 147–148.

77. Whyte, *Organization Man,* 376. For the mix of groups in Park Forest, see Gregory C. Randall, *America's Original GI Town: Park Forest, Illinois* (Baltimore: Johns Hopkins Univ. Press, 2000), 104–139.

78. William M. Dobriner, *Class in Suburbia* (Englewood Cliffs, N.J.: Prentice Hall, 1963), 92.

79. Harold L. Wattel, "Levittown: A Suburban Community," in *The Suburban Community,* ed. William M. Dobriner (New York: G. P. Putnam's Sons, 1958), 299.

80. Herbert J. Gans, *The Levittowners: Ways of Life and Politics in a New Suburban Community* (New York: Pantheon Books, 1967), 162.

81. See Whyte, *Organization Man;* John Keats, *The Crack in the Picture Window* (Boston: Houghton Mifflin, 1956); Robert C. Wood, *Suburbia: Its People and Their Politics* (Boston: Houghton Mifflin, 1958); Harlan Paul Douglass, "The Suburban Trend," in *The Suburban Community,* ed. William M. Dobriner (New York: G. P. Putnam's Sons, 1958), 103–104.

82. McCoy and Ruetten, *Quest and Response,* 164–170.

83. Charles B. MacDonald, "Novels of World War II: The First Round," *Military Affairs* 13 (Spring 1949): 42–46.

84. Donald Weber, "Memory and Repression in Early Ethnic Television," in *The Other Fifties: Interrogating Midcentury American Icons,* ed. Joel Foreman (Urbana: Univ. of Illinois Press, 1997), 144–162.

85. Becker and Thobaben, *Common Warfare,* 188.

86. Mormino and Pozzetta, "Ethnics at War," 158; and Mormino and Pozzetta, *Immigrant World of Ybor City,* 305.

87. *HSUS,* pt. 1, 401.

88. See Robert D. Putnam, *Bowling Alone: The Collapse and Revival of American Community* (New York: Simon and Schuster, 2000), chap. 14; Theda Skocpol,

*Diminished Democracy: From Membership to Management in American Civil Life* (Norman: Univ. of Oklahoma Press, 2003); Theda Skocpol, Ziad Munson, Andrew Karek, and Bayliss Camp, "Patriotic Partnerships: Why Great Wars Nourished American Civic Voluntarism," in *Shaped by War and Trade: International Influences on American Political Development,* ed. Ira Katznelson and Martin Sefter (Princeton, N.J.: Princeton Univ. Press, 2002), 134–180; and Theda Skocpol, Marshall Ganz, and Ziad Munson, "A Nation of Organizers: The Institutional Origins of Civic Voluntarism in the United States," *American Political Science Review* 94 (Sept. 2000): 527–546. See also Mettler, *Soldiers to Citizens;* and Suzanne Mettler, "Bringing the State Back in to Civic Engagement: Policy Feedback Effects of the G.I. Bill for World War II Veterans," *American Political Science Review* 96 (June 2002): 351–365. For longer trends, see Williams, *American Society,* 466–473.

89. *HSUS,* pt. 1, 401.

90. Skocpol, *Diminished Democracy,* 154–155.

91. *HSUS,* pt. 1, 391–392.

92. Stephen J. Whitfield, *The Culture of the Cold War* (Baltimore: Johns Hopkins Univ. Press, 1991).

93. "Resolution on Church Attendance and Observance of 'Go to Church' Sunday," Oct. 1951, Americanism-Religion-Divine Guidance Program, Microfilm, AL.

94. William S. Graebner, *The Age of Doubt: American Thought and Culture in the 1940s* (Boston: Twayne, 1991).

95. "Religious Emphasis Week," Jan. 10, 1958, Americanism-Religion-Divine Guidance Program, Microfilm, AL.

96. Harry S. Truman to Rev. Dr. Roy G. Ross, July 2, 1945, President's Personal File 1684, Box 530, Papers of Harry S. Truman, HST.

97. Herberg, *Protestant—Catholic—Jew.*

98. Charles Floyd to Friends, Oct. 23, 1950, Americanism-Religion, Microfilm, AL.

99. David M. Heer, "Intermarriage," in *HEAEG,* 516–517.

100. Nelli, "Italians," 559.

101. Mann, "Melting Pot," 313.

102. See the individual essays on the various white ethnic groups in *HEAEG.*

103. Foster, "Struggle for American Identity," 262.

104. Brodkin's parents were not veterans, but it is likely that many or even most of her classmates had fathers who had served in the military during the war. Brodkin, *How Jews Became White Folks,* 35–36.

105. William McLauglin Personal Account, Americal Division, USAMHI, 4.

106. Donald Dehn Questionnaire, 17.

107. Skocpol, *Diminished Democracy,* 154–155.

108. On the rise of pro football, see Michael MacCambridge, *America's Game: The Epic Story of How Pro Football Captured a Nation* (New York: Random House, 2004).

109. Blunt, *Foot Soldier,* 278.

110. Eugene Lawton to Mr. and Mrs. Lawton, Aug. 31, 1944, in *War Letters: Extraordinary Correspondence from American Wars,* ed. Andrew Carroll (New York: Scribner, 2001), 238.

111. Richard O. Davies, *America's Obsession: Sports and Society since 1945* (Fort Worth, Tex.: Harcourt Brace, 1994), 109–110, 118; and Benjamin G. Rader, *American Sports: From the Age of Folk Games to the Age of Televised Sports* (Upper Saddle River, N.J.: Prentice Hall, 2004), 241–244.

112. Horace G. Eakins Diary, 2nd Armored Division Questionnaire Files, USAMHI.

113. *HSUS,* pt. 1, 396.

114. Ibid., 397.

115. Easton, *Love and War,* 305.

116. Blunt, *Foot Soldier,* 252.

117. Mark H. Rose, *Interstate: Express Highway Politics, 1941–1956* (Lawrence: Regents Press of Kansas, 1979); Mark S. Foster, *A Nation on Wheels: The Automobile Culture in America Since 1945* (Belmont, Calif.: Thomson-Wadsworth, 2003), 94–99; Tom Lewis, *Divided Highways: Building Interstate Highways, Transforming American Life* (New York: Viking, 1997); and Frank Donovan, *Wheels for a Nation* (New York: Thomas Y. Crowell, 1965).

118. Myron Taylor, who had been sent by President Roosevelt in 1940 (see chapter 2). "Methodists Scout a Communist Link," *NYT,* Dec 30, 1947, 18. See also "Religious Tensions," *Washington Post,* July 12, 1946, 6.

119. James T. Patterson, *Grand Expectations: The United States, 1945–1974* (New York: Oxford Univ. Press, 1996), 17–18.

120. McCoy and Ruetten, *Quest and Response,* 290–291. See also Walter Waggoner, "Gen. Clark Named First Ambassador of U.S. to Vatican," *NYT,* Oct. 21, 1951, 1.

121. It was a very controversial issue in the election, passing 83,370 to 78,031. "Clerical Garb Banned," *NYT,* July 2, 1948, 14; and "North Dakota Nuns to Adopt Civilian Dress," *NYT,* July 12, 1948, 21.

122. Although the general conclusion of the report was favorable. "B'nai B'rith Lists U.S. Anti-Semitism," *NYT,* Apr. 18, 1949, 27.

123. McCoy and Ruetten, *Quest and Response,* 294.

124. James S. Olson, *The Ethnic Dimension in American History* (St. James, N.Y.: Brandywine Press, 1999), 265.

125. Caute, *Great Fear,* 164–165.

126. For a study of anti-Semitism and racist feelings toward African Americans among veterans in 1955, see the "Dynamics of Prejudice," by Bruno Bettelheim

and Morris Janowitz. Bettelheim and Janowitz found some stereotyping and passive anti-Semitism among the veterans and a very little intense anti-Semitism, 4 percent. Unfortunately, they do not measure change in attitudes from before the war or compare the veterans to nonveterans, so the study is of limited use. Reprinted in Bruno Bettelheim and Morris Janowitz, *Social Change and Prejudice, including Dynamics of Prejudice* (New York: Free Press, 1964), 99–290.

127. R. M. MacIver, *The More Perfect Union: A Program for the Control of Inter-group Discrimination in the United States* (New York: Macmillan, 1948), 29.

128. Ibid., 32–39.

129. Lubell, *Future of American Politics,* 257.

130. "Barkley Extols conquest of Bias," *NYT,* Feb. 21, 1953, 14.

131. Herberg, *Protestant—Catholic—Jew.* See also Martin E. Marty, *The New Shape of American Religion* (New York: Harper and Brothers, 1958).

132. E. Digby Baltzell, *The Protestant Establishment: Aristocracy and Caste in America* (New York: Random House, 1964), 277–314.

133. Higham, *Send These to Me,* 171.

134. J. Wayne Dudley, "'Hate' Organizations of the 1940s: The Columbians, Inc.," *Phylon* 42 (3rd Qtr. 1981): 262–274.

135. Irving Spiegel, "B'Nai B'rith Told of Decline in Bias," *NYT,* Oct. 20, 1951, 15. See also the beginning of the trend in Rose, *Studies in Reduction of Prejudice,* 70–74.

136. Robin M. Williams Jr., *Strangers Next Door: Ethnic Relations in American Communities* (Englewood Cliffs, N.J.: Prentice Hall, 1964).

137. See Bettelheim and Janowitz, *Social Change and Prejudice,* 4–10. See also George Gallup, "Anti-Semitism Found Negligible in U.S.," *Los Angeles Times,* Jan. 22, 1960, 9; and Gallup, "Prejudice in Politics Declining," *Washington Post,* Oct. 26, 1958, A1.

138. Spencer Blakeslee, *The Death of Antisemitism* (Westport, Conn: Praeger, 2001), 41–59. On anti-Semitism, lingering prejudices, and emerging issues for Jewish Americans in the postwar period, see Dinnerstein, *Antisemitism,* 150–174; and Hasia R. Diner, *The Jews of the United States, 1654 to 2000* (Berkeley and Los Angeles: Univ. of California Press, 2004), 259–304.

139. Harry S. Truman to William B. Lampe, Apr. 29, 1946, President's Personal File 260, Box 449, Papers of Harry S. Truman, HST.

140. "Religion in American Life" Address, Oct. 29, 1949, President's Personal File 260, Box 449, Papers of Harry S. Truman, HST. See also correspondence in President's Personal File 260-A, Box 449; President's Personal File 5119, Box 595; and President's Personal File 196-A, Box 180, all in Papers of Harry S. Truman, HST.

141. Harry S. Truman to Nicholas J. Wagener, Apr. 11, 1950, President's Personal File 1577, Box 528, Papers of Harry S. Truman, HST.

142. Harry S. Truman, "Address at a Luncheon of the National Conference of Christians and Jews," Nov. 11, 1949, *Public Papers*, American Presidency Project online.

143. Harry S. Truman, "Address in Philadelphia Upon Accepting the Nomination of the Democratic National Convention," July 15, 1948, *Public Papers*, American Presidency Project online.

144. Gil Loescher and John A. Scanlan, *Calculated Kindness: Refugees and America's Half-Open Door, 1945 to the Present* (New York: Free Press, 1986), 8–13.

145. Susan M. Hartmann, *Truman and the 80th Congress* (Columbia: Univ. of Missouri Press, 1971), 174–179.

146. Truman, "Address in Philadelphia," July 15, 1948.

147. See, for example, "Address at Public Square Park, Wilkes-Barre, Pennsylvania," Oct. 23, 1948, quoted in Steve Neal, ed., *Miracle of '48: Harry Truman's Major Campaign Speeches and Selected Whistle-Stops* (Carbondale: Southern Illinois Univ. Press, 2003), 138–142; and Willard Edwards, "Truman Tells East Coasters He Hates Reds," *Chicago Tribune*, Oct. 28, 1948, 4.

148. "Wiley Pledges GOP to a Fair DP Law," *NYT*, Aug. 13, 1948, 6. In 1950, a bipartisan effort in Congress expanded the total number refugees allowed in by the act and removed the Baltic preferences. Loescher and Scanlan, *Calculated Kindness*, 22.

149. In the campaign of 1948, one presidential nominee did base his candidacy on an appeal to bigotry. Strom Thurmond and the Dixiecrat States' Rights Party opposed the civil rights platform of the Democrats and through an openly racist and often anti-Semitic campaign found support in the Deep South, but not enough to effect the outcome of the election. On the 1948 campaign, see Irwin Ross, *The Loneliest Campaign: The Truman Victory of 1948* (New York: New American Library, 1968); and Zachary Karabell, *The Last Campaign: How Harry Truman Won the 1948 Election* (New York: Alfred A. Knopf, 2000). On Truman's strategy in the campaign, see Dennis Merrill, ed., *Documentary History of the Truman Administration: Running From Behind: Truman's Strategy for the 1948 Presidential Campaign* (Washington, D.C.: Univ. Publications of America, 1997), especially "The Politics of 1948," by James Rowe, Sept. 18, 1947, 29–61.

150. David Wyman, *Paper Walls: America and the Refugee Crisis, 1938–1941* (Amherst: Univ. of Massachusetts Press, 1968).

151. Divine, *American Immigration Policy*, 158.

152. Statement of William Floyd, Feb. 27, 1946, Official File 3144, Box 1750, Harry S. Truman Papers, HST.

153. Quoted in Divine, *American Immigration Policy*, 167.

154. Quoted in ibid., 184.

155. On the effect of World War II on racialized restrictions, especially toward Asians, see Reed Ueda, "The Changing Path to Citizenship: Ethnicity and Naturalization

during World War II," in *The War in American Culture: Society and Conscious-ness During World War II,* ed. Lewis A. Erenberg and Susan E. Hirsch (Chicago: Univ. of Chicago Press, 1996), 202–216. See also Hutchinson, *Legislative History,* 298–313.

156. Divine, *American Immigration Policy,* 189.

157. U.S. Department of Justice, Immigration and Naturalization Service, *Special Naturalization Benefits for Veterans . . .* (Washington, D.C.: GPO, 1959); and American Council for Nationalities Service, *How to Become a Citizen of the United States* (Dobbs Ferry, N.Y.: Oceana Publications, 1963), 49–51.

158. Quoted in Divine, *American Immigration Policy,* 181.

159. Steve Neal, *Harry and Ike: The Partnership That Remade the Postwar World* (New York: Scribner, 2001), 274–276. See also Dwight D. Eisenhower, *The Papers of Dwight David Eisenhower: The Presidency: Keeping the Peace,* ed. Albert D. Chandler Jr. (Baltimore: Johns Hopkins Univ. Press, 2001), 18:1389fn.

160. "Senators Ask for Bias Ban," *NYT,* Oct. 22, 1952, 19. See also "GOP Chairman Pledges Bigotry Will Be Banned," *Washington Post,* Aug. 19, 1952, 20; and "Reli-gious Prejudices in the Campaign," *Chicago Tribune,* Oct. 25, 1952, 10.

161. "Program of Service, Back to God," Feb. 1, 1953, White House Central Files, General File 120 American Legion 1952–53 (1), Box 700, Dwight D. Eisenhower Papers, DDE.

162. See for example, "New Jersey VFW Gathers," *NYT,* June 19, 1947, 27.

163. Leonard Demchak, Catholic War Veterans to the President, July 27, 1957, White House Central Files, General File 120 Catholic War Veterans, Box 704, Dwight D. Eisenhower Papers, DDE; Patterson, *Grand Expectations,* 329.

164. Mark Silk, "Notes on the Judeo-Christian Tradition in America," *American Quarterly* 36 (Spring 1984): 65–85.

165. Dwight D. Eisenhower, "Address at the American Jewish Tercentenary Dinner," Oct. 20, 1954; "Address at the Alfred E. Smith Memorial Dinner," Oct. 21, 1954; and "Remarks at the First National Conference on the Spiritual Foundations of American Democracy," Nov. 9, 1954, all in *Public Papers,* American Presidency Project online.

166. Eisenhower to Milton Eisenhower, Mar. 11, 1957, in Dwight D. Eisenhower, *The Papers of Dwight David Eisenhower: The Presidency: Keeping the Peace,* ed. Albert D. Chandler Jr. (Baltimore: Johns Hopkins Univ. Press, 2001), 18:88–89.

167. On the development of the idea of the Judeo-Christian tradition, see Moore, "Worshipping Together," "Jewish GIs," and *GI Jews;* Silk, "Notes on the Judeo-Christian Tradition"; and Martin E. Marty, *Modern American Religion,* vol. 3, *Under God, Indivisible, 1941–1960* (Chicago: Univ. of Chicago Press, 1996). The most famous opposition to the theological ramifications of what he saw as the misunderstanding and misuse of the idea was Herberg, *Protestant—Catholic—Jew,* 270–289.

168. James Reston, "LaFollette Holds Wisconsin Favor," *NYT*, Aug. 13, 1946, 18.

169. See Thomas C. Reeves, *The Life and Times of Joe McCarthy* (New York: Steyn and Day, 1982), 45–108.

170. John Fenton, "Cross Blamed by Maine G.O.P.," *NYT*, Sept. 15, 1954, 22.

171. *Biographical Dictionary of the United States Congress, 1774–Present*, http://www.bioguide.congress.gov/.

172. Ibid.; "Democrats Hold Minnesota Edge," *NYT*, Nov. 2, 1958, 81; John H. Fenton, *The Catholic Vote* (New Orleans: Hauser Press, 1960), 88.

173. Holmes Alexander, "Lausche's Rival," *Los Angeles Times*, Sept. 7 1954, A5.

# Conclusion

1. Lubell, *Future of American Politics*, 220–226.

2. Stuart Chase, *American Credos* (New York: Harper and Brothers, 1962), 165–166. See also Gallup, "Prejudice in Politics Declining," A1.

3. Paul Blanshard, *God and Man in Washington* (Boston: Beacon Press, 1960). For new responses, see "Catholics Now No. 1 Smear Target, Fair Campaign Group Reports," *Washington Post*, Sept. 15, 1959, A2.

4. "Catholic Candidate Is Termed an Asset," *NYT*, July 24, 1956, 19.

5. Arthur Krock, "Maneuvers for Position in Political Derby," *NYT*, Oct. 28, 1955, 24; Arthur Krock, "The Democratic Party and the 'Catholic Vote,'" *NYT*, July 5, 1956, 24; James Reston, "2 Problems on Kennedy: Democrats May Lose Votes in 1960 by Nominating a Catholic or Not," *NYT*, Jan. 1, 1959, 28; Joseph Alsop, "Outlook for Catholic Candidates," *Washington Post*, Aug. 24, 1958, E5. See also Alexander, "Lausche's Rival," A5.

6. Eisenhower to Edward Bermingham, Mar. 14, 1956, in Dwight D. Eisenhower, *Papers of Eisenhower: The Presidency: The Middle Way* (Baltimore: Johns Hopkins Univ. Press, 1996), 16:2074. On Eisenhower's appeal to Catholics, see William B. Prendergast, *The Catholic Voter in American Politics: The Passing of the Democratic Monolith* (Washington, D.C.: Georgetown Univ. Press, 1999), 120–134.

7. Theodore C. Sorenson, *Kennedy* (New York: Harper and Row, 1965), 127.

8. Russell Baker, "Kennedy in Race; Bars Second Spot in Any Situation," *NYT*, Jan. 3, 1960, 1.

9. Some anti-Catholic pamphlets circulated in the state during the primary, but according to the *New York Times*, the pamphlets "bore no resemblance to the highly personalized attacks made upon Governor Smith and his religion in 1928." W. H. Lawrence, "Humphrey Seeks Catholics' Votes," *NYT*, Mar. 22, 1960, 20.

10. Donald Janson, "Religion Big Factor In Kennedy Victory," *NYT*, Apr. 6, 1960, 1. See also "Catholic Weekly Sees Bloc Voting," *NYT*, Apr. 15, 1960, 11

11. Leo Egan, "The 'Catholic Vote': How Important Is It?" *NYT,* Apr. 17, 1960, E4.

12. "Texts of Speeches," *NYT,* Apr. 22, 1960, 16.

13. Quoted in Theodore H. White, *The Making of the President—1960* (New York: Atheneum, 1961), 117.

14. Kenneth P. O'Donnell and David F. Powers, *"Johnny, We Hardly Knew Ye": Memories of John Fitzgerald Kennedy* (Boston: Little, Brown, 1970), 166–167.

15. White, *Making of the President,* 118.

16. Dan B. Fleming Jr., *Kennedy vs. Humphrey, West Virginia, 1960: The Pivotal Battle for the Democratic Presidential Nomination* (Jefferson, N.C.: McFarland, 1992).

17. See articles in the *NYT:* "Catholics Criticized," Apr. 11, 1959, 24; "Warning by Baptists," Aug. 23, 1959, 4; "Political Criticism of Catholic Backed," Feb. 6, 1960, 9; "Heads of 2 Groups Warn On Catholic," Apr. 27, 1960, 27; "Baptists Question Vote for Catholic," May 21, 1960, 12; "Baptists Bar Catholic," June 23, 1960, 12; "Kennedy Is Attacked," July 4, 1960, 4; "A Catholic Is Opposed," Aug. 4, 1960, 11; "A Catholic President Opposed," Aug. 5, 1960, 7; "Baptist Hits Kennedy," Aug. 10, 1960, 20; "25 Ministers Fight Catholic's Election," Aug. 24, 1960, 19; "Baptist Group Acts," Sept. 2, 1960, 8; "Religious Issue Raised," Sept. 3, 1960, 20; "Arkansas Baptists to Oppose Kennedy," Sept. 7, 1960, 32;

18. Henry Jackson to Brent Spence, Sept. 15, 1960, Democratic National Committee File, 1960, Brent Spence Papers, KL.

19. John Wicklein, "Vast Anti-Catholic Drive Is Slated Before Election," *NYT,* Oct. 16, 1960, 1; John Wicklein, "Anti-Catholic Groups Closely Cooperate in Mail Campaign to Defeat Kennedy," *NYT,* Oct. 17, 1960, 24; John Wicklein, "Anti-Catholic Mail Is Rising on Coast," *NYT,* Nov. 5, 1960, 9.

20. Thomas J. Carty, *A Catholic in the White House: Religion, Politics, and John F. Kennedy's Presidential Campaign* (New York: Palgrave, 2004), 49–66.

21. Religious Freedom Statement, Republican Convention, Civil Rights, 1960, Box 580, John Sherman Cooper Papers, KL.

22. See 1960 Campaign, Box 5, National Republican Committee Series, Thurston Ballard Morton Papers, KL.

23. Dwight D. Eisenhower, "President's News Conference," Apr. 27, 1960, *Public Papers,* American Presidency Project online.

24. Dwight D. Eisenhower, "President's News Conference," Aug. 24, 1960. See also his news conference of September 7, 1960, *Public Papers,* American Presidency Project online.

25. Carty, *Catholic in the White House,* 88–89.

26. Anthony Lewis, "Nixon Seeks Date to End All Talk of Religion Issue," *NYT,* Sept. 12, 1960, 1.

27. Speech quoted in full in White, *Making of the President,* 427–430.

28. Carty, *Catholic in the White House*, 83.

29. Ibid., 91–92.

30. "Democrats Back Leaflet Charges," *NYT*, Oct. 25, 1960, 29; Leo Egan, "Religion: U.S. Campaign," *NYT*, Oct. 30, 1960, E4; and Thomas C. Reeves, *A Question of Character: A Life of John F. Kennedy* (New York: Free Press, 1991), 191–193.

31. "The Nation," *NYT*, Sept. 18, 1960, E2.

32. "Third Kennedy-Nixon Presidential Debate," Oct. 13, 1960, *Presidential Candidates Debates*, American Presidency Project online.

33. Ibid.

34. Leo Egan, "Candidates Term Religion Less of an Issue Than in '28," *NYT*, Oct. 20, 1960, 1.

35. Carty, *Catholic in the White House*, 96.

36. Resolutions of the North Carolina Department of AMVETS, May 21, 1960, White House Central Files, General File 120 AMVETS (2), Box 701, Dwight D. Eisenhower Papers, DDE.

37. See the *NYT* articles: "3 Rabbis Assail Electoral Bias," Sept. 11, 1960, 68; "Protestant Group Assailed," Sept. 10, 1960, 8; "Religious Issue Target of Attack," July 15, 1960, 11; "Rabbis Counsel Fairness in Vote," Nov. 6, 1960, 33; "20 Lutherans Support Kennedy; Deplore Injection of Faith Issue," Nov. 6, 1960, 67; "Protestant Pulpits Divide on Kennedy," Oct. 31, 1960, 1; "Protestant Hits Anti-Catholicism," Oct. 29, 1960, 12; "Church Unit Hits Religion As Issue," Oct. 21, 1960, 14; "Issue of Religion Barred by Poling," Oct. 17, 1960, 22; "Religious Vote 'Bad,'" Sept. 29, 1960, 22; "Rosh ha-Shanah Messages Ask End to National Campaign Bias," Sept. 21, 1960, 24; and "General Assembly Meets," May 3, 1960, 1.

38. Egan, "Religion: U.S. Campaign," E4.

39. Even the paranoid Nixon had a point when he wrote, "I was not prepared for the blatant and highly successful way the Kennedys repeatedly made religion an issue in the campaign even as they professed it should not be one. Led by Robert Kennedy, they managed to turn the election partially into a referendum on tolerance versus bigotry." Richard M. Nixon, *RN: The Memoirs of Richard Nixon* (New York: Grosset and Dunlap, 1978), 226.

40. Ibid., 215. He made the same argument in his earlier memoir, *Six Crises* (Garden City, N.Y.: Doubleday, 1962), 366–367, 392–393, 421.

41. See Fenton, *Catholic Vote*. See also Ithiel de Sola Pool, Robert P. Abelson, and Samuel L. Popkin, *Candidates, Issues, and Strategies: A Computer Simulation of the 1960 Election* (Cambridge, Mass: MIT Press, 1964); Prendergast, *Catholic Voter*, 135–148; Carty, *Catholic in the White House*.

42. Carty, *Catholic in the White House*, 95.

43. This breakdown is derived from Brooks, *Defining the Peace*.

44. Harvey Lites to the President, Mar. 10, 1948, Official File 190-A 1948–53 (2 of 3), Box 803, Harry S. Truman Papers, HST.

45. "Resolution of VFW Clarke-Lyon Post, 1954," White House Central Files, General File 120 VFW (1), Box 712, Dwight D. Eisenhower Papers, DDE.

46. See Chalmers, *Hooded Americanism,* 325–385; Wade, *Fiery Cross,* 276–306.

47. Gerstle, *American Crucible,* 234–235.

48. Robert Carr to the President's Committee on Civil Rights, June 13, 1947, Correspondence with American Veterans Committee, Box 10, Records of the President's Committee on Civil Rights, HST.

49. "J. W. V. Still Fights for You," 1948, Correspondence—Jewish War Veterans, Box 165, James Roosevelt Papers, FDR.

50. Pittsburg Veterans Committee to the President, Feb. 17, 1948, Official File 190-A 1948–53 (2 of 3), Box 803, Harry S. Truman Papers, HST.

51. Tony Badger, "Fatalism, Not Gradualism: The Crisis of Southern Liberalism, 1945–65," in *The Making of Martin Luther King and the Civil Rights Movement,* ed. Brian Ward and Tony Badger (New York: New York Univ. Press, 1996), 67–90.

52. Brooks, *Defining the Peace,* chap. 3.

53. Reed, *Seedtime,* 339.

54. Gunnar Myrdal, *An American Dilemma: The Negro Problem and Modern Democracy* (New York: Harper and Brothers, 1944).

55. Gary Gerstle wrote on this issue, "One is therefore impelled to ask whether civic nationalism [concerning African Americans] would have enjoyed somewhat more sway in the immediate postwar period had black and white men learned to fight alongside each other in the military, to experience each other as friends and buddies, and to begin the delicate process of imagining each other as neighbors. It is impossible to know the answer to that question with any certainty; but it is difficult to avoid the conclusion that an opportunity had here been lost." Gerstle, *American Crucible,* 236. See also Saxe, *Settling Down,* 155–190.

56. Silk, "Notes on the Judeo-Christian," 79–85.

57. Philip Gleason, "Sea Change in the Civic Culture of the 1960s," in *E Pluribus Unum? Contemporary and Historical Perspectives on Immigrant Political Incorporation,* ed. Gary Gerstle and John Mollenkopf (New York: Russell Sage Foundation, 2001), 110.

58. Pozzetta, "My Children Are My Jewels," 75.

59. Moore, *GI Jews.*

60. Nathan Glazer and Daniel Patrick Moynihan, *Beyond the Melting Pot: The Negroes, Puerto Ricans, Jews, Italians, and Irish of New York City* (Cambridge, Mass.: MIT Press, 1963). See also Barkan, *And Still They Come,* 112–196.

61. Michael Novak, *The Rise of the Unmeltable Ethnics: Politics and Culture in the Seventies* (New York: Macmillan, 1972); Schlesinger, *Disuniting of America;* Tamar Jacoby, ed., *Reinventing the Melting Pot: The New Immigrants and What It Means to Be American* (New York: Basic Books, 2004). See also Higham, *Send These to Me,* 233–248; David A. Hollinger, *Postethnic America: Beyond Multiculturalism* (New York: Basic Books, 1995); and Mann, *One and the Many.*

62. Peter Novick, *The Holocaust in American Life* (Boston: Houghton Mifflin, 1999), 19–123. See also Piehler, *Remembering War,* 126–153.

63. Robert Abzug, the leading scholar of American troop reactions to the concentration camps, wrote, "Had an accident of history denied British and American soldiers their naked confrontation with the camps, it is reasonable to assume that the Holocaust might have become like the Soviet camps, the Turkish slaughter of the Armenians, or the massacres of Cambodians in Southeast Asia—reported and put out of mind, known and dismissed, prey to every denial or charge of political manipulation." *Inside the Vicious Heart,* x–xi.

64. *Whom We Shall Welcome,* Report of the President's Commission on Immigration and Naturalization (Washington, D.C.: GPO, 1953), 263.

65. Ibid., xiii.

66. Frank Gigliotti to the President, Sept. 9, 1952, Official File 3144, Regular Veterans Association, Box 1750, Harry S. Truman Papers, HST

67. Quoted in Harry N. Rosenfield, "The Prospects for Immigration Amendments," *Law and Contemporary Politics* 21 (Spring 1956): 405.

68. "Javits Fears Coup by G.O.P. Rightists," *NYT,* Oct. 23, 1955, 45.

69. A Gallup poll from 1955 suggested that the broader population also reflected this change. The American Legion continued to oppose lifting restrictions. The AVC, Catholic War Veterans, and Jewish War Veterans came out in favor of reform. Rosenfield, "Prospects," 405–426.

70. Dwight D. Eisenhower, "Annual Message to the Congress on the State of the Union," Jan. 5, 1956, *Public Papers,* American Presidency Project online.

71. Perlmutter, *Divided We Fall,* 244.

72. Hutchinson, *Legislative History,* 314–379; Daniels, *Coming to America,* 338–344; Loescher and Scanlon, *Calculated Kindness,* 72–74.

73. C. R. Burton to John Sherman Cooper, July 29, 1959, Judiciary Committee, Immigration Legislation, 1959–1960, Box 503, John Sherman Cooper Papers, KL.

74. But he made no indication either way that he was a veteran. Ibid.

75. John Sherman Cooper to C. R. Burton, Aug. 7, 1959, Judiciary Committee, Immigration Legislation, 1959–1960, Box 503, John Sherman Cooper Papers, KL.

76. Robert Schulman, *John Sherman Cooper: The Global Kentuckian* (Lexington: Univ. Press of Kentucky, 1976), 27–29.

# BIBLIOGRAPHY

## Primary Sources

### Archives

American Legion National Headquarters. Indianapolis, Ind. .

Cornelius Ryan Collection. Alden Library. Ohio University, Athens.

Dwight D. Eisenhower Presidential Library and Museum. Abilene, Kans.
    Dwight D. Eisenhower Papers
    President's Commission on Veterans' Pensions Papers

Eisenhower Center. University of New Orleans. New Orleans, La.

Franklin D. Roosevelt Presidential Library and Museum. Hyde Park, N.Y.
    Adolf Berle Papers
    Francis Biddle Papers
    Democratic Party National Committee Papers
    Stephen Early Papers
    Harry Hopkins Papers
    Louis Howe Papers
    Joseph Lash Papers
    Isidor Lubin Papers
    William McReynolds Papers
    Eleanor Roosevelt Papers
    Franklin D. Roosevelt Papers
    James Roosevelt Papers
    Samuel Rosenman Papers
    James Rowe Papers
    Caroline Ware Papers

Harry S. Truman Presidential Library and Museum. Independence, Mo.
    Records of the President's Committee on Civil Rights
    Harry S. Truman Papers

National Archives and Records Administration II. College Park, Md.
    Record Group 44: Records of the Office of Government Reports
    Record Group 160: Records of the Army Service Forces
    Record Group 247: Records of the Chief of Chaplains
    Record Group 407: Records of the Adjutant General

University of Kentucky Archives. Margaret I. King Library. Lexington, Ky.
    Alben Barkley Papers

John Sherman Cooper Papers
Thruston Ballard Morton Papers
Brent Spence Papers
Wilson Wyatt Papers

U.S. Army Military History Institute/Army Heritage Center. Carlisle Barracks, Carlisle, Pa.

Youngstown State Oral History Program. William F. Maag Jr. Library. Youngstown State University, Youngstown, Ohio. http://www.maag.ysu.edu/oralhistory/oral_hist.html.


## Memoirs, Oral Histories, Diaries, Polls, Published Speeches, and Published Letters

Ambrose, Stephen E. *To America: Personal Reflections of an Historian.* New York: Simon and Schuster, 2002.

Armstrong, Frank H. *Payoff Artillery—WWII.* Burlington, Vt.: Bull Run, 1993.

Baker, Vernon. *Lasting Valor.* Columbus, Miss: Genesis Press, 1997.

Becker, Carl M., and Robert G. Thobaben. *Common Warfare: Parallel Memoirs by Two World War II GIs in the Pacific.* Jefferson, N.C.: McFarland, 1992.

Biddle, Francis. *In Brief Authority.* Garden City, N.Y.: Doubleday, 1962.

Bland, Larry I., ed. *The Papers of George Catlett Marshall.* Vol. 1. Baltimore: Johns Hopkins Univ. Press, 1981.

Blunt, Roscoe C. *Foot Soldier: A Combat Infantryman's War in Europe.* Cambridge, Mass.: De Capo, 2002.

Bowen, Sidney. *Dearest Isabel: Letters from an Enlisted Man in World War II.* Manhattan, Kans.: Sunflower Univ. Press, 1992.

Brawley, John. *Anyway, We Won.* Marceline, Mo.: Walsworth, 1988.

Carroll, Andrew, ed. *War Letters: Extraordinary Correspondence from American Wars.* New York: Scribner, 2001.

Coughlin, Gene. *Assistant Hero.* New York: Thomas Y. Crowell, 1944.

Darby, William O., and William H. Baumer. *Darby's Rangers: We Led the Way.* San Rafael, Calif.: Presidio Press, 1980.

Easton, Robert, and Jane Easton. *Love and War: Pearl Harbor Through V-J Day.* Norman: Univ. of Oklahoma Press, 1991.

Eisenhower, Dwight D. *The Papers of Dwight David Eisenhower: The War Years.* Vol. 4. Edited by Albert D. Chandler. Baltimore: Johns Hopkins Univ. Press, 1970.

———. *The Papers of Dwight David Eisenhower: NATO and the Campaign of 1952.* Vol. 13. Edited by Albert D. Chandler Jr. Baltimore: Johns Hopkins Univ. Press, 1989.

————. *The Papers of Dwight David Eisenhower: The Presidency: The Middle Way.* Vol. 16. Edited by Albert D. Chandler Jr. Baltimore: Johns Hopkins Univ. Press, 1996.

————. *The Papers of Dwight David Eisenhower: The Presidency: Keeping the Peace.* Vol. 18. Edited by Albert D. Chandler Jr. Baltimore: Johns Hopkins Univ. Press, 2001.

Elevitch, M.D. *Dog Tags Yapping: The World War II Letters of a Combat GI.* Carbondale: Southern Illinois Univ. Press, 2003.

Fort Custer Army Illustrators. *As Soldiers See It.* New York: American Artists Group, 1943.

Gantter, Raymond. *Roll Me Over: An Infantryman's World War II.* New York: Ivy Books, 1997.

Giangreco, D. M., and Kathryn Moore. *Dear Harry . . .: Truman's Mailroom, 1945–1953.* Mechanicsburg, Pa.: Stackpole Books, 1999.

Grant, Ulysses S. *The Personal Memoirs of Ulysses S. Grant.* Old Saybrook, Conn.: Konecky and Konecky, n.d.

Gray, J. Glenn. *The Warriors: Reflections on Men in Battle.* 1959. Reprint, Lincoln: Univ. of Nebraska Press, 1998.

Gurley, Franklin L. *Into the Mountains Dark: A WWII Odyssey from Harvard Crimson to Infantry Blue.* Bedford, Pa.: Aberjona Press, 2000.

Hill, Robert M., and Elizabeth Craig Hill. *In the Wake of War: Memoirs of an Alabama Military Government Officer in World War II Italy.* Univ. of Alabama Press, 1982.

Hoffman, Daniel. *Zone of the Interior: A Memoir, 1942–1947.* Baton Rouge: Louisiana State Univ. Press, 2000.

Hoover, Herbert. *The Memoirs of Herbert Hoover: The Cabinet and the Presidency.* New York: Macmillan, 1952.

Huebner, Klaus H. *Long Walk Through War: A Combat Doctor's Diary.* College Station: Texas A&M Univ. Press, 1987.

Huff, H. Stanley. *Unforgettable Journey: A World War II Memoir.* Fort Wayne, Ind.: Bridgeford Press, 2001.

Hynes, Samuel. *The Growing Season: An American Boyhood Before the War.* New York: Viking, 2003.

Ickes, Harold L. *The Secret Diary of Harold Ickes: The Inside Struggle, 1936–1939.* New York: Simon and Schuster, 1954.

Joy, Dean P. *Sixty Days in Combat.* New York: Presidio Press, 2004.

Kahn, E. J. *G.I. Jungle: An American Soldier in Australia and New Guinea.* New York: Simon and Schuster, 1943.

Kelly, Charles E. *One Man's War.* New York: Alfred E. Knopf, 1944.

Klein, Isaac. *The Anguish and the Ecstasy of a Jewish Chaplain.* New York: Vantage Press, 1974.

Kotlowitz, Robert. *Before Their Time.* New York: Anchor Books, 1997.

Leinbaugh, Harold, and John D. Campbell. *The Men of Company K.* New York: William Morrow, 1985.

Lydgate, William A. *What America Thinks.* New York: Thomas Y. Crowell, 1944.

MacArthur, Douglas. *Reminiscences.* New York: McGraw Hill, 1964.

Major, John Russell. *The Memoirs of a Forward Artillery Observer.* Manhattan, Kans.: Sunflower Univ. Press, 1999.

Manchester, William. *Goodbye Darkness: A Memoir of the Pacific War.* Boston: Little, Brown, 1979.

March, Peyton C. *The Nation at War.* Garden City, N.Y.: Doubleday, 1932.

Mathias, Frank F. *The GI Generation: A Memoir.* Lexington: Univ. Press of Kentucky, 2000.

Mauriello, Christopher E., and Roland J. Regan Jr. *From Boston to Berlin: A Journey through World War II in Images and Words.* West Lafayette, Ind.: Purdue Univ. Press, 2001.

Merrill, Dennis, ed. *Documentary History of the Truman Administration.* 20 vols. Washington, D.C.: Univ. Publications of America, 1995–.

Miller, Arthur. *Situation Normal . . .* New York: Reynal and Hitchcock, 1944.

Millis, Walter, ed. *The Forrestal Diaries.* New York: Viking Press, 1951.

Montgomery, Bernard Law. *The Memoirs of Field-Marshal Montgomery.* Cleveland: World Publishing, 1958.

Murphy, Audie. *To Hell and Back.* New York: MJF Books, 1949.

Neal, Steve, ed. *Miracle of '48: Harry Truman's Major Campaign Speeches and Selected Whistle-Stops.* Carbondale: Southern Illinois Univ. Press, 2003.

Nixon, Richard M. *RN: The Memoirs of Richard Nixon.* New York: Grosset and Dunlap, 1978.

———. *Six Crises.* Garden City, N.Y.: Doubleday, 1962.

O'Donnell, Kenneth P., and David F. Powers. *"Johnny, We Hardly Knew Ye": Memories of John Fitzgerald Kennedy.* Boston: Little, Brown, 1970.

O'Donnell, Patrick K. *Into the Rising Sun.* New York: Free Press, 2002.

Parillo, Mark P., ed. *We Were in the Big One: Experiences of the World War II Generation.* Wilmington, Del.: Scholarly Resources, 2002.

Perkins, Frances. *The Roosevelt I Knew.* New York: Viking, 1946.

Peters, Robert. *For You, Lili Marlene.* Madison: Univ. of Wisconsin Press, 1995.

Price, A. Preston. *The Last Kilometer: Marching to Victory in Europe with the Big Red One, 1944–1945.* Annapolis, Md.: Naval Institute Press, 2002.

*Public Papers and Addresses of Franklin D. Roosevelt.* 13 vols. New York: Random House, 1938–1950.

Puzo, Mario. *The Godfather Papers: And Other Confessions.* London: Heinemann, 1972.

Ridgway, Matthew B. *Soldier: The Memoirs of Matthew B. Ridgway.* New York: Harper and Brothers, 1956.

Rosenman, Samuel I. *Working with Roosevelt.* New York: Harper and Brothers, 1952.

Sledge, E. B. *With the Old Breed.* Oxford Univ. Press, 1981.

Smith, Alfred E. *Up to Now: An Autobiography.* New York: Viking, 1929.

Stevens, Michael E., ed. *Letters from the Front, 1898–1945.* Madison: State Historical Society of Wisconsin, 1992.

Stoup, Russell Cartwright. *Letters from the Pacific: A Combat Chaplain in World War II.* Columbia: Univ. of Missouri Press, 2000.

Tapert, Annette, ed. *Lines of Battle: Letters from American Servicemen, 1941–1945.* New York: Times Books, 1987.

Terkel, Studs. *Hard Times: An Oral History of the Great Depression.* New York: Pantheon Books, 1970.

———. *"The Good War": An Oral History of World War II.* New York: New Press, 1984.

Truman, Harry S. *Memoirs: Years of Trial and Hope.* Vol. 2. Garden City, N.Y.: Doubleday, 1956.

Wilson, George. *If You Survive.* New York: Ivy Books, 1987.

Wolfe, Don M., ed. *The Purple Testament.* Garden City, N.Y.: Doubleday, 1947.

## Printed Government Sources

American Historical Association. *Can We Prevent Future Wars?* EM 12. GI Roundtable. Washington, D.C.: AHA, 1944.

———. *Is Your Health the Nation's Business?* EM 29. GI Roundtable. Washington, D.C.: AHA, 1946.

———. *Shall I Go Back to School?* EM 34. GI Roundtable. Washington, D.C.: AHA, 1945.

———. *What Shall We Do with Our Merchant Fleet?* EM 25. GI Roundtable. Washington, D.C.: AHA, 1946.

———. *What Will Your Town Be Like?* EM 33. GI Roundtable. Washington, D.C.: AHA, 1945.

———. *Will There Be a Plane in Every Garage?* EM 37. GI Roundtable. Washington, D.C.: AHA, 1945.

———. *Will There Be Work For All?* EM 22. GI Roundtable. Washington, D.C.: AHA, 1944.

———. *Why Do Veterans Organize?* EM 6. GI Roundtable. Washington, D.C.: AHA, 1946.

*Armed Forces Talk,* 1947–1955.

*Army Lessons in English.* Bks. 1–6. Camp Upton, N.Y.: Recruit Educational Center, 1920.

*Army Lessons in English: Military Stories.* Camp Upton, N.Y.: Recruit Educational Center, 1920.

*Army Talk,* 1943–1947.

*Biographical Dictionary of the United States Congress, 1774–Present.* http://www.bioguide.congress.gov/.

*The Chaplain.* Technical Manual No. 16-205. Washington, D.C.: War Department, Apr, 1941.

Fair Employment Practice Committee (FEPC). *First Report, July 1943–December 1944.* Washington, D.C.: GPO, 1945.

Grove, Robert D., and Alice M. Hetzel. *Vital Statistics Rates in the United States, 1940.* Washington, D.C.: GPO, 1968.

*Historical Statistics of the Veteran Population, 1865–1960—A Compendium of Facts About Veterans.* Washington, D.C.: GPO, 1961.

*The Hoover Commission Report.* New York: McGraw Hill, n.d.

Jones, J. Morris. *Americans All . . . Immigrants All: A Handbook for Listeners.* Washington, D.C.: United States Office of Education, n.d.

———. *Americans All . . . Immigrants All: A Manual.* Washington, D.C.: United States Office of Education, n.d.

Kenderdine, John D. *Your Year in the Army: What Every New Soldier Should Know.* New York: Simon and Schuster, 1940.

Kreidberg, Marvin A., and Merton G. Henry. *History of Military Mobilization in the United States Army, 1775–1945.* Washington, D.C.: Department of the Army, 1955.

*The Officers' Guide.* 9th ed. Harrisburg, Pa.: Military Service Publishing, 1942.

President's Commission on Higher Education. *Higher Education for American Democracy.* Vol. 2, *Equalizing and Expanding Individual Opportunity.* Washington, D.C.: GPO, 1947.

President's Commission on Veterans' Pensions. *Veterans in Our Society: Data on the Conditions of Military Service and on the Status of the Veteran.* Washington, D.C.: GPO, 1956.

President's Research Committee on Social Trends. *Recent Social Trends in the United States.* New York: McGraw-Hill, 1933.

*Principles, Plans and Purposes of the Educational Program.* Camp Upton, N.Y.: Recruit Educational Center, 1920.

Reynolds, Alfred. *The Life of the Enlisted Soldier in the United States Army.* Washington, D.C.: GPO, 1904.

*Selective Service and Victory: The Fourth Report of the Director of Selective Service.* Washington, D.C.: GPO, 1948.

*Selective Service in Wartime: The Second Report of the Director of Selective Service,* Washington, D.C.: GPO, 1943.

Selective Service System. *Conscientious Objection: Special Monograph No. 11.* Washington, D.C.: GPO, 1950.

———. *Problems of Selective Service: Special Monograph No. 16.* Washington, D.C.: GPO, 1952.

———. *Special Groups: Special Monograph No. 10.* Washington, D.C.: GPO, 1953.

*The Soldier's Handbook.* New York: Thomas Y. Crowell, 1941.

U.S. Bureau of Education. *Report of the Commissioner of Education, 1919.* Washington, D.C.: GPO, 1919.

U.S. Bureau of the Census. *Census of Religious Bodies, 1936, Part I: Summary and Detailed Tables.* Washington, D.C.: GPO, 1940.

———. *Historical Statistics of the United States: Colonial Times to 1970.* Washington, D.C., 1975.

U.S. Congress. House. Hearings, Select Committee Investigating National Defense Migration. 77th Cong., 1st sess., 1941. Washington, D.C., GPO.

U.S. Department of Justice. Immigration and Naturalization Service. *Special Naturalization Benefits for Veterans . . .* Washington, D.C.: GPO, 1959.

U.S. Department of Labor. *Handbook for Agencies Selecting Men for the Civilian Conservation Corps.* Washington, D.C.: GPO, 1936.

U.S. Senate. Committee on Banking and Currency. *Housing Act of 1954—Hearings.* Washington, D.C.: GPO, 1954.

———. Committee on Veterans' Affairs. *Medal of Honor Recipients, 1863–1978.* Washington, D.C.: GPO, 1979.

U.S. War Department. *Military Training.* Field Manual 21-5. Washington, D.C.: GPO, July 1941.

*Veterans in the United States—1960.* Washington, D.C.: GPO, 1967.

*War Department Annual Report.* Washington, D.C.: GPO, 1890–1930.

*What the Soldier Thinks.* 15 vols. Washington, D.C.: Morale Services Division, Army Services Forces, 1943–45.

*Whom We Shall Welcome.* Report of the President's Commission on Immigration and Naturalization. Washington, D.C.: GPO, 1953.

# Secondary Sources

## Books

Abrams, Charles. *The Future of Housing.* New York: Harper and Brothers, 1946.

Abzug, Robert H. *Inside the Vicious Heart: Americans and the Liberation of Nazi Concentration Camps.* Oxford Univ. Press, 1985.

Adamic, Louis. *From Many Lands.* New York: Harper and Brothers, 1940.

Alexander, Charles C. *Breaking the Slump: Baseball in the 1930s.* New York: Columbia Univ. Press, 2002.

———. *The Ku Klux Klan in the Southwest.* Norman: Univ. of Oklahoma Press, 1965, 1995.

———. *Nationalism in American Thought, 1930–1945.* Chicago: Rand McNally, 1969.

———. *Our Game: An American Baseball History.* New York: MJF Books, 1991.

Allen, Frederick Lewis. *Only Yesterday: An Informal History of the Nineteen-Twenties.* New York: Blue Ribbon Books, 1931.

———. *Since Yesterday: The Nineteen-Thirties in America.* New York: Harper and Brothers, 1939.

Allen, James Paul, and Eugene James Turner. *We the People: An Atlas of America's Ethnic Diversity.* New York: Macmillan, 1988.

Allport, Gordon W. *The Nature of Prejudice.* Cambridge, Mass: Addison-Wesley, 1954.

Allswang, John M. *The New Deal and American Politics.* New York: John Wiley and Sons, 1978.

Ambrose, Stephen E. *Band of Brothers.* New York: Simon and Schuster, 1992.

———. *Citizen Soldiers.* New York: Simon and Schuster, 1997.

American Council for Nationalities Service. *How to Become a Citizen of the United States.* Dobbs Ferry, N.Y.: Oceana Publications, 1963.

American Eugenics Society. *American Eugenics Today.* New York: American Eugenics Society, 1939.

———. *Practical Eugenics.* New York: American Eugenics Society, 1938.

Anderson, Karen. *Wartime Women: Sex Roles, Family Relations, and the Status of Women during World War II.* Westport, Conn: Greenwood Press, 1981.

Anderson, Kristi. *After Suffrage: Women in Partisan and Electoral Politics before the New Deal.* Chicago: Univ. of Chicago Press, 1996.

———. *The Creation of a Democratic Majority, 1928–1936.* Chicago: Univ. of Chicago Press, 1979.

Anderson, Lars. *The All-Americans.* New York: St. Martin's Press, 2004.

Asahina, Robert. *Just Americans: How Japanese Americans Won a War at Home and Abroad.* New York: Gotham, 2006.

Avrich, Paul. *Sacco and Vanzetti: The Anarchist Background.* Princeton, N.J.: Princeton Univ. Press, 1991.

Baker, Newton Diehl, Carlton Joseph Huntley Hayes, and Roger Williams Straus, eds. *The American Way: A Study of Human Relations Among Protestants, Catholics, and Jews.* Chicago: Wilett, Clark, 1936.

Ballard, Jack Stokes. *The Shock of Peace: Military and Economic Demobilization after World War II.* Washington, D.C.: Univ. Press of America, 1983.

Baltzell, E. Digby. *The Protestant Establishment: Aristocracy and Caste in America.* New York: Random House, 1964.

Barkan, Elliot R. *And Still They Come: Immigrants and American Society, 1920 to the 1990s.* Wheeling, Ill.: Harlan Davidson, 1996.

———, ed. *Immigration, Incorporation, and Transnationalism.* New Brunswick, N.J.: Transaction Publishers, 2007.

Barr, Ronald J. *The Progressive Army: US Army Command and Administration, 1870–1914.* New York: St. Martin's Press, 1998.

Basinger, Jeanne. *The World War II Combat Film: Anatomy of a Genre.* New York: Columbia Univ. Press, 1986.

Bayor, Ronald H. *Neighbors in Conflict: The Irish, Germans, Jews, and Italians of New York City, 1929–1941.* Baltimore: Johns Hopkins Univ. Press, 1978.

———, ed. *Race and Ethnicity in America: A Concise History.* New York: Columbia Univ. Press, 2003.

Belasco, Warren, and Philip Scranton, eds. *Food Nations: Selling Taste in Consumer Societies.* New York: Routledge, 2002.

Bell, Daniel. *The End of Ideology: On the Exhaustion of Political Ideas in the Fifties.* 1960. Reprint, New York: Free Press, 1962.

———, ed. *The Radical Right.* Garden City, N.Y.: Doubleday, 1963.

Bendersky, Joseph W. *The "Jewish Threat": Anti-Semitic Politics of the U.S. Army.* New York: Basic Books, 2000.

Benjamin, Robert Spiers, ed. *I Am an American: By Famous Naturalized Americans.* 1941. Reprint, Freeport, N.Y.: Books for Libraries Press, 1970.

Bennett, Michael J. *When Dreams Came True: The GI Bill and the Making of Modern America.* Washington, D.C.: Brassey's, 1996.

Berger, Bennett M. *Working-Class Suburb: A Study of Auto Workers in Suburbia.* Berkeley and Los Angeles: Univ. of California Press, 1960.

Bergerud, Eric. *Touched with Fire: The Land War in the South Pacific.* New York: Viking, 1996.

Bernstein, Alison R. *American Indians in World War II*. Norman: Univ. of Oklahoma Press, 1991.

Berube, Allan. *Coming Out Under Fire: The History of Gay Men and Women in World War Two*. New York: Free Press, 2000.

Bettelheim, Bruno, and Morris Janowitz. *Social Change and Prejudice, including Dynamics of Prejudice*. New York: Free Press, 1964.

Billington, Ray Allen. *The Protestant Crusade, 1800–1860: A Study of the Origins of American Nativism*. New York: Macmillan, 1938.

Blackwell, James A. *On Brave Old Army Team*. Novato, Calif.: Presidio Press, 1996.

Blakeslee, Spencer. *The Death of Antisemitism*. Westport, Conn: Praeger, 2001.

Blanshard, Paul. *God and Man in Washington*. Boston: Beacon Press, 1960.

Blum, John Morton. *V Was for Victory: Politics and American Culture During World War II*. New York: Harcourt Brace Jovanovich, 1976.

Boemeke, Manfred F., Roger Chickering, and Stig Förster, eds. *Anticipating Total War: The German and American Experiences, 1971–1914*. New York: Cambridge Univ. Press, 1999.

Bogle, Lori Lyn. *The Pentagon's Battle for the American Mind: The Early Cold War*. College Station: Texas A&M Press, 2004.

Bohn, Thomas William. *An Historical and Descriptive Analysis of the "Why We Fight" Series*. New York: Arno Press, 1977.

Botjer, George F. *Sideshow War: The Italian Campaign, 1943–1945*. College Station: Texas A&M Univ. Press, 1996.

Bottoms, Bill. *The VFW: An Illustrated History of the Veterans of Foreign Wars of the United States*. Rockville, Md.: Woodbine House, 1991.

Bowers, David F., ed. *Foreign Influences in American Life*. Princeton, N.J.: Princeton Univ. Press, 1944.

Boyer, Paul. *By the Bomb's Early Light: American Thought and Culture at the Dawn of the Atomic Age*. New York: Pantheon Books, 1985.

Boylan, James. *The New Deal Coalition and the Election of 1946*. New York: Garland, 1981.

Brigham, Carl C. *A Study of American Intelligence*. Princeton, N.J.: Princeton Univ. Press, 1923.

Brinkley, Alan. *The End of Reform: New Deal Liberalism in Recession and War*. New York: Alfred A. Knopf, 1995.

———. *Voices of Protest: Huey Long, Father Coughlin, and the Great Depression*. New York: Alfred A. Knopf, 1982.

Brodkin, Karen. *How Jews Became White Folks: And What That Says about Race in America*. New Brunswick, N.J.: Rutgers Univ. Press, 1998.

Brooks, Jennifer E. *Defining the Peace: World War II Veterans, Race, and the Remaking of Southern Political Tradition.* Chapel Hill: Univ. of North Carolina Press, 2004.

Brown, Francis J., and Joseph Slabey Roucek, eds. *One America: The History, Contributions, and Present Problems of Our Racial and National Minorities.* New York: Prentice Hall, 1945.

———. *Our Racial and National Minorities: Their History, Contributions, and Present Problems.* New York: Prentice Hall, 1937.

Buenker, John D. *Urban Liberalism and Progressive Reform.* New York: Charles Scribner's Sons, 1973.

Burner, David. *The Politics of Provincialism: The Democratic Party in Transition, 1918–1932.* New York: Alfred A. Knopf, 1968.

Burnham, Walter Dean. *Critical Elections and the Mainsprings of American Politics.* New York: W. W. Norton, 1970.

Burns, James MacGregor, *Roosevelt: The Lion and the Fox.* New York: Harcourt, 1956.

Burton, William L. *Melting Pot Soldiers: The Union's Ethnic Regiments.* 2nd ed. New York: Fordham Univ. Press, 1998.

Bushman, Richard L., Neil Harris, Barbara Miller Solomon, and Stephan Thernstrom, eds. *Uprooted Americans: Essays to Honor Oscar Handlin.* Boston: Little, Brown, 1979.

Callahan, David. *Kindred Spirits: Harvard Business School's Extraordinary Class of 1949 and How They Transformed American Business.* Hoboken, N.J.: John Wiley and Sons, 2002.

Campbell, Angus, Gerald Gurin, and Warren E. Miller. *The Voter Decides.* Evanston, Ill.: Row, Peterson, 1954.

Carter, Paul A. *Politics, Religion, and Rockets: Essays in Twentieth-Century American History.* Tucson: Univ. of Arizona Press, 1991.

Carty, Thomas J. *A Catholic in the White House: Religion, Politics, and John F. Kennedy's Presidential Campaign.* New York: Palgrave, 2004.

Caute, David. *The Great Fear: The Anti-Communist Purge Under Truman and Eisenhower.* New York: Simon and Schuster, 1978.

Chalmers, David M. *Hooded Americanism: The First Century of the Ku Klux Klan, 1865–1965.* Garden City, N.Y.: Doubleday, 1965.

Chambers, John Whiteclay, II. *To Raise an Army: The Draft Comes to Modern America.* New York: Free Press, 1987.

Chase, Stuart. *American Credos.* New York: Harper and Brothers, 1962.

———. *For This We Fought.* New York: Twentieth Century Fund, 1946.

Chicago Public Library Omnibus Project. *The Chicago Foreign Language Press Survey.* Chicago: Works Project Administration, 1942.

Chyz, Yaroslav J. *225 Years of the U.S. Foreign Language Press: Notes on Its Influence, History and Present Status.* New York: American Council for Nationalities Service, 1959.

Clary, Jack. *Army vs. Navy: Seventy Years of Football Rivalry.* New York: Ronald Press, 1965.

Clifford, J. Garry. *The Citizen Soldiers: The Plattsburg Training Camp Movement,* Lexington: Univ. of Kentucky Press, 1972.

Clifford, J. Garry, and Samuel R. Spencer Jr. *The First Peacetime Draft.* Lawrence: Univ. Press of Kansas, 1986.

Coffman, Edward M. *The Old Army: A Portrait of the American Army in Peacetime, 1784–1898.* New York: Oxford Univ. Press, 1986.

———. *The Regulars: The American Army, 1898–1941.* Cambridge: Belknap Press of Harvard Univ. Press, 2004.

Cohen, Lizabeth. *A Consumer's Republic: The Politics of Mass Consumption in Postwar America.* New York: Knopf, 2003.

———. *Making a New Deal: Industrial Workers in Chicago, 1919–1939.* Cambridge Univ. Press, 1990.

Cole, John Y., ed. *Books in Action: The Armed Services Editions.* Washington, D.C.: Library of Congress, 1984.

Colley, David P. *Blood for Dignity: The Story of the First Integrated Combat Unit in the U.S. Army.* New York: St. Martin's Press, 2003.

Common Council for American Unity. *Foreign Language Publications in the United States.* New York: Common Council for American Unity, 1956.

———. *What's Cooking in Your Neighbor's Pot.* New York: Common Council for American Unity, 1944.

Cook, Blanche Weisen. *Eleanor Roosevelt.* Vol. 2, *1933–1938.* New York: Viking, 1999.

Cooke, James J. *The All-Americans at War: The 82nd Division in the Great War, 1917–1918.* Westport, Conn.: Praeger, 1999.

Cooper, Jerry M. *The Army and Civil Disorder: Federal Military Intervention in Labor Disputes, 1877–1900.* Westport, Conn.: Greenwood Press, 1980.

Costello, John. *Virtue Under Fire: How World War II Changed Our Social and Sexual Attitudes.* Boston: Little, Brown, 1985.

Covello, Leonard. *The Social Background of the Italo-American School Child.* Edited by Francesco Cordasco. Leiden, Netherlands: E. J. Brill, 1967.

Craig, Douglas B. *After Wilson: The Struggle for the Democratic Party, 1920–1934.* Chapel Hill: Univ. of North Carolina Press, 1992.

Creighton, Margaret S. *The Colors of Courage: Gettysburg's Forgotten History—Immigrants, Women, and African Americans in the Civil War's Defining Battle.* New York: Basic Books, 2005.

Crosby, Donald F. *Battlefield Chaplains: Catholic Priests in World War II.* Lawrence: Univ. Press of Kansas, 1994.

Dalfiume, Richard M. *Desegregation of the United States Armed Forces.* Columbia: Univ. of Missouri Press, 1969.

Daniel, Clete. *Chicano Workers and the Politics of Fairness: The FEPC in the Southwest, 1941–1945.* Austin: Univ. of Texas Press, 1991.

Daniels, Roger. *The Bonus March: An Episode in the Great Depression.* Westport, Conn: Greenwood Press, 1971.

———. *Coming to America: A History of Immigration and Ethnicity in American Life.* New York: HarperCollins, 1990.

———. *Not Like Us: Immigrants and Minorities in America, 1890–1924.* Chicago: Ivan R. Dee, 1997.

———. *Prisoners Without Trial: Japanese Americans in World War II.* New York: Hill and Wang, 1993.

David, Paul T. *Party Strength in the United States, 1872–1970.* Charlottesville: Univ. Press of Virginia, 1972.

David, Paul T., Malcolm Moos, and Ralph M. Goldman, eds. *The National Story: Presidential Nominating Politics in 1952.* Baltimore: Johns Hopkins Univ. Press, 1954.

Davies, Richard O. *America's Obsession: Sports and Society since 1945.* Fort Worth, Tex.: Harcourt Brace, 1994.

Davis, Kenneth C. *Two-Bit Culture: The Paperbacking of America.* Boston: Houghton Mifflin, 1984.

Davis, Mike. *Prisoners of the American Dream: Politics and Economy in the History of the Working Class.* London: Verso, 1986.

Dawley, Alan. *Struggles for Justice: Social Responsibility and the Liberal State.* Cambridge, Mass: Belknap Press, 1991.

De Grazia, Alfred. *The Western Public: 1952 and Beyond.* Stanford, Calif: Stanford Univ. Press, 1954.

Denning, Michael. *The Cultural Front: The Laboring of American Culture in the Twentieth Century.* London: Verso, 1996.

Derthick, Martha. *The National Guard in Politics.* Cambridge: Harvard Univ. Press, 1965.

D'Este, Carlo. *Patton: A Genius for War.* New York: HarperCollins, 1995.

Deutsch, Monroe E. *Our Legacy of Religious Freedom.* New York: National Conference of Christians and Jews, 1941.

Dew, Charles B. *Apostles of Disunion: Southern Secessions Commissioners and the Causes of the Civil War.* Charlottesville: Univ. Press of Virginia, 2001.

Dickson, Paul, and Thomas B. Allen, *The Bonus Army: An American Epic.* New York: Walker, 2004.

Diggins, John Patrick. *Mussolini and Fascism: The View from America*. Princeton, N.J.: Princeton Univ. Press, 1972.

Dillingham, William Pyrle. *Federal Aid to Veterans, 1917–1941*. Gainesville: Univ. of Florida Press, 1952.

Diner, Hasia R. *Hungering for America: Italian, Irish, and Jewish Foodways in the Age of Migration*. Cambridge: Harvard Univ. Press, 2001.

———. *The Jews of the United States, 1654 to 2000*. Berkeley and Los Angeles: Univ. of California Press, 2004.

Dinnerstein, Leonard. *Antisemitism in America*. New York: Oxford Univ. Press, 1994.

DiStasi, Lawrence, ed. *Una Storia Segreta: The Secret History of the Italian American Evacuation and Internment during World War II*. Berkeley, Calif.: Heydey Books, 2001.

Divine, Robert A. *American Immigration Policy, 1924–1952*. New Haven, Conn.: Yale Univ. Press, 1957.

Dobriner, William M. *Class in Suburbia*. Englewood Cliffs, N.J.: Prentice-Hall, 1963.

———, ed. *The Suburban Community*. New York: G. P. Putnam's Sons, 1958.

Donovan, Frank. *Wheels for a Nation*. New York: Thomas Y. Crowell, 1965.

Donovan, Robert J. *Conflict and Crisis: The Presidency of Harry S. Truman, 1945–1948*. New York: W. W. Norton, 1977.

Doubler, Michael D.. *Closing with the Enemy: How GIs Fought the War in Europe, 1944–1945*. Lawrence: Univ. Press of Kansas, 1994.

Dower, John W. *Embracing Defeat: Japan in the Wake of World War II*. New York: W. W. Norton, 1999.

———. *War Without Mercy: Race and Power in the Pacific War*. New York: Pantheon Books, 1986.

Dreisziger, N. F., ed. *Ethnic Armies: Polyethnic Armed Forces from the Time of the Habsburgs to the Age of the Superpowers*. Waterloo, Ont.: Wilfrid Laurier Press, 1990.

Dudziak, Mary L. *Cold War Civil Rights: Race and the Image of American Democracy*. Princeton, N.J.: Princeton Univ. Press, 2000.

Edgerton, Alanson H. *Readjustment or Revolution?* New York: McGraw-Hill, 1946.

*Editions for the Armed Services: A History*. New York: Editions for the Armed Services, 1948.

Ellis, Joseph J. *Founding Brothers: The Revolutionary Generation*. New York: Vintage Books, 2000.

Erenberg, Lewis A., and Susan E. Hirsch, eds. *The War in American Culture: Society and Consciousness During World War II*. Chicago: Univ. of Chicago Press, 1996.

Eulau, Heinz. *Class and Party in the Eisenhower Years: Class Roles and Perspectives in the 1952 and 1956 Elections*. New York: Free Press, 1962.

Feaver, Peter D., and Richard H. Kohn, eds. *Soldiers and Civilians: The Civil Military Gap and American National Security.* Cambridge, Mass: MIT Press, 2001.

Feifer, George. *Tennozan: The Battle of Okinawa and the Atomic Bomb.* New York: Ticknor and Fields, 1992.

Feingold, Henry L. *A Time for Searching: Entering the Mainstream, 1920–1945.* Baltimore: Johns Hopkins Univ. Press, 1992.

Fenton, John H. *The Catholic Vote.* New Orleans: Hauser Press, 1960.

Fielding, Raymond. *The March of Time, 1935–1951.* New York: Oxford Univ. Press, 1978.

Flanagan, Richard W. *AMVETS: 50 Years of Proud Service to America's Veterans.* Lanham, Md.: AMVETS National Headquarters, 1994.

Fleming, Dan B., Jr. *Kennedy vs. Humphrey, West Virginia, 1960: The Pivotal Battle for the Democratic Presidential Nomination.* Jefferson, N.C.: McFarland, 1992.

Fletcher, Marvin E. *America's First Black General: Benjamin O. Davis, Sr., 1880–1970.* Lawrence: Univ. Press of Kansas, 1989.

Flynn, George Q. *American Catholics and the Roosevelt Presidency, 1932–1936.* Lexington: Univ. of Kentucky Press, 1968.

———. *The Draft, 1940–1973.* Lawrence: Univ. Press of Kansas, 1993.

———. *Lewis B. Hershey, Mr. Selective Service.* Chapel Hill: Univ. of North Carolina Press, 1985.

———. *Roosevelt and Romanism: Catholics and American Diplomacy, 1937–1945.* Westport, Conn.: Greenwood Press, 1976.

Foote, Shelby. *The Civil War: A Narrative, Red River to Appomattox.* New York: Vintage Books, 1974.

Ford, Nancy Gentile. *Americans All! Foreign-born Soldiers in World War I.* College Station: Texas A&M Univ. Press, 2001.

Foreman, Joel, ed. *The Other Fifties: Interrogating Midcentury American Icons.* Urbana: Univ. of Illinois Press, 1997.

Foster, Mark S. *A Nation on Wheels: The Automobile Culture in America Since 1945.* Belmont, Calif.: Thomson-Wadsworth, 2003.

Fousek, John. *To Lead the Free World: American Nationalism and the Cultural Roots of the Cold War.* Chapel Hill: Univ. of North Carolina Press, 2000.

Fox, Stephen. *America's Invisible Gulag: A Biography of German American Internment and Exclusion.* New York: Peter Lang, 2000.

———. *The Unknown Internment: An Oral History of the Relocation of Italian Americans during World War II.* Boston: Twayne, 1990.

Frank, Richard B. *Downfall: The End of the Imperial Japanese Empire.* New York: Random House, 1999.

Frederiksen, Norman, and W. B. Schrader. *Adjustment to College: A Study of 10,000 Veteran and Nonveteran Students in Sixteen American Colleges.* Princeton, N.J.: Educational Testing Service, 1951.

Fried, Richard M. *Nightmare in Red: The McCarthy Era in Perspective.* New York: Oxford Univ. Press, 1990.

Fussell, Paul. *Thank God for the Atom Bomb and Other Essays.* New York: Summit Books, 1988.

———. *Wartime: Understanding and Behavior in the Second World War.* New York: Oxford Univ. Press, 1989.

Gambone, Michael D. *The Greatest Generation Comes Home: The Veteran in American Society.* College Station: Texas A&M Univ. Press, 2005.

Gans, Herbert J. *The Levittowners: Ways of Life and Politics in a New Suburban Community.* New York: Pantheon Books, 1967.

———. *The Urban Villagers: Group and Class in the Life of Italian-Americans.* New York: Free Press, 1962.

Gardiner, Juliet. *"Overpaid, Oversexed, and Over Here": The American GI in World War II Britain.* New York: Canopy Books, 1992.

Gerber, David A., ed. *Disabled Veterans in History.* Ann Arbor: Univ. of Michigan Press, 2000.

Gerstle, Gary. *American Crucible: Race and Nation in the Twentieth Century.* Princeton Univ. Press, 2001.

Gerstle, Gary, and John Mollenkopf, eds. *E Pluribus Unum? Contemporary and Historical Perspectives on Immigrant Political Incorporation.* New York: Russell Sage Foundation, 2001.

Glazer, Nathan, and Daniel Patrick Moynihan. *Beyond the Melting Pot: The Negroes, Puerto Ricans, Jews, Italians, and Irish of New York City.* Cambridge, Mass: MIT Press, 1963.

Goldberg, Samuel. *Army Training of Illiterates in World War II.* New York: Teachers College, Columbia Univ., 1951.

Goldman, Eric F. *The Crucial Decade—and After: America, 1945–1960.* New York: Vintage, 1960.

———. *Rendezvous with Destiny: A History of Modern American Reform.* New York: Alfred A. Knopf, 1952.

Goldstein, Eric L. *The Price of Whiteness: Jews, Race, and American Identity.* Princeton, N.J.: Princeton Univ. Press, 2006.

Goodman, Jack, ed. *While You Were Gone: A Report on Wartime Life in the United States.* New York: Simon and Schuster, 1946.

Goodwyn, Lawrence. *Democratic Promise: The Populist Movement in America.* Oxford Univ. Press, 1976.

Goulden, Joseph C. *The Best Years, 1945–1950.* New York: Atheneum, 1976.

Graebner, William S. *The Age of Doubt: American Thought and Culture in the 1940s.* Boston: Twayne, 1991.

Greeley, Andrew M. *Why Can't They Be Like Us?: America's White Ethnic Groups.* New York: E. P. Dutton, 1971.

Greenberg, Milton. *The GI Bill: The Law that Changed America.* New York: Lickle, 1997.

Greenfield, Kent Roberts, Robert R. Palmer, and Bell Irvin Wiley. *The Organization of Ground Combat Troops.* Washington, D.C.: GPO, 1947.

Griffith, Robert. *The Politics of Fear: Joseph R. McCarthy and the Senate.* Lexington: Univ. Press of Kentucky, 1970.

Griffith, Robert K., Jr. *Men Wanted for the U.S. Army.* Westport, Conn.: Greenwood Press, 1982.

Guerin-Gonzales, Camille. *Mexican Workers and American Dreams: Immigration, Repatriation, and California Farm Labor, 1900–1939.* New Brunswick, N.J.: Rutgers Univ. Press, 1994.

Guglielmo, Jennifer, and Salvatore Salerno, eds. *Are Italians White? How Race is Made in America.* New York: Routledge, 2003.

Guglielmo, Thomas A. *White on Arrival: Italians, Race, Color, and Power in Chicago.* Oxford Univ. Press, 2003.

Gusfield, Joseph R. *Symbolic Crusade: Status Politics and the American Temperance Movement.* Urbana: Univ. of Illinois Press, 1963.

Gushwa, Robert L. *The Best and Worst of Times: The United States Army Chaplaincy, 1920–1945.* Washington, D.C.: Department of the Army, 1977.

Guterl, Matthew Pratt. *The Color of Race in America, 1900–1940.* Cambridge: Harvard Univ. Press, 2001.

Hamby, Alonzo L. *For the Survival of Democracy: Franklin Roosevelt and the World Crisis of the 1930s.* New York: Free Press, 2004.

———. *Man of the People: A Life of Harry S. Truman.* New York: Oxford Univ. Press, 1995.

Handlin, Oscar. *Al Smith and His America.* Boston: Little, Brown, 1958.

———. *The Uprooted: The Epic Story of the Great Migrations that Made the American People.* Boston: Little, Brown, 1951.

Hansen, Marcus L. *The Problem of the Third Generation Immigrant.* Rock Island, Ill.: Augustana Historical Society, 1938.

Harbaugh, William Henry. *The Life and Times of Theodore Roosevelt.* 1961. Reprint, New York: Collier Books, 1963.

Harding, Warren G. *Our Common Country: Mutual Good Will in America.* Columbia: Univ. of Missouri Press, 2003.

Hartmann, Susan M. *The Home Front and Beyond: American Women in the 1940s.* Boston: Twayne, 1982.

———. *Truman and the 80th Congress.* Columbia: Univ. of Missouri Press, 1971.

Havighurst, Robert J., Walter H. Eaton, John W. Baugham, and Ernest W. Burgess. *The American Veteran Back Home.* New York: Longmans, Green, 1951.

Heineman, Kenneth J. *A Catholic New Deal: Religion and Reform in Depression Pittsburgh.* University Park: Pennsylvania State Univ. Press, 1999.

Herberg, Will. *Protestant—Catholic—Jew: An Essay in American Religious Sociology.* Garden City, N.Y.: Doubleday, 1955.

Herrick, Arnold, and Herbert Askwith, eds. *This Way to Unity: For the Promotion of Good Will and Teamwork among Racial, Religious, and National Groups.* New York: Oxford Book Co., 1945.

Hicken, Victor. *The American Fighting Man.* New York: Macmillan, 1969.

Hicks, John D. *The Populist Revolt: A History of the Farmers' Alliance and the People's Party.* Univ. of Minnesota Press, 1931.

Higham, John. *Send These to Me: Immigration in Urban America.* 1975. Rev. ed., Baltimore: Johns Hopkins Univ. Press, 1984.

———. *Strangers in the Land: Patterns of American Nativism, 1860–1925.* Rev. ed. New York: Atheneum, 1967.

Higham, Robin, and Carol Brandt, eds. *The United States Army in Peacetime.* Manhattan, Kans.: Military Affairs/Aerospace Historian, 1975.

Hochschild, Jennifer L. *Facing Up to the American Dream: Race Class and the Soul of the Nation.* Princeton, N.J.: Princeton Univ. Press, 1995.

Hoffmann, Frank, Dick Carty, and Quentin Riggs. *Billy Murray: The Phonograph Industry's First Great Recording Artist.* Lanham, Md.: Scarecrow Press, 1997.

Hofstadter, Richard. *The Age of Reform: From Bryan to F.D.R.* New York: Alfred A. Knopf, 1955.

Holland, Kenneth, and Frank Ernest Hill. *Youth in the CCC.* Washington, D.C.: American Council on Education, 1942.

Hollinger, David H. *Postethnic America: Beyond Multiculturalism.* New York: Basic Books, 1995.

Holt, Michael F. *The Rise and Fall of the American Whig Party.* New York: Oxford Univ. Press, 1999.

Honeywell, Roy J. *Chaplains of the United States Army.* Washington, D.C.: Department of the Army, 1958.

Houle, Cyril O., Elbert W. Burr, Thomas H. Hamilton, and John R. Yale. *The Armed Services and Adult Education.* Washington, D.C.: American Council on Education, 1947.

Hovland, Carl I., Arthur A. Lumsdaine, and Fred D. Sheffield. *Studies in Social Psychology in World War II.* Vol. 3, *Experiments on Mass Communication.* Princeton, N.J.: Princeton Univ. Press, 1949.

Hunter, Robert. *Poverty: Social Conscience in the Progressive Era.* New York: Macmillan, 1904. Reprint edited by Peter d'A. Jones. New York: Harper Torchbooks, 1965.

Huntington, Samuel P. *The Soldier and the State: The Theory and Politics of Civil-Military Relations.* Cambridge, Mass.: Belknap Press, 1957.

Hutchinson, E. P. *Legislative History of American Immigration Policy, 1798–1965.* Philadelphia: Univ. of Pennsylvania Press, 1981.

Ignatiev, Noel. *How the Irish Became White.* New York: Routledge, 1995.

Irons, Peter. *Justice at War.* New York: Oxford Univ. Press, 1983.

*Italy and America, 1943–44: Italian, American and Italian American Experiences of the Liberation of the Italian Mezzogiorno.* Naples, Italy: La Citta Del Sole, 1997.

Jackson, Kenneth T. *Crabgrass Frontier: The Suburbanization of the United States.* New York: Oxford Univ. Press, 1985.

———. *The Ku Klux Klan in the City, 1915–1930.* New York: Oxford Univ. Press, 1967.

Jacobson, Matthew Frye. *Whiteness of a Different Color: European Immigrants and the Alchemy of Race.* Cambridge: Harvard Univ. Press, 1998.

Jacoby, Tamar, ed. *Reinventing the Melting Pot: The New Immigrants and What It Means to Be American.* New York: Basic Books, 2004.

Janowitz, Morris. *The Professional Soldier: A Social and Political Portrait.* New York: Free Press, 1960.

Jeffries, John W. *Testing the Roosevelt Coalition: Connecticut Society and Politics in the Era of World War II.* Knoxville: Univ. of Tennessee Press, 1979.

Karabell, Zachary. *The Last Campaign: How Harry Truman Won the 1948 Election.* New York: Alfred A. Knopf, 2000.

Karsten, Peter, ed. *The Military in America.* New York: Free Press, 1980.

Katznelson, Ira, and Martin Sefter, eds. *Shaped by War and Trade: International Influences on American Political Development.* Princeton, N.J.: Princeton Univ. Press, 2002.

Kaufman, Isidor. *American Jews in World War II: The Story of 550,000 Fighters for Freedom.* New York: Dial Press, 1947.

Kazin, Michael. *The Populist Persuasion: An American History.* New York: Basic Books, 1995.

Keats, John. *The Crack in the Picture Window.* Boston: Houghton Mifflin, 1956.

Keegan, John. *The Face of Battle.* New York: Penguin Books, 1976.

Keene, Jennifer D. *Doughboys, the Great War, and the Remaking of America.* Baltimore: Johns Hopkins Univ. Press, 2001.

Keller, Christian. *Chancellorsville and the Germans: Nativism, Ethnicity, and Civil War Memory.* New York: Fordham Univ. Press, 2007.

Kennedy, David M. *Freedom from Fear: The American People in Depression and War, 1929–1945.* Oxford Univ. Press, 1999.

————. *Over Here: The First World War and American Society.* New York: Oxford Univ. Press, 1980.

Kerr, K. Austin, ed. *The Politics of Moral Behavior: Prohibition and Drug Abuse.* Reading, Mass: Addison-Wesley, 1973.

Kerston, Andrew Edmund. *Race, Jobs, and the War: The FEPC in the Midwest, 1941–46.* Urbana: Univ. of Illinois Press, 2000.

Kevles, Daniel J. *In the Name of Eugenics: Genetics and the Uses of Human Heredity.* Cambridge: Harvard Univ. Press, 1985, 1995.

Killigrew, John W. *The Impact of the Great Depression on the Army.* New York: Garland, 1979.

Kincheloe, Samuel C. *Research Memorandum on Religion in the Depression.* New York: Social Science Research Council, 1937.

Kindsvatter, Peter S. *American Soldiers: Ground Combat in the World Wars, Korea, and Vietnam.* Lawrence: Univ. Press of Kansas, 2003.

Kington, Donald M. *Forgotten Summers: The Story of the Citizens' Military Training Camps.* San Francisco, Calif.: Two Decades, 1995.

Koppes, Clayton R., and Gregory D. Black. *Hollywood Goes to War: How Politics, Profits and Propaganda Shaped World War II Movies.* Berkeley and Los Angeles: Univ. of California Press, 1987.

Krakau, Knud, ed. *The American Nation, National Identity, Nationalism.* New Brunswick, N.J.: Transaction Publishers, 1997.

Kuhl, Stefan. *The Nazi Connection: Eugenics, American Racism, and German National Socialism.* New York: Oxford Univ. Press, 1994.

Kurzman, Dan. *No Greater Glory: The Four Immortal Chaplains and the Sinking of the Dorchester in World War II.* New York: Random House, 2004.

Kuznick, Peter J., and James Gilbert, eds. *Rethinking Cold War Culture.* Washington, D.C.: Smithsonian Institution Press, 2001.

Kyvig, David E. *Daily Life in the United States, 1920–1939: Decades of Promise and Pain.* Westport, Conn.: Greenwood Press, 2002.

————. *Repealing National Prohibition.* Univ. of Chicago Press, 1979.

LaGumina, Salvatore, ed. *Wop!* San Francisco: Straight Arrow Books, 1973.

Lasch, Christopher. *The New Radicalism in America, 1889–1963: The Intellectual as a Social Type.* New York: Vintage Books, 1965.

Lasch, Robert. *Breaking the Building Blockade*. Univ. of Chicago Press, 1946.

Lee, Ulysses. *The Employment of Negro Troops*. Washington, D.C.: GPO, 1966.

Leffler, Melvyn P. *A Preponderance of Power: National Security, the Truman Administration, and the Cold War*. Stanford, Calif: Stanford Univ. Press, 1992.

Lemann, Nicholas. *The Promised Land: The Great Black Migration and How It Changed America*. New York: Vintage Books, 1991.

Lerda, Valeria Gennaro, ed. *From "Melting Pot" to Multiculturalism*. Rome: Bulzoni Editore, 1990.

Leuchtenburg, William E. *The FDR Years: On Roosevelt and His Legacy*. New York: Columbia Univ. Press, 1995.

———. *Franklin D. Roosevelt and the New Deal*. New York: Harper and Row, 1963.

———. *The Perils of Prosperity, 1914–1932*. 1958. 2nd ed. Chicago: Univ. of Chicago Press, 1993.

Lewis, Tom. *Divided Highways: Building Interstate Highways, Transforming American Life*. New York: Viking, 1997.

Lichtman, Allan J. *Prejudice and the Old Politics: The Presidential Election of 1928*. Chapel Hill: Univ. of North Carolina Press, 1979.

Linderman, Gerald F. *The World Within War: America's Combat Experience in World War II*. New York: Free Press, 1997.

Link, Arthur S. *Woodrow Wilson and the Progressive Era, 1910–1917*. New York: Harper and Brothers, 1954.

Lipset, Seymour Martin, and Gary Marks. *It Didn't Happen Here: Why Socialism Failed in the United States*. New York: W. W. Norton, 2000.

Lipsitz, George. *Rainbow at Midnight: Labor and Culture in the 1940s*. Urbana: Univ. of Illinois Press, 1994.

Lipstadt, Deborah E. *Beyond Belief: The American Press and the Coming of the Holocaust, 1933–1945*. New York: Free Press, 1986.

Lisio, Donald J. *The President and Protest: Hoover, Conspiracy, and the Bonus Riot*. Columbia: Univ. of Missouri Press, 1974.

Loescher, Gil, and John A. Scanlan. *Calculated Kindness: Refugees and America's Half-Open Door, 1945 to the Present*. New York: Free Press, 1986.

Longmate, Norman. *The G.I.'s: The Americans in Britain, 1942–1945*. New York: Charles Scribner's Sons, 1975.

Lonn, Ella. *Foreigners in the Confederacy*. 1940. Reprint, Chapel Hill: Univ. of North Carolina Press, 2002.

———. *Foreigners in the Union Army and Navy*. Baton Rouge: Louisiana State Univ. Press, 1951.

Lotchin, Roger W., ed. *The Way We Really Were: The Golden State in the Second Great War*. Urbana: Univ. of Illinois Press, 2000.

Lubell, Samuel. *The Future of American Politics.* New York: Harper and Brothers, 1951.

Lynn, John A. *Battle: A History of Combat and Culture.* Boulder, Colo.: Westview Press, 2003.

MacCambridge, Michael. *America's Game: The Epic Story of How Pro Football Captured a Nation.* New York: Random House, 2004.

MacGregor, Morris J., Jr. *Integration of the Armed Forces, 1940–1965.* Washington, D.C.: Center of Military History United States Army, 1981.

MacIver, R. M. *The More Perfect Union: A Program for the Control of Inter-group Discrimination in the United States.* New York: Macmillan, 1948.

MacLean, Nancy. *Behind the Mask of Chivalry: The Making of the Second Ku Klux Klan.* New York: Oxford Univ. Press, 1994.

Mann, Arthur. *The One and the Many: Reflections on the American Identity.* Univ. of Chicago Press, 1979.

Mansoor, Peter R. *The GI Offensive in Europe: The Triumph of American Infantry Divisions.* Lawrence: Univ. Press of Kansas, 1999.

Martin, Ralph G. *The GI War, 1941–1945.* Boston: Little, Brown, 1967.

Marty, Martin E. *Modern American Religion.* Vol. 3, *Under God, Indivisible, 1941–1960.* Univ. of Chicago Press, 1996.

———. *The New Shape of American Religion.* New York: Harper and Brothers, 1958.

Mattox, Henry E. *Army Football in 1945: Anatomy of a Championship Season.* Jefferson, N.C.: McFarland, 1990.

May, Elaine Tyler. *Homeward Bound: American Families in the Cold War Era.* New York: Basic Books, 1988.

May, Lary. *The Big Tomorrow: Hollywood and the Politics of the American Way.* Chicago: Univ. of Chicago Press, 2000.

McCoy, Donald R. *Calvin Coolidge: The Quiet President.* New York: Macmillan, 1967.

McCoy, Donald R., and Richard T. Ruetten. *Quest and Response: Minority Rights in the Truman Administration.* Lawrence: Univ. Press of Kansas, 1973.

McGerr, Michael. *A Fierce Discontent: The Rise and Fall of the Progressive Movement in America, 1870–1920.* New York: Free Press, 2003.

McManus, John C. *The Americans at D-Day.* New York: Forge, 2004.

McNeill, William H. *Keeping Together in Time: Dance and Drill in Human History.* Cambridge: Harvard Univ. Press, 1997.

Mead, Margaret. *And Keep Your Powder Dry: An Anthropologist Looks at America.* New York: William Morrow, 1942.

Menand, Louis. *The Metaphysical Club.* New York: Farrar, Straus and Giroux, 2001.

Mettler, Suzanne. *Soldiers to Citizens: The G.I. Bill and the Making of the Greatest Generation.* New York: Oxford Univ. Press, 2005.

Millis, Walter. *Road to War: America 1914–1917*. Boston: Houghton Mifflin, 1935.

Mills, C. Wright. *The Power Elite*. New York: Oxford Univ. Press, 1956.

Mills, Nicholas. *Their Last Battle: The Fight for the National World War II Memorial*. New York: Basic Books, 2004.

Minott, Rodney G. *Peerless Patriots: Organized Veterans and the Spirit of Americanism*. Washington, D.C.: Public Affairs Press, 1962.

Moley, Raymond, Jr. *The American Legion Story*. New York: Dell, Cloan and Pearce, 1966.

Moore, Deborah Dash. *At Home in America: Second Generation New York Jews*. New York: Columbia Univ. Press, 1981.

———. *GI Jews: How World War II Changed a Generation*. Cambridge: Belknap Press of Harvard Univ. Press, 2004.

Moore, Edmund A. *A Catholic Runs for President: The Campaign of 1928*. New York: Ronald Press, 1956.

Moore, John Hammond. *Over-Sexed, Over-Paid, and Over Here: Americans in Australia, 1941–1945*. St. Lucia: Univ. of Queensland Press, 1981.

Morin, Raul. *Among the Valiant: Mexican-Americans in WW II and Korea*. Alhambra, Calif.: Borden, 1963.

Mormino, Gary R., and George E. Pozzetta. *The Immigrant World of Ybor City: Italians and Their Latin Neighbors in Tampa, 1885–1985*. Urbana: Univ. of Illinois Press, 1987.

Mosch, Theodore R. *The G.I. Bill: A Breakthrough in Educational and Social Policy in the United States*. Hicksville, N.Y.: Exposition Press, 1975.

Murphy, Gardner, ed. *Human Nature and Enduring Peace*. Boston: Houghton Mifflin, 1945.

Murray, Robert K. *The Politics of Normalcy: Governmental Theory and Practice in the Harding-Coolidge Era*. New York: Norton, 1973.

Myrdal, Gunnar. *An American Dilemma: The Negro Problem and Modern Democracy*. New York: Harper and Brothers, 1944.

National Conference of Jews and Christians. *Public Opinion in a Democracy*. New York: National Conference of Jews and Christians, 1937.

Neal, Steve. *Harry and Ike: The Partnership That Remade the Postwar World*. New York: Scribner, 2001.

Nichols, David, ed. *Ernie's America: The Best of Ernie Pyle's 1930s Travel Dispatches*. New York: Random House, 1989.

Novak, Michael. *The Rise of the Unmeltable Ethnics: Politics and Culture in the Seventies*. New York: Macmillan, 1972.

Novick, Peter. *The Holocaust in American Life*. Boston: Houghton Mifflin, 1999.

O'Brien, David J. *American Catholics and Social Reform: The New Deal Years.* New York: Oxford Univ. Press, 1968.

O'Brien, Kenneth Paul, and Lynn Hudson Parsons. *The Home-Front War: World War II and American Society.* Westport, Conn: Greenwood Press, 1995.

Odom, William O. *After the Trenches: The Transformation of U.S. Army Doctrine.* College Station: Texas A&M Univ. Press, 1999.

Oliver, Alfred C., and Harold M. Dudley. *This New America: The Spirit of the Civilian Conservation Corps.* London: Longmans, Green, 1937.

Olson, James S. *The Ethnic Dimension in American History.* St. James, N.Y.: Brandywine Press, 1999.

Olson, Keith W. *The G.I. Bill, the Veterans, and the Colleges.* Lexington: Univ. Press of Kentucky, 1974.

Oshinsky, David M. *A Conspiracy So Immense: The World of Joe McCarthy.* New York: Free Press, 1983.

O'Sullivan, John. *From Voluntarism to Conscription: Congress and Selective Service.* New York: Garland, 1982.

Palmer, Robert R., Bell I. Wiley, and William R. Keast. *The Procurement and Training of Ground Combat Troops.* Washington, D.C.: GPO, 1948.

Patterson, James T. *Congressional Conservatism and the New Deal: The Growth of the Conservative Coalition in Congress, 1933–1939.* Lexington: Univ. of Kentucky Press, 1967.

———. *Grand Expectations: The United States, 1945–1974.* New York: Oxford Univ. Press, 1996.

Pearlman, Michael. *To Make Democracy Safe for America: Patricians and Preparedness in the Progressive Era.* Urbana: Univ. of Illinois Press, 1984.

Peel, Roy V., and Thomas C. Donnelly. *The 1928 Campaign: An Analysis.* New York: R. R. Smith, 1931.

Pells, Richard H. *The Liberal Mind in a Conservative Age.* New York: Harper and Row, 1985.

Pencak, William. *For God and Country: The American Legion, 1919–1941.* Boston: Northeastern Univ. Press, 1989.

Perlmutter, Philip. *Divided We Fall: A History of Ethnic, Religious, and Racial Prejudice in America.* Ames: Iowa State Univ. Press, 1992.

Piehler, G. Kurt. *Remembering War the American Way.* Washington, D.C.: Smithsonian Institution Press, 1995.

Pogue, Forrest C. *George C. Marshall: Education of a General, 1880–1939.* New York: Viking, 1963.

———. *George C. Marshall: Ordeal and Hope, 1939–1942.* New York: Viking, 1965.

Polenberg, Richard. *One Nation Divisible: Class, Race, and Ethnicity in the United States since 1938.* New York: Viking, 1980.

Pollack, Norman. *The Humane Economy: Populism, Capitalism, and Democracy.* New Brunswick, N.J.: Rutgers Univ. Press, 1990.

Pool, Ithiel de Sola, Robert P. Abelson, and Samuel L. Popkin. *Candidates, Issues, and Strategies: A Computer Simulation of the 1960 Election.* Cambridge, Mass: MIT Press, 1964.

Potts, E. Daniel, and Annette Potts. *Yanks Down Under, 1941–45: The American Impact on Australia.* New York: Oxford Univ. Press, 1985.

Prendergast, William B. *The Catholic Voter in American Politics: The Passing of the Democratic Monolith.* Washington, D.C.: Georgetown Univ. Press, 1999.

Pugliese, Stanislao G., ed. *Frank Sinatra: History, Identity, and American Culture.* New York: Palgrave Macmillan, 2004.

Putnam, Robert D. *Bowling Alone: The Collapse and Revival of American Community.* New York: Simon and Schuster, 2000.

Rader, Benjamin G. *American Sports: From the Age of Folk Games to the Age of Televised Sports.* Upper Saddle River, N.J.: Prentice-Hall, 2004.

Randall, Gregory C. *America's Original GI Town: Park Forest, Illinois.* Baltimore: Johns Hopkins Univ. Press, 2000.

Rappoport, Leon. *How We Eat: Appetite, Culture, and the Psychology of Food.* Toronto: ECW Press, 2003.

Rauchway, Eric. *Murdering McKinley: The Making of Theodore Roosevelt's America.* New York: Hill and Wang, 2003.

Reardon, Carol. *Soldiers and Scholars: The U.S. Army and the Uses of Military History, 1865–1920.* Lawrence: Univ. Press of Kansas, 1990.

Reed, Merl E. *Seedtime for the Modern Civil Rights Movement: The President's Committee on Fair Employment Practice, 1941–1946.* Baton Rouge: Louisiana State Univ. Press, 1991.

Reeves, Thomas C. *The Life and Times of Joe McCarthy.* New York: Steyn and Day, 1982.

———. *A Question of Character: A Life of John F. Kennedy.* New York: Free Press, 1991.

Reynolds, David. *Rich Relations: The American Occupation of Britain, 1942–1945.* New York: Random House, 1995.

Rieder, Jonathan. *Canarsie: The Jews and Italians of Brooklyn against Liberalism.* Cambridge: Harvard Univ. Press, 1985.

Roback, A. A. *A Dictionary of International Slurs.* Cambridge, Mass: Sci-Art Publishers, 1944.

Roediger, David R. *The Wages of Whiteness: Race and the Making of the American Working Class.* New York: Verso, 1991.

———. *Working Toward Whiteness: How America's Immigrants Became White*. New York: Basic Books, 2005.

Rose, Arnold M. *Studies in Reduction of Prejudice: A Memorandum Summarizing Research on Modification of Attitudes*. Chicago: American Council on Race Relations, 1948.

Rose, Mark H. *Interstate: Express Highway Politics, 1941–1956*. Lawrence: Regents Press of Kansas, 1979.

Rosenberg, Emily S. *A Date Which Will Live: Pearl Harbor in American Memory*. Durham, N.C.: Duke Univ. Press, 2003.

Ross, Davis R. B. *Preparing for Ulysses: Politics and Veterans during World War II*. New York: Columbia Univ. Press, 1969.

Ross, Irwin. *The Loneliest Campaign: The Truman Victory of 1948*. New York: New American Library, 1968.

Rumer, Thomas A. *The American Legion: An Official History, 1919–1989*. New York: M. Evans, 1990.

Runyan, Timothy J., and Jan M. Copes, eds. *To Die Gallantly: The Battle of the Atlantic*. Boulder, Colo.: Westview Press, 1994.

Salmond, John A. *The Civilian Conservation Corps, 1933–1942: A New Deal Case Study*. Durham, N.C.: Duke Univ. Press, 1967.

Saxe, Robert Francis. *Settling Down: World War II Veterans' Challenge to the Postwar Consensus*. New York: Palgrave Macmillan, 2007.

Schaffer, Ronald. *America in the Great War: The Rise of the War Welfare State*. New York: Oxford Univ. Press, 1991.

Schlesinger, Arthur M., Jr. *The Disuniting of America: Reflections on a Multicultural Society*. Knoxville, Tenn: Whittle Direct Books, 1991.

———, ed. *The Coming to Power: Critical Presidential Elections in American History*. New York: Chelsea Hill, 1971.

Schrijvers, Peter. *The GI War Against Japan: American Soldiers in Asia and the Pacific during World War II*. New York Univ. Press, 2002.

Schulman, Robert. *John Sherman Cooper: The Global Kentuckian*. Lexington: Univ. Press of Kentucky, 1976.

Severo, Richard, and Lewis Milford. *The Wages of War*. New York: Simon and Schuster, 1989.

Shelton, Peter. *Climb to Conquer: The Untold Story of World War II's 10th Mountain Division Ski Troops*. New York: Scribner, 2003.

Sherwood, Robert E. *Roosevelt and Hopkins: An Intimate History*. New York: Harper and Brothers, 1948.

Silva, Ruth C. *Rum, Religion, and Votes: 1928 Re-examined*. University Park: Pennsylvania State Univ. Press, 1962.

Skocpol, Theda. *Diminished Democracy: From Membership to Management in American Civil Life.* Norman: Univ. of Oklahoma Press, 2003.

Slayton, Robert A. *Empire Statesman: The Rise and Redemption of Al Smith.* New York: Free Press, 2001.

Slotkin, Richard. *Lost Battalions: The Great War and the Crisis of American Nationality.* New York: Henry Holt, 2005.

Smith, Chellis V. *Americans All: Nine Heroes who in the World War showed that Americanism is Above Race, Creed, or Condition.* Boston: Lothrop, Lee and Shepard, 1925.

Smith, Graham. *When Jim Crow Met John Bull: Black American Soldiers in World War II Britain.* New York: St. Martin's Press, 1987.

Sobel, Robert. *Coolidge: An American Enigma.* Washington, D.C.: Regnery, 1998.

Somers, Herman Miles. *Presidential Agency: Office of War Mobilization and Reconversion.* Cambridge: Harvard Univ. Press, 1950.

Sorenson, Theodore C. *Kennedy.* New York: Harper and Row, 1965.

Sowell, Thomas. *Ethnic America: A History.* New York: Basic Books, 1981.

Sperry, Willard L. *Religion in America.* Boston: Beacon Press, 1946, 1963.

———, ed. *Religion and Our Racial Tensions.* Cambridge: Harvard Univ. Press, 1945.

Sperry, Willard L., John LaFarge, John T. McNeill, Louis Finkelstein, and Archibald MacLeish. *Religion and Our Divided Denominations.* Cambridge: Harvard Univ. Press, 1945.

Stegner, Wallace. *One Nation.* Boston: Houghton Mifflin, 1945.

Stein, Harry. *The Girl Watchers Club: Lessons from the Battlefields of Life.* New York: HarperCollins, 2004.

Sterba, Christopher M. *Good Americans: Italian and Jewish Immigrants during the First World War.* New York: Oxford Univ. Press, 2003.

Stouffer, Samuel A. *Communism, Conformity, and Civil Liberties: A Cross-section of the Nation Speaks Its Mind.* Garden City, N.Y.: Doubleday, 1955.

Stouffer, Samuel A., Edward A. Suchman, Leland C. DeVinney, Shirley A. Star, and Robin M. Williams Jr., eds. *Studies in Social Psychology in World War II: The American Soldier.* 2 vols. Princeton, N.J.: Princeton Univ. Press, 1949.

Stover, Earl F. *Up from Handymen: The United States Army Chaplaincy, 1865–1920.* Washington, D.C.: Department of the Army, 1977.

Strecker, Edward A., and Kenneth E. Appel. *Psychiatry in Modern Warfare.* New York: Macmillan, 1945.

Strong, Donald S. *Organized Anti-Semitism in America: The Rise of Group Prejudice During the Decade 1930–1940.* Washington, D.C.: American Council on Public Affairs, 1941.

Takaki, Ronald. *A Different Mirror: A History of Multicultural America.* Boston: Little, Brown, 1993.

Tashjian, James H. *The Armenian American in World War II.* Boston: Hairenik Association, 1953.

Thernstrom, Stephan, Ann Orloy, and Oscar Handlin. *Harvard Encyclopedia of American Ethnic Groups.* Cambridge, Mass: Belknap Press, 1980.

Thornton, Francis Beauchesne. *Sea of Glory: The Magnificent Story of the Four Chaplains.* New York: Prentice-Hall, 1953.

Timberlake, James H. *Prohibition and the Progressive Movement.* Cambridge: Harvard Univ. Press, 1963.

Tugwell, Rexford G. *The Democratic Roosevelt.* Garden City, N.Y.: Doubleday, 1957.

Tuttle, William M., Jr. *"Daddy's Gone to War": The Second World War in the Lives of America's Children.* Oxford Univ. Press, 1993.

Utley, Robert M. *Frontier Regulars: The United States Army and the Indian, 1866–1891.* Bloomington: Indiana Univ. Press, 1973.

van Creveld, Martin. *Fighting Power.* Westport, Conn.: Greenwood Press, 1982.

van der Vat, Dan. *The Atlantic Campaign: World War II's Great Struggle at Sea.* New York: Harper and Row, 1988.

Van Ells, Mark D. *To Hear Only Thunder Again: America's World War II Veterans Come Home.* Lanham, Md.: Lexington Books, 2001.

Vecoli, Rudolph J., and Suzanne M. Sinke, eds. *A Century of European Migrations.* Urbana: Univ. of Illinois Press, 1991.

Vedder, Richard K., and Lowell E. Gallaway. *Out of Work: Unemployment and Government in Twentieth-Century America.* 1993. Updated ed., New York Univ. Press, 1997.

Wade, Wyn Craig. *The Fiery Cross: The Ku Klux Klan in America.* New York: Simon and Schuster, 1987.

Walker, Helen M. *The CCC Through the Eyes of 272 Boys.* Cleveland: Western Reserve Univ. Press, 1938.

Waller, Willard. *The Veteran Comes Back.* New York: Dryden Press, 1944.

Ward, Brian, and Tony Badger, eds. *The Making of Martin Luther King and the Civil Rights Movement.* New York: New York Univ. Press, 1996.

Ward, Stephen R., ed. *The War Generation: Veterans of the First World War.* Port Washington, N.Y.: Kennikat Press, 1975.

Warner, W. Lloyd, and Leo Srole. *The Social Systems of American Ethnic Groups.* New Haven, Conn: Yale Univ. Press, 1945.

Watts, Martin. *The Jewish Legion and the First World War.* New York: Palgrave Macmillan, 2004.

Weatherford, Doris. *American Women in World War II*. New York: Facts on File, 1990.

Weber, Paul J., and W. Landis Jones. *U.S. Religious Interest Groups: Institutional Profiles*. Westport, Conn.: Greenwood Press, 1994.

Wecter, Dixon. *When Johnny Comes Marching Home*. Cambridge, Mass: Riverside Press, 1944.

Weigley, Russell F. *Eisenhower's Lieutenants*. Bloomington: Univ. of Indiana Press, 1981.

———. *History of the United States Army*. New York: Macmillan, 1967.

Weir, Margaret, Ann Shola Orloff, and Theda Skocpol. *The Politics of Social Policy in the United States*. Princeton, N.J.: Princeton Univ. Press, 1988.

Westbrook, Robert B. *Why We Fought: Forging American Obligations in World War II*. Washington, D.C.: Smithsonian Books, 2004.

White, Theodore H. *The Making of the President—1960*. New York: Atheneum, 1961.

Whitfield, Stephen J. *The Culture of the Cold War*. Baltimore: Johns Hopkins Univ. Press, 1991.

Whyte, William H., Jr. *The Organization Man*. New York: Simon and Schuster, 1956.

Wiebe, Robert H. *The Search for Order, 1877–1920*. New York: Hill and Wang, 1967.

———. *Who We Are: A History of Popular Nationalism*. Princeton, N.J.: Princeton Univ. Press, 2002.

Wilentz, Sean. *Chants Democratic: New York City and the Rise of the American Working Class, 1788–1850*. New York: Oxford Univ. Press, 1984.

Williams, Michael. *The Shadow of the Pope*. New York: Whittlesey House, 1932.

Williams, Robin M., Jr. *American Society: A Sociological Interpretation*. New York: Alfred A. Knopf, 1951.

———. *Strangers Next Door: Ethnic Relations in American Communities*. Englewood Cliffs, N.J.: Prentice-Hall, 1964.

Wilson, Joan Hoff. *Herbert Hoover: Forgotten Progressive*. Boston: Little, Brown, 1975.

Winkler, Allan M. *Life Under a Cloud: American Anxiety About the Atom*. New York: Oxford Univ. Press, 1993.

Wong, K. Scott. *Americans First: Chinese Americans and the Second World War*. Cambridge: Harvard Univ. Press, 2005.

Wood, Robert C. *Suburbia: Its People and Their Politics*. Boston: Houghton Mifflin, 1958.

Woodward, C. Vann. *Tom Watson: Agrarian Rebel*. 1938. Reprint, New York: Oxford Univ. Press, 1963.

Woofter, Thomas Jackson. *Races and Ethnic Groups in America*. New York: McGraw Hill, 1933.

Wyman, David. *Paper Walls: America and the Refugee Crisis, 1938–1941*. Amherst: Univ. of Massachusetts Press, 1968.

Wyman, Mark. *Round-Trip to America: The Immigrants Return to Europe, 1880–1930.* Ithaca, N.Y.: Cornell Univ. Press, 1993.

Wynn, Neil A. *The Afro-American and the Second World War.* New York: Holmes and Meier, 1975.

Yenne, Bill. *Rising Sons: The Japanese American GIs Who Fought for the United States in World War II.* New York: Thomas Dunne, 2007.

Ziemke, Earl F. *The U.S. Army in the Occupation of Germany, 1944–1946.* Washington, D.C.: GPO, 1975.

## Theses and Dissertations

Beekman, Scott M. "Silver Shirts and Golden Scripts: The Life of William Dudley Pelley." Ph.D. diss., Ohio Univ., 2003.

Brown, Richard C. "Social Attitudes of American Generals 1898–1940." Ph.D. diss., Univ. of Wisconsin, 1951.

Bruscino, Thomas A., Jr. "The Greatest and the Toughest: American Rifle Company Commanders and the War Against Germany, 1942–1945." Master's thesis, Ohio Univ., 2002.

Frydl, Kathleen J. "The G.I. Bill." Ph.D. diss., Univ. of Chicago, 2000.

O'Brien, Marjorie A. "An Evaluation of the Civilian Conservation Corps as an Educational Institution." Master's thesis, Ohio Univ., 1970.

White, William Bruce. "The Military and the Melting Pot: The American Army and Minority Groups, 1865–1924." Ph.D. diss., Univ. of Wisconsin, 1968.

## Newspapers, Articles, Paper Presentations, and Pamphlets

Alpers, Benjamin L. "This Is the Army: Imagining a Democratic Military in World War II." *Journal of American History* 85 (June 1998): 129–163.

*American Legion Magazine,* 1941–1960.

Angrist, Joshua, and Alan B. Krueger. "Why Do World War II Veterans Earn More than Nonveterans?" *Journal of Labor Economics* 12 (Jan. 1994): 74–97.

*Army and Navy Register,* 1879–1948.

Baird, Nancy Disher. "An Opportunity to Meet 'Every Kind of Person': A Kentuckian Views Army Life during World War II." *Register of the Kentucky Historical Society* 101 (Summer 2003): 297–318.

Berthoff, Rowland. "A Rejoinder on Wartime Anti-Semitism." *Journal of American History* 77 (Sept. 1990): 590.

Brookover, Wilbur B. "The Adjustment of Veterans to Civilian Life." *American Sociological Review* 10 (Oct. 1945): 579–586.

Brotz, Howard, and Everett Wilson. "Characteristics of Military Society." *American Journal of Sociology* 51 (Mar. 1946): 371–375.

Bruscino, Thomas A., Jr. "The Analogue of Work: Memory and Motivation for World War II Soldiers." Paper presented at the Society for Military History Conference, The Citadel, Charleston, S.C., Feb. 24–27, 2005.

Canaday, Margot. "Building a Straight State: Sexuality and Social Citizenship under the 1944 G.I. Bill." *Journal of American History* 90 (Dec. 2003): 935–957.

*Chicago Tribune*, 1872–1965.

*Christian Science Monitor*, 1908–1965.

*CMTC: Memoirs of the Citizens Military Training Camps.* Chicago: Military Training Camp Association, 1935.

Coffman, Edward M. "A Younger Brother of the Greatest Generation." *Register of the Kentucky Historical Society* 100 (Spring 2002): 129–38.

Conzen, Kathleen Neil, David A. Gerber, Ewa Morawska, George E. Pozetta, and Rudolph J. Vecoli. "The Invention of Ethnicity: A perspective from the U.S.A." *Journal of American Ethnic History* 12 (Fall 1992): 3–42.

Crespi, Leo P., and G. Schofield Shapleigh. "'The' Veteran—A Myth." *Public Opinion Quarterly* 10 (Aug. 1946): 361–372.

Cuber, John F. "Family Readjustment of Veterans." *Marriage and Family Living* 7 (May 1945): 28–30.

Dudley, J. Wayne. "'Hate' Organizations of the 1940s: The Columbians, Inc." *Phylon* 42 (3rd Qtr. 1981): 262–274.

Easterbrook, Arthur E. "Reconversion of Men: Restoring the Veteran's Individuality." *Vital Speeches of the Day* 11 (Aug. 1, 1945): 610–612.

Eaton, Walter H. "Research on Veterans' Readjustment." *American Journal of Sociology* 51 (Mar. 1946): 483–487.

Educational Policies Commission. *The Civilian Conservation Corps, the National Youth Administration, and the Public Schools.* Washington, D.C., 1941.

Elder, Glen H., Jr. "War Mobilization and the Life Course: A Cohort of World War II Veterans." *Sociological Forum* 2 (Summer 1987): 449–472.

Elkin, Henry. "Aggressive and Erotic Tendencies in Army Life." *American Journal of Sociology* 51 (Mar. 1946): 408–413.

*Ex-CBI Roundup*, 1945–1960.

Fleegler, Robert L. "'Forget All Differences Until the Forces of Freedom Are Triumphant': The World War II–Era Quest for Ethnic and Religious Tolerance." *Journal of American Ethnic History* 27 (Winter 2008): 59–84.

Ford, Nancy Gentile. "'Mindful of the Traditions of His Race': Dual Identity and Foreign-born Soldiers in the First World War American Army." *Journal of American Ethnic History* 16 (Winter 1997): 35–57.

*Fortune*, 1935–1965.

Foster, Stuart J. "The Struggle for American Identity: Treatment of Ethnic Groups in United States History Textbooks." *History of Education* 28 (Sept. 1999): 251–278.

Freeman, Howard E., and Morris Showel. "Differential Political Influence of Voluntary Associations." *Public Opinion Quarterly* 15 (Winter 1951–52): 703–714.

Gerber, David A. "Caucasians Are Made and Not Born: How European Immigrants Became White People." *Reviews in American History* 27 (Sept. 1999): 437–443.

Gilbert, G. M. "Stereotype Persistence and Change Among College Students." *Journal of Abnormal and Social Psychology* 46 (1951): 245–254.

Gleason, Philip. "Americans All: World War II and the Shaping of American Identity." *Review of Politics* 43 (Oct. 1981): 483–518.

Goldin, Miton. Review of *The "Jewish Threat": Anti-Semitic Politics of the U.S. Army*, by Joseph W. Bendersky. H-Net, H-Antisemitism. Feb. 2001. http://www.h-net.org/reviews/.

Grandstaff, Mark R. "Making the Military American: Advertising, Reform, and the Demise of an Antistanding Military Tradition, 1945–1955." *Journal of Military History* 60 (Apr. 1996): 299–323.

Hansen, Marcus L. "The Third Generation in America." *Commentary* 14 (Nov. 1952): 492–500.

Hapak, Joseph T. "Selective Service and Polish Army Recruitment during World War I." *Journal of American Ethnic History* 10 (Summer 1991): 38–61.

*Hartford Courant,* 1900–1965.

Hill, Frank Ernest. *The School in the Camps: The Educational Program of the Civilian Conservation Corps.* New York: American Association for Adult Education, 1935.

*In the Nation's Service: A Compilation of Facts Concerning Jewish Men in the Armed Forces During the First Year of the War.* 1942. Reprint, New York: National Jewish Welfare Board, 1943.

Jacobs, James B., and Leslie Anne Hayes. "Aliens in the U.S. Armed Forces: A Historico-Legal Analysis." *Armed Forces and Society* 7 (Winter 1981): 187–208.

James, George F. *Eleven Years of the CMTC: A Brief Account of the Citizens' Military Training Camps, 1921–1931.* Chicago: Military Training Camps Association, n.d.

Jensen, Richard J. "'No Irish Need Apply': A Myth of Victimization." *Journal of Social History* 36 (Winter 2002): 405–429.

*Jing Bao Journal,* 1945–1960.

Johnson, Charles W. "The Army, the Negro and the Civilian Conservation Corps: 1933–1942." *Military Affairs* 36 (Oct. 1972): 82–88.

Kazal, Russell A. "Revisiting Assimilation: The Rise, Fall, and Reappraisal of a Concept in American Ethnic History." *American Historical Review* 100 (Apr. 1995): 437–471.

Klavan, Andrew. "The Lost Art of War." *City Journal* 18 (Winter 2008). http://www.city-journal.org (accessed Feb. 5, 2008).

Lee, R. Alton. "The Army 'Mutiny' of 1946." *Journal of American History* 53 (Dec. 1966): 555–571.

*Los Angeles Times,* 1890–1965.

Loss, Christopher P. "Reading Between Enemy Lines: Armed Service Editions and World War II." *Journal of Military History* 67 (July 2003): 811–834.

MacDonald, Charles B. "Novels of World War II: The First Round." *Military Affairs* 13 (Spring 1949): 42–46.

"The Making of the Infantryman." *American Journal of Sociology* 51 (Mar. 1946): 376–379.

Marshall, Charles C. "An Open Letter to the Honorable Alfred E. Smith." *Atlantic Monthly* 139 (Apr. 1927): 540–549.

Mettler, Suzanne. "Bringing the State Back in to Civic Engagement: Policy Feedback Effects of the G.I. Bill for World War II Veterans." *American Political Science Review* 96 (June 2002): 351–365.

Moore, Deborah Dash. "Jewish GIs and the Creation of the Judeo-Christian Tradition." *Religion and American Culture* 8 (Winter 1998): 31–53.

———. "Worshipping Together in Uniform." Paper presented at the Swig Lecture, Univ. of San Francisco, Sept. 2001. http://www.usfca.edu/judaicstudies/lectures. html.

*New York Times,* 1890–1965.

Onkst, David H. "'First a Negro . . . Incidentally a Veteran': Black World War Two Veterans and the G.I. Bill of Rights in the Deep South, 1944–1948." *Journal of Social History* 31 (Spring 1998): 517–543.

Ortiz, Stephen R. "The 'New Deal' for Veterans: The Economy Act, the Veterans of Foreign Wars, and the Origins of New Deal Dissent." *Journal of Military History* 70 (Apr. 2006): 415–438.

Perkins, Bradford. "Impressions of Wartime." *Journal of American History* 77 (Sept. 1990): 563–568.

Perlmann, Joel. *The Romance of Assimilation? Studying the Demographic Outcomes of Ethnic Intermarriages in American History.* Working Paper no. 230. New York: Jerome Levy Economics Institute of Bard College, June 2001.

Perlmann, Joel, and Roger Waldinger. "Second Generation Decline? Children of Immigrants, Past and Present—A Reconsideration." *International Migration Review* 31 (Winter 1997): 893–922.

*Public Opinion Quarterly,* 1937–1965.

Riemer, Svend. "Married Veterans Are Good Students." *Marriage and Family Living* 9 (Feb. 1947): 11–12.

Roberts, Harry V. "Prior-Service Attitudes Toward Whites of 219 Negro Veterans." *Journal of Negro Education* 22 (Autumn 1953): 455–465.

Rodgers, Thomas E. "Billy Yank and G.I. Joe: An Exploratory Essay on the Sociopolitical Dimensions of Soldier Motivation." *Journal of Military History* 69 (Jan. 2005): 93–121.

Rose, Arnold. "The Social Structure of the Army." *American Journal of Sociology* 51 (Mar. 1946): 361–364.

———. "Studies in the Reduction of Prejudice." Chicago: American Council on Race Relations, 1948.

Rosenfield, Harry N. "The Prospects for Immigration Amendments." *Law and Contemporary Politics* 21 (Spring 1956): 401–426.

Ross, Edward Alsworth. "The Old World in the New." 6 pt. series. *Century Illustrated Magazine* 87 (Nov. 1913–Apr. 1914): 28–35, 225–232, 392–398, 615–622, 712–718, 949–955.

Ruger, William, Sven E. Wilson, and Shawn L. Waddoups. "Warfare and Welfare: Military Service, Combat, and Marital Dissolution." *Armed Forces and Society* 29 (Fall 2002): 85–107.

Salyer, Lucy E. "Baptism by Fire: Race, Military Service, and U.S. Citizenship Policy, 1918–1935." *Journal of American History* 91 (Dec. 2004): 847–876.

Saxe, Robert Francis. "'Citizens First, Veterans Second': The American Veterans Committee and the Challenge of Postwar 'Independent Progressives.'" *War and Society* 22 (Oct. 2004): 75–94.

Shalloo, J. P., and Donald Young, eds. *Minority Peoples in a Nation at War.* American Academy of Political and Social Science *Annals* 223 (Sept. 1942).

Silk, Mark. "Notes on the Judeo-Christian Tradition in America." *American Quarterly* 36 (Spring 1984): 65–85.

Skidmore, Rex A., Therese L. Smith, and Delbert L. Nye. "Characteristics of Married Veterans." *Marriage and Family Living* 11 (Aug. 1949): 102–104.

Skocpol, Theda. "The G.I. Bill and U.S. Social Policy, Past and Future." *Social Philosophy and Policy* 14 (Summer 1997): 95–115.

Skocpol, Theda, Marshall Ganz, and Ziad Munson. "A Nation of Organizers: The Institutional Origins of Civic Voluntarism in the United States." *American Political Science Review* 94 (Sept. 2000): 527–546.

Slotkin, Richard. "Unit Pride: Ethnic Platoons and the Myths of American Nationality." *American Literary History* 13 (Autumn 2001): 469–498.

Smith, Alfred E. "Catholic and Patriot: Governor Smith Replies." *Atlantic Monthly* 139 (May 1927): 721–729.

Smith, Mapheus. "Populational Characteristics of American Servicemen in World War II." *Scientific Monthly* 65 (Sept. 1947): 246–252.

Somit, Albert, and Joseph Tanenhaus. "The Veteran in the Electoral Process: The House of Representatives." *Journal of Politics* 19 (May 1957): 184–201.

Stavisky, Sam. "Where Does the Veteran Stand Today?" American Academy of Political and Social Science *Annals* 259 (Sept. 1948): 128–135.

Summers, Robert E., and Harrison B. Summers, comps. *Universal Military Service.* The Reference Shelf. Vol. 15, no. 2. New York: H. W. Wilson, 1941.

Thomason, John W. "The Case for the Soldier." *Scribner's Magazine* 97 (Apr. 1935): 208–213.

*Time,* 1925–2005.

Truman, Harry S. "An Investment for Peace: Military Program Is a Bulwark Against Communism." *Vital Speeches of the Day* 15 (Sept. 1, 1949): 674–676.

Tyler, Robert L. "The American Veterans Committee: Out of the Hot War and Into the Cold." *American Quarterly* 18 (Autumn 1966): 419–436.

*Washington Post,* 1890–1965.

Wood, Leonard. "Heat Up the Melting Pot." *Independent* 87 (July 3, 1916): 15.

*Yank: The Army Weekly,* 1942–1945.

## Fiction

### Novels, Short Stories, Plays, Poetry

Benét, Stephen Vincent. *We Stand United and Other Radio Scripts.* New York: Farrar and Rinehart, 1945.

Fussell, Paul, ed. *The Norton Book of Modern War.* New York: W. W. Norton, 1991.

Hersey, John. *A Bell for Adano.* 1944. Reprint, New York: Alfred A. Knopf, 1967.

Zangwill, Israel. *The Melting-Pot.* New York: Macmillan, 1909.

### Films

*Battleground.* Directed by William Wellman. MGM, 1949.

*The House I Live In.* Directed by Mervyn LeRoy. RKO, 1945.

*Knute Rockne, All American.* Directed by Lloyd Bacon. Warner Brothers, 1940.

# INDEX

Page numbers in **boldface** refer to illustrations.

# A NATION FORGED IN WAR